The Open Society
along the Arduous Path of Modernity

א A L E F
Series of works on universal logic and philosophy directed by
Michele Malatesta and Rocco Pezzimenti
A   Allgemeine Logik Und Philosophie
L   Universel Logik Og Filosofi
E   Logica Universale E Filosofia
F   Logica Universal Y Filosofia

Volume 3: Rocco Pezzimenti, *The Open Society along the Arduous Path of Modernity, with letters from Isaiah Berlin and Hilary Putnam*

In memory of my friend Adriano Paglietti

The Open Society along the Arduous Path of Modernity

with letters from Isaiah Berlin and Hilary Putnam

Rocco Pezzimenti

GRACEWING

First published in 2011

Gracewing
2 Southern Avenue
Leominster
Herefordshire HR6 0QF
United Kingdom
www.gracewing.co.uk

All rights reserved. No part of this publication may be reproduced, stored in a retrieval system, or transmitted in any form, or by any means, electronic, mechanical, photocopying, recording, or otherwise, without the written permission of the publisher.

©2011 Rocco Pezzimenti

ISBN 978 0 85244 741 3

Contents

First Part

1. The Problem of Modernity.   13

   A) *Introduction with letters from I. Berlin and H. Putnam.*   13
   B) *Defence of the Republican Ideal: F. Guicciardini.*   23

2. Between the Medieval and Modernity.   49

   A) *Needs for Renewal.*   53
   B) *The Problem of Power and the "right of the peoples".*   60

3. The Change of one Century.   87

   A) *The Preliminaries.*   87
   B) *The first Self-Assertion of Liberalism.*   93
   C) *The rise of civil society.*   104
   D) *The Balance of Innovation and Tradition: D. Hume.*   113
   E) *Relationships between Economy and Politics: A. Smith.*   127
   F) *Conservative Liberalism: E. Burke.*   140
   G) *Towards the Age of Reforms: J. Bentham.*   150

4. The Aristocratic Republic in Vico and Montesquieu.   157

   A) *The Approach of Croce.*   157
   B) *The role of the Aristocracy.*   163
   C) *The Genesis of Law.*   167
   D) *The eternal Law of the Fiefs.*   171
   E) *The Aristocratic Republics.*   173
   F) *Almost the Pursuit of an Analysis.*   176

G) *The Historical and Political Teachings of Rome.* 177
H) *The Reasons for the Crisis
   and the Reasons for Tolerance.* 181
I) *The Relevance of the Thought concerning the Elites.* 193

5. The Eighteenth Century in Italy: Age of Reforms. 197

   A) *In the South.* 197
   B) *In the North.* 206
   C) *Beyond the Enlightenment: V. Cuoco.* 211

6. The Open Society Crosses the Ocean. 223

   A) *The Greatness of the Mixed Government: J. Adams.* 225
   B) *The Federalist Papers.* 230
   C) *The government based on the Constitution:
      T. Paine.* 237

7. The Consolidation of Liberalism. After the Revolution 243

   A) *Reflections on the Revolution.* 243
   B) *The Demands of the Bourgeoisie.* 252
   C) *Representation and Liberty; B. Constant.* 258
   D) *The Bourgeoisie Consolidates its Primacy:
      F. Guizot.* 268
   E) *Liberty and Equality: A. de Tocqueville.* 276
   F) *The Debate on Christianity and Liberty: J. Balmes.* 299

8. Religion and Liberty 307

   A) *The Multifaceted Patrimony of French Catholicism.* 311
   B) *Religion as the Basis of Liberty: F. R. de Lamenais.* 312
   C) *The Difficult Existence
      of Italian Liberal Catholicism.* 314
   D) *The Italian Renewal: V. Gioberti.* 317
   E) *Political society and its rationality: A. Rosmini.* 320
   F) *Liberty and History: C. Balbo.* 329

9. Liberty and Democracy from History to the Future. 333

   A) *The Economy between Liberty and Equality:*
      J. Stuart Mill. 333
   B) *Religion and Politics: Lord Acton.* 346
   C) *Liberty, Democracy and the Industrial Society:*
      H. Spencer. 355

10. Socialism and the Open Society. 363

   A) *A Precursor, Saint-Simon.* 365
   B) *Evil as a Social Problem: R. Owen.* 368
   C) *The first Denunciation of the Communist*
      Weltanschauung: *P.J. Proudhon.* 370
   D) *The* Sozialdemokratie: *E. Bernstein.* 374

Second Part

11. From Absolutism... 381

   A) *The Need for Power and the Problem of Security*
      at the Time of the Reformation. 381
   B) *The Birth of the State and the Need for Absolutism:*
      J. Bodin. 387
   C) *Absolute Power and the Catholic Reform:*
      J. B. Bossuet. 390
   D) *The Aberrations of Absolutism: the Leviathan.* 392

12. ...to Totalitarianism 403

   A) *The Defence of God the Person.* 403
   B) *The realization of truth.* 406
   C) *The Road to Salvation.* 415
   D) *Humanity is made Divine and is Reconciled*
      (Interpreters of Hegel). 417
   E) *Towards the Idea of the God as All:*
      the Liberation of Humanity. 422

F) *"Rigorousness" of the Dialectical Method (Historical Materialism).*   428
G) *Labour and Revolution.*   432
H) *Constructivism as a Social Theory: A. Comte.*   435

Third Part

13. Utopia or the Need for a Different World.   441

   A) *The Island of Utopia T. More.*   442
   B) *The* Nova Atlantis: *F. Bacon.*   448
   C) *The* Civitas Solis: *T. Campanella.*   451
   D) The Commonwealth of Oceana: *J. Harrington.*   455

Fourth Part

14. The Republican Ideal confronting the Raison d'État.   461

15. Politics and Holy Scriptures in Spinoza.   479

16. *The Abstract Society of the Just.*   487

17. The Individual, Society and the State.   501

   A) *Formal and Substantial Law: I. Kant.*   501
   B) *The Regulating State: J. G. Fichte.*   515

Works cited   521

Index of Names   557

FIRST PART

1. The Problem of Modernity.

A) *Introduction with letters from I. Berlin and H. Putnam.*

1.1 The political institutions of Rome and England have had a great influence on the history of politics in general. Their greatness comes from the fact that these two juridical entities grew little by little. They were capable of adapting to events and deal with needs in new situations. Indeed, they represent the two most representative and flexible constitutions in history (cf. Bryce, Ch. I). An analysis of political history whether practical or theoretical would be impossible without them. Both have given the greatest possible impulse in the history of law not only with their historical documents capable of describing entire eras, but also with that *ius non scriptum* that characterizes their rich tradition and brings out the moral greatness of their peoples. This statement must not be considered rhetorical since flexible constitutions are such if they can be modified, bent and altered in their form, but manage to keep their main features unchanged (cf. Bryce, Ch. III). Both of their forms of government were never specified in their entirety, an evident indication of the fact that the two powers, Roman and English, had a sense of basic limitations consolidated in tradition. It is this strong sense of tradition that, on the one hand, gave these institutions a conservative appearance, and, on the other, made them the ultimate examples of a system that could be modified and adapted more quickly than others, furthermore, in the simplest possible way. This means that in Rome and in England there is a strong sense of nation, which is not to be confused with nationalism, but which means respect for ancient customs considered an indispensable premise for any changes, customs without which any flexible constitution would have been the source of considerable instability. This explains why those institutions have been capable of overcoming difficult moments, even with the suspension of some rights which, in keeping with tradition, were restored as soon as the emergency had passed. These flexible constitutions were capable of foreseeing and thus comprehending changes without giving rise to revolutions that might have totally destroyed the past (cf. Bryce, Ch. V).

1.2 In the preceding volume, I pointed out that the stability of Roman institutions and those subsequently inspired by them comes from the fact that some aristocratic elements were safeguarded even where energetic popular participation was provided for. These were evident in the Senate and, in England, in the House of Lords. Not a few authors, Vico and Montesquieu for example, have referred to these institutions, in terms of aristocratic Republics. These aristocracies were obviously open ones, to which one could accede on the basis of merit. They have prevented what Tocqueville would call democratic tyranny or that perverse form of totalitarian democracy that was experienced in the past century. This form of democracy condemned certain positions based on merit as something reactionary, and ended up creating new ones, not only static and closed, but based on the crudest form of brutality covered by the alleged force of numbers that no-one could ever verify. Based on these premises, it can be said that open societies were born and grew out of those civilisations which, in the opinion of many, were able to combine a solid juridical mentality, respect for tradition and merits and an acute, practical sense. In the world of today, these aspects seem to have been inherited from American constitutionalism and that which is associated with that tradition. The only difference, and it would be too long to analyse here, lies in the fact that the United States created a rigid constitution, whereas the two glorious experiences of the past operated in the realm of two flexible "constitutions", for different reasons.

1.3 Some have referred to the American Revolution as one without ideologies. The writings that inspired it were mostly juridical and constitutional in nature. The problems dealt with are concrete ones and there is no getting round them. It is no accident that what characterizes the frontier experience, as with the preceding Roman and English experiences, and what constitutes the true cultural background, is private law (cf. Matteucci, RA, 86-90 and 212). Private law itself is what leads to "separation between sovereignty (public) and property (private) hence the rigorous drawing of boundaries for the sphere of power of the State" (Pellicani, HSB, 3). The distinction between public and private, the everlasting conquest of Latinity, avoids the dangers of totalitarian democracy itself, an appeal from the Sirens to which not a few representatives of western culture, from Rousseau on, will fall prey to. That distinction has been fulfilled in the world of today in American constitutionalism which, not by chance, has been considered as a natural result of the course of European history up to the Renaissance, shattered on the old continent after the various reforms (cf. Acton, EFP, 136).

1.4 The distinction between public and private law is highly important not only because it limits the potestative sphere of the State, but also because it allows for reflection and political action that the philosophies, which supinely refer to Aristotelian premises of man as a political animal or those that oppose them cannot guarantee, philosophies springing from the reflections of Machiavelli or Hobbes, which see man as a ferocious beast who needs to be subjugated by the strength of a Leviathan, whether singly or as a totality, in order to live in peace. There is another way, perhaps an intermediate one, already implicit in Cicero and made explicit in Vico, that visualizes man as slowly coming out of the savage state and, having a natural propensity for sociality, succeeds in accomplishing this only by giving himself rules that are solid enough to be obeyed. As I wrote in the preceding volume (cf. point 1.33), "as will happen in the case of Hobbes, Cicero lives in a moment of enormous civil conflict, but the solution he proposes will not, as is the case for the English thinker, be an authoritarian system. True peace cannot be guaranteed outside of law. Peace is not accomplished by delegation of powers; it comes from the base. "Peaceful coexistence (…) is the primary goal of social living, and a State must aim at this through laws and institutions (Cicero, DR, IV, 3). Dictatorships and forms of authoritarianism ensure neither peace nor order. On the contrary, they are death certificates for democracies now devoid of their basic substance". This position, which I shall discuss in the first part and particularly in authors such as Vico and Montesquieu, makes of political philosophy practically a profession of life that neither conjures up ideal states that never materialize nor does it support monstrous solutions that, in the name of an alleged peace that never turns out to be that, justify any act of an authority considered above everything in so far as it is in possession of the truth. This wise philosophy of life has not, for all too long, seemed even worthy of being called philosophy so that even Bryce wondered at the fact that no-one had considered the existence of the philosophy of law of the Romans.

1.5 As far as the first part is concerned I can say that I have considered thinkers who fear that the lessons of the past may be forgotten, but they do not, for that reason, think that they can be revived in mechanical fashion. These authors, as happens in the United States but not only there, evoke the classical term of republic in order to set it off from that of democracy. This distinction is not specious because, upon closer examination, the term democracy refers to forms of direct participation and popular governments, whereas republic is associated with mechanisms of representation typical of the large modern States (cf. Mioni, 7 and 32). A curious aspect comes out here: some of the authors taken into consideration were neglected, since they did not enjoy the fame of great thinkers and philosophers. One need only think of those philosophers of the Enlightenment that some American statesmen deemed unworthy of consideration, according to whom their error was that of not having been theoretical spirits, even though they brought about enviable institutions. It is the same presumption as that of some Greek thinkers who did not take Latin ones into consideration. They were the ones, however, to which these great statesmen referred. John Adams, for example, regretted the loss of much of Cicero's book on the republics because, based on what little has remained, we can say that there is no-one else who undertook the analysis of such a form of government as did he. Not only that, but the first analysis of the separation of powers is to be found in Cicero, as well as consideration of an aristocratic component that ensures stability for republican institutions (cf. Adams, IV, 295 ff.). In the ancient world obviously in a nascent state that had room for improvement, there is also that distinction between confederation and federation that will be of such great interest to the moderns. The former apply to alliances among the various Greek city-states which had various features in common, but which remained jealous of their independence and thereby ended up being the victims of their own weakness. The latter apply to the Latin federations, or the Roman-Italic one, based on different premises with a strong central governing authority for foreign and military policy as well as considerable juridical and administrative autonomy.

1.6 Concerning Cicero, I wish to recall that McIlwain maintains that the word constitution is used in the modern sense for the first time in a passage of *De Repubblica*. In speaking of the mixed form he tells us that this constitution (*haec costituo*) contains a considerable measure of equity, without which it would be difficult for people to remain free. Moreover, after defining the State as a *vinculum iuris* we are also told that in time a law must precede the power of sanction. Even more surprising is McIlwain's observation that between Aristotle's reflection on the constitution and Cicero's, there is an abyss that cannot conceivably be overcome. Quoting Carlyle, he reaches the point of saying that in political thought, there is no change as astonishing, in its completeness, as that which takes place from Aristotle to Cicero to Seneca, to the point that the division between ancient and modern thought is to be found in the different philosophies of these authors and in the period between them (cf. McIlwain, Chs. II and III). I pass over the fact that McIlwain, again (cf. Appendix I of his writing), believes that even the Whigs, wanting to justify the extension of the powers of Parliament, made use of a rather approximate quotation from Cicero. Vico was to understand this quite well and, on the subject, I wish to quote a few lines from Sir Isaiah Berlin.

Dear Professor Pezzimenti,
....
I agree with all that you say. Not only can there be, for Vico, no real progress in the field of the arts: each culture is what it is and not another one. But you are right in saying that the 'spirit', whether collective or individual, is not capable of progress (unlike rational enquiries) save in the very narrow sphere of a particular ingredient of a particular culture or the experience of a particular individual – so that we must be allowed to say that one work of art is more perfect (or even exhibits something progressive) in relation to another or earlier work of art within a given school of art, a given period, a given group of artists- but not beyond this.

So apart from this I do entirely agree with you; and this too perhaps cancels the possibility of the Utopian dream of perfection. Your are quite right that it is in Vico's legal writings, in particular on Roman law, that one finds 'the germ' of the plurality of cultures, conceptions, forms of behaviour and everything which goes with a particular mode of living or feeling or thinking.

If you do want to publish my letter of November 1992 I have no objection, indeed, I feel flattered, but do please make the corrections which I give in the earlier part of this letter.

Yours sincerely,

Sir Isaiah Berlin

(The first part of the letter, with the corrections requested is published in the preceding volume).

1.7 This work also aims at assuming a position in relation to the age-old problem of modernity and the accusations, by and large appropriate, that the so-called postmodern period has levied against it. The question I wish to raise and, I hope, demonstrate, is that true modernity consists of a slow and arduous process which, amidst many contradictions, gives life to – improves – and amends that intricate path taken by rights that I delineated in the first volume and its roots are ancient. This path, which what has far too long been considered the true modernity, and is, on the contrary, a parody of it, has tried to destroy. For this reason, I have divided this work into four parts of which only the *first one* traces the difficult progress of the open societies indicating the positive component of modernity; the *second one* brings out the enemies of that effort; the *third* deals with those who, while not agreeing with the enemies of the open society, have taken refuge in utopias, raising problems that are no less serious than those that conflicted with progress towards liberty; the *fourth*, finally, examines several thinkers, who can be considered truly paradoxical because of the contradictions inherent in their political and moral thought. Why this part?... because I am convinced that it is proper to state: "closed societies are cruel realities (…) just as those societies designed by utopians are cruel and violent" (Antiseri, 11). This is not enough, however, since several paradoxical statements of certain exponents of modern culture are no less dangerous when, upon closer examination, they end up expressing absurdities replete with dramatic consequences. The second, third and fourth parts, altogether, represent *that modernity* which *is justly criticized* by many people, in its totality or in part, because it has ventured to re-found mankind and society *ab imis* ending up with those aberrations that history has dramatically put on display for everyone to see. In the second part, I have placed various exponents of reforms, whether Protestant or Catholic, among the enemies of open societies. It is not that I am convinced that all religions contain the germs of closed societies, otherwise I would not have placed exponents such as those of the School of Salamanca or other Anglicans or Protestants in the first part, but, as I have sought to show in the third chapter of the preceding volume, *in religious tradition two different ways of thinking* come into conflict, which revive the ancient dispute that arose between Eusebius of Caesarea and the Bishop of Hippo as well as their followers. The former perceives a close link between religion and politics giving rise to a dangerous dependency; the latter – a separation and, even in moments of cooperation, mutual autonomy, the only condition that is capable of ensuring true liberty. A propos of the fourth part, I quote a few lines of Hilary Putnam concerning Kant. In general, I agree, but hope to have shown, in Chapter XVII, the reasons for some perplexity on my part.

Dear Dr. Pezzimenti
I enclose a paper on Non-Scientific Knowledge which I delivered at Cerisy Lasalle this summer: as you will see it deals with the relation between law and morality, as well as the relation between science and non-scientific knowledge (these relations, as I see them, are intimate; but I would not wish to simply assimilate morality, law, and rationality, as you may be urging me to do). Perhaps it will be of interest to your colleagues and students.

Re Kant: although a totalitarian government may be indifferent to the categorical imperative, I do not agree with you that that formula is "only empty words" where no liberal tradition exists. As William James wrote, "I am against all big organizations as such, national ones first and foremost; against all big successes and big results: and in favour of the eternal forces of truth which always work in the individual and immediately unsuccessful way, under-dogs always, till history comes after they are long dead, and puts them on the top"[1] It seems to me that the categorical imperative, or rather the moral image that it captures is one of those eternal forces of truth that works in individuals in even the most tyrannical regimes.

....
Sincerely yours,

Hilary Putnam

(The letter continues, dealing with other subjects).

1.8 Along this tortuous path towards modernity it is necessary to avoid what Vico called the dangers of absolutization in consideration of the crucial periods of history. For example, in dealing with periods such as the Enlightenment we must not make the mistake of those who demonize it because some figures are abstract, "totalitarian", or of those who exalt it without perceiving its contradictions. Such clearcut statements are the result of that Manichean conception which dies hard even in the most enlightened minds. We should depart from the assumption that many of our acquisitions and accomplishments did not suddenly appear in the modern world out of nothing. I agree with Pellicani when he says the Modernity "is a civilisation *sui generis*, whose basic characteristics are 1) electoral action, 2) nomocracy or the rule of law, 3) the universalisation of the rights to citizenship, 4) the institutionalism of change, 5) cultural secularisation, 6) the autonomy of subsystems and 7) rationalisation" (Pellicani, DdM, 20), but may of these subjects are already pre-modern. The civilisation of law is in the DNA of our history. I, too, was criticised for the mistake of absolutizing one aspect while giving too little emphasis

---

[1] - Letters of William James, II (p.90), written in 1899. In the same letter James writes that "The bigger the unit you deal with, the hollower, the more brutal, the more mendacious is the life displayed".

to others. Among the many reviews received, the detailed one of P. Marcos F. Manzanedo underscored the fact that I had praised the juridical course of the Latins excessively, neglecting the philosophical one of the Greeks. This is probably true, but my purpose was to bring out an aspect of classical culture that has received too little consideration, if it has not actually been neglected, by political thinkers and scholars in general. I consider this sin unforgiveable and I willingly subscribe to a maxim of my reviewer "*más che causa eficiente, el mal tiene una causa deficiente*" (Manzanedo, 23).

B) *Defence of the Republican Ideal: F. Guicciardini.*

1.9 Not many exponents of sixteenth-century European culture have, like Guicciardini, an awareness of the profound changes that were taking place then. Even fewer of those who intuited the new developments of the era sought to oppose the rampant absolutism. For this reason, as well as his republican and aristocratic ideals, Guicciardini often seems to us a character alien to his era even if now, *a posteriori*, we are less inclined to call him a person nostalgic for the past and we admire him for some remarkable things he foresaw. His anti-absolutionism can be viewed in the wake of those Florentine humanists, inspired by republican ideals, who range from Coluccio Salutati (1331-1406) with *De tyranno* to the works of Leonardo Bruni (1370-1444), both capable of furthering the analysis of Bartolo da Sassoferrato (1314-1357) who, with *De Tyrannide*, had examined the remedies that can be used against tyrannical power.

Francesco Guicciardini was born in 1483 of an aristocratic family involved in Florentine politics. Thanks to the friendship of Father Piero with Marsilio Ficino, he got his start in humanistic studies, eventually to take up juridical ones. After his studies in Padua and Ferrara he devoted himself with success to the practice of law. In 1508 he married Maria Salviati, a member of one of Florence's most prominent families. Between 1511 and 1513 he was appointed ambassador of the Florentine Republic at the court of the King of Spain. That was the start of political activity that would lead him to fill many prestigious posts some of which on behalf of the Popes, up to 1538, when he would refuse Paul III's offer to become the head of a regional government of the Papal States, in order to devote himself entirely to the composition of his *Storia d'Italia (History of Italy)*. He died in 1540. Aside from the masterpiece mentioned above, there are, among his works, the memorable: *Storie fiorentine (First History of Florence)* to which he devoted himself for a long time, the *Dialogo del Reggimento di Firenze (Dialogue on the Government of Florence)* (1524), *Considrazioni intorno ai discorsi del Machiavelli sopra la prima Deca di Tito Livio (Considerations on the Discourses of Machiavelli, on the First Ten Books of Titus Livius)* (1529-1530). Among others, the *Discorsi politici (Political Discourses)*, the *Discorsi sul Reggimento di Firenze (Discourses on the Government of Florence)* and, obviously, *I Ricordi (The Memoirs)* are noteworthy.

1.10 "Politics for Guicciardini is a form of cognition that requires particular aptitudes ("discretion"), long experience and careful study" (D'Addio, SDP, I, 312), of history above all, not just through the classics, but also through the analysis of historical events in individual nations. Despite the uncertainties the future holds, politics, within the limits of its capacity and in the face of myriads of difficulties, is the science of forecasting and forecasts can be made only after careful study of the complex human events. Hence, political activity is, contrary to what people think, delicate and difficult. Not everyone is capable of performing it. It has been said that "Guicciardini views the people with a totally aristocratic diffidence" (D'Addio, SDP, I, 312), but in actual fact, although political life requires the involvement of many, few are capable of taking important initiatives. We could say that, even within a republican idea, Guicciardini intuits the role played by several *élites,* whether mercantile political or intellectual, without which there can be no thrust toward real progress or innovation. This is anything but reactionary because it is based on the need for improvement which, for Guicciardini, is innate in every human being. This desire for improvement is also present in his way of studying and writing, to such an extent that even considering the *Storia d'Italia* a masterpiece, the components of his thought are difficult to understand if his historical works are not examined in their entirety (cf. Lugnani Scarano, 11-12), because Guicciardini's thought is continually enriched both from the point of view of methodology and content. Thus, even his aristocratic mentality seems incomprehensible if account is not taken of the fact that "experience is the quality most needed by the man of affairs" (Gilbert, 278). Only proven experience, if aided by innate intuition, makes possible the new developments of the times. Many politicians are lacking in these qualities so that "the Italian rulers were no longer initiators of events but rather were subject to them" (Gilbert, 287).

1.11 The *History of Italy* is one of the masterpieces of modern historiography, not only because of the meticulous attention devoted to the entire work but also because Guicciardini shows, on more than one occasion, a foresightedness about the future of the political events he examines, which is truly unusual. His pages on the discovery of the new world are a remarkable example of this. From the accounts of the navigators he concludes that the natives of the new world "are almost nothing but tame animals, easy prey for anyone who assails them" (Guicciardini, SdI, 617) and since, in those lands "extremely rich veins of gold have been discovered", people have begun to exploit these to such an extent that the European powers will dispute over their supremacy on the new continent itself. What is of greatest interest is the fact that those discoveries will have cultural, political and economic consequences without precedent. As far as the first aspect is concerned, with "these expeditions the ancients have shown themselves to have made many errors in many things as far as learning about the earth is concerned" (Guicciardini SdI, 618); as for the second aspect, Guicciardini views with dismay the inability of Italian politicians to interpret the times and their failure to understand that the Mediterranean, the economic and commercial centre of gravity is losing its prime role thereby causing great harm to our republics and ports. Suffice it to realise "that war of the Turks had not created so much trouble for the Venetians as had interception of the spice trade by the King of Portugal" (Guicciardini, SdI, 614). Guicciardini's use of the word *intercetto* is highly effective in underscoring the fact that, for a trading port like Venice, the interruption of traffic (*intercetto* in other words) was more harmful than a war.

1.12 To all this must be added the political and military crisis that involved Italy. There was a crisis of authority without precedent all over the country and "reverence for the Pope had been lost from the hearts of men (…) and conquerors had free rein in using their victories (…) for a long time in those highly dense times they have been the means for causing wars and new conflagrations in Italy" (Guicciardini, SdI, 472). A new *raison'dêtre* was taking over from the divine and terrestrial authorities: the State. The conclusions are lucid and bitter: "neither the fear of God nor respect for the esteem of men can do more than the interest of the State" (Guicciardini, SdI, 513). Here, too, the new developments are not understood by Italian princes, who, lost in their "*particolare*", do not perceive the political developments of the times. It would almost seem that this inability to interpret the times came from the dangerous moral crisis which was gripping our Principalities. "The infirmities of Italy were such, and her strength was so weakened, that these could not be treated with mild medicines; (...) all over Italy (...) there followed infinite killings, sacking and massacres in many cities and lands, military license no less pernicious to friends than to enemies, religion desecrated, sacred things treated with less reverence and respect than profane ones" (Guicciardini, SdI, 733). The greatest shame is that of not having understood (and there are splendid pages on the subject: cf. Guicciardini, SdI, 789 ff.) that the good and salvation of private individuals is inseparable from that of a Republic and vice versa.

1.13 There was little hope that the Italian situation could take a more positive turn. Several tools were lacking, such as the military for example, which, for lack of political foresightedness was drifting out of control. Here the close link between political institutions and power which, and this was also a conviction of Machiavelli's, had been one of the strong points of Roman greatness. Thus "it was more reckless than prudent to hope that Italian armies, lacking in virtue, discipline, reputation, captains of authority, not in conformity with the wills of their Princes, would be sufficient to drive the conqueror out of Italy" (Guiciardini, SdI, 961). The conqueror not only brought insecurity, hence peril for trade and commerce, political change, very cruel massacres, "but even new habits, new customs, new and bloody ways of making war, infirmities unknown up to that time; (...) the instruments of Italian peace and harmony which failed to be re-ordered, offered other foreign nations and barbarian armies the possibility of treating her miserably and devastating her" (Guicciardini, SdI, 157-158). The task was easy for the conquerors who faced only the armies of mercenaries inclined, to be sure, to avoid taking too many risks (cf. among many writings, Guicciardini, SdI, Ch. XI) and enable them to reap the fruits of their useless service. None of that is surprising since paid soldiers promise, "as is their custom, to do a great deal more, then they usually accomplish in actual fact" (Guicciardini, SdI, 1533-1534). What is worse is that, wanting to serve their own interests exclusively, they no longer distinguish between enemies and friends, and, if necessary, they even lay waste to (*desolano*) those who pay them with their peoples (cf. Guicciardini, SdI, 1670). It should be observed that they took as their model the politicians of the time, since "as is customary for all Princes, utility (prevailed over) honesty" (Guicciardini, SdI, 1598).

1.14 The continual ferment that troubled the Italian Principates was often aroused by those incapable of perceiving new developments in history, who had turned nostalgically to the past. Often the ancient aristocratic republics aroused turbulence of various sorts. The crisis "was enflamed by many noble citizens who disliked the government in power, and the fact that a single family had arrogated power over the entire republic" (Guicciardini, SdI, 173). In the final analysis, the Italian situation reflected not only an international political crisis and geopolitical changes in the economy, but also internal crises not easy to resolve. The rebellions spread from the cities to the country where the interests of the nobles, and the people tied to the aristocracy, made themselves strongly felt. Although Guicciardini viewed the situation with remarkable clarity, he seemed at times to accept the impressions of those who supposed that peace and security could be restored by means of a return to the authorities of the past. The ambitions of the Hapsburg Emperor reawakened the dreams of an Empire capable of regaining the "peace of the subjects and, with respect for the things of the infidels, to the benefit of the entire Christian republic" (Guicciardini, SdI, 1307). The reference to the Empire, but also the use of the term Christian Republic, one of the banners of the Middle Ages were curious. He also recalls an Italian history, which made our cities great and very wealthy even if they were at the mercy of the "Barbarians". The description of Milan and her duchy is noteworthy: "for the number and nobility of her subjects, for the considerable revenues, for the ability to feed all the armies of the world, she is superior to many kingdoms; (...) for highly sumptuous adornments, those of women and men alike, for the nature of the inhabitants given to festivities and pleasures, not only full of joy and light-heartedness but extremely florid and happy to a greater degree than in any other town in Italy" (Guicciardini, SdI, 1605 and 1664), but weak in institutions and, like our other cities, she became easy prey to foreigners militarily speaking.

1.15 Decadence in Italy was everywhere and, in addition to the political scene, it also affected the moral state; "and no wonder, because people were so weary of past turbulence, that falling into an ordered way of living, everyone willingly rested" (Guicciardini , SF, 62). Resignation became the expression of weariness and, to have a bit of peace, anyone capable of ensuring it was accepted. The Italian aristocracy itself and the great mercantile forces sought only to defend what they could, such that "rich men and ones who expected nothing from the state, lamenting the fact of having to sustain the City and having money extorted from them by the City, desired a life in which, whosoever governed it, did not disturb them in their privileges (...) because those who took their profits also placed greater burdens upon them" (Guicciardini, SF, 187 and DRF, 327). Is this not the sort of analysis of those from Hobbes to the present that justified the advent of dictatorships as a necessity, in an order capable of guaranteeing the safety of goods and people? The solution proposed by Guicciardini is extremely different. As a man of law and a history scholar he realises that the securest of governments cannot be arbitrary even if this can then offer some guarantees, because those guarantees must be the characteristic of good governments."One of the main fruits obtained from good governments is security itself and of that which belongs to it and the ability to dispose of it as one wishes; (…) and he who depends on the good will of others never has full security, since true security lies in the fact that things are such that one citizen cannot be abused and offended by another. These evils do not arise in a free government, because no-one forces you, no-one punishes you wrongly" (Guicciardini, DRF, 387-388).

1.16 Guicciardini thus introduces one of the basic characteristics of a policy that is respectful of human dignity: *the certainty of law.* His considerations leave no doubt. "Mistaken is he who believes that the law is put up to the decision – that is at the free will – of the judge, because it never makes him the master to give and to take away" (Guicciardini, R, 760). Where there is law there is no arbitrariness because even the judges must submit to it. It is not by chance that Guicciardini puts private individuals on their guard of notaries who could, either for their own interests, or under pressure, alter documents. "It is, however, a good expedient to defend oneself from that, the moment the instrument or the writing has been prepared, to have an authenticated copy made to keep in one's possession" (Guicciardini, R, 762). This advice is given for an uncertain era in which even the law must be defended to save one's security and to protect oneself from coercion. Indeed "the sage legislators found the rewards and penalties: out of hope and fear to keep men in their natural inclination" (Guicciardini, R, 766). It is superfluous to add that effectiveness of the rewards and penalties comes not just from their actual application, but also the fact that they be known of in advance, another characteristic of the certainty of law, far from any arbitrariness.

1.17 In those circumstances, it was understandable how great "the fallaciousness of human discourse was, when, judging uncertain matters, it was said that if one had proceeded differently, the desirable effect would have been attained or what had happened would not have taken place" (Guicciardini, SdI, 833). In a discourse that anticipates the methodological analyses of our times, we can say that Guicciardini is speaking almost of the end of certainties, at least in the political and social realms, maintaining, as Boudon would say, that the intentions of individuals are often followed by consequences that are anything but intentional. The fact remains certain, however, that in some areas sure and absolute rules cannot exist. "It is a great error to speak of the matters of the world indistinctly and absolutely and, so to speak, according to the rules; because almost all have a distinction and an exception because of the variety of circumstances, which cannot be judged in accordance with a single measure" (Guicciardini, R, 729). Indeed it is often said: "if it had been done or not been done in that way, such a thing would have happened or would not have happened!" (Guicciardini, R, 734), but we can say so only because we cannot verify the contrary.

1.18 Uncertainty exists in human as well as political affairs, even if people act as if everything were extremely certain. Yet, "*de futuris contingentibus non est determinata veritas*

(...) You do not have a future thing whether certain or even highly certain in appearance, (...) because things often occur beyond common opinion" (Guicciardini, R, 745 and 751). Experience with its "particularities" manages to surpass any form of imagination and, those who suffer from it most greatly, are politicians subject more than others to changing contingencies, even if they, more than others, believe themselves to be scientists. Guicciardini bitterly and cryptically comments on their claims to certainty: "they make pronouncements about the future *in scriptis*, and when these are made by those who know, they seem very beautiful to those who read them; nonetheless, they are highly fallacious because, each depends on the conclusion from the other. If one is lacking, all those deduced from it become vain; and any minimum detail that varies, is likely to lead to a variation in the conclusion. However, the matters of this world cannot be judged from afar, they must be judged day by day" (Guicciardini, R, 761). The age-old word of wisdom emerges once again to the effect that every day has its torment and there is no need to procure new ones.

1.19 If uncertainty in human affairs were given rigorous consideration a great many errors would be avoided. But, especially in politics, presumption holds sway and thus "people often are led to set off on a path because of difficulties that, if they had imagined even an eighth of these, would have fled a thousand miles away: but, since they have set off, it is not within their power to withdraw" (Guicciardini, R. 772). Indeed, in politics, there is this that is dramatic: the ways out are not always smooth or always ready, because everyone entertains the illusion of succeeding in carrying out his or her designs, but does not understand that there is nothing more difficult to translate into reality than what one supposes, especially in politics in which all people believe that they can accomplish excellent things. "How many there are who speak well but are unable to act! So many, seated on the benches and in the *piazza* seem to be excellent people, but when employed, produce only shadows!" (Guicciardini, R, 775). Guicciardini well knows how easy it is for anyone to improvise, and how few there are capable of foreseeing the risks. Those who improvise are agitated but cannot conclude any venture, with the sole result that, most times, they have only managed to worsen the situation (cf. Guicciardini, R, 777).

1.20 The presumptuous pride of the politician was accompanied, in Guicciardini's time, by the presumption that one could also plan military policy which, by its very nature, is far more uncertain than civilian matters. The worst enemy of wars is the "belief of those who have begun them that they have been won; because they may appear very easy and safe, but they are subject to a thousand accidents" (Guicciardini, R, 780). In war, but in politics as well, one generally cannot proceed with pre-conceived ideas that are inadaptable to changing situations. This does not mean, however, that one can proceed haphazardly. "Be it known that those who govern haphazardly find themselves in a haphazard situation at the end" (Guicciardini, R, 782). On the contrary, every event and condition must be considered, even the slightest one. Thus, to govern is a tiring enterprise and difficult because, when political conditions change governments or institutions, it is not easy and certainly does not depend on the design or thought that someone has taken into his or her head since those intuitions cannot fall neatly into reality (cf. Guicciardini, R, 801 and 791) which has characteristics of its own and ones so changeable as to create difficulties for various projects. This is the reason why "things that are not universally desired are rarely successful" (Guicciardini, R, 803).

1.21 The designs on the future, as Boudon would say, must take into account many variables, hence it is impossible that they be made in clear-cut and precise fashion otherwise "you do not succeed in the change which is far from what you had planned (...) Make no plans for what you do not have, nor spend from future gains, because many times they do not come to pass" (Guicciardini, R, 810). Politics thus requires the greatest possible prudence because, aside from the unintentional consequences of intentional human actions, it must also be recalled that realities "not premeditated move without comparison more than those foreseen" (Guicciardini, R, 812). With these prudence is certainly not enough, but a certain dose of *promptitude* and *inventiveness* is needed which certainly cannot be improvised and which rests on meticulous and serious preparation. It follows that it is "an honourable and manly thing not to promise more than you expect (...). The affairs of the world are so varied and depend on so many accidents, that it is difficult to pass judgements on the future, and experience teaches us that the conjectures of sages are almost always fallacious" (Guicciardini, R. 818 and 821).

1.22 Insecurity in the present and uncertainty about the future do not make Guicciardini pessimistic to the point where he would seek an authoritarian and absolutist political system and yield his own liberty to this system in exchange for security, because he is convinced that "it is more natural for people to seek liberty first in itself than domination over others" (Guicciardini, SF, 126). It would thus be unnatural to give up liberty even if this requires definite rules in order to survive. These rules must be set forth and known first, especially when they must define the behaviour of political bodies. In every political system there must be what we, nowadays after the teaching of constitutionalism, call basic rules. They cannot be changed easily and haphazardly, because, if politicians do not feel themselves bound by laws, they easily become arbitrary. Indeed there are those who "having been freely elected would not like to be bound themselves; but first the orders should be made, then the person who had to live under them, not the person left free, that it be left up to this person to be ordered, bound or otherwise" (Guicciardini, SF, 189). In an age when absolutism all over Europe advocated that the sovereign be released, *ab-solutus*, from the law since he himself is the law, these statements are a rare example of legality and the search for guarantees on behalf of the individual.

1.23 In a good republic, where civilized life is well ordered, one cannot tolerate "a universal license to do ill with little respect and fear of the law and magistrates; since a way is not open for people virtuous and capable to demonstrate and practice their virtue (…) is a presumption to want to interfere in all public affairs of any importance whatsoever" (Guicciardini, DdL, 250). Herein lies that mentality typical of the Italian mercantile world, so clearly brought out, which wishes a minimum interference of the political world in those activities that can be achieved more easily when managed by private individuals. Left free to operate well, they would be "an appetite and a stimulus in the minds of people to act properly and want to have those qualities that would lead them to high rank and the greatest glory" (Guicciardini, DdL, 286). In this context, Guicciardini makes it quite clear that a truly properly functioning republic is one of merit, because "it must be universally seen as something to be valued" (Guicciardini,DdL, 286) otherwise idleness and malice are encouraged. If that does not happen, there is no sense in speaking of liberty at all and it is understandable why "people often allow themselves to be deceived by titles" (Guicciardini, DRF, 336), since, in a society which does not recognize merits, only arrogance and presumption remain and everything is left up to the primordial instinct of superiority. This is all that counts so that in a society of this sort, the citizens "will find that superiority rather than liberty is more highly regarded as the ultimate goal" (Guicciardini, DRF, 336).

1.24 If there are no rules, there is no point in being free. The development of intelligence is not encouraged, only ignorance. Nothing can cause greater fear, "there is more reason to fear ignorance, since, as I said above, it has no measure nor any rule" (Guicciardini, DRF, 350). The reference to measure as well as rule is quite singular. Guicciardini means that *legality in itself* is not enough because *it could be a justification for immobility*. Proper timing and opportunities in politics, as in life, must go hand in hand with the rules. Suffice it to consider that "the very enterprises that are highly difficult or impossible when performed outside the proper time become very easy when coinciding with the time and the opportunity" (Guicciardini, DRF, 447) so that doing them not at the opportune moment can not only be foolish, but also dangerous. It is a great gift for the politician as for any person who acts in social and economic areas to seize the moment to act rapidly, intelligently and effectively.

1.25 *Rules, liberty* or *good government* cannot exist separately since they are closely interconnected; but they are not sufficient by themselves without a pedagogical force involving the future generations. The Florentine historian's observations on the subject are very clear: no type of virtue would ever have existed "if education in that had not been good, nor can education be good when the laws are not good and properly conserved, and where this is to be found, it cannot be said that the government order is bad" (Guicciardini, DRF, 450). There is, therefore, a sort of interconnection among all these elements that guarantee the proper functioning of civilized life and of institutions as well. The historical praise of the Roman republic confirms that. It is curious, however, that Guicciardini not only exalts the institutions, the military discipline, the clear and effective laws, but also the customs behind which a civilized, active and secure society is to be noted, in which conflicts themselves could be regulated by law and "never go to the extremes that throw into disorder all that is good in the city" (Guicciardini, DRF, 458). The life of civilized society was permeated with a morality coming from a spirit that was religious by nature. It seems that in Guicciardini there is the regret that the people of his time have lost the true sense of religion and of the Church whose value, at least institutionally speaking, has been lost sight of by Italian Princes. "You have the Church close by, which is too great for you to measure, and the reverence and authority of he who will never die; if at times one of its basic reasons for being has become a thing of the past or is almost forgotten, its time and its law return fresher and more powerful than ever" (Guicciardini, DRF, 461). Here is the torment of a religious soul which sees even the traditional religiosity of the Italians as something lost, with great harm to civil society, as well.

1.26 Liberty is also applied and defended through the proper functioning of the institutions. The same is true for equality which, for Guicciardini, means above all the possibility of participating in the managing of public affairs and of filling any position. This is why one of the most important "bases of liberty is the equality of the citizens, that no-one exceed another beyond a certain degree, and there can be no equality where there is the perpetuity of the magistrates, that is that they are the same in government, whereas change is necessary" (Guicciardini, DdL, 259). This *statement* is truly *singular* when absolutism was pressing for the idea that power was perpetual, but certainly not naïve because Guicciardini quite well knows the risks of power that perpetuates itself all too easily since "the affairs of the State require experienced men to attend to them" (Guicciardini, DdL, 259), especially in a period of such frequent and unexpected changes. Participation and continuity are the two watchwords in an efficient republic. Guicciardini speaks in no uncertain terms of a sort of Senate (a kind of House of Lords) which would ensure the continuity lacking in those other bodies that, on the contrary, must guarantee the greatest possible participation and change. Thus, "that a senate be elected that will deal with arduous matters, that which may be the pride of the prudent, noble and rich men of the city; let it be perpetual or at least last for a very long time" (Guicciardini, CDM, 611). The newness is ensured by the fact that, not only for the high positions, "the optimum must not always be the same lineages and families, but that they be from the entire body of the city, that is from all those who according to the law are competent to participate as magistrates" (Guicciardini,CDM, 611). It is a bit like the Roman Republic where the aristocratic component blended with the "popular" one ensuring stability and continuity. Guicciardini sets forth some stratagems for this historical experience which might have avoided, even though proof to the contrary is impossible to obtain, some conflicts that were too bitter and ended up in bloodshed. If the great Roman families "had opened up the way by which the leading plebes might have been made patricians at certain times, perhaps these tumults would not have taken place" (Guicciardini, CDM, 620). There is, in the final analysis, the wish to ensure a social osmosis that brings about greater attachment to institutions and guarantees change in continuity.

1.27 Guicciardini fears a form of government that might drift towards despotism, but he is equally fearful of one that might drift towards populism, "because if everyone were given the freedom to persuade and dissuade there would be great confusion" (Guicciardini, DdL, 264). Rules for everyone are needed in other words, for the government as for the people, for the institutions as for the individual. In the *Dialogue of the Government of Florence*, Capponi sums up this vision with extreme lucidity: "Our intention was to rid the city of the power of one and bring it back to liberty, and so it was done. It is true that we wished not to place the government absolutely in the hands of the people, but in those of leading and citizens of the highest quality, so that it would be a state of good people rather than entirely of the people, yet not restrict it to so few that it would not be a free government" (Guicciardini, DRF, 316), hence, a moderate republic that becomes all the more comprehensible when one thinks of the role that the new like the old aristocracy played in Italy during the Renaissance. In any case, such considerations cannot be deemed pure verbal exercises. Guicciardini is a great realist and not a self-deceived utopian. "A government that gives birth to better effects always receives greater approval and praise (...) the effects the governments bring about are what lead to the final judgment" (Guicciardini, DRF, 339), meaning that one must always look at the results in order to pronounce a judgment on governments.

1.28 "There are then three bases for a good and free government of the republic; a greater council, the substantiality necessary for liberty, a lifetime or at least a long-term gonfalonier, the deputation of a large number of citizens to advise and determine all the important matters of the state" (Guicciardini, DdL, 261). Only this way do the aristocratic and popular elements blend leading to a stable government. Care must be taken that the gonfalonier elected to a life – or to a long term ensure continuity to be sure, but that he have *very limited powers* "because he who is the head of a closed state (closed [*stretto* trans. note] = government of one or a few) has no end other than his particular aggrandizement and does whatever he likes in order to keep this, with no respect whatsoever of God, the country or people" (Guicciardini, DRF, 329). It is impossible to live under such a government so that "it would be better to abandon the country than live that way" (Guicciardini, DRF, 352), since it is impossible to be engaged in politics, defend oneself or be engaged in any other activity. This is why *despotic governments deprive the State itself of those great men who have always been the true wealth of a nation* as a careful reading of both ancient and modern history can amply demonstrate (cf. Guicciardini, DRF, 393-394).

1.29 For Guicciardini, despotism and populism are equally dangerous and can only give rise to mediocrity. This is proven by the fact "that great matters are not to be dealt with by the council of the multitude, from which a popular solution would be found, and it would limit the gonfalonier. So it should arrogate for itself and deal with too much of the affairs of state" (Guicciardini, DdL, 260). Mediocre systems also go against logic because they end up spending too much and badly while not succeeding in accomplishing simple and immediate goals. "You shall see with how little order revenues will be managed, and how much negligence and thievery there will be; because one cannot expect anything more from such a government that has no order and a constant leader" (Guicciardini, DRF, 374), and because no-one answers directly for what is done and so no-one is induced to perform a true control. Guicciardini, anticipating Tocqueville, thus rejects mass demagogy, as we would call it today. He is also opposed to those Athenian government experiences which he deems "merely popular", while, on the contrary, he appreciates the Roman republican experience, because it was able to arrive at a measured and balanced system which, in his view, seems more modern. It happened because "in Rome, although the people had their role, the authority of the Senate was great, and the plebes provided a check on the power of the nobility" (Guicciardini, CDM, 643). This separation of roles and duties between the democratic and aristocratic components, guarantees, for Guicciardini, a respective and efficient system. Among the many passages in which he maintains this conclusion, one need only read the 4th chapter of the *Considerations on the "Discourses" of Macchiavelli* in which, concerning the Roman Republic, he reaches the point of saying, that "perhaps it has never happened that a republic has had a perfect order from its beginning" (Guicciardini, CDM, 617). This statement sounds historically and politically absurd given the institutional changes and adaptations that the republic brought about within itself, but it is surely true from the point of view of political philosophy since it is true that the republic, ever since its birth, showed that ductility that made it great and made it prosper. *Continuity being open to the new in stability* were its features.

1.30 Guicciardini draws experience for his own time from this historical experience of checks and balances. For example, when speaking of the gonfalonier, he maintains that if he absolutely must be elected for life, "it is necessary to regulate the other members and, above all, take care that they be so organized that he cannot take for himself too much authority; (...) that that diligence and continued vigilance that will lack in this person, will be compensated for by those balances" (Guicciardini, DRF, 413 and 389). Even more explicitly, he maintains that it is necessary to think of legislative devices that enable citizens to "make the appropriate laws free of his will" (Guicciardini, DdL, 274). What counts most of all, however, is that in a political system thus balanced the "honest ambition in the great spirits [be kept safe] and that they be given the chance to perform great deeds" (Guicciardini, DdL, 274). There is still the customary concern to *avoid the flight of intelligences*, those capable of giving lustre, with their authority, to the entire Republic. The play of checks and balances leads to a sort of division of powers that can certainly not be improvised, but which is perhaps easy to accomplish in the Italian tradition. "I believe that in the government of a city similar to ours three things must be considered above all: how justice is equitably administered, how appropriately the distribution of public expenses and earnings are distributed, and how external affairs are governed" (Guicciardini, DRF, 323). These tasks can obviously not be carried out by the same body.

1.31 Concerning the administration of justice, Guicciardini is convinced that a spirit of greater rigour is to be found in the republics that have more competent and less ostentatious institutions, thanks to the separation of powers. In despotic systems justice is non-existent because it is based on caprice, but the situation in popular systems is equally serious. "And popular governments under some impulses are more readily raging or bestial than severe; when they make rash judgments, and maximum ones where charges of scheming against the state are involved, and then there is the danger that they may commit some injustice and greatly whimsical act, especially against powerful men with authority, whom they ruin because of vain suspicions" (Guicciardini, DRF, 357). In other words, under the two extremes of despotism and populism prudence disappears, and prudence, in the eyes of the Florentine thinker (a great many pages are devoted to this subject), is the main virtue of a moderate State capable of safeguarding liberty and security.

1.32 It should also be pointed out that, in Guicciardini's opinion, despotism and populism often converge to the point of becoming a single system. This happens when some seek to "ingratiate themselves with the multitude", which willingly exalts such individuals who are not so concerned about evaluating whether what they are doing is proper or mistaken as they are about pleasing the multitude. It has happened on occasion that the alliance between despotism and the multitude had some good effect, but most often they have produced extremely great evils and great scandals (cf. Guicciardini, DRF, 433-434). For this reason the election of some officials, such as that of the gonfaloner, must be taken away from the people, but must be carried out by a "greater council" in which the Senate and popular representation are present (cf. Guicciardini, DRF, 435). The Senate is a sort of intermediate body capable of mollifying despotic demands or populist whims. As if to show that he is not behind the times, Guicciardini looks at the Venetian republic in addition to the Roman one. The executive of the former cannot be called a "merely popular government" but, at the same time, it "defends itself from the ambition of the Doges and all those who aspire to tyranny" (Guicciardini, DRF, 405).

The aristocracy and merchant class are a bulwark against the two forms of extremism which not infrequently manage to combine. History itself bears witness to all of that. In the past, "there has been no lack of Doges and others who aimed at tyranny, but they have quickly been put down because of the good regulation of the government" (Guicciardini, DRF, 407).

1.33 The "greater council" must have guarantees that its legislating will not encounter pressures that can, through fear or blackmail, alter its will. Since ancient times, voting took place in the open. In modern times it is necessary to offer greater guarantees of liberty. "And opinions are obtained either by voice or by counting beans; the ancients voted by acclamation, the modern republics have used beans or secret voting. There are different reasons for using each of these methods, but in order not to speak at overly great length on every matter I am more inclined to praise the beans" (Guicciardini, DRF, 424). This cryptic statement is intended to defend autonomy and the political force of this fundamental institution. There is another reason, however, one of extreme importance. This sort of political discretion is not only justified by the insecurity of the times, but it also advises anyone who performs political activity to exercise a certain moderation, especially when the people are involved. In the long run, the people do not accept too much ostentation. History teaches this, too: when the patricians did not make moderate use of their authority, conflicts could not be resolved (cf. Guicciardini, DRF, 452). In addition to prudence, moderation is another virtue that anyone involved in politics, in a Republic, cannot and must not neglect.

1.34 The appeal on behalf of the virtues in the life of a Republic, leads Guicciardini to anticipate the observations that Montesquieu will make on the subject. If a republican system really wants to survive and prosper, everything that "alienates the souls in their search for virtue and leads them into a thousand forms of usurpation and dishonesty" (Guicciardini, DdL, 294) must be kept at bay: these things have destroyed more than one republic as the ancient historians show us. A basic duty of a great Republic will be that of teaching in favour of and producing conditions to encourage a life of great works. On the contrary, "A government shall be blameworthy and detested when it takes extremely great care to subdue any form of generosity and any virtue!" (Guicciardini, DRF, 333). As in his times, anyone who sought to take away this love of virtue and liberty reducing a Republic "to a form of Princedom, would take away its soul, its life and would weaken and shatter it to the greatest possible extent" (Guicciardini, DRF, 377). Here is to be found the typical conviction of the western world that *order*, is an *interior condition*, before being an *exterior* one: if the one does not exist, the other is impossible. That conclusion, which I would call typically Augustinian, is borne out by the fact that not even the search for the useful can be conceived of above and beyond virtue (cf. Guicciardini, C, 506). When this sort of upbringing is lacking, the very limits of civil life founder and there is no force of law that can guarantee the survival of a Republic.

1.35 Aside from these considerations that will be dissected by Montesquieu, it is quite singular that Guicciardini anticipates other subjects that will be dealt with in the centuries to follow. What can one say of the concept that Tocqueville will be so fond of according to which "men naturally love equality and thus (Guicciardini uses the term 'però' here in the sense of 'thus') are unwilling to agree to have to recognise others as superiors"? (Guicciardini, DRF,

318). In other words, men may become satiated with liberty, but they are never so with equality. What can one say, then – as Locke will point out – about the legislative body that since "this council cannot be gathered together at any hour, and matters require continued diligence and labour, and many things that are deliberated on must be practiced and require swiftness and secrecy, a more particular magistracy is necessary" (Guicciardini, DRF, 417), in other words, an executive which is always performing its tasks and which has particular duties for unexpected matters as well. These and other perceptions make Guicciardini a far-sighted spirit capable of analyzing the past and the present experience in order to make useful suggestions for a future that can safeguard various forms of liberty and progress. This spirit was not listened to because it was overcome by absolutism which was then more actual, even if more tragic, but which certainly appears more modern today, and more capable of involving us. This is a great difference from many of his contemporaries.

1.36 While absolutism in various forms is arising all over Europe, other voices are rising up to recall that man is naturally free and inclined to mature in social relations. If he now lives in a state of servitude this can be considered the result of several historical contingencies which have, over time, brought about a tendency towards tyranny. Servitude has thus become a sort of later form of human nature which, in many cases, covers over and cancels the former one. These are the conclusions reached by Etienne de La Boétie (1530-1562) in *De la servitude volontaire*. The author speaks not only of those moments when, through threats and violence, the people are forced to live under a tyrant not daring even to enquire about what it has lost. On the contrary, by voluntary servitude, he means that situation, unfortunately not very infrequent either, in which peoples, now resigned, passively accept tyranny. The tyrant does not even need to make a show of force. It is accepted as such because the yearning for liberty has been snuffed out, due to a series of more or less noble circumstances. The subjects are so brutalized that they have the illusion of living well and have all they require, since their very imaginations have been impaired. Tyranny has managed to destroy what nature had instilled in the human spirit. With a handful of accomplices, the tyrant thus creates a pyramid-like system of obedience and bonds that are difficult to evade and against which passive resistance is helpless. For this reason tyrants manage to reduce those who had been citizens first to the condition of subjects and finally, that of beasts. These observations will be taken up again by Montesquieu. Guillaume Postel (1510-1581) is certainly to be remembered alongside La Boétie. In his *De Concordia: primo, religionis christianae placita rationibus philosophicis docentur*, he proposes to reunite Islam with a simplified and rationalized form of Catholicism. This latter operation becomes necessary since the Christian religion can no longer count on the special means that enabled it to propagate itself at the beginning. From this comes the objective of setting forth a form of natural law valid for everyone, which will form the basis for a new, universal religion. This is a cosmopolitan approach to be put into practice and France will have to play a fundamental role. Nationality and cosmopolitism become the crucial ingredients in this reflection. He has in view a universal monarchy which, establishing itself as the sole authority, will be able to guarantee an effective harmony. In addition to the pressures to reform characteristic of that period, there are also suggestions, even if re-adapted to the times, that take us back to various authors of the past among whom there are Dante and Cusanus.

2. Between the Medieval and Modernity.

2.1 Political thought concerning the great themes of peace and moralisation of political life has a long history even though every era has experienced it in terms of the particular problems to be faced. In the modern world those subjects are seen in relation to the power of the State whereas they had been seen in relation to the two great forms of universality: the Papacy and the Empire. It must be said, however, that as the Medieval era came to an end, these subjects were dealt with in a new way. Along with the two great parties to the conflict, there are more particular political subjects concerning the problems of the individual states. One can think of Catherine of Siena, for example, (1347-1380) who did not lose sight of what concerned the action of the Pope or the Emperor and addressed herself to sovereigns such as the King of France or politicians from the various Italian governments reminding them of their fundamental duties. The first was to maintain civil harmony and peace through concrete means to the point where politicians should be considered "adempitori d'essa pace" [peacemakers] (Catherine, 464). Then, politics in the sense of a service, which is possible only if the politician listens, "*since you possess* (addressing herself directly to the people governing) *your realm as something loaned to you and not your own (...) That you maintain health and true justice and that this is not to be destroyed because of your pride, or by flattery or any human pleasure*" (Catherine, 309). It need hardly be pointed out that Catherine considered power not a personal matter (the realm as something loaned to one) but an instrument that could be granted to- or administered by others. Only thus could one hope to pursue the common good (cf. Catherine, 487-491).

2.2 The common good can be more easily obtained when, in addition to peace, there is a good government and all are convinced that this is necessary to achieve justice. The subjects were dealt with again in the fifteenth century first by Bernardino of Siena (1380-1444) and then Girolamo Savonarola, one of the most controversial and brilliant figures of his time. In his preaching and treatises there is a clear appeal to return to legality in an era which seemed more and more to pave the way towards absolutism. Taking up ancient reflections on tyranny, receiving criticism based on new reasoning, he was of the opinion that Florence should carry out political renewal aimed at restoring true liberty. "The first thing that you (Florence) must do among others is make laws to the effect that no-one in the future can make himself the leader, otherwise, you will be founded on sand. And you must do so in a way that no-one can set himself up such that others must bow before him as before a superior, but that authority be solely virtue" (Savonarola, PsA, 132). Therefore, it has been correctly said that Savonarola's can be considered a form of moral theocracy (cf. Sarubbi, 134), based on the necessity for internal renewal in turn based on the best tradition of Christianity.

Girolamo Savonarola was born in Florence in 1452. After entering the Dominican order, he became the Prior of the famous monastery of St Mark's in Florence, actively and passionately taking part in the political affairs of the city, with his fiery preaching. He seemed a prophet to not a few, but since he had touched upon the consolidated interests of several Catholic parties and come into conflict with several religious authorities, he was condemned to be hanged and burned at the stake. The sentence was carried out in Piazza della Signoria in 1498. The author of notable philosophical and theological works, it is useful, in this context, to recall his preaching, and among these *Prediche sopra Aggèo (Preaching on Haggai)* and the *Trattato circa il reggimento e il governo della città di Firenze (Treatise on Law and Government of the City of Florence)*.

2.3 The concern to avoid tyranny comes from Savonarola's great respect for the intelligence of the Florentines. They should be offended at the mere idea of being dominated by a ruler especially when he is a tyrant and thus lacking all those moral, religious and even intellectual prerequisites. This saps the city of its most promising possibilities. Suffice it to think tyrants often govern, neglecting the abilities of their leading citizens and, since "they cannot know the contingent or future problems, or many particular things that can happen" (Savonarola, PsA, 224), they turn to astrology, because they trust no-one, not even the most intelligent people. Thus, resignation ends up running rampant, weakening intelligence and the will to perform good works, until there is revolt and killing in the fury of dramatic events. "Let it be said that the people under a tyrant are like water held back by force, which finds a hole from which to spring, impetuously creating ruin as it bursts forth" (Savonarola, PsA, 225). The tyrant governs with every means, even the most perfidious, because he considers politics and the State to be his only ends and does everything possible to keep from losing hold of them (cf. Savonarola, T, 457), when it should be one of the many ways of attaining the supreme goal of salvation. This is why the tyrant is basically a godless person, even if, in a statement that seems to anticipate Machiavelli, "he seeks to appear religious and devoted to the divine cult" (Savonarola, T, 460) A comparison with the future Florentine secretary does not come as a surprise: the points of contact between the two, despite the difference in the objectives, are quite frequent (cf. Weinstein, 251-264).

2.4 Another very import reflection is that the tyrant cancels out the very reason for community living. He aims to sew disharmony, divide families and groups, forgetting that society itself was born to move from the phase of discord to that of harmony (cf. Savonarola, T, 459). Not only that, but offending intelligence and favouring mediocrity, he plunges the people into poverty, because he takes from them the will to improve. This is true since there exists no certainty that they will reap the benefits or their work, and there is no certainty for the future. "In the final analysis, nothing is stable under a tyranny, since everything is governed according to his will, which is supported not by reason but by passion" (Savonarola, T, 465). Clearly, the certitude of law is the first thing to be lost: "He seeks to corrupt all the good laws, since they are contrary to his unjust government, and he continually makes new laws for his own benefit" (Savonarola, T, 463).

2.5 Hence, the Florentines are called upon to create a republic that is good. This is certainly not easy and "it must be well governed" (Savonarola, PsA, 212). At this point comes the reflection on the sense of limits typical of States in which the law governs, since it clarifies the sense of liberty which, thanks to the rules, forestalls the dangers of tyranny and of anarchy as well. These laws must then be obeyed as long as they exist. Indeed "where there is no charity, the citizens do not like one another; where there is no obedience, they separate and do not have nor can they have among them sage council for the division that exists among them" (Savonarola, PsA, 219). Here, too, taking up a classical subject once again he reiterates the conviction that society is based on a precise political order which becomes disjointed, first for internal reasons. This is why Savonarola favours a form of aristocratic republic, as long is it is based on consensus. Despite the fact that everyone can administer the State and many wish to do so, in actual fact not everyone "is appropriate for the task". Political activity requires a moral tension which not everyone can achieve. For this reason, one can, in connection with Savonarola, speak of "a substantial identity between Christianity, political and civil liberty which confers a precise ethical and civil liberty on the needs for renewal of religiosity" (D'Addio, SDP, I, 255)

A) *Needs for Renewal.*

2.6 Even before Savonarola, the problem of renewing the shaky imperial political system, with consideration for the greater and more just needs of the individual imbued with humanistic expectations, was put forth by Cusanus, surely one of the most open and systematic minds of his time. For him, the social inclinations of mankind are important not only on the political level, but also and especially on the cultural one: "Every feeling arises from an encounter" (Cusanus, C, II, 141), he says explicitly in his *Conjectures*. This encounter gives rise to a mutual enrichment, given the diversity of the individuals, whose equality must be considered in a logical sense and, if one wishes, a legal one, otherwise there would be the worst possible levelling off. "There would be no otherness if there were exact equality" (Cusanus, C, II, 168). Development is always the fruit of a never-ending search for improvement, exactly like the search for divine perfection (cf. Cusanus, C, II, 167) the true driving force in human betterment.

Nicola Cryfts was born in Cusa (hence the Latinization of his surname **Cusanus**) in 1401. After studying in Heidelberg, he completed his studies of canon law at the University of Padua. His having known Pope Martin V was of fundamental importance and, above all, that of his having heard some of the preaching of San Bernardino of Siena.

After returning to Germany, he crowned his studies with the discovery, in Cologne, of speeches of Cicero, works of St Cyprian and twelve unknown comedies of Plautus. In 1432 he took part in the Council of Basel. In the mid fourteen thirties, he wrote the *De concordantia catholica* concerned with, among other things, the problem of Papal supremacy. In 1437 he went to Constantinople to set once again in motion the dialogue for the reuniting of the two Churches. It was for his efforts to recreate the unity of the Church that he was named Cardinal. Among his other works, *De docta ignorantia* (1438-40), *Apologia doctae ignorantiae* (1450), *De pace fidei* (1453), should be mentioned as well as numerous scientific and mathematical writings.

2.7 The quest, a characteristic of human nature is certainly not without obstacles. "Religion, too, fluctuates unstably between spirituality and temporality" (Cusanus, C, II, 149), it is thus necessary to take action to create those conditions of stability which make possible the real improvement of mankind. The quest for the unity of Christians departs from this point, but this unity is not to be accomplished by offending the diversity and intelligence of people. Suffice it to remember that "although the tie that binds the Church in unity is faith, nonetheless the variety of opinions held without obstinacy may, at times, co-exist with that unity" (Cusanus, DCU, 151). Cusanus presents the term "community" combining it with *universitas* whose root lies in the idea of seeking the convergence of multiplicity into unity. "Indeed, a multiplicity assembled in units for convergence towards one becomes a universitas" (Cusanus, DCU, 195). All of this applies on the religious and, obviously, the political level. Thus, everyone, whether in the Councils or in Assemblies, must be guaranteed freedom of speech (cf. Cusanus, DCU, 203). The guarantee is for everyone, since everyone is born free and equal. Hence, any power is based on agreement and consensus as well as on the possibility of electing those who are to wield the power (cf. D'Addio, SDP, I, 222-223).

2.8 This understanding of power recalls the suggestions of Roman jurists who viewed the people as the real holders of power. But the will of the people is the expression of a rationality which is then codified into law. That is why laws are manifestations of the common consensus of all. There is in Cusanus the entirely humanistic confidence that the people, or more often its majority, will always succeed in expressing in laws what is most useful (cf. Cusanus, DCU, 393). It follows that "it is better for a State to be governed by laws rather than by an excellent ruler" (Cusanus, DCU, 397-398). The institution of the Empire itself, then, had to looked at again to give it new strength to carry on with its duties, but only on the condition that it considered the people the true source of power.

2.9 Departing from such positions, but then arriving at the conviction that the power of the Principate had now become definitively consolidated, Erasmus of Rotterdam, more than any other person, interpreted the need for far-reaching renewal in his time, and this had to involve all the areas of civil life. Like few others, he was able to ascribe value, even theoretical, to pacifism to the point of condemning every policy of power pursued by the nascent national States. Thus he succeeded in pointing out the responsibilities of sovereigns in a period in which their action conditioned that of the entire State and involved the entire political community. He succeeded in this intent bringing to bear the finest tradition of Christian and Medieval humanism as well as that of his own era. Suffice it to think of the suggestions coming from Petrarch, Ficino and Cusanus. From these, he had pursued the ideals of *docta pietas* and *docta religio* (cf. Petruzzelis, 7).

Geert Geertsz was born in 1466. He Latinized and Hellenized his name to **Desiderius** and **Erasmus of Rotterdam**, the city of his birth. After the death of his parents, he entered the Augustinian Canons Regular at Steyn where he was ordained as a priest in 1492. After completing some studies in Paris, he travelled for several years, first to England, where he met Thomas More, then he returned to France and there published the first edition of the *Adagia* and, finally, to Italy, where he met the great Italian humanists. Among them were Giovanni dei Medici, the future Leo X, who would later dispense him from his monastic obligations, allowing him to leave the order to live a life devoted to travel and study. From this period comes Μωρίας 'Εγκώμιov id est Stultitiae Laus that is *In Praise of Folly*. In 1518 he published the *Institutio Principis Christiani*. In 1524 his *De libero arbitrio* appeared. It was in open conflict with Luther, who replied with his *De servo arbitrio,* which Erasmus, in 1529, countered with *l'Institutio christiani matrimonii* in which he repeated his theses. After a series of vicissitudes and disagreements with the various religious formations conflicting with one another in that period, and other publications, he died in 1536 in Basel.

2.10 Erasmus, the profound religious spirit, was intransigent against all forms of religious Pharaism and formalism, but this led him to renew rather than contest. Suffice it to think of the conflict with Luther in which he recognizes that free will has been wounded, but not stifled, in agreement with all of Catholic thought (cf. Petruzzellis, 12). Basically, he remains fully orthodox. Erasmus himself confirms this fact when he maintains that for too many theologians neither the Gospel nor Saint Paul, nor the Fathers nor even Saint Augustine or Saint Thomas are sufficient; and, instead of striving to be Saints as they had been, they work day and night splitting hairs not even finding the time to look for a moment at the Gospel or the Epistles (cf. Erasmus, M'ESL). In his devastating satire, Erasmus not only attacks religious Pharaism, but, to some extent, all of the society of his time: laymen, politicians, philosophers, the military, men, women, all unmasked in their exteriority and considered in their passions. Among these the first is the passion for money and not by chance Folly declares herself to be the daughter of Pluto the God of wealth. Her land is where all things grow without sowing and ploughing, and so without fatigue. What comes after results from vanity, adulation, forgetfulness, laziness, voluptuousness, failure to reflect, gluttony, pleasure-seeking and heavy slumber. All of these vices even command the princes (cf. Erasmus, M'ESL, VII-VIII-IX) who, on the contrary should have dominance over them. It is the portrait of a society in need of an appeal to return to those Christian values that it has forgotten and which, in Erasmus' opinion, one which needs to be ridiculed so that it will re-discover them.

2.11 Erasmus' satire makes reference here and there to subjects already dealt with in other works or ones that he will deal with later. His considerations on the folly of war or that of philosophers is worthy of note. Everything, however, is laid out with sharp realism and he never loses himself in chimeras or utopias that could be still more dangerous. Certain statements leave no doubts: "Has there ever existed a State, that adopted the laws of Plato and Aristotle, or the dogmas of Socrates?" (cf. Erasmus, M'ESL, XXVII). Hence he appeals to the princes, the consolidation of whom was now taken for granted, and which was to the detriment of representative political systems, to remind them of those duties, unfortunately neglected, that would be recalled with precision in *Institutio Principis Christiani*. Erasmus shows preferences for a mixed constitution since the sovereign's power here is tempered by the aristocracy and by democracy. When the power of the prince is not moderated by other bodies, the state easily drifts towards tyranny. To keep this from happening, the private lives of the citizens must be freed from the influence of politicians to the greatest possible extent. For this reason, the prince's tax policy must be as moderate as possible, and he will have to attempt to make the handling of the resources as transparent as he can, showing that they indeed serve the public (cf. Erasmus, IPC, IV).

2.12 The political activity of the Christian prince should be transparent and clear, starting from legislative activity that must be kept in conformity with the principle which not only needs a few laws for the proper conducting of affairs of state, but also, these laws must be totally comprehensible. Those provisions must then function to prevent crimes. It is not enough to threaten the guilty, one must persuade those who vacillate. The law must therefore perform a true educational function "inflaming (the souls of the citizens) with the passion for good" (cf. Erasmus, IPC, VI). Laws must take social change into account, so they must adapt to the real situation of the people on whom laws of other peoples cannot be imposed, laws which would require excessively abrupt changes. Indeed, could not be proposed because they would only manage to upset the social context which, on the contrary, needs continually to be kept serene. Social and "international" peace are the main subjects dealt with in the last two parts of the *Institutio Principis Christiani*. Here, Erasmus reveals all of his Augustinian upbringing because it is in peace that the unity of the Christian world is created and consolidated. Thus, peace must not be threatened for any reason. The position of those who maintain that if it is acceptable to castigate the individual evil doer, it must also be acceptable to punish a collective body through war is senseless. It is senseless because, while the guilty and convicted party pays by law, in war, each of the two sides accuses the other, believing that it is in the right and, furthermore, the punishment affects only the guilty party in the first case, in the second, the innocent are also punished. Moreover, while legal actions aim at the individual seeking to protect the community, war, whose aim had been to punish someone who will perhaps remain without punishment, is directed against a community (cf. Erasmus DBI, 974-991).

2.13 These points must first of all be explained to sovereigns. Erasmus pursued this aim throughout his life. Already long before the *Institutio Principis Christiani* he had written, in the *Aut regem aut fatuum nasci oportere,* that it is difficult to encounter, over the centuries, a prince who did not distinguish himself for his idiocy (cf. Erasmus, ARAF, 90-91). Hence, it is necessary to prepare him to assess matters properly, to then be horrified by infamy, and to be inclined towards the virtues (cf. Erasmus, ARAF, 130 ff.). This educative process must begin immediately in the earliest childhood, so that there is time to mould the prince to perform his difficult tasks. With the aid of Christian civilisation and tradition, he will have to be able to recognize merit and fend off useless conflicts and, obviously, wars (cf. Erasmus, ARAF, 239 up to the very end). This apprenticeship is slow and fatiguing but it is the future prince's duty to undertake it for his own good and that of his people. This was the only aim of the advice referred to above and with which Erasmus started a veritable literary style. For example, it led to so-called "preceptism" in Spain which influenced minds of the greatness of a Cervantes. Proof of this can be found quite simply in Chapters XLII and XLII of the second part of his *Don Quijote*. In general, it is all of Erasmus that provided ideas for all of the great European literature; selections from his Μωρίας Ἐγκώμιον *id est Stultitiae Laus*, on considerations of life as a theatrical representation, find their way to the pages of Shakespeare. On that subject, it must not be forgotten that the aforementioned work was dedicated to Thomas More and widely read in England.

B) *The Problem of Power and the "right of the peoples".*

2.14 Up to what point could the Spanish conquest of the New World be considered legitimate and to what extent was it right to impose the Catholic faith on those new populations? These two questions led to a re-examination of the very nature of political power and its aims, and were carefully analysed in Francisco De Vitoria. Attempting to discover the basis of power itself, De Vitoria summarized the Thomist conception of politics with the Stoic one on the society of nature, pointing out that the need to provide for vital necessities gives mankind the inclination to gather together in a society to meet those needs as well as they can. Political power is justified by its ensuring unity and stability, for the very purpose of satisfying the needs mentioned above. This power, or *summa potestas,* is what distinguishes the political community from other forms and it is always thought of as power which makes use of all the means necessary to carry out its aims. De Vitoria also rejects the points of view typical of other reformers bent on demonstrating that the original inequality of people did not allow any form of political power (cf. D'Addio, SDP, I, 334-335). As the Fathers had already said, this position would lead society to disintegrate to the point of losing its reason for being.

Francisco **De Vitoria** was born in 1492 in Burgos. Between 1510 and 1523 he entered the order of Preaching Friars and was ordained. He performed many functions in Paris among the theological disciplines taught at the Sorbonne. After returning to Spain, he taught first in Valladolid then, from 1526 to his death in 1546, at the University of Salamanca. Among his works dealing with political questions *De potestate civili* and, obviously, the *Relectio De Indis* that came from courses he taught between 1534 and 1539 should be recalled.

2.15 The need for power does not take from it the limits that are inherent in it to achieve the ends desired by the community. The sovereign is always obliged to obey the laws, including those which he himself had enacted. This comes about from the nature of law as a contract and it means that every "political community must be considered completely autonomous, capable, in other words, of governing itself" (D'Addio, SDP, I, 336). Therefore, power is not conferred by superior authorities whether they be the Empire or the Papacy. Nor can the Aristotelian consideration apply, which states that the native populations of America are slaves "by nature", because they are inferior, and must therefore be governed by Europeans. These arguments do not hold up because these populations may be more primitive, but not barbarous or slaves from a nature point of view and so are capable of governing themselves (cf. De Vitoria, I, 1, 16). Nor can violent conquest be justified even for religious reasons such as that of the propagation of the faith: *"per bellum barbari non possunt moveri ad credendum"*, but they will feign to believe this monstrous and sacrilegious thing *"quod immane sacrilegium est"* (De Vitoria, I, 2, 20).

2.16 In support of this conviction, De Vitoria replaces the Medieval conception of the *Imperium christianum* with that of the Society of all people which he calls *Totus orbis*. Here he is bringing back the Roman juridical conception that sees in the formation of the *societas* the irreplaceable action of individuals supported here by the Christian message which conceives of the political order as something achieved through the common effort of all. "The new theory he proposes is based on a profound and new reflection about mankind, which for De Vitoria is radically free" (Castaño, 106). Starting from this original liberty, De Vitoria also fights all those, theologians or jurists, who continue to support the theocratic theory: *Pope non est dominus civilis aut temporalis totius orbis.* The fact that mankind is *radically* free, means that it is necessary to free theological reflection from the area of pure jusnaturalism. For him, the latter is part of a precise historical discussion since it cannot escape the just evolution and achievement of liberty, even though it is based on natural law (cf. Castaño, 107 and 112). Thus, when De Vitoria speaks of a *pactum politicum et sociale,* "it is implicit in the contract stipulated between governing and governed bodies, that the latter ascribe to the former public powers only, and not the right to interfere *ad libitum* in their private sphere" (Luppi, 488) which, ever since ancient times, has belonged to the *ius privatorum.* Here the solid Roman juridical conception is brought back (whose references to the *Digest* are eloquent on the subject) "not in the primary sense of the role of the will, but in *ius,* which, as Cicero explains, indicates *dignitas*" (Composta, 274-275). This aspect has succeeded in uniting natural law *mos maiorum,* with common law and with the gradual transformation of the concept of *societas*, itself.

2.17 What has been said thus far also applies to the *ius gentium,* which must benefit from the three characteristic notes of *semper, ubique* and *apud omnes.* This means that the *ius gentium* "can be considered as belonging to natural law even if it has been derived from other sources. De Vitoria is, furthermore, aware of the pactician and consensual aspect of the law which governs the relations between nations, and as such it can also be considered a positive law" (Castaño, 114). This is why, in the formulation of *ius gentium*, the bases of modern law can be perceived. Suffice it to think that for De Vitoria and his contemporaries, those relations that we now call international, were governed by the *ius gentium.* In that era, this law included the present-day international law, since it contained the various *norms* present in treaties.

2.18 The Hispanic-American Alonso De Veracruz (1507-1584), the best known disciple of De Vitoria and the author of *De dominio infidelium et iusto bello*, is considered in some way the *Fundador De la Universidad De México* because, as a philosopher, theologian and missionary, he devised an actual theoretical defence of the Indios from an American viewpoint. In exploring his master's teachings, De Veracruz develops a theory of private property, which, in some cases, may encounter some limitations where the political authority and the priorities of the common good identify prerogatives that may concern the whole community. The common good and the community in its entirety may have aims and objectives which, at times, override those of the States themselves in so far as there exists a *bonum commune totius orbis* that crosses over rigid political boundaries and belongs, as some United Nations provisions maintain today, to all of Humanity (cf. Cerezo De Diego, 260-261). The greatest merit of De Veracruz's work is that he wrote in America about things which concern the new continent, of which he now had direct knowledge, since he had absorbed the mentality, usages and customs.

2.19 The subjects dealt with by De Vitoria were explored from the juridical point of view by Ferdinando Vasquez (1512 ca -1569). For him, if the political authority had been set up to achieve the common good of society, this means that it cannot think solely about working to its own advantage. The purpose of the written laws was to place limits on the enormous power that the sovereigns had increased as they wished. This could happen because the legitimate Principate had, over time, turned into a tyranny, forgetting that its nature lay, according to Cicero's authority, in consensus. Consensus shows that power, in so far as it is conferred, can be revoked when the aims of the community are not pursued. Power, therefore, has a pactician nature which binds whoever wields it to obeying the rules (cf. D'Addio, SDP, I, 338-389). What has been said is corroborated by history in which Vasquez identifies three phases: in the first, the natural law and peoples are created; in the second, political authority is created; in the third, written law, that is, civil law, is formulated (cf. Cedroni, 885). Here, too, one of the themes is treated, which Roman juridical tradition is fond of: law as a synthesis of natural premises and historical process slowly determined by tradition.

2.20 Characteristic of the birth of the modern State is the re-discovery of the juridical tradition. It is no longer seen as a person on a larger scale in an organic view, but considered as an actual person with all his prerogatives. Law, which to some extent constitutes its spirit, is determined by the need for self-preservation, self-governance and defence (cf. Quadri, 39). These are all governed by laws, which bind, as Domingo De Soto (1495-1560) maintained, even the Prince himself. That the state has the characteristics of a person is a conception that will be developed by Navarro after De Vitoria (Martín De Azpilcueta named Navarrus 1493-1586) and Alonso De Castro (1495-1558). In these authors, there is the conviction later developed by the theorists of sovereignty, that the State is the original holder of the power and so, the primary subject of political authority. Soto, is extremely clear about this: *"Diregere autem in commune bonum proprium est reipubblicae"* (Soto, I, 1, q.1, a.3). Navarro, too, agrees that the *potestas* emerges when the *communitas* is established, thus it comes about before law is consolidated. Characteristics such as equality and liberty come before juridical recognition by any State, since they are elements making up the original community.

Soto is clear here, too: "*Omnes enim nascuntur liberi*" (Soto, I, 4, q.4, a.2). Indeed, De Vitoria had been decidedly critical of Aristotle for his justification of slavery which is not understandable from the point of view of natural law and even less so from that of divine law.

2.21 The idea of equality and liberty bring up another important subject in the political debate: is the transfer of power an obligation or can it be merely advantageous and necessary? The answer to this question creates a division among authors of the time: next to Soto and Molina (1535-1600), who consider democratic wielding of power inadmissible, there are Navarro, Castro and then Suarez who maintain the direct opposite. For example, Navarro supports the idea that the law of nature grants authority to the State, but it does not, in any way, specify how it is exercised or transferred. Thus, democracy, even direct, is not opposed to natural law.

2.22 From the beginning of the sixteenth-century, the Dominican community of the island of Hispaniola devoted itself to evangelizing that community of natives which, from the viewpoint of the missionaries, were people born free and so, had to be treated accordingly. It was in that period that Bartolomé De Las Casas, who had departed with the group of Diego Velasquez as military chaplain, began to have a new look at the original rule of his Order and had a personal conversion experience (cf. Cantù, 64-65). This re-examination was to lead him, with total clarity, to enjoin the colonists immediately to give up the Indians that had been assigned to them as slaves, if they wanted to avoid eternal damnation, but if not, he would deny the sacraments to those who refused to release them and compensate them for the harm suffered (cf. Acutis, 11 and 13).

Bartolomé **De Las Casas** was born in 1474. He went to America for the first time in 1502. In the new continent, a sermon given by a Dominican Father radically transformed him to such a degree that he took holy orders in 1510. He then carried on a firm struggle against the *encomienda*. In his defence of the Indios he was accused of having proposed the replacement of weak natives by black people for hard labor to save their race, while he repeatedly said that he wanted to attenuate a more serious ill which was bound to manifest itself in what would later be called ethnic cleansing. He received some land on which experimentally to apply his standards of colonisation, but this failed since, in his absence, the criteria he had set forth were clearly denied. His *Brevisima relación De la destruyción De las Indias,* published in 1552, was translated into several languages. In the last part of his life he also wrote the *Apologetica,* in which he wanted to include a geographical description of the Indies, as well as the *Historia De las Indias.* In these last works there are not a few mistakes, since he was writing from memory at an advanced age, but this takes nothing away from the vivacity and realism characteristic of his writing. He died in Madrid in 1566. Many works remained unpublished for a long time and some still have not been.

2.23 His action was supported by many fellow brothers, ecclesiastics, theologians, and even the authority of the Church. The bull *Sublimis Deus* of 1537 issued by Paul III reiterated the fact that Indians were real people. They could thus rebel against all the impositions placed on their shoulders. Las Casas' words leave no room for doubt: "And I know from certain and infallible knowledge that the wars of the Indians against the Christians were always highly just, while not a single one of those waged by the Christians against the Indians has been so" (Las Casas, DI, 42). The words of the missionary and theologian describing the conquest, or, as he better expresses it, the destruction of the Indies was highly dramatic because it shows with unequaled crudity and realism the horrors perpetrated in those distant lands. In one of the points where his judgement is more serene, his words convey all the weight of the atrocities committed: "and what they call by this name (conquest) is no other than brutal invasions by cruel tyrants, condemned not only by the law of God but also by any just human being, and far worse than the actions of the Turks aimed at destroying the Church of Christ" (Las Casas, DI, 61). Moreover, it is the missionary's firm conviction that the Holy Scriptures themselves prohibit any sort of harassment of the subjects (cf. Las Casas, DRP, II, X, l), so certainly, of other peoples who however primitive they may be, are free.

2.24 It must be recalled that for Las Casas, any power is such because it encounters very precise limitations in its exercise. Suffice it to recall that no sovereign can, without just cause, enter the area of all that belongs to private individuals. He cannot give away or negotiate with the goods of the subject without having requested and legally obtained explicit consent (cf. Las Casas, DRP, II, XI, 1) This affirmation is likewise justified in Roman law. So there is no regal authority that can justify what is being done to the Indians. All that would not be justified even if it were authorized by the Pope in person, who, in fact, has no right to make concessions. (cf. Las Casas, DRP, app. VI). Thus not only can people not be deprived of their natural liberty without just cause, but no governing or other prominent figure can be deprived of their own dignity and regal states (cf. Las Casas, DRP, app. VII). The only path to follow is that of civil dialogue. Las Casas refuses any type of violence in the pedagogical method because that procedure does not enable people sincerely to accept faith (Henkel, 381).

2.25 Many have observed that Suarez makes a fundamental contribution to political, moral, and juridical thought, but there are probably three points where he succeeds in providing possible solutions to problems raised in his time. First of all, contract theory, which becomes in him decidedly institutional; then his theory of the right of peoples, progressively obligatory, and applying to the area of public law as well as private; finally, a new proposal in new terms of so-called indirect power which, transcending theocratic and overly regalist theses, acknowledges the enjoyment of its rights to the civil authority and appropriate means for the preaching of the Gospel to the Church (cf. Mesnard, II, 437-438).

Francisco Suarez was born in Granada in 1548. He studied in Salamanca then continued to explore theology in the Company of Jesus. He occupied many positions in various universities and colleges thanks to his recognized abilities. Between 1601 and 1603 he wrote his first work, in Coimbra. This work, the *Tractatus De legibus ac De Deo legislatore,* was published in 1612 after three revisions. His *Defensio fidei catholicae erga sectae anclicanae errores,* written in opposition to the claims of James I, the King of England is fundamental on the political level. The king supported the idea of the divine right of kings. Suarez died in 1617 in Lisbon.

2.26 Suarez's political conception also takes into consideration the components of the Protestant reform in order to criticize their reductive idea of the State that some reformers wanted, as well as the theocratic approach sought by others. The traditional distinction between spiritual and temporal power is enhanced by the conviction that there may be a distinction such that one power cannot interfere with another, but the State, too, is capable of orienting mankind towards good (cf. Suarez, PP, III, 9, 4). Furthermore, the nobility of the political organization comes from the fact that Suarez conceives of this as an actual *corpus* which, analogous to the mystical body of the Church, has a precise reason for being (cf. Elourduy y Pereña, CLII). The power of this State, its *soma potestas,* comes from this community and it is on this union which, as Cicero would say, society and law are based.

2.27 The political community surpasses all other forms of intermediate communities starting with the family itself, which cannot be considered a form of *communitas perfecta,* since it cannot meet all the needs of the individual. But the simple *communitas politica* cannot consider itself perfect either. Aristotle cannot satisfy a modern person and a Christian. The stoics and Cicero in particular (cf. Elourduy y Pereña, CLXXVIII ff.) saw that the social components of the *polis* went far beyond politics, but only Christianity identified the ultimate goal of mankind in a perspective beyond this world. This goal can be more easily attained when the *communitas* finds itself once again in that *iuris consensus*, which facilitates the achievement of the goals desired. *Consensus* must arise from the will of those associated, so that one cannot think that sovereignty is granted directly by God to the monarchs, but the latter obtain it from the community, *per modum pacti.* Thus, it cannot only be granted, but also revoked if the reasons for the pact no longer exist (cf. Suarez, PP, III, 2, 12). This is *the most serious argument against monarchical absolutism* so that the right to resist the monarch who has violated the pact always exists albeit in properly qualified ways and through qualified individuals.

2.28 All depends, therefore, on the will of the community, even the forms of government or constitutions based on positive law. The monarchy, the aristocracy and democracy are chosen by the community depending on the need of the moment and how they succeed in meeting the needs of the community itself. It must, however, be added that whereas the monarchy and aristocracy arise from human positive law, democracy, on the contrary is the original constitution of the community and is based on natural law. From that consideration, it follows that the law of nature is the source of positive law, but also the fact that any form of government is, in fact, almost "constitutionalized", in the sense that the executive can act only within those laws that govern it. Concerning the moment of volition, it is useful to recall that it precedes the institutional moment because, first of all, people must form a community, political power, and the rules that define it come after establishment of the body politic. That explains why reason can find legitimacy in various political systems since power in itself is not tied to a single person, or a more or less numerically determined group, as comes out quite clearly in some passages of the *Defensio fidei* (cf. Quadri, 70). There is another, no less important reason to explain what has been said up to now. There is, in mankind, a perfective component, which can never completely satisfy it. Suffice it to think that each person is inclined to go beyond even the area of his or her own natural family, finding it not up to fully realizing his or her own self. It is to be remembered that *civitas* does not consist of a simple juxtaposition with a family unit. Even though family and State have the same nature, they have distinctly different ends. Moreover, the *civitas* presupposes a moral as well as political union of its members in view of the eventual association in a society (cf. Quadri, 28).

2.29 Organizing the political community and taking cognizance of the fact that human nature is not perfect but, as has been said, perfectible, one realizes the need for the *auctoritas* without which it would be difficult to keep under control some, whose will "*saepe contraria sunt bono communi*" (Suarez, DDL, I, 3, c.l, n.5) and direct them towards the desired goals. These are the ones who make authority necessary since these goals cannot always be identified by individuals in general: "*Quia sine gubernatione politica vel ordine ad illam non potest intelligi unum corpus politicum*" (Suarez, DDL, I, 3, c.2, n.4). As can be seen from the definition, the social order is not created without authority, as is written subsequently, *unitas*, the real element making up the body politic. So the *auctoritas* presents itself as a *vis ordinatrix* of the body politic to the point of being called its spirit. In other words, authority is not only an element making up the political dimension but is almost the premise upon which it rests so that, "once the free will has been determined, the citizens cannot prevent the creation of the authority " (Quadri, 44).

2.30 This authority must be able to impose its *voluntas* in accordance with the law. Its strength is and must always be a legal one and it must legally resolve the conflicts among the parties that submit to it. Pure and simple force, outside of what is permitted by law, is typical of barbarity and not of a civil political dimension. Thus, authority is the expression of the political community, but it is so not only on a national level. It is or must become so on a universal level as well. The United States, too, will have to give up trying to use wars to resolve their highly serious conflicts and arrive at forms of international arbitration. This shows that Suarez, and his contemporaries theorizing about the laws of peoples, was more interested in universal problems than in those of national states and their policies of power (cf. Schumpeter, II, 2, 4). It also shows that juridical subjects were never divorced from moral ones and vice-versa. The very fact that there are moral subjects, as well as juridical questions, that do not come within the sphere of action of the State bears witness on the one hand to the autonomy of bodies such as the Church, which have the right and duty to educate consciences and on the other, the need to devise worldwide bodies with jurisdiction to solve those problems that are not covered under the *summa potestas* of the individual States.

Suarez is the first to deny that there can be valid reasons, even religious ones, for justifying war: the right to war can be justified only within natural law and is not the exclusive prerogative of the prince (cf. Cedroni, 886 and 889).

2.31 It has been appropriately observed that, despite the crises of medieval universalisms, Suarez cultivates the grandiose idea of the political unity of the Christian peoples in an entity now extremely remote from that ideal because, for one thing, as a result of the reforms, a subjectivist view had spread in law and politics – but I would say in culture in general, which made it very difficult to formulate objective criteria capable of providing the basis for a new unity. In Suarez's opinion, the fundamental goal is to acknowledge the sociable nature of man which determines social relations and society itself. From this comes the very founding principle of law. The *ubi societas ibi ius,* as well as its corresponding *ubi ius ibi societas,* places the terms in an extremely close correlation so that it is not possible to separate one without eliminating the other: between these there is an actual ontological correlation (cf. Messineo, 472-476). However, individuals depart from a level of equality in a society, and the same happens for the States in an international society. The latter is made up of perfect societies (the State, republics and kingdoms were described in these terms by the Scholastics) which are therefore primary subjects in the international context thanks to their sovereignty, to be understood, however, differently from that *summa potestas legibus soluta* of which Bodin speaks (cf. Messineo, 477 and 483). This is sovereignty in the law which, in the original community, allows individuals to pursue the common and their own personal good on an international level for the general well-being and that of the individual States.

2.32 A decisive contribution to the concept of the superiority of the *communitas civium* over the claims of the monarchy is offered by Mariana with a study of the origins of society and the State. It is worth noting that the premises for his reflections are an *unicum* in his era. Anticipating some statements that will be characteristic of Vico, Mariana is of the opinion that primitive humanity sought a political form in a still-confused vision whose sensibility was one typical of wild beasts, *ferarum ritu* (cf. Mariana, Ch. I). Only with the passage of time was the value of cooperation and its necessities discovered.

Juan De Mariana was born in 1535 near Toledo at Talavera de La Reina and he died in Toledo in 1624. He taught theology and Holy Scripture in various parts of Europe. His first master work, finished in 1592 after approximately twenty years of effort, is *Historiae de rebus Hispaniae*. In 1599 he published *De rege et regis institutione* (the part quoted here is from a partial edition written in Spanish) in which his tyranicide theory stands out. This created several problems for him. Among other works, there is *Tractatus VII* in *De mutatione monetae* in which he sharply criticizes the Spanish government for its currency devaluation policy. This shows that he is not only sensitive to moral and theological problems, but also to economic, not to mention political ones, and this was something new for the era.

2.33 For Mariana, the people can put the king on trial, since the king obtains his power from the people. When new laws are set forth, and they are not in contrast with the intentions of the people or with the oath by which the king and his successors were in vested by the people with the rights inherent in sovereignty, the people are obliged to obey and stand by *consensus* on which civil life is based. If this does not happen disobedience is appropriate and that explains the great merit of those in history who have opposed tyrants and sought to eliminate them (cf. Mariana, 43). Surely political stability is a condition which one must always cherish and that means that the sovereigns must not be changed, or, more in general governments on any occasion, but when the holders of power are public enemies they can be overthrown in any manner by taking away from them the power that they had acquired through violence (cf. Mariana, 45). It is quite easy to recognise who is a tyrant, from a juridical point of view. Tyrants believe that their authority is greater than that of the entire community whereas an upright prince will, on the subject of authority, always maintain that "*siempre es mayor la autoritad del pueblo que la suya*" (Mariana, 47). Whoever thinks differently is on the side of the tyrant.

2.34 These ideas – expressed in the first book of *De rege* – caused Mariana a few problems. He hastened to emphasize that the necessity for and justification of tyranicide must not lead to the belief that the lives of princes can be in constant danger. They must simply not be continually reputed to be tyrants. The judgment of tyranicide does not, in fact, come from the private decision of anyone whomsoever or the opinion of an angered multitude, but from the opinion of learned or authoritative people capable of discerning the nature of consent and its bases. The philosopher is concerned with avoiding anarchical hypotheses or civil-war like situations, but also with keeping princes alert to a problem such as that of sovereignty, which cannot be exclusively subject to their caprices.

2.35 The problems with which Mariana deals in the second book of *De rege* are less actual. In discussing the education of the Christian prince, not only does he bring in problems of an Erasmian sort, but also subjects that were strongly felt in his era. The same is true of the subjects in the third book although in this case one can always say that questions such as the administration of a State can arouse interest that goes well beyond the era in which the author was writing. Mariana believes that the choice of magistrates is fundamental to the success of a State. Thus, the sovereign must consider above all competence, honesty and experience not considering recommendations and pressures of various sorts. Even before that, he must take care, even if he has worthy and meritorious functionaries, not to assign too many positions to a single individual. That turns out to be harmful and unproductive: harmful because the person becomes too powerful, unproductive because too many positions end up distracting his attention from problems that could turn out to be mistakenly underestimated (cf. Mesnard, 277). Among the other subjects already dealt with previously, Mariana returns to the importance of religion considered determining from the social point of view as well and, therefore, worthy of being put in a condition to benefit from total respect in order to safeguard that dualism between temporal and spiritual which constitutes the true premise for any form of liberty. The clergy, then, must manifest divine dignity in an irreprehensible fashion.

2.36 Bellarmino is one of the most representative figures of his time, among other things, for the wide variety of interests that he was able to pursue and the balance he showed in circumstances that were not easy. The trial of Galileo was one. He showed benevolence and understanding. His political thought, inspired by the doctrine of natural law, brings out the role of the people in the formation of the Sate laying out the limits of the wielding of power and manifesting the possibility of resisting any abuses that the powers might perpetrate. The forms and methods of this resistance, which can even lead to tyranicide, are, however, subject to legal limits in order to avoid continued instability in the political community, although power resides in it, and also for reasons of necessity or efficiency, power is delegated to specific bodies.

Saint **Roberto Bellarmino**, born in Montepulciano in 15421, and who died in Rome in 1621, a professor for a long time in the college of the Jesuits, an order to which he belonged, was named cardinal in 1599. Although Thomism was his inspiration, he was strongly influenced by the thought of Saint Augustine. He pursued the aims of Spanish Scholasticism with a clear and rigorous style. For a knowledge of his basic thought, there are the *Disputationes de controversiis christianae fidei adversus huius temporis haereticos* (1586-1593) in three volumes, whose definitive publication, in 4 volumes, came out in Venice in 1596. In the century that followed, this work went through about thirty editions, and was fundamental in the doctrinal debate of his time. The political works in the *Controversie* of 1610 and the *De officio principis christiani* of 1619.

2.37 Synthesizing the classical approach, Bellarmino considers mankind naturally inclined to live not only in the political dimension, but also the social one: "*homo fuisset naturaliter animal civile et sociale*" (Bellarmino, De laic., c. 7). This natural propensity gives rise to that consensus which not only gives society its form, but, concretely, authority as well, without which society would disintegrate. It is in the order of things that society realize itself to the full, an order obviously within the bounds of legality, which recalls the classic Latin distinction between people and multitude. "*Societas est multitudo ordinata, non enim dicitur societas multitudo confusa et dispersa*" (Bellarmino, De laic., c. 5). The criterion for authority comes out of this society to govern, above and beyond individual wills and independently of the other forms of society even if these are based on consensus, all those matters that require a single direction, one which is ready and efficient and obviously invested with coercive force (cf. Quadri, 27-28 and 37-38).

That force concerns solely the temporal sphere; indeed, in combating absolutism, Bellarmino not only brings up the value of consensus, but also removes spiritual life from any sort of political interference, to justify, among other things, the independence of the Church.

2.38 The problem of political subjection arises from this force of coercion which is not at all in opposition to the original freedom of mankind. It is despotic subjection that means the end of liberty because, in this case, force is exercised outside of legality. Political subjection, claimed by the legitimate political authority, does not mean oppressing the citizen, but is intended to make him or her pursue his or her interests within the realm of the general interest of the community to which he or she belongs (cf. Quadri, 52-53). This consideration on subjection, for Bellarmino, made possible the interest of Christians in a legally exercised power and made it possible scientifically to base the arguments against those, for example Anabaptists and Trinitarians, who claimed that it was not legitimate for Christians to become involved in matters of political power (cf. Bellarmino, SP, 225). Based on what was said, first about human nature, laying down such a prohibition would be the equivalent of having the pretension of changing nature itself thereby destroying it. What is more serious is that it would mean preventing any possible development and progress in the human spirit, because who can doubt that even the sciences and the arts were created over a long time and through the cooperation of many? Without a political organization, who could then guarantee the pursuit of those objectives which the community intends to attain? (cf. Bellarmino, SP, 231-232). If political life and participation in it were not something good, who could maintain that political power comes from God?

2.39 Against some reformers, Calvin for example, Bellarmino maintains that civil laws, too, bind the conscience. Although civil law is less stable and lasting than divine law, and can be abrogated, it still imposes such an obligation. Obligatoriness is indeed fundamental to law, without which it would be a simple recommendation and would never be able to achieve its goals. It must be kept in mind that if the purpose of religion is the salvation of souls, politics, properly practiced, does not have a less noble goal since it aims first of all at maintaining social peace and preserving civil life (cf. Bellarmino, SP, 244-245).

2.40 Bellarmino was keenly concerned about the safeguarding of civil life to the point that all those disturbing factors that could somehow have threatened it had to be eliminated, even if they were claimed to be religiously motivated in some way. It was a case of unjustifiable interference. The Pope himself has no possibility, even in divine law, of directly wielding power in the temporal order (cf. Bellarmino, 302). It is true that the two powers have been joined in the same hands in history, just as they have been separated at other times, but that was due to particular historical contingencies. The rule should be the distinction: as political power has its principles, its laws, its legal processes, etc., so ecclesiastical power has its bishops, its canons, trials, the goal of which is not temporal peace, but eternal salvation (cf. Bellarmino, SP, 137-138). The arguments against Barclay are to be interpreted along these lines. Bellarmino expressly states that the Pope directly exercises, *directe,* his religious and political authority only in Rome, in the State of the Church. Sovereigns can rest assured of their own thrones, the Pope will never depose anyone. Kings are well advised, however, that there is a higher spiritual authority that keeps them under control so that they will not abuse their power (cf. Giacon, 245). This is that indirect power of the Pope with sovereigns which, even if never exercised, serves the peoples who, in view of the influence that the ecclesiastical authority can wield indirectly, *indirecte,* feel protected in the face of dangerous cases of regression towards tyranny. As Pietro Pallavicino Sforza (1607-1667) would say quite eloquently, and taking up some of Bellarmino's subjects, these peoples feel more secure in republics than in kingdoms because they believe that one who has all the power in hand can more easily interpret the law in terms of his caprices.

2.41 In the relationship between religion and politics the highly fortunate work of Botero (1544-1617) is worthy of mention. *Della ragion di Stato* aims at criticizing those who associated Michiavelli's Reason of State with that of Tacitus since the intention of the latter was to unmask the tyrannical arts used by Tiberius Caesar (cf. Continisio, XXVII ff.). While Botero had in common with Macchiavelli the experience of the historical laboratory, he departs "from a highly ethical perspective, which reaffirms the subordination of politics to religion" (Continisio, XXII). As in Machiavelli, the problem of founding, preserving and increasing the domain of a State is posed, but it is all placed in the framework of the excellence of the virtues as they were understood by Tridentine Catholicism to be (cf. Botero, beginning of Book I and, in the same book, the paragraphs devoted to the problem of the virtues). The analysis of the interdependency of the State and the power is equally noteworthy.

2.42 The political works of Althusius had assumed a position against the absolutism reigning at the time and had claimed, in opposition to authors such as Bodin, the theory of popular sovereignty, but they were not attacked by the constituted authorities as happened in the case of other writings, published in France and England that dealt with the same subjects as the German scholar. That is probably due to the fact that Althusius did not write a work of propaganda or political passion, but a purely doctrinal one. Only after the death of the author in 1638 was the *Politica methodice digesta* the object of extremely sharp attacks from various critics such as Hermann Conring, Giovanni Enrico Boecler, Ulrico Huber and others (cf. Gierke, 21-22).

Johannes Althaus, or Althus or also Althusen, but certainly known by the name **Althusius**, was born in 1557 in Dieden Hausen, in Westphalia. He studied in Basel, but it can be supposed that he also spent time in Geneva where he studied the rigid Calvinist spirit. In Von Gierke's opinion (op. cit. 27), his theological concerns as a strict Calvinist, oriented him toward the Old Testament and Jewish institutions. In 1586 he published an important law work *De arte iurisprudentiae Romanae methodice digesta libri II*. He held posts as a university professor for several years. In 1603 the *Politica methodice digesta* appeared (the actual title is much longer) which went through many other editions, basically the one of 1614 in which the study became a veritable political tract. He wrote many other works where a juridical, theological, philosophical and humanistic culture transpires, but he also showed himself to be practical and highly capable, and indeed served successfully as the mayor of Emden where he died in 1638.

2.43 As early as the *Preface to the third edition* Althusius underscores the close tie between religion and politics to the point that the precepts of the former infuse into the latter the "vital spirit" which sustains the association of symbiotic life. This reference to the association is fundamental. "Politics is the art by means of which people associate for the purpose of establishing, cultivating and preserving social life with one another." For this reason it is called symbiotic (...) The end of the symbiotic politician is a holy symbiosis, just, comfortable and happy, that is, not lacking in the useful and necessary things" (Althusius, I, 1 and 3). The subjects of this political entity are called symbiotic, that is those who cooperate and associate, bound by the rules and with the intention of communicating with one another what is necessary. "Thus, Cicero wrote that 'the people are a group of people associated by consensus, under a single law and in the communication of useful things'" (Althusius, I. 7, d. and also point 6). Law can also be called the law of association and it codifies those necessities that induced people to form a union. It is curious that, in a Protestant environment, a passage from Aquinas concerning *De Regimine Principum* is cited (cf. Althusius, I, 33).

2.44 Next to a purely natural form of association, one can think of the example of the family, there exist forms of civil association such as corporations which are created through the mutual consent of individuals. Those forms of society are, by their very nature, transitory and temporary, to the extent necessary, because they are spontaneous and voluntary, that is, they last as long as those who create them desire (cf. Althusius, IV, 1-2-3). Here, too, Roman law must be referred to since, quoting the *Digest*, one can say that individuals who associate to set up a corporation are called colleagues or members and it is through communication that they help one another to carry out the desired goals; it is obviously the communication of services for the purpose of mutually promoting business, advantages and communicating duties (cf. Althusius, IV, 5,8 and 12); hence private associations which are distinct from public ones. Returning to some definitions from the *Digest*, this political association resulting from the joining together of various private associations can be referred to as a political community. "This is an associated body, the political association par excellence, permitted and approved by the law of the peoples. This does not die until only one sole person is surviving, nor is it changed by the change in individual people, but is perpetuated as they are replaced" (Althusius, V, 2,3). This last word, replacement, is of crucial importance (*Digesta*, I, 1, 76), because it enables Althusius to achieve a new understanding of sovereignty, as he argues against Bodin. Local-type associations also exist. "Among these, he orders territorial communities in the three degrees of 'vicus', 'pagus' and 'oppidum'" (Gierke, 38-39). These associations place themselves in a relationship with the State so as to give rise to a federal conception in which sovereignty belongs to the entire community, even if single individual members appear as subjects thereby conforming to the saying of the Pandicts: *quod universitati debetur, singulis non debetur* (cf. Gierke, 41).

2.45 Before taking up the problem of sovereignty, Althusius insists on the importance of mixed societies made up in part of private associations and in part, of the public society. This is called a general association: "this is identified with the people united in a single body through the consensus of the numerous symbiotic associations and particular bodies, gathered and joined together under the same law" (Althusius, IX, 3). To say that "this identifies itself with the people" is of major importance since for Althusius it is always so whether a republic or any other political system, including a kingdom, is involved. "Indeed, the property of the kingdom belongs to the people, while its administration is the duty of the king" (Althusius, IX, 4) administrating by law and over a particular territory whose boundaries are well defined. That law is also called the law of sovereignty (cf. Althusius, IX, 13-14). Here, the German jurist goes beyond the conception of sovereignty as it had been set forth by the absolutist Bodin. "The law of sovereignty applies not to individuals, but to all of the members together, that is, to the entire body in the kingdom. Since the general association cannot be made up of only one member, but several members together, that law applies not to individuals but to all in so far as it is a community" (Althusius, IX, 18). This is also confirmed in the *Digest* (cf. III, 4, 7, 1) and corroborates two fundamental convictions of Althusius: the *first* that, although there are legal traditions such as Jewish, Roman or German ones, now, most European States operate under Roman Law (cf. Althusius, XXI, 33); the *second* that the sovereignty of the people is founded on that law and by that law tyranicide is justified (cf. Althusius, through the entire Ch. XXXVIII). Still, it is the argumentation against Bodin that is emphasized: "Thus, it is the king who represents the people and not, on the contrary, the people who represent the king, since, in the final analysis, the power and forces of many are greater than those of one person. All of this means that the monarch is required to answer for his administration" (Althusius, IX, 24). From this comes a remarkable conclusion from Althusius who considers Bodin's distinction between form of State and form of government contrived: since the sovereign rights are always of the people, all the differences concerning the forms of states are simply reduced to differences among forms of government (cf. Gierke, 49).

2.46 The idea of sovereignty thus conceived leads to a particular reflection on law which, in order to acquire value, must follow a precise itinerary in order to be accepted and recognized after being promulgated. Only then does law become a rule that prescribes, both singly and collectively, what is to be done to preserve justice and, as Seneca said, the bond which holds the State together (cf. Althusius, X,

3, 4). In order for this to be, law must also have the force to punish those who attack its essence. That force is produced "in assigning to suitable ministers, imposing upon them, and entrusting them with, the care for, government and administrations of the laws of the State, respecting certain conditions or laws, binding them to the State through an oath" (Althusius, XVIII, 5). Here is to be found that concept of limits that guides those who have always aimed at defending a society of law. The ministers are established with the utility of the general association in mind. They receive a sort of proxy that allows them to administrate so as not to harm the State. There are two types of administrators: the Ephors and the Highest Magistrate. Ephors must be understood to mean all those authorities, variously named and everywhere present who, invested by the people, operate in their name (cf. Gierke, 45). "The Ephors are elected and appointed with the consensus of all the people" (Althusius, XVIII, 59). They decide together and have a precise series of duties, among them that of electing the Highest Magistrate and "they must keep him within the limits and boundaries of his office, as custodians, defenders of and claimants of liberty and rights which the people have not transferred to the Highest Magistrate, but have reserved for themselves (…) The Ephors themselves, however, cannot take any decision pertaining to the affairs of State without the consent and approval of the Highest Magistrate in the fullness of his functions" (Althusius, XVIII, 63). In case the Highest Magistrate is incapable of administering the State, however, the Ephors have the duty of administrating during the interregnum. They can even remove him if he becomes a tyrant, but they must also defend his rights when he is deserving of this.

2.47 It could be said that Althusius sees law as the foundation of the State, as with all the tradition of the preceding centuries examined thus far. Doubtless this is true, but of this law, "the ultimate basis is the divine order of the world, which manifests itself in nature" (Gierke, 36). This conclusion places Althusius' works among those that anticipated modern *jusnaturalism*, which sees the deepest reasons for human life in common as traceable back to the natural essence of human beings, that is, in that reason whose characteristics, far above and beyond contingencies, is worth more than what the legislator can will, even if the latter, as Grotius maintains, is God himself (cf. Grotius, Proleg., § 11). It is here that the school started by Althusius, and carried on by Grotius and Pufendorf, differs from tradition: law decidedly takes on a rationalistic and lay character in which the relationship with transcendence will gradually be eliminated until it is possible to speak of *iusrationalism* of which Kant would be the most authoritative representative.

2.48 The work of Grotius (1585-1645) comes at a point where the traditional position is reversed. Law no longer appears anchored to a preceding metaphysical position which indeed becomes entirely alien to the future forms of *jusnaturalism* (cf. Giacon, 283). It may be false to deny the existence of God, but it is absolutely not useful to have recourse to Him to have the source of natural law: "*non esse Deum aut non curari ab eo negotia humana*" (Grotius, Proleg., § 11). The reference to the simple *negotia* shows us that society is basically more and more to be understood as that locus where the individual pursues his own interests without asking himself whether the perfecting of his personality implies a reference to and role for transcendence. Interests which determine that instinct for sociality, *appetitus societatis*, which is present in every human being (cf. Grotius, Proleg., §§ 6-9). It is always these interests which confer a sort of rationalistic subjectivism on law, in a way different from scholastic objectivism, to the point that the hypothesis itself of a contract is seen as something contingent and variable. Furthermore, all political life, the State, civil law itself and even the body politic, taken as a gathering of free people, are considered as a function of the peaceful enjoyment of rights into order to pursue good for all (cf. Grotius, L. I, Ch. I, § XIV, 2). What is to be found at the beginning of the *De iure belli ac pacis* is the guiding theme of the entire work, so that in the conclusion, when the need to seek peace and thus the obligation to keep one's word are reaffirmed, it is repeated that losing hope in peace is dangerous, a peace of which not only the States derive benefit, but of the greater society in its entirety, that embraces all Nations and all people (cf. Grotius, L. III, Ch. XXV).

2.49 The position of Samuel von Pufendorf (1632-1694) seems even more explicit: for him, the basis of natural law, intrinsically universal, cannot be religious in nature. Religion varies in time and place. Natural law, on the contrary depends on reason which, in turn, is to be distinguished from revelation. Mere human ends are the responsibility of law, so that a purely human science provides the way of understanding and interpreting it. How can it be forgotten that the basic aim of human beings already in the ancient world was to make life more comfortable and salutary, by means of some useful inventions as well? (cf. Pufendorf, L. III, Ch. III, §§ 1-2). The same law served to formulate those rules that could guarantee all of this not only whenever possible, limiting the competences of sovereigns, but also setting forth certain rules which, by means of written laws or customs, would guarantee the functioning of democracies and their assemblies (cf. Pufendorf, L. VII, Ch. VI, §§ 7-8).

3. The Change of one Century.

A) *The Preliminaries*.

3.1 The hundred years between the two *Treatises on Government* (1690) of Locke to the famous *Reflections* (1790) of Burke are the high point of political writing on the subject of what we could call modern, open societies. Naturally, dates concerning historical periods of particular significance cannot be as rigorous as those of the birth and death of an individual. Throughout the eighteenth century there are elements that serve as prologues and others, in retrospect, become evident in subsequent thinkers such as Bentham, Mill and Acton. If we reach the roots of the first and see the fruits in the second, the fact remains that the trunk of the tree goes back to those hundred years, of a contradictory nature at times, in which the features of liberalism and modern democracy were debated.

3.2 Shortly before the mid eighteenth century, in a climate that was dramatic, and which would justify the writing of the *Leviathan* in many ways, a discussion arose among those whom we can consider the harbingers of the modern and contemporary political debate. All that would make our age great and tragic seems already to be found in the famous *Putney Debates,* which tell us what the different positions in English politics and the programmes of many future parties were at the time. The position which, in the course of a few decades, won out is that of the Whigs "marked by a relationship of close identification with the classes arising out of incipient mercantile capitalism" (Revelli, XVIII), but also the expression of the nascent bourgeois society, in the broadest sense of the term and not strictly ideological, as it has been presented up to now. In the debate, there are some subjects, other than the specific ones of the moment, that would become matters for discussion even in the present time. Among these and aside from those debated in the second day, we can recall the possibility, later to be called constructivist, of designing "a rationally and wilfully constructed society", the role of the army and its "advice" in a revolutionary phase, the need to have laws that cannot be modified and that serve as fundamental laws for a State (cf. Revelli, XI ff.) All of these presuppositions, especially the first two are expressions of the most radical wing of the revolution.

3.3 The debate of the second day merits a consideration of its own. It begins with the institutional problems concerning the King and the Peers (subjects taken up again in the third day) and come to problems concerning property. People like Rainsborough have words of firmness and passion and help us to understand how similar problems were felt. These became words of wisdom, but also fiery ones, when the subject turned to representation: "Every person born in England cannot and must not, either from the Law of Nature, or that of God, be excluded from the choice of those charged with making laws". Representation and property became the crucial points in the discussion because the first seemed to be seen in terms of the other to the point that, for some, extending the vote to everyone would be the equivalent of destroying property. The Law of Nature and the Law of God seemed at times to follow the same line, at times to be in conflict with one another until there were those, like Ireton, who wisely maintained that Divine Law could not be extended to particular things. There were even people who referred to Ancient Rome with its experience with an aristocratic Republic, and proposed a sort of Locke vote, a system that would be suggested in a way rather similar to that of Harrington in his *Oceana* (cf. Revelli, 86). Then, among the various problems brought up, one stands out: concerning whether or not it is just to bind oneself to a law when consent for the election of those who must make laws for everyone is not granted to everyone. The position of Petty is one of great dignity. According to him, if a constitution exists for which the people are not free, that constitution must be eliminated. These subjects would be taken up with greater calm after the upheaval of 1789. What is surprising, however, is the fact that the serious problem of *poverty,* or, if one prefers, *the lack of adequate well-being, which does not enable actual liberty* arises, even though it is not given an adequate theoretical basis. The question of consensus is in the air for all these subjects and it has always been the crucial question of all free societies.

3.4 Consensus is one of the subjects which, according to not a few exponents of the period, has religious roots since the conscience must have the opportunity to accept the various principles freely and without any type of political pressure. This is one of the great subjects of the action of John Lilburne (1614-1657) for whom the great subjects of politics are justice and liberty, which cannot be taken away even from enemies. More extreme reflections departed from religious presuppositions, such as those of Gerrard Winstanley who, with his ideal of a small farming and artisan community, seemed not only to anticipate ideals of agrarian communism, but also a nostalgia for a simple world, that would ban the so-called speculative sciences, and would return to a sort of myth of the noble savage.

3.5 Thomas Smith (1513-1577), with his *De Republica Anglorum,* is the first authoritative voice in support of the Parliament, considered the supreme and absolute power of the Kingdom of England. The king may only approve all those provisions that the Parliament deem useful to the community of citizens. The power of Parliament may be compared to that of the Roman people in the *comitia centuriata et tributa* (cf. D'Addio, SDP, I, 414). It is not by chance that reference to the Republic is made in the title, and certain not by chance that all of those, whom we could call the fathers of modern constitutionalism, make reference to the definition of *res public* given by Cicero (Matteucci, OPL, 2) and, over and above the importance of the reformed religions or religion in general, the rediscovery of Roman Law cannot be ignored. The political organization corresponds to the needs of the community and from this approach comes the return of the classical concept of society, as the "doing together", then that of sovereignty which belongs to the community in its entirety and to one of the individual institutions that only partially represent the community. This is why no political body, least of all that of the King, can pretend to wield absolute power, but, at the least, a part therefore, the executive power, whereas the legislative and judiciary ones belong to Parliament and the Magistracy (cf. D'Addio, SDP, I, 415-416). Before the great liberal eighteenth-century thinkers, Smith took up and newly formulated the classical separation of the three powers that would be the basis of modern constitutional States. It must not be forgotten that Smith had studied in Padua where he had learned and admired the ideal of the classical political thought of the mixed State. The division into classes of English society is also attributable to Smith: "in the first he places, the upper nobility on one side, and on the other, the knights, the gentlemen, the *gentry*; in the second, the citizens and the bourgeoisie; in the third the small landowners; and finally in the forth category the peasants, artisans, labourers, who did not have the right to participate in government" (Matteucci, OPL, 18).

3.6 To Edward Coke (1552-1634) surely goes the merit of having formulated the principle of the sovereignty of the law which, being based on the tradition and customs of the English people, came to be a sort of expression of *mos maiorum*, of *common law* to which all people had to refer. The primary duty of Parliament was to control everything that is to serve as an actual High Court of Justice. *Common law* necessarily came into conflict with the claims of primacy of the Crown and the latter had no possibility of judging matters known only to judges (cf. D'Addio, SDP, I, 417-418). Judges, in other words, had to have autonomy and independence in order to re-affirm the primacy of law over politics, and this meant "autonomy of the judiciary power over the executive" (Matteucci, OPL, 64).

3.7 It is important to emphasize that the new political ideas came, in those predicaments, not from Academic spheres, but from civil society which was changing and which wanted to change political structures to make them correspond more closely to reality. It is no accident, as comes out in *The Agreement of the People*, that consent is periodically renewed (it is not granted once and for all as in Hobbes) and public offices are subject to rotation to enable the people to exercise control and participate constantly. *The Commonwealth of Oceana* of James Harrington (cf. Schiavone, 15-17) can be read with this in mind. This work had its contradictions, forced points, and, I would say, not a few Platonic influences. As was the case for other utopian works, it expressed a need for the liberation of mankind.

3.8 At a time when the truly free voices all over Europe were rare to a certain degree, the *Areopagitica* of John Milton (1608-1674), engaging in the political struggles and conflicts of idea of his time, constitutes a first statement of the liberty of reason, in the name of religious principles as well. More specifically, he fights for freedom of the press and against any sort of censorship considering the latter seriously harmful to the Church and the State, because *"killing" a book is no less serious than killing a person*. A printed text is indeed something vital produced by that living intellect whose fruits go well beyond the natural lifespan, so killing a book is the same as killing reason itself (cf. Milton, 168). The English poet takes this conviction from a fervent conversation with the ancients (the considerations on Plato are interesting: cf. Milton, 176) and a careful analysis of history. Censorship seems to him a mistake which the reformed religions must not make, hence the appeal to the English Parliament, which would otherwise render vain the attempts made by reformers (cf. Milton, 185). The reformers did not succeed in avoiding this error as the existential adventures of Milton himself and his repeated prison terms show. It was almost as if Milton had hoped to reform the Reformation itself (cf. Gatti M. and H, XIX).

3.9 In Milton the connection between knowledge and liberty appears indivisible and vital because both, if authentic, feed upon truth. The latter fears no type of conflict. When truth and untruth contend with one another, who has ever seen the former succumb in a free and open conflict? Untruth is eliminated only through confutation (cf. Milton, 189).

This is the arm that truly demeans anyone who wants to eliminate truth and not unmotivated censorship because, where there are no valid and convincing reasons, no-one can accept the falseness of a position. This is why Milton does not at all deny that it is of vital importance for the Church and the State to control books, as ill-doers are controlled, (cf. Milton, 168), but forms are needed, which do not discourage, as does censorship, liberty and intelligence.

B) *The first Self-Assertion of Liberalism.*

3.10 The state of nature to which Locke refers in order to speak of the birth of civil society is not similar to that of Hobbes since it is governed by a law of nature to which all are bound (cf. Locke, TTG, II, 6). This state of nature, extremely different from the state of war of everyone against the other which the author of the *Leviathan* speaks of, is characterized by the fact that a clear definition of liberty is lacking. Thus, one seeks to achieve the political society in which liberty, coming out of its undetermined nature, consists in having a stable law by which to abide, common to all the members of that society and created by the legislative power instituted therein: the freedom to carry out my will in which the law makes no pronouncement (cf. Locke, TTG, II, 22). Attribution of the work to Locke (considered by some as his first work) is probably not certain, but the fact remains that here, concerning Roman law, the words of Cicero are once again echoed *"Legum servi sumus ut liberi esse possimus"* (Cicero, OpC, 53) in other words we are servants of the laws in order that we may be free". Locke says this clearly stating that to be truly free, one cannot be subject "to the inconstant, uncertain, imponderable, arbitrary will of others (cf. Locke, TTG, II, 22). If one goes from the state of nature to civil society it is to be freed of this imponderability, to have certainty of law, to be better off. Indeed, once the civil society is set up, no-one can elude the force of law by means of his authority, once it has been instituted; nor, out of a claim to superiority, can one ask for exemptions aimed at justifying ones own misdeeds or those of persons dependent on this person. No-one in civil society can be exonerated from the law (cf. Locke, TTG, II, 94). It is no accident that the word "ribellantes" is used to describe those who oppose the laws (cf. Locke, TTG, II, 227) in the sense that if they want to leave the state of legality, they cause society to plunge once again into the state of uncertainty and war (they propose *bellum* once again) which at times is characteristic of the state of nature. Anyone who uses force without law places himself in a state of war with those against whom he uses it, and in that state all the preceding bonds are cancelled (cf. Locke, TTG, II, 232). It should be kept in mind that these limits involve not only the liberty of individuals, but also the action of the powers provided for and exercised, otherwise it becomes usurpation itself: Anyone who comes to exercise any portion of power whatsoever following other paths that are not those that the laws of the community have prescribed, has no right to receive obedience, even if he keeps the form of the State intact (cf. Locke, TTG, II, 198).

John Locke was born in Somersetshire (Bristol) in 1632. His father, an attorney and Justice of the Peace, certainly had an influence on his son's sense of the importance of law. After studying Philosophy and Literature at Oxford, he took up the study of medicine and science in London. In the capital, he met Anthony Ashley Cooper, thanks to whom his life took a course quite different from what had been planned. His first *Essay concerning Toleration* dates from this period. In 1672 Locke became a political advisor of Ashley Cooper, who was created Earl of Shaftesbury, whom he followed to Holland after the latter's arrest and liberation. Here, he confirmed and developed the Whig programme of the Earl. He returned in England in 1689 with William of Orange whom he had met in Holland. The following year the *Two Treatises of Civil Government* and the *Essay concerning human Understanding* appeared. Before his death in 1704, he wrote, among other things the famous *Letters concerning Toleration*.

3.11 It has been said by many that Locke's political conception reflects the rise of bourgeois society because the need to defend private property lies behind the certainty of law. That seems quite oversimplified. Law does not protect property alone, it protects all the conditions capable of ensuring prosperity and progress, peace first of all. As I already said *à propos* of Roman law and Cicero (cf. vol. I, point 1, 32), peace is not obtained when all powers are delegated; it arises from beneath like positive law. Arguing against Hobbes it can be said that various types of authoritarianism do not guarantee peace or order since they suppress liberty and do not limit it by legal means. Those forms of authoritarianism are only the death certificate of democracy and constitute a step backwards in history. Labour, too, manifests itself differently in a society based on law and not force. Indeed, it is after the contract that a new way of working develops as well as a new way of understanding economic activity, hence the possibility of producing wealth. First (in the state of nature) people were content mainly with what nature offered to meet their needs without help (cf. Locke, TTG, II, 45). As the world of labour gradually developed, with its consequent division and thus the possibility of satisfying an increasing number of needs, a sense of utility grew and law increasingly improved more and more "and all that could safeguard the property of all the members of that society, in so far as possible" (cf. Locke, TTG, II, 88).

3.12 The fact that individuals, in order to transfer a prerogative of theirs to law, waive punishment of those who damage the various types of property means that the State acquires the power to decide what punishment fits the various violations that occur among the members of that society (cf. Locke, TTG, II, 88). Individuals have thus given up their right, typical of the state of nature, to punish the violations. Here, too, it is not simply a limitation of a power. From the contract, the power to punish increases on a par with liberty, because it is not just a case of punishing anyone who violates the laws of nature, but also the positive laws that represent the perfecting of political society. In other words, a new right to make laws comes out of the contract, which goes beyond the laws of nature, and to punish, which also involves those who violate the universally accepted rules. Thus the origin of the legislative and executive power are determined. All that does not happen solely when a certain number of people associate to make up a single people (here, too, the famous adage *ubi societas ibi ius* finds an echo), but also when an individual is incorporated into an already existing society accepting its laws and inviting it, tacitly, to make laws in conformity with the needs of the public good (cf. Locke, TTG, II, 89). It would almost seem that the individual, once placed in a social context, can only be represented by his legitimate representatives whose directives he then accepts. Locke, however, who, among other things, justifies the Glorious Revolution against absolutism, maintains that bodies such as the legislative and executive, too, have very precise limits on their work. The people conserve that supreme power that also determines the right to revolt whenever the legislative branch, and obviously the executive one act in a manner contrary to their mandate (cf. Carpenter, XIII).

3.13 Here too, there is notable progress compared to Hobbes. Waiving one's powers is not a definitive and irreversible act for individuals unless a state of insecurity is created, as is the case for the author of the *Leviathan*. On the contrary, according to Locke, certain rights are waived only to increase the good of society itself. Indeed, since each person does this with the intention of better safeguarding his or her liberty and property, it is right to expect that the power of society, or the constituted legislative body, will never go beyond the limits of the common good (cf. Locke, TTG, II, 131). The problem of *limits* reappears once again confirming that in no society can the arbitrary domination of any power whatsoever be accepted. The legislative, which is indeed the superior power and must be such to provide laws that bind the other powers, cannot go against the will of those who have elected it, otherwise it would lose its legitimacy (cf. Locke, TTG, II, 149-150). These statements are also understood when one returns to the true nature of the contract at the origin of political society. People tend to constitute one sole body politic convinced that in that body the majority has the right to decree and decide for the rest (cf. Locke, TTG, II, 95). That majority and the consensus on which it is based, becomes the golden rule within which there is no room for arbitrariness. There are words that leave no doubt on the subject, what gives rise to a political society, and actually institutes it, is nothing other than the consent of a certain number of free men, capable of a majority (cf. Locke, TTG, II, 99). This, for Locke, is a legitimate government.

3.14 Examples of free and independent people who have created political societies can be found in history once again proving that the contract, Locke's point of departure, is not a mere hypothesis used as a point of departure that can justify a fascinating thesis in the abstract. On the contrary, it is the result of an empirical analysis which determines concrete powers out of which highly precise and not illusory laws arise. It has been said that, from this point of view, Locke represents a synthesis between the speculation of Aristotle and the Roman juridical sense. "Political theory is purely philosophical in nature, whereas the art of politics leads back to historical and juridical considerations" (Pareyson, 29). Locke himself corroborates an observation of the sort. In his opinion the origins of Rome, Venice and the United States confirm that those institutions are the results of a union among some free people (cf. Locke, TTG, II, 102). Indeed, when political societies have arisen from natural liberty and the consensus of individuals, those systems have been more stable and longer lasting (cf. Locke, TTG, II, 104). This happens not only in those environments in which republics have been created, but also electoral-type monarchical systems, that is ones in which the heir of the deceased or deposed king has been chosen because the king has been incompetent or weak (cf. Locke, TTG, II, 105). That happened during the monarchy in Rome or among the kingdoms of the new world. Presenting these two different forms of government is useful to Locke so that he can argue against those who maintained the erroneous conviction that power is monarchical by nature and belongs to the father (cf. Locke, TTG, II, 106). On the contrary, since power is based on consensus, it can assume different characters and, even at the beginning, be presented as an elective monarchy. This shows that the peaceful beginnings of political power were all founded on the consent of the people (cf. Locke, TTG, II, 112). It is always history and juridical tradition, however, that gives Locke the cue for another important statement: not only power and its forms of government come out of consent, but they receive force and continue to live on the basis of consent. When obedience becomes illogical and pressing, people escape their bonds and all this is shown in sacred and profane history (cf. Locke, TTG, II, 115). Consent is the soul of a true, legitimate political system in the sense that the laws it expresses find themselves in harmony with a people's way of feeling and being. Thus, it is certainly not forcing this issue to say that a true *consensus iuris* is involved.

3.15 This *consensus iuris* establishes itself only when there is the certainty of law. Locke is extremely clear on the subject. If it is true that people submit to a government to safeguard property, they do so because for that purpose the state of nature is inefficient in many respects. First of all, stable, fixed and known law is lacking, accepted and recognised by common consent as a criterion for the just and unjust and as a communal measure to decide on every controversy (cf. Locke, TTG, II, 124). Furthermore, in the state of nature a recognised and impartial judicial authority is lacking, one which obtains its authority from the established laws. Then, force is lacking, this, too, coming from law, capable of sustaining and supporting the just sentence and rendering it operational (cf. Locke, TTG, II, 125-126). This is the real feature of a truly anti-absolutionist society, more important yet than forms of government that can be composite or mixed, depending on what seems appropriate. What is important is to see the nature and place of the supreme power, which is the legislative one (cf. Locke, TTG, II, 132). Here, too, the juridical nature of such a political society is fundamental. Such a State must be founded on law and this for Locke means not a democracy or another form of government, but an independent community, what the Latin civilisation designated under the term *civitas* (cf. Locke, TTG, II, 133). It hardly need be recalled that *civitas*, which could be translated as a condition capable of allowing enjoyment of the rights of citizenship, sums up in one word that concept of a society of rights, *ubi societas ibi ius,* which is at the heart of the historical process that accompanies the difficult road taken by open societies.

3.16 Here lies the importance of the legislative power on which not only the birth, but the safeguarding of the society itself depends. In virtue of this principle, that power encounters quite precise limits in the area of its action. Whether this is in the hands of one or more people, whether it acts at times or is always in operation, what counts is that it cannot exercise arbitrary power over the lives and property of the people and expropriate for itself the power to govern by means of extemporaneous acts or arbitrary decrees (cf. Locke, TTG, II, 135-136); and it cannot take from people any part of their property without their consent. It hardly need be recalled that property, which comes from the term *proprius*, characterizes something that not only belongs to the owner but shows that owner's very nature strictly connected to the utility which he or she obtains from that possession. From this comes that private law which governs the utility of private individuals as Ulpian's adage quite effectively recalls: *privatum (ius) est quod al utilitatem privatorum interest.* That utility, like all property is never safe if the one who governs has the power to take from a private individual that portion of property that he wants and use and dispose of it as he sees fit (cf. Locke, TTG, II, 138). Thus, the just expenditures of the government must also be made with the consent of those who support them (cf. Locke, TTG, II, 140-141). These are the limits that the mandate from society and divine and natural law impose on the legislative power in every State and in every form of government (cf. Locke, TTG, II, 142). As is pointed out below these limits consist in the following points: a) laws promulgated and determined and not subject to continual variation (the Latin criterion of notoriety and juridical certain should be recalled here) must apply to all; b) all laws must have as their sole purpose the good of the people; c) the legislative power cannot place taxes on property without the direct consent of the people or its legitimate representatives (it should be recalled that this was to be one of the causes of the American Revolution and the principle that would be supported by not a few English intellectuals); d) finally, the legislative cannot transfer its power to others, having received it from the people in the name of whom it performs its functions.

3.17 Laws are made to last for a certain period of time and it is for this reason that they require a force of execution as well as constant and lasting obedience; it is necessary that there be a power always in effect that presides over the carrying out of the laws which have been made and which continue to be in effect. For this reason, the legislative and executive powers are often separate (cf. Locke, TTG, II, 144). Side by side with these two distinct powers, Locke places another one, the federative, which "can also be called natural" and implies the power over war and peace, leagues and alliances and all negotiations with all persons and communities that are outside the State (cf. Locke, TTG, II, 146). Although this power is distinct from the others, it is difficult to separate it from the executive because it cannot be put in the hands of others, needing as it does force.

3.18 Among the less often remembered points in Locke's thought there are the reflections on tyranny in which not a few ideas anticipate certain conclusions of Montesquieu. From the lapidary definition of tyranny – there is tyranny when he who governs, in whatever name, establishes not law, but his own will as the norm – comes the conviction that it is a mistake to believe that this mistake is inherent only to monarchies (cf. Locke, TTG, II, 199 and 201) that are degenerating. It can be concluded that more or less dangerous tyrannies take root whenever their powers go beyond the confines within which they must act. If, in theses cases, revolutions come to pass, these are legitimate. Indeed, Locke is not so alarmed as those who maintain that for the multitudes every occasion is fit for rebelling. Men are not induced to abandon their old institutions as easily as some tend to maintain (cf. Locke, TTG, II, 223). The risks of revolutions are such that they are accepted only if the political situation becomes unsustainable. It is on the risks and dangers that the English philosopher concentrates to keep the various powers within their own limits. Thus the best way to prevent evil is to show its dangers and iniquity to those who are tempted to perform it (cf. Locke, TTG, II, 226). All in all, it is symptomatic that to keep a society within the realm of legality there must be the certainty of punishment for anyone who falls into error.

3.19 Locke's thought also reveals itself to be highly innovative in the area of religious problems, not so much for that tolerance that turns out to be somewhat limited on the practical level, to the point of excluding believers from other confessions such as Catholics and also free thinkers who refuse the idea of divinity itself, as for those basic reasons that justify tolerance itself and which were to lead the English philosopher to theorize that secularity of the State that placed him in conflict with by no means few thinkers of his time. The point of departure for an analysis on tolerance can be considered natural law and its tradition, but, as has appropriately been pointed out, to the natural law from the Stoa and the Fathers of the Church, Locke adds the great stimuli of the rising English bourgeoisie since "the law of nature imposes obligations because it has been commanded by God and because violation of it prevents mankind from becoming happy" (Euchner, 191). For this reason, Locke disputes the advanced conceptions of the Presbyterians and Independents of what was then called "indifferent actions". If the result of those actions is to put in jeopardy the peace, tranquillity and well-being of those associated, the magistrate must intervene because the very roots of civil coexistence are called into question. On this subject there cannot be the slightest doubt: the power and authority of the magistrate are granted to him so that he could make no use of them other than on behalf of good, the conservation and peace of people in that society which place him in charge (cf. Locke, in Fox Bourne, 174). All the other actions have a right to tolerance; but only to the extent to which they do not tend to disturb the State, or cause more harm than offer advantages to the community (cf. Locke, in Fox Bourne, 178).

3.20 At this point, a rather delicate problem arises. It is clear that the magistrate commands the practice of the virtues, not because these are virtuous forms of behaviour and place obligations on consciences, or because they are the duties of man to God as well as a way to obtain his pardon and his favour, but because they are advantageous in the relationships of man to man (cf. Locke, in Fox Bourne, 182). In a too hasty analysis all that would appear to be a reduction of religiosity to a utilitarian morality whereas for Locke religion is much more than a simple utilitarian presupposition for society. Here too his words are extremely clear; belief in a divinity must not be counted among the purely speculative opinions, because it is the basis of all morality. If it is true, then, that Locke forcefully sets forth the reality of a lay State, with the ideals of tolerance he promotes real respect for those religious themes that constitute the premise for civil life. This aspect also seems to me to recall one of those crucial points in western tradition that refused compromises or, in any case, overly close ties between politics and religion. These ended up granting the latter those claims to perfection which, when it confined itself to its authentic teachings, it placed in the dimension of an afterlife. In that perspective religion, rejecting all utopian temptations, ended up being a constant critical and therefore liberal component of politics itself. This is why there must be tolerance. Belonging to a religious creed is the result of embracing it intimately and spontaneously. "The care of souls cannot belong to the civil magistrate, because all his power consists in constriction. But true and salutary religion consists in the internal faith of the soul, without which nothing has value before God. The nature of human intelligence is such that it cannot be constricted by any outside force" (Locke, ALcT, 114). Now it is clear why Locke rejected atheistic positions in any case, because along with other liberals like Constant and Tocqueville, he considered religion not only the foundation, but also a bastion of the defence of liberty.

C) *The rise of civil society.*

3.21 At the risk perhaps of going against current thought, I think that the work of Mandeville is not to be included among those who have contributed to the formation of modern societies open to the development of philosophical thought around individualism which, not a few times, appears exaggerated and questionable, but for other reasons to be found here and there in his works, have caused English culture to ask itself questions about a series of problems to which some – and I am thinking of Hume – have provided more balanced solutions and which are better suited to a modern-style liberal society.

Bernard de Mandeville was born in 1670 in Rotterdam in a very prominent family of politicians and doctors. He also received a degree in medicine in 1791. After moving to London he took up the practice of medicine with success and, after marrying, settled definitively in the English capital. After translating the *Fables* of La Fontaine, he published various writings concerning the disorders of hysteria and hypochondria. In 1714, he published *The Fable of the Bees, or, private Vices, publick Benefits* a work, which, through several editions and reprinting, aroused considerable interest. Among other things, he also published *Free Thoughts on Religion* in 1720. Aside from his writings, very little is known of his private life. He died near London, in Hackney, in 1733.

3.22 It would seem plausible to say that the point of departure in Mandeville's thought is, in certain respects, quite close to the anthropological conceptions of Machiavelli and Hobbes even though he differs from them especially in the conclusions about how to organize society. The fact remains that that way of judging humanity, both in its single and overall aspects, is very close to those "universal categories" found in the *Prince*. Concerning human beings, Machiavelli was used to saying that *in universale*, that is usually, they behaved the same way. What almost always changes is the insignificant, the basic, vices, qualities and defects, remain the same. Mandeville has the same opinion: humanity has remained the same for many eras, despite the many instructive and elaborate writings by means of which attempts have been made to correct it (cf. Mandeville, 9). Behind appearances, every individual hides his wickedness, slyness and will to obtain his own personal advantage, to the detriment of anyone else. His verses in *The Unhappy Beehive* are famous: "These were call'd Knaves, but bar the Name / The grave Industrious were the same. / All and Place knew some Cheat, / No Colling was without Deceit / The Lawiers, of whose Art the Basis / Was raising Feuds and splitting Cases" (Mandeville, 20).

3.23 It would almost seem that Mandeville's pessimism is along the lines of Hobbes' to the point of considering the human being practically a beast: being an extraordinary selfish and obstinate animal as well as sly, however much it can be subdued with greater force, it is not possible, with force alone, to make it docile and make it accomplish the progress of which it is capable (cf. Mandeville, 41-42). For Mandeville, all this appears to be a universal and necessary category, such that he wishes, in the *Introduction* as well as elsewhere, to advise the reader once and for all: when I say men I do not mean Jews or Christians, but simply man in the state of nature and since human nature continues to be identical as it has been for so many thousands of years, we have no good reasons to expect a future change as long as the world lasts (cf. Mandeville, 40 and 229). Who could deny this since if I undertook seriously to analyze men I would find calumny, envy, wickedness and gluttony, drunkenness and impure acts as well (cf. Mandeville, 154). All of that makes man a fickle and cowardly animal, and millions of these animals well united together make up a strong Leviathan more inclined towards idleness and pleasure than to labour, when not driven to this by pride and avarice (cf. Mandeville, 179 and 194).

3.24 It would almost seem that on the political level it is necessary to strive to understand how to make a beast of this sort manageable: the first concern of all governments its to keep in check his ire by means of severe punishments when he causes damage and, thus, increasing his fears, to prevent the ills that he could cause. Thus, the only useful passion that man possesses for the peace and tranquillity of a society is fear (cf. Mandeville, 206). The same standard of justice can be true only if it refers to a future life, but it is false if one wants it to refer to the present world (cf. Mandeville, 273, even though here, in actual fact, the author is criticizing the sentence: it is better that five hundred guilty parties escape just punishment, than if one innocent person is punished). It is useless to believe that education makes a human being morally better. Those who are destined to a life of fatigue could be made worse through studies and, by keeping them in ignorance, they will more easily bear certain hardships (cf. Mandeville, 288-289 and 317).

3.25 Equally surprising is the fact that Mandeville proposes an almost Platonic solution to escape such a situation. On a par with the Philosopher Kings, " politicians succeed in gaining acceptance for the concepts of honour and infamy as the greatest good and the greatest evil, relating them to actions performed based on reason and with the public good in mind" (Magri, XVII). Furthermore, if an honest society is desired, one must seek to create a frugal one which will keep its original simplicity, a society which prevents contact with superfluous things, that can somehow arouse desires, and with foreigners, especially if they are rich and devoted to commercial activities. They develop avarice and luxury; where there is a great amount of trade, there is a great amount of fraud (cf. Mandeville, 185), just as, where there is little or a lot of money, certain choices will be made on the basis of this, such as those of parents who are thinking about the future of their children (cf. Mandeville, 158).

3.26 Yet, despite this dark pessimism, development of society departs from these assumptions: If you wish to make a society of men strong and powerful, you must touch their passions (cf. Mandeville, 184). These are what dictate human actions, even spontaneous ones, and from these comes the best society which, in Mandeville's view, "is evidently not the result of human planning" (Hayek, I, 20).

The fact that acting depends on pursuing a certain form of utility should come as no surprise because this is what many other illustrious spirits had maintained before Mandeville. Among these was Cicero who, in lapidary fashion, said, *à propos* of justice, that it was a *"habitus animi, communi utilitate conservata"* (passage from *De Inventione*, 2, 53, quoted by Hayek, II, 154, nr. 9). On this subject, it is useful to recall that Cicero is among the very few authors who was praised in connection with the *Fable of the Bees*, because the Roman world is among the most distinguished that has ever appeared under the heavens (cf. Mandeville, 334 ff. and 50). Private law itself is the continual analysis of all the human desires and passions aimed at the search for utility and this is not only the fruit of the virtues, but also of the vices (cf. Mandeville, 48). Economic activities themselves are functions of this complex of passions, trade, too which is the most important but not the only condition for the greatness of a nation (cf. Mandeville, 116). Aside from trade, anticipating conclusions that Smith would reach, Mandeville maintains that the greatness of a nation consists in giving each person an opportunity to find work the well-being of all societies will always depend on the fruits of the earth, and the labour of people (cf. Mandeville, 197); on labour value itself seems to depend (cf. Mandeville, 286-287). In such a highly developed society, one that seeks to develop more and more which has requested that property be well guaranteed, justice administered with impartiality and the interest of the nation tended to in every matter (cf. Mandeville, 249).

3.27 The fact that societies, with their structures, are the fruits of human actions, which, however, do not abide by any design will be one of the favourite subjects of some English eighteenth-century thinkers. Among these is Adam

Ferguson (1723-1816). According to him nations arise from institutions which are certainly the result of the action of men, but are not the realization of any human design (cf. Ferguson, 187). Such a conviction is the premise for further exploration into one of the subjects latent in Mandeville's thought; that is, the fact that society is the result of what the Latin civilisation called a *concordia discors*. In other words, if, on the one hand, there is the great multiplicity of human desires, on the other there is the continued opposition that human beings encounter in satisfying them. This is a sort of sociable unsociability which had been partly anticipated by Lucanus (cf. vol. I, point 2.24). In the final analysis, the dialectic of human action has two opposing characteristics: on the one hand dissent and animosity, on the other, affection, disinterestedness and generosity. This dynamism is indeed vital and, if it is cut off, liberty itself is lost. Indeed, it disappears not when despotism emerges, and despotism is the visible expression of its demise, but even before that, when the longing of mankind to conquer and defend its rights is extinguished.

3.28 Speaking of Mandeville, it is appropriate to recall that the passions are not always the stimulus to the development of a society. There are others which must be concealed on behalf of the proper functioning and decorum of that society (cf. Mandeville, 68-69). If that does not occur, it almost seems as if society has taken a step backward which can lead to a crisis. There seem to emerge several reasons typical of Vico's thought in the *Fable of the Bees*. Furthermore there are not a few contradictions in a certain phase in the development of a beehive. All places first occupied by three, that watch over the common mischief, and often from affinity, they help one another to steal, they are now held successfully by one. And at this point a few thousand others go off (cf. Mandeville, 31). Greater efficiency is rewarded with growing malcontent; too many well adapted ones end up suffering privations that they had not expected. Thus, a society is achieved that can no longer offer what it had promised. Anticipating conclusions that will be those of Schumpeter in the *Fable* we read: Whoever spends a great amount of his youth learning to read, write and do accounts, expects, not without reason, to find a job in which the things he has learned are of some utility (cf. Mandeville, 289). These prophetic statements show the complexity of a thinker who prophesies the qualities and defects of a society which has yet to define itself. The great insights about the moral needs of the new society have not yet acquired a certain rigour from a philosophical point of view. It will be the task of Hume to set forth the experimental study of human nature on the basis of knowledge itself seizing the very close tie that exists between morality as a science of feelings, and politics, in the sense of a science of social man (cf. Abbondanti-Ghiringhelli, 104-105).

3.29 A person such as Bolingbroke should not enjoy the status of those who fought on behalf of an open society. Considered a reactionary for a long time if not an anti-historical figure, in so far as he supported ideas not in keeping with the times, he was recently reputed to be almost a populist or, in any case, an exponent of "democratic-popular Toryism" (Capozzi, 6). The fact remains that, having lived in a turbulent era, Bolingbroke was able to accept some anti-absolutionist elements that are highly visible in his work. In particular, the ethical and religious treatment in his *Fragments*, from the last years of his life, deserves to be remembered. Here, he specifies the "reflection on the essence of society and government, on the relationship between these and the natural order" (Capozzi, 9). In his last writings, Bolingbroke recovers the sense of national tradition in a view that makes him seem to be "a supporter both of the mixed State as a form of government, and the division of powers, as that which presides over liberty" (Compagna, IP, 97).

Henry Saint John, Viscount **Bolingbroke**, was born in 1678 at Battersea where he died in 1751. A prominent exponent of the Tories he took part in all the events in the first half of the eighteenth century. At first he had noteworthy political successes ending, after the death of Queen Anne, in a period of disgrace that eventually led him to be sentenced for high treason, with exile in France. When he returned to England in 1726 he founded the *Craftsman*, the first party and opposition newspaper, in which Pope, Swift and William Pulteney were involved. In opposition to Walpole, he attempted to bring together the moderates of the Tories and Whigs. Noteworthy among his works are *Remarks on the History of England* (1730-1731), *Dissertation upon the Parties* (1733-34), and *The Idea of the Patriot King* published in 1749, having already come out in clandestine form in 1738. The important *Fragments*, or *minutes of essays* were published posthumously.

3.30 Bolingbroke earned himself a place in history as a representative of theism. In his opinion, the existence of the one God the creator can be achieved only *a posteriori*. The same consideration applies to other reasoning as well. One need only think, for example that "the limited nature of human reason excludes the fact that individuals may be capable of perceiving *a priori*, the essence of natural law" (Capozzi, 14). The same reasoning applies to social aggregation and its rules. Societies originated from instinct and were perfected by experience and in tacit agreements making up what can conveniently be called the law of nations (cf. Bolingbroke, 40). This experience, which is also juridical experience, marks the return to Ciceronian Stoicism, which sees in natural law the possibility of giving rise to universal principles of aggregation in total opposition to the vision based on a selfish impulse of natural law characteristic of Hobbes (cf. Capozzi, 12). There can be no doubts about this conclusion: I do not believe that men have ever lived in a state of absolute, individualistic isolation at any moment preceding the institution of civil society. "Men were never out of society" (cf. Bolingbroke, 43 and 46). For Bolingbroke the difference between natural society and political society is not so great as one might imagine and, if nature has created the former, "we cannot doubt that reason and experience improved it" (Bolingbroke, 75). If law and liberty rest on natural premises it is in the area of historical origin that they improve and mature.

3.31 More than for those ideas, Bolingbroke is famous for the *Idea of a Patriot King* which, despite the dispute with Filmer no less sharp than with Locke, makes him seem a sort of national populist, yet, for him, power is to be conceived of as "an authority in which the need for the security of a multitude of already-existing communities is congealed, rather than the founder of a society departing from single individuals" (Capozzi, 17). This, too, differentiates him from Hobbes and it could be said that brings him closer on the one hand, to the Roman juridical experience based on the *gens*, and on the other, to Vico's conception of the contrast between major and minor peoples; one need only think that for him, civil governments were set up not by the association of individuals, but by that of families. "Families kept men out of that state of individuality which Hobbes, and even Locke, supposes" (cf. Bolingbroke, 65 and 81). The nation that finds in the King the guarantor of their *raison d'être* comes from these families. That monarch-legislator gives rise to a constitutional monarchy which is based on a sort of national aristocracy, in turn based not on rank but on merit. From that institution, seen from an anti-oligarchic point of view, comes the national and popular regeneration of the *country*, which is capable of opposing governmental and parliamentary corruption (cf. Compagna, IP, 93). Here the need to define a balanced or mixed political system re-emerges. If one prefers, a system of checks and balances is needed, capable of curbing the excessive power of the emerging institutions and their corruption as well.

3.32 The *raison d'être* of all bodies of power and, obviously, non-tyrannical ones, depends on consensus or, if one prefers, the support of the community. On this subject, Bolingbroke's definition of the constitution has become famous: "By constitution we mean, when we speak with propriety and precision, that sum total of laws, institutions and customs, coming from certain immutable principles of reason and aimed at certain immutable ends for the public good, that constitute the complex of the system according to which the community has agreed and accepted to be governed" (Bolingbroke, quoted by Compagna, IP, 89). Whatever the government may be, it must operate within the constitution, the expression of the community's feeling, but, at the same time, it must be the expression of the confines that the activities of government must never exceed. Here, that concept of limit returns and is typical of the noblest western tradition, and will be one of the cornerstones of the future experiences of liberal democracy. All of this appears certainly tied to a sort of institutional patriotism, the expression of that *country-party,* which was to have eliminated all possible divisions (cf. Compagna, IP, 88).

D) *The Balance of Innovation and Tradition: D. Hume.*

3.33 The gnoseology of Hume appears in a new form, different from the past; it ignores the analysis of first principles because it considers that impossible. This applies to science as well as to religion: the relativity of scientific knowledge drags theological and metaphysical knowledge along with it. Religion can no longer give valid support to science and both seem destined to lose any and every objective value. The metaphysical foundations of science are called into question to the point of casting doubt on the very logical structure of science (cf. Cassirer, 83-85). However, this position does not give way to scepticism. Hume is criticizing a now inadequate and outmoded way of pursuing science, but when he supports the value of ideas in the gnoseological area, he does not do so by exalting the subjective approach to knowledge, even if this is the first step. Indeed, if "it is not always possible directly to indicate the original of a given idea, however much this may be hidden, there is no doubt that it exists and that we must search for it" (Cassirer, 131). This is what comes out quite clearly from a careful reading of the *Treatise of Human Nature,* in the famous second section of the third part of the first book, when reference is made to the *relationships* that exist between objects in the relations to the idea of causality. Furthermore, when Hume maintains that seeking certain truths can turn out to be extravagant and vain, he never does so by criticizing the uselessness of the search for truth, but simply pointing out that, given the lack of balance in the research, it turns out to be senseless most of the time. "Much of humanity can be divided into two classes; that of the *superficial* thinkers, who remain outside of truth, and that of the *abstruse* thinkers, who go beyond it" (Hume, EMPL, II, 285). For this reason, rather than arguing about the utility of research, one must investigate a methodology capable of attaining the few possible certainties, keeping in mind the clear limits of our reason and our way of operating.

3.34 The same must be said as far as the problem of faith is concerned. This is not based on rational and universally valid principles, but always remains a primary stimulus of human nature that cannot be eliminated. Upon closer examination it is from here that tolerance must arise. Religion cannot be fully understood, even as an historical phenomenon, based on an exclusively rationalistic analysis, as the Enlightenment claimed to be able to do. Hume also does not like the exalting of a *religio naturalis*, so dear to not a few figures of the Enlightenment. The "*religio naturalis* is not at all natural nor is it as ancient as creation and even less is it a religion. Religion, in Hume's words, is *Faith,* faith in the Christian sense. Natural religion had existed only in the imagination of the Deists" (Nicolai, 14). Furthermore and quite clearly, in the *Inquiry concerning Human Understanding* we read that "*Our most holy religion is based on Faith not on reason (...) Mere reason is insufficient to convince us of its necessity*" (Nicolai, 57). Hume shows the greatest respect for this religion of faith without the slightest form of scepticism. On the contrary, people regretted that religion based on faith was too often criticized by exaggerating its errors and contradictions without ever underscoring the fact that such a religion "pursues its natural tasks, its operations that, although infinitely appreciable, and secret and silent, rarely come into historical consciousness" (Nicolai, 59). It is understandable why, and certainly not by accident, Jacobi calls Hume a "master of faith" (Nicolai, 57).

3.35 The fact that religion is also linked to passions and feelings, such as hope and fear, that instilled religious feeling in humans and keep them bound to this, does not mean an element of weakness for religion itself. It can be recalled that Vico, too, had aired the same considerations with results that were anything but irreligious. Moreover, the passions are a fundamental component in the analyses of Hume. It must not be forgotten that his love for certain

Latin classics came from their profound analyses of the passions and thus from their genuine respect for mankind, hence his admiration for Cicero, especially for his "probabilism", and for Seneca. Believing is an interior acceptance which, at times, leaves reason bewildered. Enlightenment rationality can do quite little when the ancient vigour of religion still rests on premises such as *credo quia absurdum*. These considerations of Hume, constitute a *unicum* in the reflections of his century and leave extremely ample space for religion which no other contemporary of his will bring out (cf. Cassirer, 240 ff.). On the level of religious philosophy as on that of the philosophy of history, Hume seems not to belong to the Enlightenment, but this does not place him in the past. His position, rejecting the claimed objectivity of abstract reason, leads him to consider the value of subjective positions. This is why it can be said that "Hume's doctrine defends the particular nature and right of the individual and seeks to make it known" (Cassirer, 304).

David Hume was born in Edinburgh in 1711. After studying law, he became interested in the historical, philosophical and literary disciplines. He was the embodiment of the English political scene not only occupying political and administrative posts for a certain period, but also facing the trials of the traditional English parties. He went from positions typical of the Whig party to those of the Tories, but, in the second circumstance as well, remained an enlightened observer who defended the principles of tolerance, civil and political liberty. He also sided with those in favour of the independence of the American colonies. He spent periods of time in the most important European capitals, too, as the secretary of English representatives, and was an undersecretary in the Grafton government. Among his numerous writings the *An Inquiry concerning the Human Understanding*, *Treatise of Human Nature*, the *Natural History of Religion*, *Research on the Principles of Morality*, the *Essays Moral and Political* and the *Political Discourses,* as well as an *History of England from the Invasion of Julius Caesar to the Revolution of 1688* are particularly memorable. He died in Edinburgh in 1776.

3.36 One of the basic tasks of Hume's gnoseology is to identify the problem of limit that involves not only the theoretical sphere, but also the practical one. From the limits of reason and those of thought come the limits of our liberty, too, such as those of law which govern liberty itself. Examining the limits of thought we become more aware of the limits of our liberty. Indeed, although our thought seems to possess this unlimited liberty, upon a more stringent examination, we will discover that it is really confined to highly restricted limits. Even creative thought, the imagination, is reduced to nothing more than the ability to compose, transport, augment or diminish the material supplied to us by experience (cf. Hume, ICHU, 19). All that comes from experience determines custom which, in many areas, is more important than reasoning. Custom is the great guide of human life. This is the sole principle that makes experience useful to us and makes us expect, for the future, a series of events similar to what has appeared in the past (cf. Hume, ICHU, 54-55). The study of custom brings us closer to history which, for Hume, is closely connected to politics such that it can be considered the true "cabinet of experimentation" of politics itself. The passions, which have given life to custom and given birth to history, are a constant in human vicissitudes so that humanity, from this point of view, is always the same at all times and in all places. Thus, Hume almost paradoxically maintains that whoever wishes to know the inclinations and feelings of the Greeks and the Romans, need only analyze the temperament and actions of the French and the English, since there is great similarity. But that is not sufficient. The study of human characteristics, as it is offered to us from reading the classics, is more useful than the reading of scientific texts which no longer correspond to our way of discovering the world. For this reason it is still highly instructive, and will always be so, to read Polibius and Tacitus (cf. Hume, ICHU, 98).

3.37 Political action must be solely a function of the daily necessities of individuals and their interests. Justice calls for the defence of property, and hence becomes an obligation. Hume therefore maintains with extreme clarity that one must confute the speculation systems that pertain to politics, widespread in this nation; as well as the religious position of one party and the philosophical one of another (cf. Hume, EMPL, II, 533). These parties are decidedly dangerous because they do not content themselves with setting forth immediate or long-term programmes to achieve contingent goals but, they have opposite views concerning the basic nature of the form of government (cf. Hume, EMPL, II, 538). From the positions arise obstinacy and points of view that risk ending up in armed combat. Those parties, moreover, base their convictions on an abstract rationality which takes into account neither history nor the specific conditions of a people and, in order to chase after forms of utopia, they risk overthrowing even the most solidly formed government that ensures stability and well being. A government of that sort, with a position which brings to mind the clear Ciceronian explanation of consent, has the infinite advantage of its successful consolidation, since the mass of people govern themselves with authority, not with reason, and never confer authority on what has not been confirmed since antiquity. All the government projects that hold out a prospect for sweeping reforms of the customs of humanity are clearly a figment of the imagination (cf. Hume, EMPL, II, 561 and 563). Among these there is necessarily a reference to all those schemes that go from the *Republic* of Plato to the *Utopia* of Thomas More.

3.38 Now it is understandable why Hume, in another passage, could state that all philosophers who have concentrated only on the theoretical can have variable fortunes in the course of time. On the contrary, those who have described the human passions, from which the concrete life of human beings come, end up in everlasting glory. Aristotle and Plato, Epicurus, and Descartes could give way one to the next, but Terence and Virgil have maintained an undisputed and universal supremacy over the spirits of human beings. The abstract philosophy of Cicero has lost credit: the vehemence of his oratory is still a subject of our discussion (cf. Hume, EMPL, I, 275). When Cicero described the passions, therefore, he gained sympathy, compassion or indignation and today it is impossible for a reader with good taste to read some of his pages without feeling sincere sympathy or grief (cf. Hume, EMPL, I, 253 and 248). The political struggle must be centred on these passions, controlled and made legitimate and the parties are their instrument and expression.

3.39 Politics are extremely complicated in their own right and should not be weighed down with speculations as audacious as they are vain. Indeed, it is quite unlikely that a choice may be made in any matter that is entirely good or entirely bad. Doubt, reservation and uncertainty are the only premises upon which (the individual) tests these phenomena (cf. Hume, EMPL, II, 554). This sort of prudence or political moderation not only makes it possible to oppose utopian absurdities, but also the ignorance, of individuals or of the multitudes, which is "confusing and dogmatic". Here that search for the "happy medium" among the various political and social forces in conflict becomes evident. The happy medium is what attenuates the claims of the extreme. It can be said that for Hume "moderation is inseparable from the very nature of the English Constitution, just as the influence of the Senate and the censors had set up one of the regular and constitutional balances that had maintained the equilibrium of the Roman government" (Compagna, IP, 107). Not only had the English system re-established such a balance, but it had also strengthened and improved it bringing to bear that antynomic tendency between Authority and Liberty that guaranteed that the House of Commons could operate as the proper driving force of the Crown, aided by other institutions that identified with tradition, and to exercise that restraint that prevented sudden and surely inopportune changes (cf. Compagna, IP, 109). Far from the dangerous utopias that led only to the most absurd refusal to co-operate and intransigence, the parties ended up backing up either the driving force or restraint and, therefore, constituted an element of stability in the English system. These are the parties of *interest*, that can be distinguished from those of *principle* (which are those that claim religious or philosophical positions) and that of *affection* (cf. Compagna, IP, 116-121). Only the former are practicable and ensure certain progress. Here is the position embraced by Hume, which accepts only merits from tradition and the Enlightenment, rejecting the absurd, extreme forms.

3.40 The relationship between authority and liberty comes from the relationship between the State and the individual. Between the two there is continual osmosis and enrichment. Indeed as private individuals draw from public authority greater security in the possession of commerce and their wealth, so the community becomes more powerful in proportion to the wealth and extension of the commerce of private individuals (cf. Hume, EMPL, II, 287). Here there seems to be a reversal of the theses of Rousseau. The development of political society has meant enrichment and development for all: consolidation of the principle of authority, legitimate obviously, has offered greater leeway to liberty and greater security in social life. An authority so thoroughly tested by history has, moreover, given rise to genuine consent in the political community showing how fallacious all those theories are that claim to invent *ex novo* the standards of liberty and civil life. Such abstract liberty often gives rise to the opposite and drags everything and everyone towards despotism and poverty. The poverty of the mass of the population is a natural if not infallible effect of absolute monarchy (cf. Hume, EMPL, II, 299). There is, therefore, an inseparable bond between legitimate authority and liberty and between the latter and progress and wealth. Furthermore, a proper relationship between power and the individual not only favours internal economic activities, but also foreign trade which with its imports supplies materials for new industries and with exports applies labour to the production of particular objects that could not be consumed domestically (cf. Hume, EMPL, II, 296). These reflections and, above all, those on labour, will be further developed with originality by Adam Smith.

3.41 It is also useful to recall that the gaining of wealth not only leads to more refined taste, but also improvement of the institutions. Barbarian peoples are not even capable of dealing with this problem. Can a government of a people that do not know how to construct a spinning wheel or make proper use of a loom be expected to be properly formed? (cf. Hume, EMPL, II, 308). Ignorance and barbarian behaviour are not even capable of grasping the needs of a free individual and his relations with institutions that are worthy of that name. Law, order, police, discipline can never reach any degree of perfection, before human reason is refined through exercise and application of the most common arts, at least those of trade and manufacture (cf. Hume, EMPL, II, 307-308). This is a strong attack on the myth of the noble savage which would have such an effect on utopian thought from Rousseau onward.

3.42 To combat the various types of utopias, it must always be kept in mind that no individual is authorized to carry out innovations through violence. They are dangerous even when the legislative body ventures to perform them. History shows us that. To avoid dangers of this sort a power so mild as that of making laws must not be left up to a sole body. Create two distinct legislative assemblies, each of which has full and absolute authority in its own area, and has no need for the concurrence of the other to confer validity on its acts. There is no need to go far to demonstrate the validity of the preceding hypotheses, since such is the case of the Roman Republic (cf. Hume, EMPL, II, 415-416). In the latter, the legislative power belonged to various types of *comitia* and allowed the people to oppose the power of the nobles that was exerted in the Senate. From this came a political system in which various powers jointly limited themselves and no-one could completely prevail over the other. Hume approved of what in the West has always been called a mixed constitution. That constitution is made up of diverse parts, it can still maintain sufficient stability, supporting itself on the aristocratic or democratic component, even if the monarchical one is altered from time to time to adapt itself (cf. Hume, EMPL, II, 530). It hardly need be recalled that the three above-mentioned components were those that ensured stability to the English system. From here arose that popular consensus that, as Cicero had already recalled, was one of the just foundations of the government (cf. Hume, EMPL, II, 518).

3.43 The question of consensus is another reason for Hume's argumentation against Rousseau. The theory of the *original contract* of the latter involved the consent of the fathers to binding their children, down to the remotest generations, but this is an aspect, which is not justified by history, or by the experience of every age or every country in the world (cf. Hume, EMPL, II, 514-515). Consent is, in fact, political and is constructed little by little and, once it has been confirmed, needs to be recalled in every circumstance because, among other things, every different historical experience enriches it with new content and new rules. That was amply demonstrated by Locke who stated that no power can take from anyone through taxes a portion of his property, without his consent or that of his representatives (cf. Hume, EMPL, II, 532). This is once again proof that even if an original contract arose from consent, it should have gradually found support in tradition and in the various crucial moments in the history of a people, once again proving that consent is not a priori, but a requisite that needs constantly to be revived and enriched.

3.44 The relationship between authority and liberty establishes a proper balance between stability and innovation. It is all concretely implemented institutionally, as well, in the division of the two Houses which are the expression of diverse interests. While the House of Lords represents tradition and thus authority, the Commons expresses the needs of the English people in the matter of innovation. With the industriousness of the English, it continually brings into existence new activities which bring progress to the entire nation. The lower House is the supporting element of our popular government, and the entire world recognizes that it owed its pre-eminent influence and consideration to the increase in trade, which brought property, thereby re-distributed, into the hands of the Commons (cf. Hume, EMPL, II, 312). That latter expression, which speaks of redistribution, is fundamental. Hume is, in actual fact, convinced that, leaving the primitive state, it was possible to proceed, however slowly, to redistribute that property more equitably which, in the primordial world and in all the political systems associated with it, was and is concentrated in a very few hands. The division of property and growth in the number of owners was possible thanks, in part, to the merchant class, "one of the most useful races of men" (Hume, EMPL, II, 338). Not only did they increase the wealth of the nation, but also took property out of the static hands of the State.

3.45 Why is their merit so remarkable? Anticipating some considerations that Smith would bring up, he goes so far as to speak, unequivocally, of work productive and unproductive even if useful. Whereas attorneys and doctors do not generate productive activities, indeed they create their wealth at the expense of others, merchants, on the contrary, promote activity and gather together a large amount of labour and goods, the creation of which they are the main means (cf. Hume, EMPL, II, 340-341). Not only does merchant activity make merchants rich, but also the entire national community and, in some respects, that of the neighbouring States. If they become rich and progress, this is to be considered a good. It is clear that the economic activity of a people cannot be harmed by the greater prosperity of their neighbours and any reason we might have for being jealous is excluded here. But I go further, and observe that, where communication among nations is kept open, it is impossible for the internal activity of each one not to be increased by the progress of the others (cf. Hume, EMPL, II, 368-369). The economic entity is so full of relations that the enrichment of one neighbouring country stimulates the other to produce in order to increase trade. On this subject, Hume maintains that he is a faithful British subject and, for this very reason, hopes for the prosperity of Germany, Spain, Italy and even France with which there had been not a few grounds for rivalry. International trade is a great stimulus to productivity: when production is performed seriously something to export profitably will always be found. But, if our neighbours have no techniques or experience, they cannot purchase from us, because they cannot give anything in exchange (cf. Hume, EMPL, II, 369). In trade, States behave like individuals: the more their wealth increases the more possibilities there are for reciprocal exchanges and interest. There is no reason, therefore to be apprehensive about the progress of a neighbouring State, on the contrary, this brings about a need for emulation which serves to keep production alive (cf. Hume, EMPL, II, 371). The variety of products stimulates their improvement and increases the trading of them.

3.46 The economic development of a community can be put in jeopardy by internal factors such as ones pertaining to taxation, more than by international matters involving the interests of neighbouring States. Hume certainly is not of the opinion, a utopian one of course, that a political community that does not pay taxes can survive, but he warns that that principle, taxation, is of such a nature as to lend itself easily to abuse (cf. Hume, EMPL, II, 384) reaching the point of irreparably harming the economy of a nation. As the great historian that he was, the English philosopher believes he can trace the fall of the Roman Empire to questions of taxation. The destruction of the Roman State departs from modification of the tax system brought about by Constantine. The people in all the Provinces were so exploited and oppressed by the Publicans, that they were happy to take shelter under the victorious arms of the Barbarians, whose dominance, was found to be preferable to the refined tyranny of the Romans, since the Barbarians had more modest exigencies and less experience (cf. Hume, EMPL, II, 388). He said that at the beginning and in its expansion and at its height, it had not at all been like that because since the Roman Empire had a positive effect, this could only come from the fact that humanity, before its foundation, was in a state of great disorder and barbarism (cf. Hume, EMPL, II, 382 note u) The Empire guaranteed that security and certainty of the rules that favoured economic activities and trade. A tax system becomes absurd when the State uses taxes not to offer services, but to pay the interest on debts that it has contracted in another way: the taxes that are levied to pay interest on these debts either serve to raise the price of labour, or oppress the poorest class (cf. Hume, EMPL, II, 398). What Hume calls a "monstrous situation" develops at this point because, among other things, in its abstractness, the State is a debtor that no individual can force to pay (cf. Hume, EMPL, II, 408). When this debtor finds itself in a situation of default, it ends up by promising more and more to the masses convinced that the latter can become a useful means of support. On this subject, and with a certain bitterness, Hume quotes Tacitus: "the common people ran open-mouthed towards the profusion of bestowals, the most improvident conquered them with money, and those who kept their heads together, considered these favours vain, since they could be neither given nor received without ruining the State" (Hist., III, 55; Hume, EMPL, II, 408). Under those circumstances, acquiring those "bestowals" means acquiring some of the debts of the State and turning our resources into public capital which is always to be found in inactive hands that live from their earnings, our securities, and in this sense, largely encourages a useless and idle life (cf. Hume, EMPL, II, 398).

E) *Relationships between Economy and Politics: A. Smith.*

3.47 Probably Smith's basic intention in writing the *Wealth of Nations* was to examine the economy in relation to the laws that govern the organization of labour. The goal was undoubtedly achieved; that does not, however, mean that his work did not have a series of repercussions, politically as well, given the very close tie between the economic and political spheres. In Smith's eyes, the latter, called the *artificial society*, while keeping its enormous importance, ended up being an emanation of the economic dimension, that is the civil *society*, the *natural* fruit of human action.

Adam Smith was born in 1723 in Kirkcaldy, Scotland, in a middle-class bourgeois family. He studied at the University of Glasgow then at Oxford. In Edinburgh, he taught literary and juridical subjects before teaching logic and moral philosophy in Glasgow until 1763. That year, as the tutor of the young Duke of Buccleuch, he departed on a long journey to Switzerland and France. Upon return to his own country, he occupied various posts such as cashier of the army, but that same year (1767) he began to write *The Wealth of Nations* which he published in London in 1776. As a writer, he engaged in many activities, even though some of his works appeared posthumously: *The Theory of Moral Sentiments,* 1759, *Considerations concerning the first Formation of Languages and the Different Genius of Original and compounded Languages,* 1761: *Essays on Philosophical Subjects*, 1795. Starting in 1788 he was also the Chancellor of the University of Glasgow. He died in 1790.

3.48 Smith caused an upheaval in what had by then become a classic and universally accepted conviction. Mankind is no longer a political animal, or as was said from Cicero on, a social animal. Playing on the latter expression, the

Scottish thinker ends up calling the human being a working animal. This a *homo oeconomicus* who only later becomes political. But that is not enough: it is the way of organizing labour that explains the anthropological dimension and, in a broad sense, every aspect of life. This life is reconsidered in its every aspect and not only, as the Enlightenment had intended, from a rationalistic point of view. Natural tendencies have enormous importance and the division of labour itself is not the outcome of reason, but of the natural propensities of mankind. The way of working determines likings, relationships and relations among individuals, in the final analysis, it determines their way of being in society.

3.49 Natural society develops through the concurrence of all those who undertake economic activities, but the latter are more effective only if political society guarantees the rules of the world of labour and, above all guarantees order and peace. This is what Smith writes with extreme clarity right from the opening lines of his classic: "Since the downfall of the Roman empire, the policy of Europe has been more favourable to arts, manufactures, and commerce, the industry of towns; than to agriculture, the industry of the country" (Smith, WoN, XXV). It is the lack of safety in the countryside, which has led to all that, because a no-longer existing authority left entire territories at the mercy of the barbarians and these were afflicted with plundering and devastation of all sorts. This principle seems to Smith evident as a logical presupposition: "In all countries where there is tolerable security, every man of common understanding will endeavour to employ whatever stock he can command" something which does not happen "in those unfortunate countries, indeed, where men are continually afraid of the violence of their superiors" (Smith, WoN, 309). Here people prefer even to bury or hide their capital to use it when it is needed. Under different conditions this capital earns and grows considerably. And this has taken place in almost all nations in all the relatively tranquil and peaceful ages (cf. Smith, WoN, 374).

3.50 A society that lives in peace favours prosperity and thus increases the size of the market as well as the *division of labour*. The latter depends on three different circumstances: first, the increase in dexterity of each individual worker; second, the time saved which is normally wasted when one moves from one type of job to another; finally, the invention of a large number of machines which facilitate and shorten work putting one person in a position to perform the work of many (cf. Smith, WoN, 7). Along with this work, other types of activity are also specialized, such as intellectual ones, so that apparently theoretical disciplines like philosophy have also performed that division. Only human beings have this propensity to divide labour, and this division has come about slowly and gradually. It comes from the need to traffic, barter and exchange one thing for another (cf. Smith, WoN, 14) which only an ever more specialized, hence divided work tends to satisfy more and more. The above makes it quite clear why, for Smith, the division of labour is determined in relation to the dimension of the market. Growths and declines lead to increase or stagnation in the division of labour.

3.51 Before continuing to deal with a problem so delicate and fundamental for a liberal society, it is fitting to point out that Smith clarifies that not even a principle such as the division of labour can be made absolute because this, too, carried to its extreme consequences, gives rise to really dangerous phenomena. His position is decidedly contrary to what, nowadays, can be called anarchical-liberal. The division of labour has indubitable merits and procures indubitable benefits, but it destroys not a few virtues, and, among these, intellectual and social ones, so that a good government must concern itself with controlling it. The division of labour leads a large number of individuals to carry out the same simple operations, hence never exercise their intellect and inventiveness. The result is that the human being generally becomes as stupid and ignorant as a human creature can. This uniformity also corrupts physical activity (cf. Smith, WoN, 840) and a people ends up becoming weaker both mentally and physically. A menace of that sort is countered above all with a serious discussion of the instruction to which Smith devotes very fine pages.

3.52 It has been said that market capacity increases with the division labour and vice versa, but that is not enough. Market capacity is proportional to exchange capacity. The more the world of labour grows, the more the possibility and need to exchange the products that are manufactured increases and this is when society itself turns into what is basically a commercial society (cf. Smith, WoN, 24). From the increase in trading and the fact that "everyone lives exchanging goods" arises the need to have an "appropriate exchange structure". Thus, after various attempts that go from the use of salt to that of precious metals, the next one is currency. It is interesting to note that currency is accepted because it has requisites of morality, and, we would say, justice, superior to other traded goods universally accepted such as gold, for example. In times when precious metals were used as a means of exchange, people always had to be exposed to the crudest of frauds and impositions and instead of a pure silver or pure copper pound they could receive in exchange for their merchandise an adulterated compound. Hence the origin of coined money and those public offices called mints. These all have the purpose of certifying, by means of a public seal, the quantity and uniform quality of this variety of merchandise when it is brought to the market (cf. Smith, WoN, 27-28). With the passing of time people went on – and the phenomenon was just getting under way in Smith's era – to replace gold coins with paper money, a much lighter instrument and "at times equally economical". The importance and value of paper money depends on the overall wealth of a country, a class or several individuals that acts as guarantors of that currency. The words of the Scottish philosopher on that subject are extremely clear: those bills come to have the same value as gold or silver money, confidence in these lies in the fact that they can be changed into gold and silver coins at any moment (cf. Smith, WoN, 318). However, as soon as one problem is solved, another arises, that of the value and utility of the goods, a value which can be called *use* or *exchange*. The discussion surrounding these two ways of understanding merchandise would never have found a solution if another way of measuring the value of goods had not been hypothesized: that of *labour*. This conclusion is reached after a consideration is made: only labour, its value never varying, is then the sole, final and real measure with which the value of all goods can in any time and place be estimated and compared. That is their real price; the currency is only their face value (cf. Smith, WoN, 36-37). It seems evident that labour becomes a universal and precise measure to establish value and, therefore, the most effective instrument, indeed the only one, for creating wealth.

3.53 An equally important condition for creating wealth is that of pursuing one's own interest. Pursuing that means increasing the interest of all the others. There is an unusual form of optimism that accompanies Smith's entire economic and political conception. There is the conviction that economic actors are "led by an invisible hand (...)

and thus, without willing it and without knowing it, they promote the interest of society, and furnish the means for the multiplication of the species" (Smith, TMS, p. IV, c.I). Subsequently, that optimism will be deemed excessive by authorities who are certainly not socialists. The fact remains that, for Smith, the economic process is ensured when, in addition to the pursuit of one's own interest, there is also the creation of capital. The latter, together with labour and land, constitute the three production factors (cf. Smith, WoN, 285-286) to which three distinct categories of individuals correspond: capitalists, salaried workers and land owners. It is concerning the first two that Smith's analysis seems particularly original. It is the profit of the capitalists which adds to the price of the merchandise an entity which increases what is simple labour value. This concept is taken up again with the greatest simplicity and clarity: in the price of goods, then, the profits from capital constitute a part, component entirely different from the salaries of labour, and governed by principles that are completely different. It is clear that an additional part must be attributed to the profits from capital, which anticipated salaries and provided the materials for that labour (cf. Smith, WoN, 55-56). Interesting and new considerations are also made on pay. The society seen by Smith is not at all static. Equal pay over time is inadmissible. It is obvious that "salaries increase with demand", but it is likewise true that, in a continually expanding society, salaries are generally higher in the new than in the old professions (cf. Smith, WoN, 132). The new insight is accompanied by a demand for new expertise and capacities and the widening of the markets including, obviously, that of labour. It is a need that Europe, however, will be slow to understand in that creating obstacles to the free circulation of labour and capital, as much as from employment to employment as from place to place (cf.

Smith, WoN, 136), will enormously delay its capacity for development. There seem here to be echoes of those recommendations for the opening up of the bourgeoisie that Marx will formulate precisely, from the *Manifesto* on. What must be emphasized here is that in Smith, civil society seems to be more mature than political society which has not yet completely become aware of the changes under way. There is another element, too (this will also be typical of Marx's analysis) which bears witness to the degree to which the political class was incapable of understanding the real changes in society and the world of labour: the new role of the city and the malleability of the citizens compared to the backwardness, mental too, of the peasant world (cf. Smith, WoN, 171 ff.) Changes are absorbed and implemented with less difficulty in the city because the social sense, the aptitude for association, come more naturally. The division of labour, the development of techniques of working and the machinery of industry progress more easily in the city.

3.54 The accumulation of capital proceeds together with the division of labour, and, in some respects, precedes it, indeed as the division of labour progresses, to ensure constant employment for an equal number of workers, an equivalent supply of victuals and a greater quantity of materials and tools than would be necessary in a more primitive state (cf. Smith, WoN, 300). In other words there is no progress without capital and without its accumulation one lives in a static and closed society. Furthermore, if the first goal of economy is to provide for subsistence, it is also true that, to ensure real development, one must go beyond the state of pure and simple subsistence. If that is not done, the economic process risks taking a step backwards, and a way out of this situation is certainly not easy to find. Political and economic crises, especially those having universal impact, are not easily overcome because they give rise to conflicts and contradictions which drag on for a long time. One could think, for example, of the Western Roman Empire, disorders that followed many revolutions lasted for a good many centuries (cf. Smith, WoN, 413) and discouraged the most important economic activity of the time, which was agriculture, causing an economic crisis, hence a political one as well, that would last for about half a millennium.

3.55 The reflection on the accumulation of capital leads Smith to the famous considerations on labour seen as a source of wealth or, to use his own words, work as "productive". There is a sort of labour which increases the value of the object to which it is destined; there is another that does not have this effect. The former, in so far as it produces value, can be called productive labour, the latter, unproductive (cf. Smith, WoN, 360). What is the relationship between these two different types of labour with capital? Here too, the Scottish philosopher is extremely clear since with productive labour capital is advanced and is generally recovered with a profit, whereas with unproductive capital it is never recovered. One becomes rich by hiring a quantity of workers, but one becomes "poor, by maintaining a multitude of menial servants" (Smith, WoN, 360). It must not be thought, however, that Smith fails to see the social value of unproductive labour since this labour, too, deserves compensation "as much as that of workers". There are many unproductive jobs for which discussion of their usefulness would be ridiculous. "Protection, the security of the pubic good" have an importance on which everyone agrees. The problem comes from the cost and dimension that certain jobs can have within the individual societies. Since only capital and productive labour create wealth and the latter must re-integrate the capital as well as guarantee profit, too, an expenditure to sustain unproductive jobs, indispensable in any case, must be precisely determined and must not exceed certain limits (cf. Smith, WoN, 361 ff.). One of the problems to solve is that of discovering the proportion between profit and earnings and the portion of the product that reconstitutes the capital. This is a principle which must always be kept in mind in order to avoid the development of conceptions, recurring ones unfortunately, based on the opinion that the national debt is added capital (cf. Smith, WoN, 1002 ff.). That way of thinking makes no sense. It would seem strange that at the heart of such an economically rigorous presentation, Smith recalls several moral motivations which he had carefully considered as a moral philosopher. Indeed, if at the basis of everything there is capital and its accumulation, it must also be said that capital is generated and increases only if there is a certain degree of parsimony which manifests itself in certain individuals more than in others. Without it there would not be saving and creation of capital. If parsimony gives rise to so many advantages, prodigality and imprudence leads to the opposite vices. The situation worsens to the point that it becomes uncontrollable when those vices are not only manifested by private individuals but also flaunted by the State (cf. Smith, WoN, 373-374) even though it is often opposed by the frugality and prudence of private individuals.

3.56 Considerations having a moral character, hence with juridical consequences are what encourage Smith to have a new look at the entire economic evolution in civil life which, at the beginning, was marked by three fundamental phases, whose characteristics have come down to us. The first society of which we are aware was that of hunters. When the relationship with the animal world became more continuous and regular it became a society of shepherds.

These two initial societies were not, however, permanent. This phenomenon was discovered and came into being in the agrarian society. At this point came the first fundamental division of labour in so far as the military force was distinguished from farming activity: the need for defence arose. This need became more and more specialized and was not only in opposition to outside enemies, but also against internal usurpers. At this point, the political society came into being when awareness came that one was defending private property and administrating justice. Where true private property does not exist, the "civil government is not so necessary" (Smith, WoN, 767). As civil society developed the fundamental tasks of politics became more evident: the defence of the country, the administration of justice and the maintenance of certain public works (cf. Smith, WoN, 745). It is clear that as natural (economic and labour) society develops, artificial society develops correspondingly, that is the society which guarantees the achievements and development of the former. It is in actual fact a structure which, as Marx will point out, consists of a superstructure depending on the former and guaranteeing it. This superstructure cannot be expected to impose the economic rules on the structure since economic activity must come under the aegis of private individuals. It is appropriate to recall that Smith justifies this conviction using a gnoseological form of reasoning, which will be taken up again, and perhaps exaggerated, by von Hayek. Economics is the science of the "particular", the momentary, even when involved in problems of a general character. It is clear that everyone, in his local condition, can judge much better than any statesman or legislator what sort of internal industry his capital can employ and which product will probably have the greatest value. The statesman who tried to direct private individuals in their use of capital would not only take upon himself a concern that is not necessary and in no place could it be more dangerous than in the hands of a man foolish and presumptuous enough to consider himself capable of pursuing it (cf. Smith, WoN, 485). He seems to be reinterpreting those statements that Guicciardini, in a different context and for different reasons made about speeches and programmes, perhaps it would be better to say proclamations, of some politicians who considered it possible to plan everything out to the slightest detail, without considering that, at times, a small unpredicted event is enough to render complicated planning vain. Such an unexpected event can be foreseen and resolved by those directly responsible more easily than by directors and bureaucrats.

3.57 In Smith's view, there is an element that leads to wealth and development of a nation which nowadays could leave us perplexed: population growth. "The most decisive mark of the prosperity of any country is the increase of the number of its inhabitants" (Smith, WoN, 80). It is from this reflection the that Scottish philosopher departs to justify the brilliant future of North America, which, aside from the population increase, obviously, can count on other requisites which guarantee sure progress. In Smith's considerations there is the regret of one who is convinced that the utility and future of the American colonies have not been fully understood by the English governments (cf. Smith, WoN, 601), but there is also the open-minded intellectual who perceives the factors that will turn those distant territories into a superpower: the abundance of land, their wealth, their population growth, good pay which provide incentives for work, but above all, that concern, imported from the old continent, to create a good government, are all features (cf. Smith, WoN, 609-610) which ensure well-being and good administration of justice. It is those institutional conditions that guarantee progress that no other colony will be able to obtain. If to that is added the fact that in those colonies people want moderate taxes and do not accept trade-monopoly conditions (cf. Smith, WoN, 616 ff.) a complete picture can be obtained that explains the need for independence that the North American colonies felt before the others. For that reasons Smith maintains that it is useless to deny independence to those territories and proposes that Great Britain voluntarily renounce its entire authority over the colonies (cf. Smith, WoN, 666) and allow them to organize themselves autonomously, with their own administration and foreign policy.

3.58 The increase in wealth of the American colonies was so great that, in little more than one century, the revenue from their taxes could exceed that of British taxes. The head of the empire would move then to that part of the empire which contributed most to its general defence and sustenance (cf. Smith, WoN, 675). This far-sighted observation encouraged Smith to propose that representation in Parliament be equal to the tax burden. It is curious that that conclusion came to him from a reflection on ancient history (which affirms the purport of what I am writing, cf. the preceding volume, too). In moments of crisis and civil wars, Rome had to deal with some populations that wanted to break off from the federation. In those circumstances those allies asked to be admitted so as to enjoy all the privileges of Roman citizens. Rome granted those privileges to most of its allies (cf. Smith, WoN, 671). This is what Smith advises the English to do, expressing the hope that they will not behave like the inhabitants of Athens. On that subject he recalls that there was never a more jealous people than the Athenians in admitting foreigners to public office (cf. Smith, WoN, 154).

3.59 The work of Adam Smith has been one of the most often discussed and "envied" of modern thought. For his opponents, who could not themselves fail to recognize the indubitable innovative merits, it was not difficult to note some contradictions. A monumental piece of writing always puts forth some weak points and others that, after just a few years, turn out to be obsolete. That does not mean that *The Wealth of Nations* must not be considered for what continues to be useful for us today. It is true that Smith had the advantage of living in a country which, given its institutions, facilitated reflection on economic subjects. It is true that this political stability led him to think that everything in economics tended towards a "stationary state"; we modern people, unfortunately, have "learned, on the contrary, that price mechanisms cannot ensure immediate and automatic settlements" (James, II, 2, § 3). It is true that often "Smith's social philosophy is contradictory and unsatisfactory, and is strongly characterized by passive resignation to social injustice" (Denis, 193), such that the poor person, like the rich one, should be satisfied with his social condition. It is true that pursuing one's own selfish instincts and interest does not mean that this will always be to the advantage of the individual alone. That does not, however, mean that confidence and respect for natural liberty, the need to protect it and with that, the conviction that the entire society must also be protected from violence and, to no less a degree, from ignorance and stupidity, all means that Smith's reflection is one of the milestones which an authentically liberal and democratic society cannot do without. For an environment so rich and capable of preparing the event, the *Wealth of Nations* appears as one of those works that have truly produced a step forward in quality (cf. Abbondanti-Ghiringhelli, 132) and subsequently it will be the very adversaries of Smith who are the first to discover that fact.

F) *Conservative Liberalism: E. Burke.*

3.60 Now that some preliminary ideological questions that led Burke's work to be labelled as reactionary have been set aside, the moment has perhaps come to analyze with greater objectivity a body of thought which, despite some conservative elements, contains not a few components of that authentic liberalism which is slowly being rediscovered. Liberty is certainly not the fruit of a miracle, as it is easy to discover in Burke and other authors, who in some ways go along with him albeit in different approaches, but it is the result of a slow conquest that can be summarized only when the basic issues of a difficult and laborious historical process are reviewed. What has been said can be confirmed by this typical statement: All that England has slowly achieved, with the aid of various peoples in a series of conquests and colonisations bringing civilization for one thousand and seven hundred years, will be doubled by America in the course of a single life! (cf. Burke, S, 233).

3.61 Burke goes so far as to say that, with the intention of constructing a society larger than the natural one, humanity "invents" laws, which can likewise be called artificial in the sense that they are produced by the art of humans. From here originate the dramatic struggles for the way of conceiving and managing power that, as various forms of government and subsequent degeneration came and went, and the mixed constitution came about, which, as many intended, was supposed to lead to a peaceful solution (cf. D'Addio, SDP, II, 74-75). On the contrary, the diffidence among the powers and the need for limitations on them was such that the state of continued instability was never overcome. This is demonstrated by the revolutionary struggles of the seventeenth and eighteenth centuries, not only European but also American.

Edmund Burke was born in Dublin in 1729. His father was a Protestant and his mother a Catholic. He was educated in literature, philosophy and history, but in 1750 went to London to study law for the purpose of pursuing his father's profession. Not many years later his first writings came out. Among these we recall *A Philosophical Enquiry into the Origin of our Ideas of the Sublime and Beautiful* (1757). The following year, he began the *An Essay towards an Abridgement of the History of England* (1757-1762), which he never finished. After being the secretary of Lord Hamilton in Ireland and Lord Rockingham, he was elected to the House of Commons in 1765. He quickly attracted attention with various qualifications. From this period come *A Speech on American Taxation* (1774) and the *Speech on Moving Resolutions for Conciliation with the Colonies*, (1775). However, his fame remains associated with his famous *Reflections on the Revolution in France, and on the Proceedings in Certain Societies in London relative to that Event*, (1790) after which he wrote, among other things, *An Appeal from the New to the Old Whigs* to reaffirm his membership in the Whig party. He died near London, in Beaconsfield, in 1797.

3.62 Burke was more than just sympathetic to the struggle of the American colonists. He took the side of that enlightened public opinion that openly criticized official English politics towards the North-American colonies. He was opposed to the use of force and warned, as did many others, that in case of a colonial war, France and Spain could obtain dangerous advantages over a weakened England. However, the motives that encouraged Burke to support the American claims are the same which, a few years later, led him to criticize the French Revolution bitterly. The Americans are not only devoted to liberty, but to a liberty seen in terms of English ideas and principles. Liberty in the abstract like so many other abstractions, does not exist. Liberty resides in some palpable object. In our country since the beginning, the greatest battles for liberty were fought over questions of taxation (cf. Burke, S, 237-238). He sympathizes with America, convinced that there, liberty has been so well forged that, thanks to the aid of religion, too, all the dangers of populism will be avoided. Anticipating some of Tocqueville's reflections, he goes so far as to say: If there had been lacking anything in the full development of this form of government, religion would have been sufficient to provide it. Religion, always a principle of energy, subsists in this new people in all its vitality (cf. Burke, S, 239). This, too, is a theme that would come back in the famous *Reflections* when he cryptically wrote that religion is at the basis of every form of associated life, the source of every good and every consolation (cf. Burke, R, 261). Thus, there is a connection between the history of the English and that of the colonists. Ignoring this leads us to deny the very foundations of English liberty. Aside from religion and the form of government, the English who insist on denying such a connection also fail to understand other causes of that rebellion such as the customs of the colonists, their upbringing and the "physical" distance from the English centre of government.

3.63 It is Burke's conviction that the people of the colonies must be made to participate in "our constitution" and not for formal or abstract reasons, always opposed by Burke, but because the Americans are calling for what we once called for and obtained since it had developed through our history. Indeed, rights are not written abstractly but codified from practical life. For example trade with America is not assured by the *Navigation Acts*, but the natural and irresistible advantages of a trade preference (cf. Burke, S, 256). This is the concreteness of life: interests are what lead to events and slow changes. When revolutions are inscribed in a history, a tradition, and do not completely reject it, they can be called transformations; when they profess to wipe out the past, as the French Revolution did, they are downright follies. The progress of history is slow (cf. Burke, S, 262): this seems to be Burke's programme for analysis and political action, one which makes it possible to understand if you will choose to build on the imagination or on reality (cf. Burke, S, 273). It is on this reality, on these practical interests that humans act and not as a result of metaphysical speculations so the Americans will no longer have any interest in opposing the greatness and glory of England, when they are no longer oppressed under her weight (cf. Burke, S, 279). This appeal to practical life will be one of the basic themes of his most famous work written not only against the French Revolution, but against the very abstract culture that caused it.

3.64 One of the primary concerns that disturbed Burke's moderately-inclined conscience after the French Revolution was that of considering it difficult, perhaps impossible, to limit the purely abstract jurisdiction of the supreme power, which was then exercised by the Parliament (cf. Burke, R, 104). French institutions seemed to him lacking in that moral support which comes from tradition. In other words, they did not have that feature typical of Great Britain, and ended up almost "depersonalizing" certain bodies: a monarch can abdicate on his or her own behalf, but not for the entire institution of monarchy, the House of Lords itself cannot give up part of its authority; nor are the Lords morally competent to dissolve their House or the other one (cf. Burke, R, 105). In the English tradition there is a sense of limits that every power has accepted and that in France, on the contrary, seems entirely non-existent. These limits, from time to time revised, are what lead to effective change. Burke does not at all believe that conserving some rules means preventing improvement, he just does not believe that this can occur through revolution. A State lacking any possibility for change does not have any way of conserving itself either. These two principles, of conservation and change, operated energetically during the two critical periods of the Restoration and the Revolution, when England found itself without a king (cf. Burke, R, 106). In France, unfortunately, harmony of the two above-mentioned principles did not come to pass. The French revolutionaries, ignorant of the true essence of political science, thought that they could build a new State by wiping out the past. The science which teaches how to construct a State (*a Commonwealth*) or recreate is an experimental science, and as such, it cannot teach *a priori* (cf. Burke, R, 152).

3.65 This abstract procedure could certainly not be accepted by Burke. Along with it, what happened to that *mos maiorum* (to which he will appeal several times to defend himself from the accusation of no longer being a Whig) which not only justified all of tradition, but even gave it meaning? This seemed to him the only criterion for legitimacy, "that is the *opinio iuris*, borne out over a long period of time, which comes from the *spirito generale* of a people, of a nation" (D'Addio, SDP, II, 84-85). This is why one must flee from any abstract presumption of momentary reason which does not at all take into account the general wealth of experience that has accumulated throughout the history of many centuries of peoples and which would suddenly be annihilated by the *philosophes*. According to them, governments would be subject to the same innocuous changeability as fashions, constitutions would no longer rest on a principle other than that of a possible advantage of the moment (cf. Burke, R, 184). It is not necessary to emphasize here that "of the moment" is the equivalent of extemporary, because the reasons of the past and possible implications for the future are unknown. Anyone who administers a state must get it into his head that he is a simple and temporary administrator of a power (cf. Burke, R, 192 ff.) which he inherits and must pass on to another in future. Power and the laws under which it is to be exercised come from ancestors and must, properly improved, be bequeathed to posterity. Can we leave a pile of ruins to one who comes after us when we were the ones to have received a precious home from someone who came before us? France did not act this way, it fought nobility but did not define its powers, it simply eliminated them; it fought the monarchy and did not think to replace the sovereign, it thought only of annihilating the institution itself; it accused religion but did not think of adapting it, it proclaimed itself atheist. Thus it placed itself outside of history with the risk of plunging once again into the bestial barbarity of a primitive world, which was savage and anything but good as the abstractions of Rousseau claimed we should believe. *Maintain* and *adapt* seem to be the two verbs dear to Burke, the only ones capable of opposing *eliminate* and *re-invent*, the actual dogmas of the Revolution.

3.66 There was an aspect typical of English liberal reflection that greatly interested and concerned Burke who unhesitatingly states: "The great source of my solicitude is, lest it should ever be considered in England as the policy of a state, to seek a resource in confiscations of any kind; or that any one description of citizens should be brought to regard any of the others, as their proper prey. Nations are wading deeper and deeper into an ocean of boundless debt" (Burke, R, 263-264). These thoughts are surely in line with those of Hume or Smith who, with more lucidity that anyone else, foresaw the drama of public indebtedness. Here too, ideas are supported, above all on the problem of property, through use of ample, albeit rewritten quotations from Cicero which also come back when the *mos maiorum* and the nobility are spoken of (cf. Burke, R, 245). Naturally the nobility is not understood here as an archaic caste that has the pretention of defending anachronistic prejudices, but as the essence of that aristocratic republic which personifies law and morality, that is tradition. It is a nobility without which no republic can exist, a nobility which, as Vico and Montesquieu would say, reappears in any republican structure worthy of that name. Today we call this nobility an *élite* and it constitutes the essence of a State, as it continually returns. Burke certainly does not have such a modern view of the problem, but he senses the impossibility of doing without such *élites* in a stable institutional structure. In this sense it is certainly true that "*Cicero was of course a favourite of Burke's*" (O'Brien, 391, note 113), that same Cicero who "*ludicrously describes*" those who sought to teach young people how to behave in public life following several philosophical paradoxes (cf. Burke, R, 283), somewhat as the abstract *philosophes* sought to re-found a State not taking its history into account.

3.67 The themes from the *Reflections* also reappear in Burke's most famous work prepared to defend his liberal principles which seemed to some to have been repudiated. History with its certitudes was still the most solid bulwark against the fickle revolutionary fashions. Considering matters in their entirety, it is safer to live under the jurisdiction of a severe but constant rule, than the imperiousness of an indulgent but capricious passion (cf. Burke, A, 77). It is as capricious as fighting religion and showing oneself to be intolerant. The irreligiousness of revolutionaries was still more dangerous than that of the ancient persecutors. The latter claimed to be inspired by the zealous urge to safeguard some other "orthodoxy", whereas the new ones were disdainful of any form of religiosity, and so were not only intolerant, but also indifferent towards religion in itself (cf. Burke, A, 83-84). The struggle against religion then became a struggle against all those governments that had any relationship with it. The result of all that was to call into question peace itself. In such a changeable situation there is such a strong tendency to leap to the dangerous extremes of *servile* complacency or *unbounded popularity* (cf. Burke, A, 104). In those situations impudence, charlatanism reigned, and what is more serious, several powers were even called into question at the expense of the balance of power itself. That delicate and difficult thing, the balance, (cf. Burke, A, 105), could not continue where there are those who live in a state of inferiority and fear, as was happening then in France. In that State the Revolution dragged everything into a state of ruin because the mania to change everything whatever the cost might be was such that people had forgotten that any spirit of reform is never more coherent in itself than when it refuses to let itself become a means of destruction (cf. Burke, A, 116). On this subject and once again to confirm the thesis of the difference between the two revolutions, Burke includes excerpts from the *Additional Declaration of the Prince of Orange* among which one reads of the concern to procure a settlement of religion and liberty and the property of the subjects on such solid foundations that there is no danger for the future that the nation will plunge back into such squalor (cf. Burke, A, 145). How could these principles be in harmony with a Revolution which based itself on atheistic principles and which, therefore, started out combating religion and finished up with fear, to call into question the very liberty that was so abstractly being exalted.

3.68 On a par with liberty, the republic, too, which, according to the French revolutionaries would replace monarchy, was an abstract ideal which did not deserve even the respectable name of republic (cf. Burke, A, 83). A comparison with several republics worthy of this name would have been sufficient. Here again history becomes the laboratory of politics, and an indispensable tool for understanding the course of events. Of himself he would say: he began very early to study the form and spirit of republics, with great care and a mind devoid of passions or prejudices. He is convinced, furthermore, that the science of governing would be badly cultivated without that study (cf. Burke, A, 114). This for Burke is the real lesson from classical liberalism to pass on. The early Whigs would surely have defended this position and the Irish liberal intends to use it to defend himself from today's Whigs (cf. Burke, A, 120). It is here that that sort of liberal-conservatism characteristic of Burke can be perceived, which distinguishes him from the positions, in some ways reactionary, of Maistre and Bonald (cf. O'Brian, 75-76). In this light it is possible to understand that, along with the appeal of the old Whigs, that of the early defenders of republican ideals can be perceived to such an extent that the author makes of what the ancients called *mos maiorum* not the only but certainly his principal political norm, to guide his judgement in all that can concern our laws (cf. Burke, A, 134). This appeal to what we could call teachings of Cicero, offers us a Burke who ends up preferring a system, which is almost that of an "aristocratic republic". In this, however, the social categories are static and immutable and certainly not dynamic like those of Vico or Montesquieu. It is a more conservative way of interpreting the Roman Republic, with the understanding that there is a need to ensure an effective division of powers. This is why the people can exercise control over the authority, but, at the same time, cannot possess it: to exercise and control it at the same time is impossible. We have seen that the exorbitant use of power cannot be effectively controlled in a popular regime (cf. Burke, A, 159) as France was showing at that time. There is an ancient wisdom in a society when it has room for those elements that begin before us and continue after use almost independently of our will. This is the place for social and civil relations. All that was true in the ancient world and is true in the modern one. What has been said of the Roman Empire is likewise true of the British Constitution: This constitution was created with the fortune and discipline of eight hundred years, and can never be destroyed without the ruin of those who would destroy it (cf. Burke, A, 196). Tacitus' words summarise quite well the political position of those who would see events in the general flow of history and not in extemporaneity.

3.69 It has been justly said that Burke made a mistake of interpretation in his critique of Enlightenment philosophy and Rousseau, in particular, he forgets that sympathy with the power of the people and for a person who lives in almost natural conditions influenced the American supporters of national independence (cf. Laski, 111). In part, this criticism is true but, at the same time, it does not recognize that other thinkers, less contradictory than Rousseau, influenced the American revolution. Remaining in the French context, one need only think of Montesquieu. I do not think I share the position at all of those who consider Burke's liberalism only apparent. Even if he is conservative he certainly remains a Whig, an *old Whig*. It certainly follows that "*Burke was not a democrat*" (Laski, 150). What has been said enables us, however, to say that different personalities of the same author, who allegedly assumed different positions depending on whether Burke was speaking of Ireland, France of America do not exist. Burke was always the same (O'Brien, 40), faithful to his basic convictions. For him tradition was always an inalienable basis and all that was related to this tradition, from religion to nobility, was likewise sacred, just as all that opposed tradition was absurd and almost demoniacal, beginning with the extemporaneous abstractions of Enlightenment reason (O'Brien, 48). In other words, Burke remained faithful to a liberalism which now seemed outmoded and which needed innovation in order to survive. This he was not able to understand and so to bring about. Burke lacks the open-mindedness of Tocqueville who, despite coming from an aristocratic and liberal dimension, and without abandoning his roots, was capable of intuiting what democratic pressure could offer that was new in a positive sense. Burke identified only the evils and did not see, as the French thinker did, the correctives and indubitable merits that that pressure brought to bear.

G) *Towards the Age of Reforms: J. Bentham.*

3.70 In the difficult years when Europe was searching for minimum prerequisites for liberal guarantees, a process of transformation got under way in Great Britain, which was to bring the English constitutional system towards a liberal and democratic one. Bentham played a particular role in this process so that he has been called the master of English reformism of radical inspiration, even though this latter appellation has perhaps been overemphasized. It is sure, in any case, that Bentham continues Hume's analysis, especially in relation to the criterion of the useful, reflecting at the same time on that complex of laws that facilitate it to see if they, and the institutions that give birth to and apply it, meet the practical needs of society instead of being empty principles destined to remain on paper (cf. D'Addio, SDP,II, 336-337).

Jeremy Bentham was born on 15 February 1748 in London. His father was a magistrate and from his youth onward the problem of legislation was crucial in his thought. In 1776 he anonymously published *A Fragment on Government* in which he put forth punctilious arguments against Bolingbroke. His first systematic work *An Introduction to the principles of Morals and Legislation* appeared in 1789. The following year he published the *Defence of Usury*. Other juridical works came subsequently and they ensured him international fame as the *Traités de législation civile et pénale* show. These were published in Paris in 1802 thanks to the involvement of his friend Dumont. In 1823 he founded the *Westminster Review* then devoted himself to a work of constitutional politics *Constitutional Code* which, however, was never completed, and was published posthumously. He died in London in 1832.

3.71 Reference to the concrete implies the radical criticism of jusnaturalism and contractualism which appeal to a meta-empirical conception of reason and which, among other things, had also led to the abstractionism of the French revolutionaries and members of the constituency. Bentham does not accept contractualism even as a hypothesis in so far as society, we could say in Ciceronian terms, subsists only when a certain number of individuals accepts a command-obedience relationship with the intention of obtaining those advantages which political organization guarantees, first and foremost, security (cf. D'Addio, SDP, II, 338-340). How can society and its legislation be derived from abstract principles when they must be aimed at concrete and feasible goals for the greatest number of people? It is from this concreteness that Bentham wants to reach the point of devising legislation that could be called scientific. Although the term 'scientific' would require a long discussion (cf. Burns-Hart, XXXVI ff.), the fact remains that for Bentham, law must constantly refer to the concrete because thanks to this, its good and efficacy can be established. From this comes the exaltation of the work of the English Parliament which, differently from the French one, does not become involved in useless disputes over matters of principle, but deals with specific problems with a view towards finding possible solutions (cf. D'Addio, SDP, II, 338).

3.72 From these considerations, it becomes quite clear that the idea of politics itself must contend with concrete matters; thus, speaking of the useful means dealing with particulars and quite precise interests that can be pursued within precise limits. This is why the "government (itself) must maintain coercive power in areas such that unhappiness, caused by its repressive action, is always less than the happiness that individuals derive from its action, aimed at guaranteeing and promoting existence, well-being, security and equality" (D'Addio, II, 341). This is why government legislation must not be involved in those areas in which the individual can enjoy his or her own liberty of action and do so better than the institutions. The same is true in those areas that come within the sphere of morality and only by this can they be condemned. In other words, there is the rejection of those statist approaches that result in paternalism, but there is also the conviction of the need for some precise rules to avoid the risk of dreaming of anarchical and libertarian aspirations that are no less dangerous than the former (cf. D'Addio, SDP, II, 341-342).

3.73 In *A Fragment on Government* it comes out quite clearly that the sole effectively valid remedy to correct the imperfections of the English government is the implementation of the "principle of utility". This is the only one that can enable achievement of the *greatest happiness* as a measure of the just and unjust in morality in general and government in particular. It must immediately be said that even if some will believe that the wish is to dust off the old concept of the common good, Bentham is clearly critical of that English political class motivated by "*sinister interest* which always and solely takes account of the interest of a few seen in direct opposition to the general interest of all the citizens*"* (Marcucci, 9). The criterion of utility does not, then, take us back to a sterile and crude empiricism, but is based on principles of a "theoretical" and "moral" sort which give Bentham's thought an "epistemological" perspective, in some ways "metaphysical" in so far as the criterion of utility cannot take into account simple personal advantage, but seems to imply far broader criteria of justice certainly not tied to momentary problems (cf. on the subject the second chapter of *An Introduction to the Principles of Morals and Legislations)*. This is why a "superior" principle of utility can be spoken of. Not only can this principle be devised, but, according to some, even calculated. It is thus understandable why an actual "rational" morality can be referred to, but in other than Kantian terms, since, in this case, rational morality also implies jurisprudence and politics that are themselves "rational" (cf. Marcucci, 13-20). Indeed, a morality that did not become regularized in the laws and implementation in politics, would be an empty, abstract exercise incapable of having any influence in actual fact.

3.74 Bentham insists that the principle of utility is not a hedonistic individual one saying unequivocally that "*it is the greatest happiness of the greatest number that is the measure of right and wrong*" (Bentham, FG, 3). In some ways, this statement harks back to the classical juridical position that, on the one hand, seeks firm juridical premises capable of opposing individual caprices and, on the other hand, seeks the validity of the principle in practice, in the form of custom as well as experienced and tested morality. This is why one should scrupulously obey and criticize freely in a really civil system – *To obey punctually, to censure freely* – (cf. Bentham, FG, 10). Failing to obey is equivalent to living in anarchy, not having the possibility of criticizing is the equivalent of denying every possibility for improvement, but is it possible to increase the possibilities for happiness without reforming what is unjust? Perhaps too, this "dialectical" relationship between obedience and liberty comes from the *"private judgment in opposition to public"* (Bentham, FG, 11, note d), that distinction between public and private that is at the heart of our civilization. Furthermore, it is the right of the private individual to judge, and that is the basis of all that every English person considers fundamental (cf. Bentham, FG, 16).

3.75 Some are of the opinion that Bentham's analysis rests on principles that seem to find support in religious or, at least public areas, in order to have greater force, and that is not rare (cf. Marcucci, 56, see note 21 commenting on note p of Bentham). However, and without wishing to force a point, I believe that it is possible to find some Augustinian motifs in Bentham. When he says: The end of which I speak is happiness; and this inclination in every action is what we call its utility (cf. Bentham, FG, 26) how can one not recall that the Bishop of Hippo himself, albeit for different reasons, maintains that every action of ours has happiness as its aim and that its inspiration is love, which that search for happiness gives birth to. This love is not necessarily of a religious sort since the *amour sui* can be a stimulus to the achievement of personal happiness without illusions that this can lead to a perfect life such as never existed in the state of nature. It should not be forgotten that a perfect state of nature can be called *"an extravagant supposition"* (Bentham, FG, 42). The English have never pursued these extravagant suppositions. This is why they created a Constitution "superior" to any others that had ever been attempted (cf. Bentham, FG, 84), even if there are those, like Cicero, who had already intuited in ancient times that the mixed form in which all the various components of society come together is good (cf. Bentham, FG, 70), even if it is difficult to achieve.

3.76 It might be said that Bentham's lesson is actually based on realism rather than an extreme utilitarianism. Analyses of societies that will never come to pass, even if profound, are of no interest. Of interest are feasible solutions for possible societies. Bentham's economic thought should also be considered in this light, especially when he speaks of usury. The latter, probably made necessary by the commercial and financial needs of the burgeoning English economic power, is justified by the fact that no-one can be prevented from performing the actions that he or she retains appropriate to obtain money (cf. Bentham, DU, *Letter I*). Today, Bentham's thoughts on usury can cause some perplexity, but it must be kept in mind that, at that time, it was necessary to support the entrepreneurial spirit and free competition not only of goods, but also capital. It must also be said, however, as is clear from *Letter X*, that the analysis of the problem of usury seems to be aimed at escaping from the stringent motivations of the moment, in function of some psychological and social implications rooted in human nature and always to be considered detrimental (cf. Buccilli-Guidi, XX and XXIV).

3.77 A propos of usury, another consideration arises that reveals perhaps even Bentham's libertarian more than liberal nature. In *Letters VI* and *VIII*, he points out that the law has always shown itself to be incapable of solving problems concerning rates of interest. Freedom of the latter will certainly not lead to a solution of the problem, but will certainly diminish it. It is to be kept in mind that the risk of sanctions reduces the number of those who want to offer money and reduces its circulation. Furthermore, the law commits an abuse because it protects the debtor, but does not in any way favour the creditor. All of these subjects find their logical conclusion in the famous *Letter XIII* addressed to Smith in which Bentham maintains that only the freedom to set the conditions for the loan guarantees the possibility for economic development and innovation in entrepreneurial activity. To be sure, positions of that sort seem highly questionable, but to understand them it is necessary to go back to a time and a tradition in which the lending of money had always been opposed and condemned.

4. The Aristocratic Republic in Vico and Montesquieu.

A) *The Approach of Croce.*

4.1 It has been appropriately said that "Croce does nothing but attribute his own historicism to Vico, that is, that history is the absolute" (Amerio, 391). I cannot fully share this judgment. There is no question of arguing against Croce, and paraphrasing him would be saying that it is "something of very little use" (Croce, 10) but there is no doubt that Vico's point of departure is the analysis of the truth, of which, and Croce himself admits it, for a Christian "only God can have full knowledge (…) because God is the prime maker" (Croce, 13). From this comes the universal gnoseological principle of Vico, that is, "the condition to know a thing is to do it, and the true is the deed itself: *verum ipsum factum*" (Croce, 14). This means that knowing and operating are closely connected with one another as intellect and will in God. All the *vis polemica* of Vico against the knowledge of his time springs from this foundation. Cartesian mathematics, for example, while being science in a certain way, does not have the concreteness that only the *true* can ensure.

Giambattista Vico was born in Naples in 1668 in a family that was certainly not well-to-do. It had to make considerable sacrifices to support him in his studies until he received his degree in jurisprudence. For several years following that, he was a tutor for a noble family in the Cilento region. After returning to Naples he continued to pursue his studies and in 1697 expressed the premises of his philosophical thought in *De nostri temporis studiorum ratione*. Then followed *La metafisica* and the *De antiquissima italorum sapientia*. Crucial in his historical and political thought are his juridical writings and the *Principi di una scienza nuova d'intorno alla natura delle nazioni* the first addition of which dates to 1725 and the third and definitive one to July 1744, a few months after his death in January.

4.2 Vico also keeps his distance from abstract rationalism in methodology. "The importance acknowledged to experimentalism, which takes Vico away from the French and Cartesian direction and brings him closer to the Italian and English one, to Galileo and Bacon, and makes him an enemy of Aristotelianism and scholasticism, as well" (Croce, 23). All of this is certainly true, but it is equally true that a series of suggestions and teachings coming from Roman historicism come together in his methodology. Suffice it to think of Tacitus, from the analysis of the dramas of history, see St Augustine, up to the Italian historicism of the Renaissance of which Vico will perform all his perceptive analysis, but also all of his firm criticism. Here it is appropriate to recall the "diffidence towards universals, understood here in the sense of general or abstract concepts" (Croce, 24) that would lead Vico to argue against Machiavelli, for his continual recourse to the "*in universale*" and, indirectly, to lead us to say that he would have accepted Guicciardini fully absorbed in the analysis of the "*particular*". Universals end up being vague and do not enable us to perceive the true meaning of reality. This is just what happened to the Machiavelli of the *Discorsi* who, for Vico, failed to understand the true nature of the Roman Republic (cf. Vico, De univ., 704).

4.3 Alongside the relationship between the true and the deed and the criticism of Cartesian abstractionism other fundamental ideas of Vichian philosophy are "the claims of the world of intuition, experience, probability, authority, of all those forms that intellectualism was unaware of or denied" (Croce, 26). All these aspects would themselves be examined and evaluated side by side with the moral sciences, morality being the criterion that accompanies the development of authority as of any other form of human action. It should be said that here, as is quite clearly set forth in the juridical writings, Vico grasps the extremely close *connection between morality and religion* both *sources of liberty and responsibility*. This is the terrain of history: "here we are in the greatest concreteness of knowing. Man creates the human world, he creates it transforming himself in civil things" (Croce, 35). From these he acquires certainty that then becomes truth, the truth of what man does. Here the Croce approach can be accepted. According to it, and paraphrasing Leibnitz, from the *vérités de raison* one goes to the *vérités de fait* (cf. Croce, 36-37).

4.4 To make these comprehensible it was necessary to go on to the other great intuition of Vico, that is to the extremely close link between philosophy and philology which, up to then, had remained something alien. Only the analysis of that link made that new empirical science, heretofore never evaluated, perceptible, and Vico was fully conscious of this. The title of his most famous work bears witness to this: *Scienza nuova*, written to argue against a presumptuous and specious way of understanding scientific knowledge which had undermined the foundations of that gnoseological enterprise since its birth. "Human science was then born of a defect in our minds, that is of its extreme narrowness, so that it is on the outside of all things, does not contain the things that it aspires to know, and, since it does not contain them, it does not translate the true things that one strives to reach. (…) From what has thus far been said, one can doubtless conclude that the criterion for – and the rule of the true consist in *having done it*" (Vico, De. ant. 68). This fact narrows our field of analysis and not only avoids our becoming dogmatic, but also sceptical: "Now it is possible to find all in infinity, but we are not given the way to find anything there" (Vico, De. ant 76)... little, then, but that little is, at least, certain.

4.5 Now it can be understood that Vico needs both to resolve the reason of doctrines of natural law critically and to found an historical reason. The latter makes it possible to arrive at a political conception which seizes the concrete foundation of becoming. On the contrary, the rationalistic and panjuridical view of doctrines of natural law ignored political realism devising a juridical abstraction (cf. D'Addio, 482). "People who do not know the truth of things endeavour to restrict themselves to the certain, because, not knowing how to satisfy the intellect with science, let the will at least be based on the conscience" (Vico, PSN, 434). The certain ends up being part of the true. Hence the recovery of a political action totally centred on prudence and wisdom (cf. D'Addio, 484) without which liberty itself would founder.

4.6 The problem of liberty is considered by the religious and moral Vico, but also by the political and juridical Vico as well. It is above all religious. "The faultiness of the idea of God is also the main argument of the criticism that Vico levels at two of those whom he greatly honoured as 'princes' of natural law, Grotius and Pufendorf. Neither the one nor the other (says he) sets forth divine providence as the prime and proper principle" (Croce, 85). Note carefully, however, this it is not an abstract religiosity born from the mind of philosophers. For Vico religion turns into practical life, for this reason it is closely linked to morality. Hence he criticises some juridical approaches of his time, since law, without religious hence moral foundations, becomes a pure and simple utilitarianism into which not only some theoreticians of the reason of State are caught, such as Machiavelli, Hobbes and others, but also Grotius and Pufendorf themselves. Furthermore civilisation and the republics have been set on their feet and held up by religion and morality and not certainly by philosophy which may have succeeded in producing great conjectures, but has never succeeded in edifying a *polis* nor keeping it alive. The *mos maiorum* has done more for the Roman Republic than the writings of Plato for the Greek *polis*.

4.7 At this point a doubt might arise as to whether Vico is not very realistic. Religion and morality indeed divorce him from that real man, filled with passions, which was so dear to the Italian realism of the Renaissance, and to the empiricists and utilitarians of his time. But that doubt is without any foundation. Here, Croce's opinion can be shared: "He always felt the supreme importance of the passions and if he could not approve giving into them, and if he always judged the epicurean morality as one 'of idle people confined to their little gardens', he likewise disapproved of overly austere moralities, such as that of the Stoics which by another way managed to be a morality of 'solitary people' and not of people living in a Republic" (Croce, 94). The same can be said for utility. In other words, the passions are fundamental. It is from studying and controlling them and the space that can be ascribed to them that arises that intrinsic right of morality and religion. Anyone who might wish proof of this need only read, for example, the pages on modesty: "refraining from exercising their beastly lust before heaven, which they greatly feared; and each of them devoted himself to dragging for themselves a woman into their grottos and keeping them as perpetual life companions; and with them exercised their lust, concealed, to use modest terms; and began to feel shame" (Vico, PSN, 520).

4.8 The feeling of shame had moral and religious repercussions immediately. Everyone soon thought that the shame had been inspired by God himself and the sense of humanity was found to be based on two principles: by liberty and by shame (cf. Vivo, De univ., 378 ff.). These feelings: religious and Christian in particular, have also played a considerable social role. The benefit offered by religion has made institutions stabler and longer-lasting (cf. De Vico, De univ., 400 ff.) Furthermore, it was from this shame that the family and aristocratic right of the major peoples was born; chapters such as the ones on "Utility is an opportunity, honesty is the origin of law and human society" or "The fundamental justice of every society" (Vico, De univ., Ch. XLVI) confirm this.

4.9 Furthermore who better than Vico has analyzed the passion of force which at times presents itself with violence and barbarity? This is what he reproaches Grotius for or those, like him, who analyze history starting from the ages of civilization neglecting the "virile" eras of great men. "Submitting the *ius gentium* to the immutable *ius naturale*, Grotius tends to place those originally voluntary elements in a secondary position" (Badaloni, XXIV). What is the effect of an analysis of that sort? – that of losing trace of a good half of history (cf. Vico PSN, 482). Vico, on the contrary, sees humanity as it is and not as it should be. He is not like Plato who ignores things ancient and past (cf. Vico, De univ., 394-396) and is so presumptuous as to found a city *ex novo*. He does as Tacitus does: analyzing the differences, he sees mankind as it is. His numerous quotations show an historian aware that he is examining real personalities and is a master of comparative history (cf. the preceding volume 2, 43). It is in this relationship with Tacitus and Latinity that Vico refers to Montesquieu when he maintains that governments must be in conformity with the nature of the people being governed, but it is from here that he again criticizes Grotius: although recognizing the importance of the *ius naturale*, he maintains that one cannot fall back on anti-historical abstractionism. In other words, there is a positive law without which the utopias of the Platonic Republic follow.

B) *The role of the Aristocracy.*

4.10 Realism led Vico to examine those *aristocratic political systems* which are the *point of departure of every civilization and their prime mover as well.* Roman history serves as a singular model. Rome itself experienced what it then went about proposing to the world with which it came into contact. What the patricians did with the plebeians, was gradually repeated in the conquered territories. The Romans "reduced the savage provinces to being clients sending them colonies, to the submissive they left the bonitarian ownership of the fields, they allowed Italy quiritarian ownership, and meritorious municipalities or cities received the same treatment of equalization as, finally, the plebeians" (Croce, 186). This was first experienced in the Urbe, then again in the Orbe except for an *aristocratic principle* which constituted the true *aspiration for those who aimed at increasing equalization.* All of that came from the original *Law of the Twelve Tables* which expressed the superiority of the *patres,* who set up the Republic, and tempered the crudity of the heroic times. For Vico, this is further proof that the aforementioned laws originated from

Rome and were not influenced by the Greek world, which flaunted an excess of culture then acquiesced in a cruel and proud way of interpreting things (a conviction which Vico repeated several times).

4.11 The fact that the original laws were "softened" as the institution of the family and that of property evolved is of interest. Family and propriety, then piety towards the deceased, were, as time passed, requirements that the plebeians, too, began to aim at since they represented the things which characterized full citizenship with relative obligations, but also rights. The laws were enforced in a way, which today we might call savage throughout the period in which the aristocracy maintained a role. It should be said, however, that the aristocratic Republic was characterized, and for Vico this would be a constant, by the small number of laws which, on the contrary, multiplied as the Republic took on characteristics of democracy. The two republics had one thing in common, even though there would be different outcomes. The strictness of the patrician laws aimed at an order capable of maintaining the privileges acquired. Once the plebeians, however, attained certain goals they feared losing them on account of periods of disorder or anarchy, and themselves called for peace and order, hopefully defences as well, if not by force of law, by weapons. Another type of aristocracy was thus generated whether or not this was desired and appeared as almost a constant in history. Here a thought directed towards Vico is perhaps not strained.

4.12 The Middle Ages cannot be labelled in haste, since they consist of various moments in history. They began with the rebirth of a natural aristocracy which found expression in those fiefs which, initially, were personal then became royal in nature. The republics characteristic of the central period of the middle era, were first aristocratic and achieved their grandeur on this premise, which went along with, not by chance, Roman law. In Vico's opinion the history of Venice is a good example of this.

4.13 The aristocratic aspect must not lead us to think that Vico is tied to archaic political and socially static models. On the contrary, he was keenly interested in the *mixed republics* where the relationship between aristocracy and democracy was tempered and each enriched the other. As a result "attention was devoted to English and Dutch models both on account of the advanced development of trade and the bond of their political forms with *libertas* (...) on the basis of a dualistic tension which tended to blend a conceptual framework of the possible political forms as well as historical and social models that were necessarily applied in them" (Badaloni, XXXII). All took place under highly precise and accepted rules. It can be said with confidence that all the juridical writings of Vico emphasize that striving to look for an order, which must always be something desired, without which everything is destined to fail. This explains why his relationships and conflicts, even when duality is being spoken of, must be viewed in terms of unity, this aspect already having been implicit in the title of his most famous juridical work which, not by chance, starts with *De Uno*. In this context it is understandable why a period of natural law in which the *meaning-reason* anthropological model is accompanied by the social one in which the other combination *force-law* predominates. The same applies to authority; initially expressed in terms of the authority of nature it is gradually integrated with the authority of reason (cf. Badaloni, XXIII). The same can be said for the natural order which, as time goes on, takes its place side by side with the rational one. The later, because it is threatened, must continually be desired and defended.

4.14 Now it becomes clear why society cannot be the mere fruit of a utilitarian, moralistic or juridical view only, but is the sum total of all this. *Utilitas* is continually threatened by the incessant search for *æqualitas* which in turn can only be moderated by the *vis iuris*. There is a vision of a harmonic unity that Vico traces back in long periods of Roman history, but there is also a wholly Christian anthropological analysis of human nature which could be said to have a clear Augustinian approach. Suffice it to read the opening remarks of the *Synopsis of Universal Law* of 1720 to realize this. For this reason Vico was always ill inclined to yield to utopian or ideal temptations because "there was all of mankind to contemplate the true eternal, turning into the corrupt man" (Vico, Sinposis, 5). Hence, three "*ius* or reasons: dominion, liberty and protection come out of the three parts that govern man's life – prudence, temperance and strength. From prudence, or the just election of the utilities, dominion; from temperance, or the moderate judgement of oneself and things, liberty; from strength, or moderate force, protection; and these three parts of justice are the sources of all the republics and all the laws" (Vico, Sinopsis, 5-6). This Trinitarian dimension is the essence of "every science, divine and human" (Vico, De univ., 32) "for its infinite power, knowledge and goodness created mankind in his image" (Vico, De univ., 92).

4.15 Vico returns several times and always with the greatest clarity to this subject. "Dominion, control, is the right that man has to dispose of his possessions as he wishes; liberty is that of living on his level; protection that of ensuring for himself, as he wishes, the person and the possessions" (Vico, De univ., 90). From this come "cognition, will and might", the three components making up the unity of human nature. Indeed, mankind would no longer be such if any one of these components were lacking (cf. Vico, De univ., 108). Here too, Augustinian ideas are considerable, but what must be emphasized is the moment of dominion "that part of authority which, in the case in point, is called *proprietas*" (Vico, De univ., 412) because it is authority and property that are the movers of history as well as their points of encounter and conflict. Among these liberty is present and acts: "(liberty) which is always present when common property is used with moderation" (Vico, De univ., 416). This reference to moderation in relation to liberty is important, liberty which it brings to the sense of "limit" expressed by laws and guaranteed by authority.

C) *The Genesis of Law.*

4.16 Liberty, authority and property are rationalized in the law which originates in Rome as a specific component of the aristocratic class. Indeed, at the beginning the "patricians kept secret among themselves the science of the laws, of the gius patri and the juridical customs (…) The jurists were appointed as the wise men of the Romans" (Vico, De univ., 24), because they preserved the essence of tradition. Thus, the study of law became a philosophy of history and practice. In Vico's opinion, these disciplines had never been studied before him (cf. Vico, De univ., 28). Where can one find the newness or, if one prefers, the delay in adopting such an approach? Vico is quite clear: "This is the real reason for the perpetual contrast between philology and philosophy, because, on one side, the philosophers have never investigated the reasons of authority, and on the other, when the philologists need the dogmas of the philosophers, however important they may be, they consider only the aspect of simple historical events" (Vico, De univ., 28). If the reference to the "reasons of authority" is noteworthy, no less important is the *unmasking of that feeling of superiority manifested by pure philosophy* a "practice" which, alas, still has idealism as an accomplice, and has continued to the present. Yet, several times Vico seems to say the practical *Romans, Venetians or English, have set up institutions that no ancient philosophy and modern rationalism either have been able even vaguely to conceive.*

4.17 What has been said also finds justification in the criterion of justice which, if it finds the noteworthy Aristotelian intuition in Greece, often and unfortunately remaining as theory, from distributive and corrective justice, in Rome this is concretized, through patrician virtue, in a justice which "is rectifying when it intervenes in matters of public interest, and equalising when in operates in those of private interest" (Vico, De univ., 78). This is why Rome was able to reject an excessively egalitarian conception of justice as well as the opposite, one which was too egalitarian, which tended to suppress merit. It is sufficient, on this matter, to recall the reflections of Cicero on *æquabilitatis* (cf. the preceding volume, 1.30 ff.) Not only were dangerous extremes thus avoided, but the law increasingly become specific in relation to, and applied legislation on to those subjects where natural law was too vague. This is the meaning of civil law as set forth by Ulpianus "'that which neither departs from all gius naturale, nor that allows everything; adding to it at times, and subtracting from it at times'; and from which comes that saying which has become banal, 'reason being the soul of law', and thus the Italians translate *ius* as 'reason'" (Vico, De univ., 98).

4.18 It is important to note that law and *auctoritas* originate at the same time. "The ancient Romans called *auctoritas* the right to command presently called 'auctoritas' (...) Many times in Roman laws, those who are called auctores are the ones from whom the right to command comes. (...) The authority which we have discussed up to now, is absolutely the first juridical acquisition of mankind, and it proceeded by far the possession of any other right; and since it was born together with mankind, it can be considered *native to* – and *innate in him*" (cf. Vico, De. univ., 108-110). Authority had, *in primis,* its divine origin and as time passed, it was sustained by human authority (cf. Vico, PSN, 480), and finally manifested itself in laws. Human history can be analyzed in the light of the principle of authority. It expresses "a philosophy of authority which is another main aspect of this Science" (Vico, PSN, 480), the New Science, in fact.

4.19 It must be added that, "taking the item authority in its primary meaning of property, that item of the law of the XII Tables is always used in that sense" (Vico, PSN, 480). It can be said that law originates to defend property and for the certainty of possession which characterizes the life and activity of the greater peoples. As time passed, these sought to pass on to others the use of force in so far, first, as "people, who lived outside of any law and took the things that they needed with their hands (*usu capiebant*) used force to keep them" (Vico, De univ., 112). This was the situation that led children to take part in what had belonged to their fathers.

4.20 From this the family was born, the first "hint of civil governments", who found in testaments the first manifestation of their will, where natural law and civil law found their first form of integration and development.

Then the governments of the optimates arose, the first "to establish themselves on the earth" and they quickly became the source of envy for those who were still living in the "extra-legal" state. As time passed, in order to flee the insecurity in which they lived, they sought protection within patrician families. Thus, the "Clienteles, the second version of civil government" were born (cf. Vico, De univ., Ch. CIV) as well as the resulting dialectical relationship among patricians and plebeians who, even in the bitterness of some moments, went on to enrich that set of rules that characterized the birth and growth of the Republic. "From that collection of all rights conveyed from each individual to universality, arose the republics. Thus the Republic must be defined as: "the sharing of every civil utility" (Vico, De univ., 126). The term "sharing" [translator's note: *accumunanza*] is noteworthy. It bears witness to the fact that republican history is characterized by the cohabitation of these two utilities: on the one hand the security of the plebeians and their rights, but on the other, the authoritativeness of the patricians who have always kept an aristocratic vein in republican institutions. Indeed, property and that right to heredity which had made the greater peoples great, were kept. All of this was moderated, since all that one possesses must offer a "common advantage, eminent domain over the possessions and persons of the citizens, which must come before any private law" (Vico, De univ., 130).

4.21 As a result, civil relations were considerably pacified thanks to the certainty of the law and the importance that all Romans ascribed to it. Indeed "so operating, thanks to the introduction of civil *gius*, the civil *podestà* succeeded in rendering those rights sure and peaceful, which naturally true but uncertain, become certain but violent because of the gius of the major peoples" (Vico, De univ., 138).

Thus juridical rationality with its certainty replaced brute force. Herein lies the true greatness of Rome, and Vico, referring to Saint Augustine, emphasises that the conquered populations, as time passed, made use of that certainty.

D) *The eternal Law of the Fiefs.*

4.22 Once the goal of physical safety was reached, the plebeians aimed to ensure the certainty of several goods which had always been the prerogative of the patricians. Hence the agrarian laws were drawn up. This is one of the crucial points in Vichian political thought, that of the *eternal law of the fiefs* or, if one wishes, of the landed aristocracy and not only them. This law survives "due to the nature of the strong to keep their acquisitions and for the others on behalf of the benefits that they can hope to obtain in civil life" (Vico, PSN, 557). In history, in other words, there is a constant which leads those who have created "their own utility" to create the tools to maintain it. In natural succession, forces of that sort are, for Vico, always operating in history. In the past they could be families, groups, leagues, or corporations. Now they can be lobbies, labour unions, groups or financial or banking conglomerates: the way of defining them may change, but not the intentions behind them. It is a true law and, as such, continues to operate. Indeed "from the clientele and the fiefs of higher people the *gius civile* derived its common origin, then Roman gius civile came from it. And when the barbarians who had come from Germany and the other northern regions had invaded Europe and placed every right in the hands of force, bringing back those same reasons related above, fiefs and duels reappeared" (Vico, De univ., 154). Fiefs reappear, albeit in different ways, in different situations and moments and it could not be otherwise since they represent the expression of that aristocracy, at times landed at times economic (today we would say financial), that has always been present in the history of civilisations and that finds its most efficacious expression in law. "As a result from the right of the greater peoples as studied, we find the principles that subsequently underwent development in the law of the minor peoples. Civil societies were based on that law, and that did not happen out of deliberate intent, but as a consequence of the old and deeply rooted customs" (Vico, De univ., 160). This reflection is highly perceptive for two reasons: first because it shows that institutions, which are aristocratically born, survive as long as they maintain their original bases. When these are destroyed, a new aristocracy, brutal perhaps at the beginning, ends up imposing other rules; secondly because it anticipates some of Boudon and Von Hayek's conclusions on the not fully worked out development of societies in so far as, in addition to the "not deliberated council" that right that developed from the customs the peoples had in common, there is the natural law of the jurists, far different from that of the philosophers, which is most severely conceived under the law of eternal reason" (Vico, De univ., 162).

4.23 These two considerations are likewise drawn from that inexhaustible laboratory that history represents, in which the Roman events constitute a sort of prototype. One need only consider the fact that the two quotations just mentioned are interspersed, as if to be justified, by a cryptic sentence of Gaius: "when governed by laws and customs every people comes to use a law of its own, and in part that law which is common to the universality of people" (Gaius, Inst., I, 1.9). This is tantamount to saying that *tradition* ends up having a *force equal to nature.* It is important to note that, for Vico, that tradition is based both on a "law of the peoples which remains uniform in any people, and at any time" and on a right that is the fruit of will and contingencies which "is changeable, but not by caprice, but as a result of changes that have occurred" (Vico, De univ., 164). This *dualism is typical of the republics created by the "optimates"* who wore those of the Romans, Venetians and English, contrary to all tyrannies and pure monarchies typical of the Orient (cf. Vico, De univ., 168 ff.).

E) *The Aristocratic Republics.*

4.24 In the republics of the "optimati" or aristocratic republics "the laws and customs are both expressions of law, but the customs are firmer and more solid interpretations of them, because they show themselves to be in accord with events, and the progress of time converts them naturally. The laws are an interpretation at times better, but still weaker, because they are dictated by a changeable will. Therefore aristocratic governments and monarchies are more tranquil, and less likely to be destroyed" (Vico, De univ., 174). Herein lie the basic reasons for Vichian gnoseology: the cogent importance of the fact, the problem of order which is never acquired once and for all and that need for continuity that makes governments stable. Stability is more prevalent in republics that maintain an aristocratic presence because, in addition to the aforementioned reasons that lead to juridical guarantees, "the state of the *optimati* refrains from undertaking wars and cultivates justice to the utmost, so that the defence of the patrician order will be its basic and constituting element" (Vico, De univ., 180). To be sure, things can degenerate into obtuse conservatism and struggles among the citizens occur, but an aristocracy that understands the signs of the times and the justice of the claims of the people can ensure a legitimate prosperity in stability.

4.25 To avoid falling back on the trivial subject of historical claims and appeals to which Vico attributes a certain importance but also allows not a few exceptions, it must be kept in mind that the birth of political institutions, too, can have its variations. That is, the aristocratic element, with its typical and vital dualism vis-à-vis the popular presents itself in a way that is different from the usual one. There is the singular analysis of the republics that we now call federal ones whose first traces come from the Roman world, then on the eve of the modern age anticipating what would become the American system. Vico clearly intuits the phenomenon submitting it, as usual, to analysis. "From the joining of several popular republics a government of optimati forms, like that of the united Dutch states" (Vico, De univ., 206). The popular and aristocratic elements are both present in that *Republic of the United Provinces* which will be a model for liberty throughout the seventeenth century. These two elements act without interfering with one another to such a degree that one can say: "if the Dutch have founded colonies in the Indies, that was the work of private merchants, and not the public potestà, the strength of trade joining those colonies to the nation that founded and rules them" (Vico, De univ., 206). Vico says the same thing as he praises the Venetian Republic (cf. Vico, De univ., 578 ff.)

4.26 It should be noted that the aristocracy plays a pivotal role in the republican system in this as in other cases both against hazardous democratic planning and against fearsome tyrannical or authoritarian thrusts. Thus, "to check the violence of one or several powerful people the optimati come and plead for the confidence of the plebeians, so as to be able to rely on their aid" (Vico, De univ., 212). This explains the prestige "of the authority of the Senate in the popular mixed and aristocratic Republic" (cf. Vico, De univ., chs. CLXI ff.) which conferred greatness on the Roman institution and made it the model for the future republics. That the Senate was an aristocratic component is proven by the fact that "the terms *patricians* and *senators* were interchangeable, as if they were the same thing" (Vico, De univ., 246). The fact that the aristocratic class jealously guarded the foundations of law was fundamental. For a long time, they had a language and culture distinct from the popular ones. Few have observed that "the Romans, whose language of laws was jealously guarded, had one language for jurists, and a different one for the populus. Cicero amply demonstrates this" (Vico, De univ., 482). On the subject of the language, it is useful to recall that Vico, demonstrating the originality of the Latin tradition, several times maintained as has already been said, that "the language of the law of the Twelve Tables is absolutely native to Latium" (Vico, De univ., 712). Those who know how important philology was for the Neapolitan philosopher can understand the importance of those statements.

4.27 History, as can be seen, fascinates Vico, too, because of its recurring novelties. Despite its methodological analysis, history is not at all rigid determinism. In addition to the well-known example of the Jewish people, there are other points where Vico hints that he is going beyond the three distinct phases of human history. When everything seems to have reached a moment of crisis and the three classical forms of government have lost their strength a new cycle can come to an end and reopen, but a new phase can also begin "a fourth type of republic, in which the well-meaning and honest are supreme and are the true, natural aristocracy" (Vico, PSN, 696).

F) *Almost the Pursuit of an Analysis.*

4.28 From an analysis "of the nature of peoples come the political forms of government" (Vico, De univ., 180). Vico and Montesquieu's thought have in common this and numerous other points. The sense of history, tradition, the love for Latinity, but above all the role of virtue in republics are the ideal heredity that Vico leaves to Montesquieu, who, enriching it with further content, will lay the basis for European liberalism. Much has been said about possible direct relationships between the work of the French thinker, especially when he travelled to Naples, and Vichian thought, but the most penetrating scholars have excluded any sort of contact. The fact remains, however, that the two works quite often seem to complement each other.

The baron of **Montesquieu** Charles de Secondat was born near Bordeaux, in the castle of La Brède in 1689. He studied law in Bordeaux and Paris. After having been the President of the section of Parliament in his city he was also appointed as a member of the city Academy. In 1721 he published *Lettres persanes* which were instantly successful. For several years he travelled in many European countries getting to know cities and famous personalities among whom, probably, were Giambattista Vico in Naples. In 1734 he published another basic work *Considérations sur les causes de la grandeur des Romains et de leur décadence* (*Considerations on the Causes of the Grandeur and Decadence of the Romans*). His everlasting fame was due to the *De l'esprit des lois* (*Spirit of the Laws*) which came out in 1748 and published in revised editions a year later. He died in Paris in 1755.

4.29 Montesquieu is a complex personality and difficult to categorize according to many critics. He inspired the American and French Revolutions, was a philosopher of history and sociologist, a republican and, at the same time, a monarchist, and so on. In actual fact all these various facets are not contradictory but are united in a man who was able to look into the past as into the present discovering what could be useful, and he sought to integrate it all. The result was a balanced personality capable of integrating the modern with the classical, the rising classes with the traditional ones, which led to the drawing of that portrait of a *moderate liberal* not pursuing utopias but at the same time, not wanting to defend absurdities, as absolutism, for example, could be, which, at this point are to be relegated to the past.

G) *The Historical and Political Teachings of Rome.*

4.30 In the far-distant and recent pasts Montesquieu, like Vico, captures those forces that were able to ensure the highest moments of civilization and which, like the Roman Senate and the House of Lords, were able to marry innovation with tradition ensuring the liberty and stability of the State. The *Dialogue de Sylla et d'Eucrate* (*Dialogue of Scylla and Eucrates*), considered one of his minor works, is a case in point. Liberty has something of the divine in it. It is granted by the gods and so is a "noble" liberty. Thus, a price must be paid for it (cf. Montesquieu, DSE, I, 503).It is an aristocratic liberty, not understandable to everyone. Scylla appears to be the champion of this liberty. Here it is not a question of whether the portrait of the dictator corresponds to historical truth or otherwise. What is important is Montesquieu's interpretation which is a sort of constant in all of his thought. Depriving the city of which I was a citizen – maintains Scylla – of liberty was the most heinous crime that could be committed. It must be emphasized that this liberty is not a result of the caprices of the times, but comes out of the *gouvernement de nos pères* (cf. Montesquieu, DSE, I, 504). Liberty is not an abstraction, but comes from tradition and that spirit of a civilization of which it is the spirit.

4.31 It is no accident that the personalities Montesquieu admires the most were those champions of the aristocratic Republic which made Rome great. The recurrent considerations on Cicero are proof of this. In the Dialogue of Scylla, however, there is another, typically aristocratic and "liberal" element: the conviction that force can and must be used to defend liberty which, in this case, is tantamount to defending a civilization and a tradition (cf. Montesquieu, DSE, I, 505-506). It is on the tormented history of all of Europe – concerning the peoples of the north see Letter 131 of the *Persian Letters* (cf. Montesquieu, LP, I, 327-329) – that liberty is based. This liberty certainly finds no equal in the history of continents such as Asia, but also not in the abstract thoughts of certain revolutionaries.

4.32 There is bitterness in Montesquieu because of the fact that aristocracies do not always manage to safeguard the great ideals, and, among these liberty first and foremost. Very often, the avidity of individuals spoils the relationships among fellow citizens, which should be based on virtue. In these cases, if one does not want to degenerate into despotism, a Republic can count on the force of the people, before whom, even the judges, although they come from the aristocratic class, must show the greatest respect if they want to enable a republic to exist. The examples taken from Roman and English history prove this and also show that history, for Montesquieu, was actually a research laboratory. The aristocracy must be driven by a strong sense of duty which also lays the basis for its sense of "limit". In this respect, too, Montesquieu shows his debt to Cicero whose works had literally fascinated him.

4.33 Cicero is the only one of his era to lament the pitiful remains of a dying liberty and puts himself forward as its defender (cf. Montesquieu, DsC, I, 93). His original philosophy – an opinion which coincides with Hume's – disdains the empty philosophizing of those who perpetrate monstrous things which have nothing human about them (cf. Montesquieu, DsC, I, 94), but which elude the presumptuous and the peoples who follow them. These considerations constitute the premise which accompanies Montesquieu as he interprets history in general and Roman history in particular. Right from the opening lines of the *Considerations on the Causes of the Grandeur of the Romans and their Decadence* modern history with its examples is related to examples from the ancient world and vice-versa (cf. Montesquieu, Cons., II, 71 and 108). However, another element is present in the *Considérations*. It is typical of all of his historical and philosophical thought: the conviction that only the prudence and wisdom of aristocratic minds like Cicero's, together with the virtue of a people which are still bound by a strong moral and religious sense, can keep a Republic alive and prolong its existence.

4.34 This rigour in customs, as with Vico, is seen by Montesquieu within traditional institutions such as the family whose cohesion gives vitality and youth to a population. In other words, it is the problem of birth-rate that brings out the strength and possibility for a future of a civilization. There are extremely clear reflections on this subject. There was a period during which Rome and Athens had approximately the same number of inhabitants. The observation, however, comes from a census taken when Rome's institutions were at the height of their development, whereas Athens was going through a period of corruption. It is noteworthy, concludes Montesquieu, that, whereas a quarter of the inhabitants of Rome were at the age of puberty, those of Athens having that age were less than a twentieth of the total (cf. Montesquieu, Cons., II, 81-82). Still in consideration of customs there is a comparison with Carthage which, having become rich before Rome, had also become corrupt first (cf. Montesquieu, Cons., II, 83).

4.35 If these elements, birth-rate and wealth, show the conditions of private individuals, they also mark the condition of public life where examples of favouritism and corruption abound. A truly free State is one in which "*il n'y a point de favoris*" (Montesqieu, Cons., II, 84). In such a State income is better administered and the laws are not evaded. During its golden age Rome well knew that "gold and silver run out, while virtue, constancy, force and poverty never do so" (Montesquieu, Cons., II, 85). Obedience to laws was not, in those times, based on fear and a noteworthy clemency accompanied the wisdom of the government. One need only realize that when the Romans came to Spain, the harshness of Carthaginian domination was such that the Iberians viewed the newcomers "*comme des libérateurs*" (Montesquieu, Cons., II, 86). Thus, after a short while, as also happened with other peoples, "*sans être compatriotes, ils étoient tous romains*" (Montesquieu, Cons., II, 108) or, better yet, "*Rome les recevoit esclaves, et les renvoyoit Romains*" (Montesquieu, Cons., II, 142).

4.36 One of the crucial aspects of Montesquieu's political thought is the relationship between the Senate and the people. In this analysis all those reflections on the aristocratic Republic which mark the synthesis between the best of tradition and the best of modernity are to be found. Montesquieu identifies in the people, as early as in ancient Rome, strength, numerical superiority in franchises, the rejection of war or the threat involved in abandoning it. This and other things were tempered by the wisdom of the senate, its sense of justice and love of country as well as its traditions which also earned the respect of the people. The Roman aristocracy was ready to grant the reasonable requests of the people and never thought to entrench itself in its privileges (cf. Montesquieu, Cons., II, 112-113). All this, together with the greatness of a judiciary as censor, made the Republic great and, for a long time, it succeeded in practicing that civic "virtue" without which no republican institution can survive. Thus a rule which showed itself to be universal was tested, namely that "*un government libre, c'est-à-dire toujours agité, ne sauroit se maintenir, s'il n'est, par ses propres lois, capable de correction*" (Montesquieu, Cons., II, 116). A propos of laws, it should be said that Montesquieu does not consider them abstractly to the point of distinguishing good laws from adequate ones (cf. Montesquieu, Cons., II, 120). There is a great difference between the two and only a concrete historical analysis can bring this out.

H) *The Reasons for the Crisis and the Reasons for Tolerance.*

4.37 The discussion of laws provides an introduction to that of the forms of government. Here too, there is a conclusion which will be found again in the *Esprit des lois*, as is the case for so many points. What is important in considering a government, is that it be capable of meeting the goals which have been set by those in charge. Hence, the perfecting of a government does not lie in the possibility of returning to one of those forms considered perfect and which are to be found in the books of some philosophers. To those people, the government of Rome seemed imperfect as a jumble of various forms of government (cf. Montesquieu, Cons., II, 1488, nr 8). That government, considered a mixed one by others, was responsible for the greatness of the Roman republic. In this mixture of various institutions there was also the Roman religion which effectively sustained the customs of the Republican era (cf. Montesquieu, Cons., II, 121). It was perhaps this deeply rooted religious feeling that led the Romans, during the Empire, too, to be tolerant towards *"toute sorte de culte"* (Montesquieu, Cons., II, 188). Religious feeling and the soundness of the institutions enabled the Republic to resist corruption for a long time (cf. Montesquieu, Cons., II, 122) which in other civilizations far earlier suffocated whatever good had been created through toil and continuity.

4.38 The crisis of the Republic lasted for a long time. The civil wars that forced everyone to turn into a soldier bears witness to this. This destroyed the diversity of roles and classes that had been the motive force of republican institutions. It is curious that speaking of civil conflicts Montesquieu puts forth opinions, for example that of Scylla, which in part come into conflict with what had been said previously (cf. Montesquieu, Cons., II, Ch XI). Once *"la loi étoit precise, les exemples reçus"* (Montesquieu, Cons., II, 131), now this certainty of the law was lacking and everything was in doubt. From free individuals, the Romans were becoming slaves. The aristocratic class was eliminated and the Republic found itself in a state of crisis. The people, or rather the plebeians, were no longer controlled by the Senate and, in general, by the patricians. They hailed the most corrupt sovereigns, as in the East, under the illusion that their government was making everyone happy (cf. Montesquieu, Cons., II, 149). This is one of the saddest moments in history: indeed, there is no power more absolute than that of a sovereign who takes over from a Republic because he can exercise all this power over a people, which is no longer capable of controlling themselves (cf. Montesquieu, Cons., II, 150).

4.39 The change is so sudden, that in Montesquieu's view, it causes an absurd situation. For this reason, it is wise to take care in changing those institutions that have been operating for a long time (cf. Montesquieu, Cons., II, 168). Changes must take tradition into account, otherwise disasters ensue. In other words, history has its logic. Referring to Machiavelli, Montesquieu believes that *"ce n'est pas la fortune qui domine le monde: on peut le demander aux Romains"* (Montesquieu, Cons., II, 173). Then, in the same text, he continues emphasizing that general, moral and physical causes exist; and when what may seem an accident leads to the ruin of a State, this means that other causes have been ignored, and that ignorance has led to the catastrophe. Here too the voice of Machiavelli can be heard with his famous reflections on fortune.

4.40 It should be reiterated here that Montesquieu's interest in history leads to a sort of comparative analysis: the ancient serves to show the incongruities of the present and, likewise, the errors of the past must put us on our guard to avoid possible and dangerous relapses. This fact of comparing has already made possible in the *Lettres persanes* judgments full of appreciation not only of the ancient republics, but also of modern ones such as Switzerland and Holland (cf. Montesquieu, LP, especially letters 122 and 136). These modern republics, to which Venice should also be added, all have the traits of so-called "mild government" which is also to be found in those monarchies, like the English one, which have been able to set limitations on themselves thereby avoiding degeneration. To avoid degeneration of this sort a good government must be sensitive to the interior spheres of individuals. In this "Montesquieu once again takes up the classic theme of treatises on tolerance, from the Reformation to Locke, that is, of the distinction between interior tolerance (i.e. acquiescence in one's inner self to a profession of faith different from what is considered orthodox), and exterior tolerance, which enables the State to remain neutral when face to face with various religions (similar to German Catholic principalities which also admitted Calvinists and Lutherans after Wesphalia)" (Postigliola, 46).

4.41 Tolerance becomes necessary because of the intrinsic nature of human action and that of history as well as for political reasons. Human action does not manifest the certainties of religion. It is a set of manifestations of great, unforeseen events. It is true that every event has a cause, but the latter is at times so remote that it is impossible to analyze it, or else it has become mixed with other concomitant causes, so that it is not easy to identify the implications of each one. The unity of these causes is a bit like the unity of a body politic which, most often seems equivocal since the concept of unity is the result of a harmonious bonding of several factors, which allow the most highly varied parts to contribute to the general good of the society autonomously, and not in a preordained fashion (cf. Montesquieu, Cons., II, 109). Only the government which departs from this historical awareness can accomplish a political order based on liberty and not slavery. They are all those concomitant causes, the results of which are not always totally foreseeable, given the difficulties involved in sifting them out from the totality which make up "the foundation of the science of society of Montesquieu, representing the key to understanding human nature not 'abstractly' (...) but in the concreteness of its historicity" (Postigliola, 91). This aspect is appropriately contrary to the abstract vision of society offered by the Enlightenment figures who, in tradition and in the past in general, saw only prejudices.

4.42 From the very beginning of his most famous writings Montesquieu has pointed out that laws are neither the function of chance, nor of extemporaneousness, but the result of *"rapports nécessaires qui dérivent de la nature des choses"* (Montesquieu, EdL, II, 232). In other words they are manifestations of a certain intelligence and a certain will. This will is more or less free. It calls for certain laws and from these obtains diverse types of government. The title of the second book brings this intention out quite clearly. In the Republic the people, in their entirety or in part, enjoy the supreme power to do all they can to *"bien faire; et ce qu'il ne peut pas bien faire, il faut qu'il le fasse par ses ministres"* (Montesquieu, EdL, II, 240). This statement is of the greatest importance because it shows first of all that the people have a precise area within which (they) *peut bien faire*, secondly that the people are obliged to delegate powers because they cannot do everything. This system that sees the people as sovereign, more than a monarchy, must *"être conduit par un conseil ou sénat"* (Montesquieu, EdL, II, 240). Here that elitist, or if one prefers aristocratic idea reappears, that accompanies liberal thought like that of Montesquieu. Anyone who doubts this should be reminded that in democracies, the people alone should be the ones that make laws, however there are so many cases in which it is necessary for a smaller body to deliberate; in fact, it is almost better that a law be tested before it is established. In Rome, the Senate's ordinances lasted first one year and then became law through the will of the people (cf. Montesquieu, EdL, II, 244). Here then is that idea of aristocratic Republic that Cicero, too, cherished. Another fundamental point comes out of what has been said, however. The more important and powerful a position is, the more limits must be placed on it: *"il faut compenser la grandeur de la puissance par le brièveté de sa durée"*

(Montesquieu, EdL, II, 246). No power, and no judiciary, is capable of keeping within its limits if these have not been set forth in clear and solemn fashion.

4.43 The aristocracy, which is an element of stability in the aristocratic Republic, plays the same role in the second form of government, the Monarchy. Here, if it is true that this form of government manages to keep within its own limits thanks to all those intermediate powers that constitute its nature, it is also true that *"le pouvoir intermédiaire subordonné le plus naturel est celui de la noblesse"* (Montesquieu, EdL, II, 247). Once again it is the aristocracy that functions as an element of balance and stability so that if in the Republic it succeeds in moderating the nature of the republican foundation, that is the people, it becomes its very nature in a monarchy, that is the basis. All of this is confirmed by that fact that when this aristocratic structure is abolished, *"vous aurez bientôt un État populaire, ou bien un État despotique"* (Montesquieu, EdL, II, 247). It is obvious that here *aristocracy is understood in the broad sense of the word.* It is not just the nobility, which is important of course, but all those intermediate bodies, for example the judges and the clergy, which constitute an ever effective barrier, when there are no others (cf. Montesquieu, EdL, II, 248). This position will arouse the enthusiasm of some critics of the French Revolution, Burke for example, who will see in the elimination of the aristocracy the failure of revolutionary expectations.

4.44 Along with the analysis of nature, there is also that of the principles of forms of government, which makes it possible to delve further into what has been said up to now. Furthermore if it is nature that makes a government what it is, it is its principle that makes it act; the former constitutes its structure, the latter comes out of the human passions that make it grow (cf. Montesquieu, EdL, II, 250). In the Republic, whether democratic or aristocratic, virtue constitutes the founding element (cf. Montesquieu, EdL, II, 254). In this system, in which the forms of liberty manifest themselves most completely, the force of the laws, as in a monarchy, of the iron fist or of arms are not sufficient, as they are in despotism (cf. Montesquieu, EdL, II, 251). That virtue is needed from which the spirit of moderation arises, without which no republic can survive (cf. Montesquieu, EdL, II, 254). It is clear that politicians, too, must contribute to the creation of this virtue but, unfortunately, nowadays, comments Montesquieu with a touch of bitterness, they think and speak to us only "*de manufactures, de commerce, de finances, de richesses et de luxe même*" (Montesquieu, EdL, II, 252).

4.45 To some extent the principle is the mainspring of a government, which in a monarchy comes from honour and from fear in despotic rule. Indeed virtue is useless and honour would be dangerous in a despotic system (cf. Montesquieu, EdL, II, 258). It is useless because how can it be carried forth in a system which takes no consideration of it at all and deems it difficult to put into practice? With extreme realism Montesquieu underscores the fact that this does not mean that "*dans une certaine république, on soi vertueux; mais qu'on devroit l'être*" (Montesquieu, EdL, II, 261). The actual functioning of republican institutions depends on the measure of virtue. The real thermometer of the phenomenon will be offered by the laws of education in every family and every State, "*elles nous préparent à être citoyens (...) C'est dans le gouvernement républicain que l'on a besoin de toute la puissance de l'éducation*" (Montesquieu, EdL, II, 261 and 266). Education must make people understand that only if a people are virtuous can a republic enjoy true happiness (cf. Montesquieu, EdL, II, 284), because only in this case will the laws offered by lawmakers be in harmony with the principle of government.

4.46 What is more, if republics were not virtuous and capable of obtaining real happiness for the citizens, why should they be preferred to forms of government that show themselves to be more efficient? A monarchical government offers greater promptness in action (cf. Montesquieu, EdL, II, 289) and more guarantees, as well, in specific areas of endeavour. What is more important, however is that, if republics do not seek to be virtuous, they degenerate, with the danger of facilitating the birth of despotism, as well. This, albeit typical of the "Asiatic" world, "*comme il ne faut que des passions pour l'établir, tout le monde est bon pour cela*" (Montesquieu, EdL, II, 297). Despotism is the only form of government that does not have to fear the corruption of its principle. The despotic government is indeed continually corrupted "*parce qu'il est corrompu par sa nature*" (Montesquieu, EdL, II, 357). Republics and monarchies, on the contrary, must fear corruption because, for these governments, it means complete degeneration. Much attention must be devoted to why the principle of a government becomes corrupted. In a republic the principle is eliminated when people want to create a spirit of extreme equality and "*chacun veut être égal à ceux qu'il choisit pour lui commander*" (Montesquieu, EdL, II, 349). In this case the people reject those who are in charge of performing some specific functions. For example, they seek to take the place of their judges and for this reason no longer respect them (cf. Montesquieu, EdL, II, 350). The result of this claim for extreme equality is that the people reject those *élites* to whom they had delegated power and seek to take their place on every occasion. In the final analysis, a democracy must, on one hand, avoid allowing the spirit of inequality to become too strong, and, on the other, avoid allowing the spirit of equality to go to an extreme (cf. Montesquieu, EdL, II, 351). Now that spirit of moderation which is the basis of every virtue and "civic" virtue in particular reappears.

4.47 The true sense of liberty comes out at this point. We can give various meanings to this word (cf. Montesquieu, EdL, II, 394) but its real meaning is essentially Ciceronian. No-one would be free if he or she could do what the laws prohibit. "*La liberté est le droit de faire tout ce que les lois permettent*" (Montesquieu, EdL, II, 395), somewhat like "*Legum servi sumus ut liberi esse possimus*" (Cicero, *Oratio pro Cluentio,* 53). All that is possible only within governments that demonstrate a spirit of moderation. Only moderate governments succeed in creating the *sense of limits* which nothing human can abstain from observing since "*la vertu même a besoin de limites*" (Montesquieu, EdL, II, 395). Only that way will no-one abuse power and the powers will reach the point of placing limits on themselves and each other (cf. Montesquieu, EdL, II, 395). This is what comes out of the analysis of the Roman and English worlds.

4.48 This sense of limits is difficult to achieve in direct democracies, but is present in republics based on the criterion of representation. Herein lies that legislative power which is the true greatness of republics as is also the case for moderate monarchies, which we would call parliamentary nowadays. In those forms of government the legislative power is limited, hence controlled by the executive and the judiciary. The true originality of Montesquieu, however, does not lie in that three-way division of powers so much as the way he presents the legislative: this brings out his aristocratic spirit perhaps, but also reveals his intention to give greater stability and force to the republic. If the legislative portion of the people is not to degenerate, it must deal with the legislative portion of the nobles. Only in a *legislative body divided in two parts* will one keep the other under control and both will be bound by the executive which, in turn, will be bound by the legislative (cf. Montesquieu, EdL, II, 404-405). This was what happened in England, too, and had happened in Rome in ancient times. This is also what aroused discussion of *aristocratic liberalism* or "pact of solidarity" between the aristocracy and the bourgeoisie (cf. Burgio, 34-37) which would enable both to coexist defending interests long acquired or recently achieved. This position is perhaps a bit restrictive.

4.49 This reflection on limits brings up another problem, however: how is the law to be understood? Where does it come from? It is certain that when speaking of laws Montesquieu is critical of classical doctrines of natural law. These doctrines were in contrast with the juridical historicism that underlies the entire work of the French thinker, who is decidedly opposed to that way of understanding law abstractly with a vaguely idealistic flavour (cf. Althusser, 57-60). Matter-of-factness is of great concern to Montesquieu who, for example, speaking of political liberty, does not consider it simply in relation to the constitution, but also in its relationship with the citizen. Indeed, there are particular laws in every constitution that can aid or run counter to liberty (cf. Montesquieu, EdL, II, 430-431). That means that it is not possible to find a perfect constitution or body of laws. All laws, and criminal laws among them, *"n'ont pas été perfectionnées tout d'un coup. Dans les lieux mêmes où l'on a le plus cherché la liberté, on ne l'a pas toujours trouvée*" (Montesquieu, EdL, II, 431). As can be seen he is contrary to any result achieved definitively or in a predetermined fashion; politics are not the area of perfectionism and every utopia of that sort is to be rejected. For Montesquieu all that concerns the sphere of political action is temporary and the political order itself must be continually desired and sought after.

4.50 Liberty is synonymous with certainty and the opposite of all that is arbitrary. Punishments themselves, which do not allow anyone to perpetrate violence on another, are not capriciously devised, but come out of the nature of things (cf. Montesquieu, EdL, II, 433). Liberty is based on an act of the conscience before which every authority has the duty to bow. It is cryptically and unequivocally written: "*Les lois ne se chargent de punir que les actions extérieures*" (Montesquieu, EdL, II, 441). Only outward appearances come under the control of the law, otherwise not a shadow of liberty remains any longer. However, even when outward appearances are judged, one must always be able to distinguish the importance of the deeds. Theses may be extremely serious in one political system and considered of minor importance in another: one need only think of satirical writings (cf. Montesquieu, EdL, II, 442-444) tolerated in democracies, avoided under despotism. Liberty may have its price, in the sense that, in order to enjoy it, the citizens voluntarily accept the necessity of paying high tributes. Liberty is a sort of quid pro quo for the dimensions of the tributes: the citizens pay, but they want to participate to the greatest possible extent in political life. The more liberty is lacking, or is entirely lacking as under despotism, the more modest the tributes must be (cf. Montesquieu, EdL, II, 466-467) because, speaking in Machiavellian terms, men bear anything except losing their substance without understanding why.

4.51 It is certain, in any case, that the spirit of liberty is indicated by the laws and these come from religion, the nature of their territory and the climate as well as tradition. But that is not enough. Returning to a fortunate insight of Cicero to be found in a letter to Atticus, the nature of the laws and the political system that determine them also depend on what type of activities a given people perform for the most part. For tradespeople and farmers, those who are self-employed, every law then, *"tous les gouvernements sont égaux, dès lors qu'ils sont tranquilles?* (Montesquieu, EdL, II, 531). People in certain social categories ask only to be left alone as they carry on with their business and derive the benefits. It is in these circumstances that legislators must show their ability because, in making laws, they must follow the spirit of a nation as long as this is not contrary to the spirit of the government obviously (cf. Montesquieu, EdL, II, 559). It is a noteworthy fact that Montesquieu senses that social change which was manifesting itself in France, after it had done so in England. This change involved the replacement of the old aristocracy by a new social *élite,* which called for new laws and legal orders. What is important, and seems evident in a moderate spirit like Montesquieu, is that these changes do not come about suddenly since peoples are attached to their traditions. Changing traditions induces the people themselves to change (cf. Montesquieu, EdL, II, 565). All the pages concerning commerce in the second part of Book XIX and Books XX and XXI, are revealing on that subject. One need only realize that commerce can be influenced by various types of government, or it itself can influence them.

4.52 Liberty also depends on the clarity with which laws are formulated. The style of the laws must be simple. If such is not the case, there is pure ostentation in the laws and only confusion is created. On the contrary, laws must stimulate the same ideas in the spirit of all men (cf. Montesquieu, EdL, II, 877). However, the finesse of human spirits also depends on how they have been brought up and the religious feeling they manifest because it is in consciences that this takes place. Now religion, as Lord Acton quite clearly shows, even though he had expressed the opposite at times, is the basis of the conscience and of liberty. Anyone who does not feel this way, should not only assemble and enumerate what bad things religion has done in its long history, but also enumerate the good things it has done; although it is useful that laws require that religion not upset the State in any way. This is possible when divine and human laws are exercised with mutual restraint, not invading each other's territory (cf. Montesquieu, EdL, II, 715, 744 and 751).

I) *The Relevance of the Thought concerning the Elites.*

4.53 What has been said up to now about the aristocracy and élites necessitates serious consideration to explain why such an analysis must not seem backward-looking. Vico's observations on the major peoples must not lead people to believe that the Neapolitan philosopher can be classified together with those scholars among the *élites* who, in this century, have put forth more or less reactionary views. Defending what I like to call the *Aristocratic Republic*, Vico means to underscore that dynamic relationship between the people and the ruling class in which the former possesses sovereignty (indeed, Cicero had already been pointing this out), and the latter – the functions of direction. Vico believes in the possibility of teaching the masses as the initial circumstances have taught and refined the major peoples. Anyone who wishes to take advantage of certain benefits, must obey certain rules without which one strays from the civil context. The manner in which change takes place must also be civil, at least as long as one lives in a system where legality prevails. Hence, the word aristocracy could be used not in a reactionary sense. Indeed, despite Vico, and Montesquieu as well, departing from historical analysis, they are not unaware, as Guizot will say, that there also exists a natural aristocracy which has little to do with the sterile and static one of privileges, an aristocracy which, among other things, is getting ready to step out of history (cf. Compagna, LA, 24).

4.54 The same could be said for Montesquieu who deceived himself as to the actual capability and importance the French nobles could bring to bear in France. As the revolution approached the kings could rule the people directly without finding intermediaries in the aristocracy; moreover the nobles, a short time thereafter, showed themselves incapable of defending themselves (cf. Bien, 720 and 724). That bears witness to the fact that between the idea of Montesquieu, England, and the actual French situation there was a gap that was difficult to fill, as the failure of the parliaments themselves during the French Revolution brings out. As Tocqueville would say, it had become too late to imagine a reform of the nobility in France. Since it was behind the times, it was on the way to departing from history (cf. Bien, 726). It was the weakness of the aristocracy that favoured the birth of absolutism differently from what had happened not only in England, but in Venice itself.

4.55 The aristocracy Montesquieu had in mind is an open and liberal body, far from what the French nobility had been at the time. This perhaps depends on the fact that the French thinker is, at least in this, far from the feelings of many other intellectuals of his age who, at times, would have more influence than he did. For example, one can recall when Montesquieu formulated his praise of commerce because it renders the manners less harsh and brings peace. The exact opposite would happen in France right after the Revolution: between '92 and '94 the austere and virtuous republic prophesied by Rousseau would be imposed (cf. Manin, 884). This has nothing in common with a modern republic based on progress and development. The latter was certainly not possible because a *modern élite* was lacking that would be capable of sensing, as happened elsewhere, the fact that times were changing. This is why the French aristocracy appears as a degenerate class and its perhaps the fact that fear of these forms of degeneration would continually recur, as, among other things, an analysis of Rome's long history taught, that meant that "there is no regime, among those which he judges to be good, in which Montesquieu did not note some imperfection here and there" (Manin, 887). As has been said, it is a bit like the fear of the disintegration of the social body, an ever present danger to be countered through the search for a political order, based on laws, that must always be desired and defended. Those laws are indeed bound by a precise logic, because of their intrinsic spirit.

4.56 The fact that each of the individual laws systematically depends on the other bears witness to the fact that an order exists in them: to some, this seemed the basis of Montesquieu's juridical thought and the real "spirit" of the laws (cf. Cassirer, 325). I believe that as far as this search for an order is concerned, one can share the opinion of those who claim that Vico, and Montesquieu, too, cannot be saddled with the label of relativism (cf. Berlin, 76 and 87). What's more, such a search starts from history. With this, the author of the *Esprit des Lois* creates a new relationship which surpasses both political utilitarianism and abstract rationalism (cf. Meinecke, 178-179). Political analysis is impregnated with that matter-of-factness that belonged to the great masters of political realism.

5. The Eighteenth Century in Italy: Age of Reforms.

A) *In the South.*

5.1 The eighteenth century, an age of reform, gave rise to a series of reflections in the South of Italy that clearly show the backwardness of a world that, at that point, seemed to be late in accepting civil and economic innovations that were coming into being in more advanced parts of Europe... backwardness to be sure, but also a desire for improvement, which led to two particular orientations. On the one hand there was a utopian current that fought against feudalism and manifested a need for liberty and equality approaching those that were the expressions of the best European culture; on the other, a more provincial school perhaps, but certainly more concrete, equally anti-feudal, but more tied to conceptions of reform coming from a new juridical approach (cf. Venturi, I, XV-XVI). The latter would anticipate one of the subjects of which romanticism was particularly fond: blaming the lack of a unified State on the decadence and poverty of Italy. Here the eighteenth century rediscovered the lesson of Machiavelli. "The legal profession, the courts, were all too often the teachers of a large portion of the Neapolitan ruling class because this path was not pursued insistently and with renewed hope" (Venturi, I, XIV). Juridical culture had to be renovated, but legalism, too, had to be fought as well as the lawyer mentality that favoured the status quo.

5.2 The two currents, and in general all those who wanted to reform the institutions had a serious concern for teaching, through which the real change of the future generations passed. Basically, the future of the State depended on how to bring together intellectuals and the people. An example of all that is offered by *Elements of the Logical and Critical Art* of Antonio Genovesi which appeared in Latin in 1745 and was addressed to young students to whom the need for liberty was clearly presented. Genovesi had dealt with matters of metaphysical interest, but from this work on, one could perceived "that 'socialitas' had taken its place as the focus of his interest as well as the problems deriving from it". This interest always remained down-to-earth without losing itself in dangerous utopias to the point of rejecting "any faith in a perfect civilization, bound to the memory of the ancient, classical world whether Greek of Roman; believing in an actual increase in well-being and civilization in the modern era" (Venturi, AGNI, 15 and 16). He well knew that since the classical age, progress, and especially commerce which would be the centre of his attention, require peace and legality. This is a lesson that he would learn from Montesquieu and he would use Montesquieu to take him back to the ancient world. That optimism came into conflict with those who thought any transformation impossible based on this conviction. It is perhaps because these people would lose those privileges that they still possessed as an old ruling class.

Antonio Genovesi was born in Castiglione (Salerno) in 1713. Ordained as a priest in 1737, he went to Naples the following year where he followed the lessons of Vico. He then taught philosophical subjects on a private basis, but was becoming more and more interested in practical and scientific disciplines. He came to teach *Civil Economics* (nowadays: political economy) in Naples, the top in Europe. Because of his studies, he had some problems with ecclesiastical authority even though he tried to remain within the confines of orthodoxy. He died in Naples in 1769. Among his many writings, we recall those of a sociopolitical nature here. These will be cited below: *Discorso sopra il vero fine delle lettere e delle scienze* (1753); *Al gentile e cortese lettore (Introduzione) della Storia del commercio della Gran Bretagna* (1757); *Lezioni di commercio o sia d'economia civile* (1765-67); *La logica per gli giovanetti* (1766).

5.3 As Cuoco would quite well summarize, in all southern-Italian culture, starting from Vico, there is a need for concreteness to escape that abstraction that was not only typical of a now archaic culture, but also of a revolutionary approach which would have to come into conflict with a context incapable of understanding it. Genovesi is an expression of that need. Addressing himself to Bartolomeo Intieri, he wrote: "From the study of ideas and sterile contemplations you have brought me back to thoughts closer to human matters (...) A certain, vain cast of mind still keeps us attached to things more specious than useful, we think that we are greater when we are admired as incomprehensible than when we are considered useful" (Genovesi, D, 86 and 101). The need to review the reason for study comes from these considerations, but also the need to give life to a political system that can favour "the industry of the inhabitants" from whom come the wealth and power of a country. The insight that between industry and good consciences there is an unbreakable bond is noteworthy to the point that there will be no industrious, great and mighty nation without keen human minds. Down-to-earth intelligence succeeds in doing what all ignorant people cannot manage to do in an infinite period of time, in a short time, and with a great saving of energies (cf. Genovesi, D, 107-108).

5.4 The true sages, that is men gifted with concrete intelligence, must be defended from two grave dangers, both with tragic political implications. They must be defended from the ignorant who "make fun of the learned, when hearing them speak of the pleasures they experience in the discovery of some beautiful and useful truth" (Genovesi, D, 122). That could discourage eager learned people and induce them to desist or to flee. For this reason it would be necessary to create an *Academy of the Learned* in Naples. These learned people must also be defended from those abstract intellectuals who seek a perfect world. "The greatest obstacle to the perfection of things human is the belief that they are of the utmost perfection (…) The desire of that which is better (…) has led them to that point where they are" (Genovesi, D, 111). If the intelligences capable of improving the life of the nation are not defended, corruption and intellectual sterility take over and one of the real forces that can improve and enrich a people is lost, hence the need to increase "knowledge and virtue and, as a consequence, our true happiness" (Genovesi, D, 129). This must be the aim of a renewed educational system. It is not a numerous people that makes a nation great, because if it is crude and uneducated, that people will always be small. At times small republics perform admirable feats even when compared to those of great monarchies. History shows this, too. Therefore, those who maintain that a more educated people, which have made "reading and writing a common thing", end up lacking farmers or artisans, should keep silent (cf. Genovesi, L, 225-230). The advanced countries of contemporary Europe are proving the opposite. It must not be forgotten that, according to Genovesi, it was necessary to "prepare future priests in seminaries with instruction in agriculture to make them useful shepherds for their flocks of farmers" (Croce, SRN, 178).

5.5 How long would such a change in mentality take? Who can answer that question: the spirit is like nature which takes its own time to mature. Acquiring true knowledge can take many years, so no time is to be wasted. Above all, it should not be thought that the practical aspects of a culture were of secondary value. A theoretical philosophy that has absolute value does not exist. Alongside it there can be a practical philosophy which is expressed, for example, on the level of institutions and laws, which has equally great value: here I feel the need to bring in a quotation which justifies this long work of mine with statements from Vico, Montesquieu or Hume. "All laws are pieces of philosophy. Ulpianus was a philosopher, Paul was, Papinianus was, etc. (...) I am pleased if the jurist knows languages, knows history: but if he is not a philosopher he will fill his commentaries with glibness" (Genovesi, LpG, 280-281).

5.6 The need for concreteness becomes more specific when the utility of commerce is referred to. This art is useful not only to trades-people or those who carry on an economic activity, but to everyone, starting from heads of families and those who govern the communities, because everyone must know how to take advantage of the activities they perform for the good of all those who live with them or whom they govern. For this reason, Genovesi, long before Smith, not only lists the reasons that make commerce useful and advantageous, but also those activities such as agriculture, manufacturing, industry and trade that increase the wealth of a nation. It is the new way of conceiving of international trade and the advantages coming from it that favours commerce (cf. Genovesi, SC, 140-159). However, commerce is a consequence of production which often comes about from the seeking of luxury, so long considered a dangerous vice for the moral life of individuals, even though, upon closer look, forms of moral degeneration are as old as the human race even when the latter, as the Bible says, lived in conditions of poverty. Genovesi considers it a "prime mover" of the economy and a way whereby, as von Hayek would later say, the rich stimulate the poor to become industrious to improve their lives. Luxury is not to be confused with weakness and laziness. What is noteworthy is that all that depends on three conditions: a) controlling the mania for the greatness of the State, b) examining real needs, c) occupying the spirit and bodies of people. Wars bear witness to the failure of the first condition and render the others useless (cf. Genovesi, L, 187-195 and 181-182).

5.7 There are numerous disciples of Genovesi who, often faced with a thousand difficulties, searched out aspects that had been brought up not only by the master but also by other European thinkers. Among them is Francesco Longano (1729-1796) famous above all for his book *On the Equality of Men* which, in the wake of Rousseau, pointed out that even in the face of the immense variety of individuals, their equality lay in the rights of each one. They were equal before the law which had to guarantee a genuine "revolution of customs" and from this was to come encouragement and support for truly useful works. Wealth, indeed, cannot be based on the accumulation of the precious metals, but on the work of production and commerce: "the superstitious man gives alms, but the politician gives work to the needy" (Longano, 378). The expression is quite clear and shows faith in the new industrial activities that favour commerce.

5.8 Among the followers of Genovesi the brothers Domenico (1735-1805) and Francescantonio Grimaldi (1741-1784) are worthy of mention. The former was able to combine his interest in economy and agriculture, supported by modern technologies, with the needs for a serious reform of education. He even spoke of "agriculture schools", nowadays "scuole di agraria" in Italian. The latter had many-sided interests. Especially in his *Riflessioni sopra l'ineguaglianza tra gli uomini* [*Reflections on Inequality among Men* (3 volumes 1779-1780)] he returns to a subject central in Rousseau maintaining that at the heart of inequality is nature herself. Compared to what happens in a natural society, civil society is a moment of enlightenment because the laws have sought to mitigate the wildness and wrongdoing of bestial man. All this is due to the laws that protect the weak and provide directives that reinforce reason. These laws need, however, to be improved because they must not be limited to repressing or punishing, they must encourage and reward people.

5.9 Gaetano Filangeri (1752-1788) deserves a place of his own. His book *La scienza della legislazione* [*The Science of Legislation*] "one of the most important books that the mature Enlightenment has ever produced" (Albertoni, 334) comparable in reputation only to *Della moneta* [*of Currency*] by the abbot Ferdinando Galiani (1728-1787). It appeared all over Europe and was the subject of debate on the part of great scholars, among whom were Constant and Franklin. One of the assumptions on which Filangeri's thought is based is that only the law ensures "social liberty" and only the certainty of law makes security possible. Roman history confirms all that. Unfortunately its greatness was spoiled not only by the barbarians (cf. Filangeri, 662-663) but also the establishment of feudalism. The barbarian invasions meant the end of legality and the authority that comes from it, but feudality meant the parcelling out of authority and sovereignty. "Who does not see (…) that feudality is a true alienation and division of sovereign power, which by its very nature is indivisible?" (Filangeri, 722). A work on the reform of legislation might have seemed unrealizable given the government's deafness and above all the "monstrous jumble" of principles of Roman jurisprudence unfortunately contaminated by barbarian legislation, the feudal system and canon law. But the need for reform, upheld by a practical philosophy, had now gained a foothold in consciences. Culture had given rise to an unstoppable movement. The bringing down of feudalism for Filangeri would lead to an opening-up to democracy. One of the first steps would be to elect magistrates by the people, ones paid, promoted and rewarded by the people. All that would be subject "to the rules, for which the need has been demonstrated, to avoid errors" (Filangeri, 674). Among these, one of the most sensational came about from the continued existence of the death penalty and torture in criminal legislation. Filangeri was not absolutely against the death penalty, but considered it valid only in exceptional cases. As far as torture is concerned "legislators must be persuaded that the most elaborate torments do nothing but make men view the law with greater bitterness, without correcting them" (Filangeri, 731). On the contrary, the law must allow what we would now call an open society. It must therefore ensure freedom of the press, which is one of the best guarantees for progress (cf. Filangeri, 748 ff.) It must allow the redistribution of earthly riches and the acquisition of property which "is what creates the citizen (...) All societies began from the distribution of lands" (Filangeri, 690 and 692). Furthermore it must also enable a religious renewal to create new moral bounds. In the wake of Rousseau, Filangeri proposes a sort of civic cult and one of social morality which, however, seems to go dangerously far. The willingness to give the State the power to regulate not only worship but also principles of dogma means confining religion within boundaries that do not even guarantee political liberty.

5.10 Francesco Mario Pagano (1748-1799) is certainly not a secondary figure. A victim of the repression following the revolution of 1799, in a moment when not a few were infatuated with the mania of a possible perfectionism, Pagano was considering human nature and its intrinsic perfectibility. From Vico, as his *Saggi politici* [*Political Essays*] demonstrate, he had learned "to look at permanence, the representation in history of some basic situations, to observe above all the great similarities between the first and second barbarisms, between the archaic and feudal worlds" (Venturi, FPNI, 802). The latter was attacked as a symbol of backwardness and the impossibility of progress, but also for its erroneous way of conceiving of property, considered the primary source of all laws as he repeats in the *Progetto di costituzione della repubblica napoletana* (cf. Pagano, PC, 910). This can prosper only in tranquillity and order, hence it must be protected by laws which, as is written in *Politicum universae romanorum nomothesiae examen*, must not only perform a function of repression but also an educational one to bring them to everyone's attention and put them on the path to doing good (cf. Pagano, PUR, 837). This operation was certainly not easy and, indeed, for some, it constituted a downright illusion. Giuseppe Maria Galanti (1743-1806) is of this opinion. He had the fortunate insight to understand that impossibility of a true reform of legislation coming from a distortion that had affected almost all Neapolitan men of law. Law study had become pure "legalism" from which everyone tried to gain his own advantage. "It can well be said that jurisprudence has become similar among us to scholasticism, and the lawyers have become so many sophists whose only task seems to be that of placing what the particular passions call for in opposition to law. Only the use of the law courts is studied, and these learn the art of defending all opinions. There is no law that cannot be opposed; there is no property that cannot be destroyed" (Galanti, 1043). Out of this comes a less and less precise culture which does not follow the progress of society which in turn, thanks to the arts, commerce and sciences, continually changes even ways of speaking and thus relations among men. This was quite well understood by Giuseppe Palmieri (1721-1793) who, with precise and unbiased realism, was able to describe the actual condition of the South in his study *Della richezza nazionale* [*of the National Wealth*] (1792). The author of this study many times called "state property a 'leftover of the barbarianism of our fathers', and advocated its transfer to private property" (Croce, SRN, 175). From this lucid work it might have been possible to set off to renew and increase the economic strength of the Kingdom of Naples without falling prey to the useless illusions of the past. This was also the profound conviction of Melchiorre Delfico (1744-1835) who expressed the wish that a reasoned history could arise, a genuine work of historical criticism capable of forgetting a history viewed as a tale of praise (cf. Carletti, 149-175) of a past that, often was certainly not to be imitated, but studied with a view to understanding and criticizing the present. For Galanti, but for Delfico as well, Croce's statement can be agreed with where he acknowledges that these intellectuals were among the few who had no illusions about the actual condition of the south of Italy (cf. Croce, SRN, 195).

B) *In the North.*

5.11 In the North of Italy, too, works were produced that, like the *Scienza delle legislazione* of Filangeri, drew attention from all over Europe. This is the case for the writings of Pietro Verri and Cesare Beccaria. Both offered a determining and original contribution to the examination of problems of law and criminal legislation following a concrete approach with precise references to historical fact. Verri (1728-1797) was the author of a text that gained consensus and aroused reactions of various sorts. His *Osservazioni sulla tortura* re-examined a problem, that of the plague-spreaders who had wreaked havoc in Milan during the plague period in 1630. The historical episode was not, however, an end in itself. It aimed at being the point of departure for criticizing methods such as torture that he considered useless and harmful, as well as ineffective. The episodes taken into consideration were not only irrational but also arbitrary because, as always when torture is involved, they were incapable of ensuring that justice would be done. From the very start of his work, the author's position is clear: there are those who maintain that if the punishment of torture were abolished many crimes would remain unpunished and judges would be barred from having a method for investigating them, whereas this writer is of the opinion that torture itself is a method that is incapable of guaranteeing that justice will be done to the guilty (cf. Verri, 52).

5.12 The problem of torture, far back in 1630, was not a problem that concerned Milan or Italy alone. It was one that had European dimensions since all of the old continent was bound up with sinister superstitious people to the point that it was possible to go so far as to incite men to kill almost arbitrarily (cf. Verri, 63-65). Torture is an infernal torment but, to some extent it is not strange that it had been considered useful for so long. In Verri's era still, the judges could have called upon it since the legislation on the subject had remained almost unchanged. This fact shocked few souls since the nature of man is such "that, once repugnance for the evils of others has been overcome and the beneficial seed of compassion suffocated, he grows ferocious and is overjoyed at his superiority before the spectacle of the misfortune of others" (Verri, 106). Over and beyond this sort of sadism, if one wants to reason properly it can be said that the practice of torture turns out to be entirely unmotivated for a series of reasons. "First, that the torments are not a means of discovering the truth. Second, that the law, and criminal practice itself do not consider torment a means of discovering the truth. Third, that even if such a method were conducive to the discovery of the truth it would be intrinsically unjust" (Verri, 110). The *first* reason can be explained by the fact that delinquents, given the savage and hard life they lead, are more accustomed to bearing up under torments. On the contrary, the innocent, who find it more difficult to bear humiliation and pain, are prepared to confess in order to avoid them, panicked as they are. This is what the accusers want, not the truth. The *second* reason is even more easily explainable insofar as torments were useless for discovering the truth, as the "Digest (maintained) and that was the opinion of the Romans our legislators and masters" (Verri, 114-115) who never tried it on free men. *Third*: it is logical that it cannot be considered just, even if it leads to the discovery of truth, when even the best law considers it repugnant.

5.13 The recovery of classical law also interested Pietro's brother, Alessandro Verri (1741-1816) with his writings appearing in *Il Caffè* among which the *Discorso sulla felicità dei Romani, Di Giustiniano e delle sue leggi* and *Di alcuni sistemi di diritto pubblico* are worthy of mention.

5.14 It has been said, with justice, that "Cesare Beccharia can be referred to as the one-book man. (...) *Dei delitti e delle pene* [*on Crimes and Punishments*] is not the work of a jurist, but one of an acute observer, a man who abhors blood and violence, who views everything from the perspective of good for all, the defence of society" (Jemolo, IB, 5 and 7) and one could add public tranquillity, as he points out in § XI of his work. Even though this work is not written by a jurist, it is singled out as one of the cornerstones of western juridical civilization; that is the principle of not allowing judges to interpret, often arbitrarily, criminal laws because the citizens feel safe "only when a set code of laws leaves it up to the judge only to investigate whether their actions are in conformity or not with the written law" (Jemolo, IB, 10). This, and not only this, ensured *Dei delitti e delle pene* fame all over Europe, because, among other things, it appeared to not a few French Enlightenment figures to be the premise for a treatise on criminal law, which Enlightenment culture was still lacking.

Cesare Beccaria was born in Milan in 1738 and studied in Parma and Pavia. He returned to Milan, and after marrying, took part, together with Pietro Verri, in the *Accademia dei Pugni*, in which Verri was the leading force. In 1764 he published *Dei delitti e delle pene* which quickly gave rise to consensus and confutations all over Europe. In '66, together with Alessandro Verri, he went to France where he was highly successful, but he was homesick and returned almost immediately. He then refused an invitation from Catherine II to go to St Petersburg. He died in Milan in 1794. At his funeral, a nephew was present who was nine years old: Alessandro Manzoni. Pietro Verri would complain that no newspaper had included a line of praise on that occasion.

5.15 After affirming that he wished to relieve judges of any discretionary power, that only the law must determine what evidence can justify detention, Beccaria introduced what would be another step forward in western juridical civilization. "A man cannot be considered guilty before the judge's sentence, nor can society take away public protection from him, unless it is decided that he violated the agreements by which this had been granted" (Beccaria,

92). The testimony against the offender must be based on serious criteria. Evidence for the various charges must be uncovered and, whenever possible, several witnesses involved. A single one could be insufficient because, for one person who charges, there is one, the offender, who defends himself (cf. Beccaria, § XIII). With some hesitation because at particular moments it is an advantage for the public good when anything may be advantageous, Beccaria is opposed to admitting secret accusation. A situation of mutual suspicion and total mistrust would arise and this would put civil life itself in jeopardy. "Anyone can suspect another of being a spy, and see an enemy in another (…) Who can be defended from calumny when this is armed with the strongest shield of tyranny, the *secret*?" (Beccaria, 89-90).

5.16 The two crucial points which gave the work its fame are related to § XVI *Delle tortura [on torture]* and § XXVIII *Della pena di morte [on the death penalty]*. Beccaria does not deal with this problem moralistically dwelling only on its atrocity or that religious idea that only God is the master of life. What he is interested in showing is its uselessness. Above all it has become a sort of show for the people more than a warning. Nor can it be said that it is so greatly feared considering the way it is faced by some hardened delinquents before a howling public. The certainty of a long and just prison term provides more food for thought, and hence fear and continually strikes one, not just at a given moment (cf. Beccaria, 119). He is also outraged against the death penalty because, more often than not, it is established by a magistrate who is both the prosecutor and the judge. All this must not lead one to think that albeit Beccaria manifests a sense of compassion and understanding for the poor and the lower classes, he is naïve. One need only think about the fact that he shows all his scepticism towards those who support the prohibition on carrying weapons which, never being accepted by delinquents, always harms those who are moderate (cf. Beccaria, 150 ff.). Crimes must not only be punished, but also prevented and one way of preventing them is to write clear and simple laws, but which are genuinely effective (cf. Beccaria, 153).

C) *Beyond the Enlightenment: V. Cuoco.*

5.17 The merits of Vincenzo Cuoco are many and they are not of secondary importance. He lived between two ages which marked a crucial moment for the cultural and political life of the south of Italy and all of Europe. These ages opened with intense cultural ferment which had not prevailed in the Italian peninsula for a long time. They came to an end in an atmosphere of disappointment and the concern that "philosophy" can do little to change the political, economic and social situation (cf. Villani, V-VI). Cuoco was not demoralized by this conclusion. Indeed, he cleansed it of all those perfectionistic conceptions intended to reform the States on the basis of preordained schemes, which could never be adapted to situations incapable of dealing with them, and whose roots were not properly adapted. All of this was not for the purpose of pursuing reactionary goals and nostalgic feelings, but to see what practical possibilities existed to improve the social conditions and institutions of Italy in general and the south in particular.

Vincenzo Cuoco was born in Civitacampomarano, in Molise, in 1770. He studied in Naples where he undertook a law career. In 1799 he declared his allegiance to the Republic, and, implicated in a plot, was imprisoned for nine months. The following year, he was sentenced to confiscation of his property and twenty years of exile. His long wanderings began. In 1801 he published the *Saggio storico sulla rivoluzione napoletana del 1799* [*Historical study of the Neapolitan*

Revolution of 1799]. After producing several minor works, in 1804 he took over the direction and was in charge of the *Giornale italiano* (many of the articles published there were gathered together in the volume *Scritti vari*, I, [*Various Writings*]), whose program he had already compiled. He published the first two volumes of *Platone in Italia* [*Plato in Italy*]. In 1805 he had received an offer for a chair at the University of Krakow. After Napoleon re-conquered Naples he obtained various positions and took over direction of the *Corriere di Napoli*. With the return of the Bourbons and stricken with dementia, he continued to live in Naples at his brother's house. He died in 1823 from gangrene resulting from a fall.

5.18 Abstractionism was one of the basic enemies against which Cuoco fought. He was convinced that "the French were deceiving themselves about the nature of their revolution, and they thought that what was actually the effect of political circumstances was an effect of philosophy" (Villani, XV). Hence there was the conviction that revolutions can be performed even without the people as if philosophy and not real needs was what moved the masses: "the people will not understand, will never follow the philosophers (...). The French were forced to deduce their principles from the most abstruse metaphysics, and they made the mistake that people ordinarily make when they pursue overwhelmingly abstract ideas: to confuse their own ideas with the laws of nature. They believed that what they had done or wanted to do was the duty and right of all people" (Cuoco, S, 30 and 39). For this reason too, Cuoco distinguishes the American Revolution from the French one, the former being primarily inspired by practical needs. The *Declaration of Human Rights* made in America speaks to the senses and not to abstract reason. This conclusion brought Cuoco's conclusions closers to those of Burke or De Maistre, but it was certainly forced. Cuoco wanted to go beyond the French Revolution returning to the prospects for reform of the best of the Italian eighteenth century by offering the possibility for a new national order (cf. Villani, VII). He was convinced that people with genuinely liberal spirits shared his opinions "for example Montesquieu would never have applauded the revolution" (Cuoco, S, 41) especially because of how it degenerated. Despite that, he supported Napoleon's efforts.

5.19 His judgment of the French Revolution, which is in any case seen as an epoch-making event, may at times seem harsh: "Such abstract ideas carry along their own drawbacks: it is easier for scoundrels to deceive themselves with them, they are more easily adapted to all the caprices of the powerful; the turbulent and factionalists will always find in them what they need to support the strangest of propensities, good men receive no protection from them. Anyone who observes the course taken by the French revolution will be convinced of that" (Cuoco, S, 40). If the revolution lost itself in its abstractionism, the inefficiency and inability to understand the times was the fault of the sovereigns. These, too, like the French *philosophes* believed that everything happened through a caprice of the intellectuals and ended up not knowing the real causes and needs for change. All the good that might have been done was compromised. The same happened in Naples where the needs of the Neapolitan nation were different from those of the French. This was not understood, just as it was not understood that "the people are not moved by reason, but by necessity" (Cuoco, S, 40). Politics is not simply rationality, otherwise the Greeks would have triumphed, but as the Italian moral and political sciences show, they are also passion, interest, feelings, etc. "Anyone whose head was filled with the ideas of Machiavelli, Gravina, Vico could neither confide in nor applaud the operations of the revolutionaries" (Cuoco, S, 40).

5.20 Cuoco's position could be referred to as that of a liberal. He is convinced that the progress of ideas cannot be held back by means of prohibitions and censoring, but this does not mean he is deceived and expects to lose himself in any novelty whatsoever. He believes that some ideas should be opposed, like the abstract ones of some revolutionaries, but without using violence. "The way to oppose contagion of ideas (this I will say) is only one: let them be discovered and discussed as much as possible. Discussion will give rise to opposite ideas; it is the effect of pride" (Cuoco, S, 41). Any other means is useless and harmful for liberty itself as well as the well-being of a people. Here some observations of Montesquieu seem to find their echo. Along with some from the Italian classics, they often recur in the pages of the *Saggio* and not only that. "Liberty is a good, because it produces many other goods, such as security, a comfortable existence, population, moderation in taxes, the growth of industry and so many other tangible goods" (Cuoco, S, 102). Here the classical concept returns according to which liberty and order can be guaranteed in a free system and not as the more or less enlightened absolutists wanted, in a paternalistic system.

5.21 The call for concreteness is noteworthy. Concreteness not only escapes the abstractionisms of a certain philosophy, but also a law which, far from real problems itself turns into abstraction losing itself in empty disputes. "All the matters of the Kingdom were discussed in the forum, and in the forum all matters were argued over. Many ills came from that. All that was not a subject for dispute in the law court was neglected: agriculture, the arts, commerce, the useful sciences" (Cuoco, S, 49). The debaters seemed to be uninterested in the progress of the State. As far as concreteness is concerned, it must also be said that, with their irreligious spirit, the revolutionaries came to be seen as enemies by the people especially when a proclamation was published in Naples inviting the population to love one another and cooperate in the defence against the invader. "The priests were given the task of reawakening those feelings in the name of God. These operations never failed to have great effects. The major phenomenon was in Naples, where an immense populace, without any profession or education, lives on nothing but government disorders and prejudices of religion" (Cuoco, S, 73-74). That fact that there were those who had everything to gain from crises of the sort does not detract from the idea that, for Cuoco, one cannot attempt to involve the people in a struggle if account is not taken of their needs, not to mention their feelings. Such people said that although the people no longer loved the king and his assistants, they "still loved their religion, loved their country and hated the French" (Cuoco, S, 78) who were offenders of the tradition of the south, bound to a religiosity that certainly could be offended or replaced with empty abstractionism. Here the considerations of Cuoco indeed coincide with those of Burke.

5.22 It has been said that Cuoco well learned the lesson of Italian historicism from Machiavelli to Vico. Chapter XIV is further proof of this. Returning to the short-sightedness of Italian politicians described by the Florentine as the balance in the Italian Renaissance political system crumbled, Cuoco compares the events of the end of the eighteenth century to those of the end of the fifteenth. Using this comparison as a point of departure he then examines why Naples did not succeed in becoming a Republic, which would have been possible "if one had wanted to derive them (the rules) from the very heart of the nation. Taken from a foreign constitution they were extremely remote from ours" (Cuoco, S, 83). It is not to be forgotten what these fundamental provisions must be. "Constitutions are like clothing; it is necessary that every individual, the every age of every individual have his own, which, if you wish to give it to others, will be inappropriate" (Cuoco, FL, 218). This *lack of a sense of tradition* is added to the *abstractness* of some revolutionary ideas and the *irreligiosity* of some propositions. All that contributes to increasing more and more the distance between the southern plebeians and the methods and objectives of the revolution itself. Immobility came about from this confusion which condemned the situation to reaching a sort of impasse. As had been the case in France, this could be overcome only through the action of an exceptional personality. The variety in ways of thinking produces a sort of immobility. "If ideas were uniform, everyone could act without cooperation, because everyone would act in terms of their own ideas; but when these differ, it is necessary that only one person act" (Cuoco, S, 83). Cuoco here foresees considerations typical of the twentieth century that would be made, for example, by Gramsci (cf. Pezzimenti, OSPG, 53-55). The nature of the chief is different from the forces that he supports and the outcome of the revolution: Lenin and Mussolini are expressions of two different outcomes of a revolutionary situation.

5.23 To the reasons for the failure of the revolution another no-less important one must be added: the rift between intellectual-patriots and the popular masses. "Since our revolution was a passive one, the only way to bring it to a successful conclusion was to win over the opinion of the people. The views of the patriots and the people, however, were not the same: they had different ideas, different customs and even different languages" (Cuoco, S, 90). The admiration of the intellectuals for French culture took them farther and farther from the people to such a degree that it could even be said that the Neapolitan nation was made up of two different peoples. Here the pre-romantic and Risorgimento Cuoco comes out. The first thing that it was necessary to copy from the French was that love of country and national pride that enabled France to stand up to the assault of the European powers. The French people had a sense of the State that was unknown to the Italian plebeians. They would have to be taught to accept responsibility. The task was not easy and much time was needed, but it was more necessary than anything else. "Despotism bases itself on the dregs of society, who, with no concern either for good or evil, sell themselves to anyone who can best fill their stomachs" (Cuoco, S, 93). Despotism is possible during or after revolutions because an unprepared people are afraid of change. "The mad desire to want to reform everything brings with itself counter-revolution: the people do not then revolt against the law, because it does not attack the general will, but rather the individual will" (Cuoco, S, 96). In the total levelling off people are afraid to think with their own heads, because they are in the minority and are threatened.

5.24 In a similar situation it seems that Cuoco sees the recurrence of crises that Vico had feared. The government acts arbitrarily, "the laws remain without effect, in contradiction with the public customs, the powers will languish: the torpor will either lead to anarchy or, in order to avoid anarchy, it will be necessary to call upon an alien force to carry out the laws, which is no longer that of the free people; and you will no longer have a republic" (Cuoco, S, 95). It is not enough consolation to say that that form of government is no longer for the people. Paraphrasing Machiavelli, Cuoco goes so far as to say that human nature, because of its changeability, is inclined to become weary of everything to the point that "all of its affections reach an extreme. They weaken and are snuffed out: due to an overly strong desire to be free, people become weary of the feeling of liberty itself" (Cuoco, S, 99). Is there anything that people never tire of? Certainly! Anticipating an astute observation of Tocqueville, Cuoco maintains that what human beings never have enough of is being equal to others, even when this demand jeopardizes liberty. "When demands for equality press and cross the confines of law, the cause of freedom becomes the cause of scoundrels" (Cuoco, S, 100). What defends liberty, and it is no accident that a conclusion of Cicero is cited, is the sense of limit sanctioned by the law and which must be defended at all costs.

5.25 The Neapolitan revolution was, then, a passive revolution and thus destined to fail. To put it into a position to obtain some results it had to be made active. "Active revolutions are always more effective, because the people are immediately attracted to what interests them the most" (Cuoco, S, 106). To accomplish that, however, the people have to be educated. They must, above all, develop a sense of justice even if they do not know how to arrive at it. Here Cuoco offers a truly original consideration that permeates his whole pedagogical vision. The people must not be allowed to destroy the classes that have oppressed them out of a just desire for justice, inevitably involving in this action useless persecutions of those who are not guilty or individuals who could be very useful to the nation. Rage against the nobility must likewise be kept within just and legitimate limits. As had been the case for Vico, support for this position comes from Roman history. "The Romans were happy to see to it that the plebeians could accede to all positions: this was just and created liberty; if they had wanted to exclude the patricians only because they were patricians, it would have been the same as wanting to restore the patricians after having destroyed their class, and wishing to cause civil war" (Cuoco, S, 113, cf. as well 164-165). One must take care not to impoverish the nation of men of genius or simply valid people because they can be useful to all, even if they belong to a class.

5.26 The reference to utility brings in one about property, one of the great subjects of the revolutionary period. A nation that begins to develop some activity must allow the purchase and distribution of property. All of this leads to a transition from a feudal system to a trace of bourgeois society (cf. Cuoco, S, 118 ff.). The thinker from the south has an original reflection here, too, that takes him back to a classical approach in Roman law. "Desiring to seek a deed in nature is the same as desiring to destroy property: nature does not recognize anything but possession, which does not become property unless it is through the consent of people" (Cuoco, S, 123). This means that property needs a title for its recognition that is accomplished in the formulation of law. Thus, property belongs to civil society, when this is governed under precise laws. However, property, anticipating a conclusion that will be shared by Fichte, must also be the expression of liberty. This had been lost during the feudal era. As a result of the great periods of insecurity and civil war, "the few free men that had remained in our regions, having neither security nor property, requested protection from the powerful and obtained it with liberty as the price" (Cuoco, S, 124). Out of this came a "custom" which distorted the proper way of understanding property itself. Here too, a genuine cultural revolution was necessary. It had to go well beyond the abolition of feudalism itself. Only law was not enough to accomplish this. There had to be a change in mentality.

5.27 The relationship between liberty and property enables Cuoco to return to the subject of religion, which the revolutionaries had by and large misunderstood. Property represents a stimulus for liberty which cannot content itself with the "chimerical equality of goods" (Cuoco, S, 127). This dream presents itself as the most abstract of all. It is still property which goes hand in hand with liberty and which requires governments that guarantee it, hence ones that recognize their own limits, if liberty is to be attained. It is moderate governments, typical of western and Christian tradition, that accomplish this. Cuoco leaves no room for doubt: Christianity "is the religion that better than any other adapts to a moderate and liberal form of government. No other known religion arouses the spirit of liberty to such a degree (...) The Christian religion was the first that said to people that God did not approve of slavery: as a result of the Christian religion, we have a sort of liberty in modern Europe that is different from the ancient form (...) It has not yet been demonstrated that a people can be without religion: if you do not offer it, one will form by itself" (Cuoco, S, 130). Curiously enough, for Cuoco, as time has passed this original tolerance of Christianity has been replaced by intolerance. Philosophy is primarily responsible for this. It is clear here, too, that the target is the abstractionism of certain intellectuals who believe that they can reform everything. Through "pure reason".

5.28 Denying this view means embarking on the path of decadence, because one goes against the natural course of things which, being against nature, neither adapt to it nor do they last. Here the lesson of Vico appears again. Even his expressions are used: "One wanted to follow a road opposite to that of nature. Nature moulds her operations in a scheme, and her design in everything precedes the execution of the parts: we wanted to construct the parts before the design had been created" (Cuoco, S, 145). A dismal picture comes out which seems, still in Vichian terms, to take us back to the considerations on barbarity of which ignorance is the primary expression. "English monopolists were seen trading our paintings, which, having been sacked, had been taken from the old owners and placed in the hands of the populace, which knew neither their merits nor their price" (Cuoco, S, 203-204). These are bitter conclusions on one of the many aspects that bear witness to the end of a nation left to its own devices. It happened not only at the end, but throughout the revolution. The people were never informed of what had to be done. The brief but dense chapter XXXV, "Lack of Communication", shows this. Here it is shown that the government neglected what was one of its most important actions: "keeping communication among the various parts of a nation free" (Cuoco, S, 155). This alone explains what happens and confers responsibility on anyone who acts in the political arena. Hence, the ancient institution of notification must be restored: "any resolution adopted by a population shall not go into effect as law until after one month" (Cuoco, FL, 234).

6. The Open Society Crosses the Ocean.

6.1 It is no use denying that in a view, which we could call inordinately Eurocentric or, more precisely we should refer to as being of Enlightenment origin, the American Revolution has too often been seen as a forerunner of the French one. The only result has been that of not perceiving its particular and original nature. It has only been for a few decades that scholars have begun to analyze the religious roots, the premises based on English tradition, the ties with Renaissance political thought (which John Pocock quite clearly brought out) and even ideas from the classical world as well as medieval juridical thought (cf. Matteucci, RA, 6-11). Yet, only ideological prejudice could keep certain typical innovations hidden. A good example is the written and rigid Constitution that aimed at being superior to the legislative power which, in contrast with the Enlightenment figures, indeed, and with the future positions of proponents of French "assemblearism" (a degenerate adherence to the institution of the assembly), is a clear reference to medieval constitutionalism. The same is true for the past to which the idea of the Empire refers, including the federal system with the consequent division of sovereignties. It certainly does not refer to the history of France. Typically American motivations must be added such as the defence of private property threatened not only by monopolistic concentrations but also all those manifestations of capital freed of rules (cf. Mateucci, RA, 21-22 and 41). A two-party system also belongs to the tradition of the colonies. It is not only the conflict between liberal and conservative ideals, but also between an agricultural world with democratic, at times even extremist, aims and a city aristocracy tied to the world of commerce and capital, which wants to defend its own privileges.

6.2 Certainly all those who wanted to refer to Enlightenment ideas synthesized in the American experience must have found it counterproductive to extol the accomplishments of ancient and medieval tradition, but it was equally uncomfortable to acknowledge influences such as those of the *Irish Catholic Confederacy,* which came out of the Irish revolution of 1641. That step was not a reactionary one because of its being Catholic, but a first case of armed conflict similar to that of the independence-seekers. As McIlwain says, it was a fundamental step in the development of American institutions. It must not be forgotten that the Irish Constitution drawn up by Darcy in 1642 is similar to the one written by the levellers in 1647-49. Not by chance the American scholar maintains that those who consider the medieval period synonymous with reaction, as do many nowadays, should think again and ponder certain writings that have been unknown to scholars heretofore (cf. Matteucci, RA, 122-123 and 127). The influence of this tradition leads us to consider a fundamental point in the American experience: a pluralistic society cannot be governed if a greater rationality revealed by the law is not recognized, above and beyond that multiplicity of interests and conceptions. This conclusion, typical of many scholars, among whom Mateucci, is nothing more or less than the Stoic conviction that Cicero so well presented. Thus, it can be said that the American Constitution is not politics, but the rules of politics. Indeed, after it was approved, this was observed by everyone, even those who, like Jefferson or others, had more democratic approaches in the discussion phase and had revealed themselves to be opposed to the position of the federalists which then won out (cf. Matteucci, RA, 66-67). This "rule" applied to any other manifestation of life beyond politics, including religion, which certainly played a fundamental role as the American State dawned, but which must be considered without exaggerations. It is indeed true that in the *Northwest Ordinance* of 1787 it is stated that "religion, morality and knowledge, being necessary to good government and the happiness of the human race, as well as schools and means of education, must be perennially encouraged"; but it is also true that when the ideals of religion come into conflict with the political situation to the point of threatening public order, the Supreme Court itself was induced to intervene. Suffice it to think of the numerous rulings against the Mormons for their practice of polygamy or the intransigence of some of their sects (cf. Negri, SP, 133, nrs 53-54).

A) *The Greatness of the Mixed Government: J. Adams.*

6.3 For not a few scholars, the American Revolution represents a truly anomalous case in the historical panorama of revolutions. That is probably due to the fact that it signifies a complete break with the past. If that had been the case, its results would perhaps have been far less significant and lasting. For this reason, some, John Adams among them, spoke of revolution "in legality", "in the sense that a revolution must not be an event subverting juridical civilization". The revolutionary experience is thus seen in the context of historical continuity. This explains why Adams in his examination of the problem of popular sovereignty, did not view the parliamentary "assemblearism" so extolled by the French revolutionaries favourably, but praised institutional methods cherished in the American experience which avoided the dangerous forms of extremism of the French Revolution (cf. Mioni, 12-13). It should be added that Adams' somewhat aristocratic nature not only induced him to distinguish what happened in America from what happened on the old continent, but gave his thought aspects bordering on the sceptical, coming from a certain eighteenth-century English culture.

John Adams was born in Merry Mount, Massachusetts in 1735. After graduating from Harvard College and having been an instructor, he devoted himself more and more to the study of jurisprudence. At the time of the *Stamp Act* (1765), he sided with the Massachusetts Whigs to defend the colonies' rights from the claims of royal power. Throughout the revolutionary period he defended the *Acts of Trade* by which the authority of Congress over trade relations, but not in the internal affairs of the colonies, was recognized. Taking the side of Washington, whom he was the first to succeed in office after a period of being the Vice-President, he was the inspiration behind foreign policy in relations with France where he spent some time, in part to sign several treaties. When relations with England were resumed, he stayed in London where he wrote his most famous work *Defense of the Constitution of the Government of the United States* (1788). Two years later he wrote the *Discourses on Davila* where he explained his ideas on the State. Opposed by Jefferson in the 1800 elections, and after being defeated, he withdrew to private life until his death on 4 July 1826, exactly fifty years since the Declaration of Independence.

6.4 Adams was a realistic thinker. He realized that people wanted a political system that would enable them to achieve happiness, but did not offer those abstract and utopian connotations that characterized some French theoreticians. He knew that happiness could be achieved, to the extent that this is possible, only by observing well defined rules that are not the result of caprice or dreams. For this reason, he is a proponent of the republic *"an empire of laws, and not of men"* (Adams, VI, 219). In this sense a republic is any political system that has a division of powers such that power will never be in the hands of a single individual. In this sense, too, what is analyzed by Cicero and, unfortunately, about which we have lost too many writings, is a republic, but the English one is also a republic, even if a *monarchical republic*. Obviously the American one is, too, and it is the best example because in it the popular ideal blends with a *monarchical* and an *aristocratic power* (cf. Mioni, 19-20). In the English tradition, Adams saw that form of aristocratic republic that Vico and Montesquieu had seen in the Roman Republic and sought to bring about this stable form of government in the United States, as well. This position, which was to be that of the Federalists, too, represented the interests of the *élites* of heavy industry and trade with Europe and was in contrast with the more popular ideals of those who represented farmers, artisans and small tradespeople. History would synthesize these two fronts which would direct, alternately, the future fates of the union. The ideal synthesis would come from the Constitution which would make it possible, in stability, to give a voice to the various forces. Stability, security, progress, well-being, all synonyms which become possible wherever there is an effective balancing of the various orders operating in a society, as can be found, in Adams' view, in every American Constitution, even preceding the one that would eventually establish the union. Here he not only sings the praises of mixed government, but also criticises those who, starting with Aristotle, considered monarchy, whenever it was in the person of a wise and capable prince, the best form of government. This is not true: when such sovereigns, balanced powers, and above all when these are defined by a Constitution exist, they constitute the best that human beings can wish for. The *rest*, including the pure democracies, *are forms of government only to be proposed in a utopian phase* (cf. Adams, IV, 286 ff.).

6.5 Democratic ideals cannot survive in their entirety. Without a strong executive, separate from other powers, the conditions for a democracy cannot be kept intact for a long time. "Assemblearism", hence inefficiency, will take over. Too many philosophers have dreamed of perfect governments, only a few tried to bring about those that were possible. If Cicero or Tacitus came back to life today, they could say that their ideas on the subject were put into practice in the English nation and the Americans sought to perfect them (cf. Adams, IV, 290 and 295). Has a perfect democracy ever existed? Adams explicitly asks himself this question. Where have the hypotheses of the philosophers turned into reality? Do there exist in modern societies villages in the state of nature or small urban agglomerates capable of governing themselves by exercising all legislative powers? What we encounter in the most advanced states is the existence of an institution which carries out governmental functions under various names, a limited body, in many cases a senate, that carries out various functions of an administrative and judiciary nature, too, and finally, a broad assembly chosen by the people according to the interests and expectations of each person... hence the criticism of Monsieur Turgot and all the French who had hypothesized a single assembly to which every type of power would be granted. What the Americans tried to do, on the contrary, was bring about a balance among all the various components. In so doing, they showed all their realism setting aside the temptations of those who had believed people to be absolutely good or evil. People have been driven to create such a system out of their weakness, rather than their goodness or evil (cf. Adams, IV, 302 and 379-382). There are other reasons for realism, too. Like so many "realistic" writers, Adams believes that there are various passions that drive the individual in his social action. Among them, the most basic one is the passion to distinguish oneself, as if one were escaping anonymity, the desire to be different. Despite what the so-called sages say, the real reason why people desire wealth, usually, is because it gives rise to consideration and attention from others (cf. Adams, VI, 232 and 238).

6.6 The aristocratic ideal of Adams must certainly not be viewed with the European tradition in mind. It could almost be called a natural aristocracy, typical of individuals capable, not only on a personal but also a political level, of orienting interests, choices, thus votes of other people or groups. It was those personalities that made it possible to divide up sovereignty, to balance it thereby making liberty effective (cf. Mioni, 23-24). For this reason, Adams would be a proponent of bicameralism. He was convinced that a nation incapable of achieving a balance among the various powers would end up with despotism. There was no alternative to a controlled rivalry, the presupposition for any true democracy, but confusion, which was also a prelude to despotism. The basis of a true free government lies in the control and regularization of rivalries (cf. Adams, VI, 280). Bicameralism makes it possible to take more carefully pondered decisions and this is one of the fundamental arguments always used in its defence. A representative body ends up cushioning the exaggerations of the other. Here, in fact, is that criterion of *checks and balances* that would be one of the cornerstones of the American system. With the intention of finding an effective cooperation among the various States of the Union, it would be an inalienable precondition of the Federalists. Now it can be seen why Adams, speaking of a republic, means a sort of "mixed government", the only one capable of preventing anyone from occupying the entire political space. Only this way could the dangers of degeneration of democracy be avoided because other institutions have precise and fundamental duties. A representative assembly makes the people genuine protagonists and avoids the dangerous forms of degeneration of popular democracies.

6.7 Not a few people have judged Adams to be a conservative, but this is surely an unjust label. There are a great many liberal elements in him; the lesson from the past was for him a point of reference but not one to restrict oneself to. What is new, for example the dynamics and conflicts among parties, could certainly not be neglected. To support liberty, innovations had to come about within the framework of the rules and develop gradually. There could be a few individuals capable of bringing them about whether due to circumstance, birth or other things and they constituted the real aristocracy of the nation. This aspect was dealt with in the famous correspondence with Thomas Jefferson for whom an *artificial aristocracy* based on conditions in part illustrated by Adams was placed in opposition to a *natural aristocracy* characterized by virtue and talents (cf. Mioni, 34 and 42-43).

B) *The Federalist Papers*.

6.8 The best summary of the political thought of the American Revolution is to be found in the debate undertaken by the three editors of the *Federalist Papers*. These are the myriads of pamphlets and articles by authors such as Otis, Dickinson, Paine, Jefferson and others who had been debating on the future of the States of the Union for years. This cogent and practical discussion shows that the Americans slowly began to doubt the omnipotence of the Assembly, and their increasing conviction that a great democracy, operating in a great State, cannot be "direct" and, furthermore, it must operate within clearly defined rules in order not to run the risk of becoming arbitrary. They had to organize power and its division in a practical way. There were two different ways of understanding democracy. On the one hand, there were the proponents of a "balanced" democracy, on the other, those in favour of a populist one, which meant, in short, the conflict between Federation and Confederation which ended with the victory of the former. This victory was possible in part thanks to the creation of a Senate which ensured equal representation to all the States and a Supreme Court which guaranteed diversity of competences (cf. Negri, SP, 133, nrs 53-54). As can be deduced from reading the *Federalist Papers*, it was also said that an anthropologically pessimistic conviction won out, that of those who shared the viewpoint of Machiavelli or Hobbes, and who did not have faith in human nature. The fact remains that, despite the pessimism, the "realism" of the victors did not give rise to justification for absolutism, but the framework of a non-utopian but possible democracy (cf. Matteucci, RA, 178-179).

Alexander Hamilton (1755-1804) took part in the war of independence and was Washington's secretary. Later, he was sent by the State of New York as a delegate in the Philadelphia Convention. Appointed, then, as the Secretary of the Treasury, he organized the Federal Bank. **James Madison** (1751-1836) was among the most zealous supporters of the idea that the United States could be saved from disintegration only by adopting a strong Constitution. He decisively condemned Confederation, and dedicated a book to the subject. He played a decisive role in the politics of the nascent State. The first ten amendments to the Federal Constitution were his initiative. During the Jefferson presidency, he was the Secretary of State after which he was elected President twice. **John Jay** (1745-1821) had roles of primary importance in the judiciary and in diplomacy. His experience was such that he became more and more convinced of the need to ensure continuity in foreign policy. He was nominated Chief Justice of the Supreme Court by Washington and held this position between 1789 and 1795. Subsequently, he was also the governor of the State of New York.

6.9 In the summer 1787 debate of the Philadelphia Convention it immediately came out that the Americans were following paths that were new when compared to those followed by the European States. These innovations appear with all their implications in the *Federalist* which can be considered the first real comment on the Constitution of the Union. The work can be divided into four parts: the *first* emphasizes the need and consequent advantages that would come about when the Constitution was enacted; the *second* underscores the urgent need to create a national government with precise aims and duties; the *third* lays out the powers and limits of the various constitutional bodies; the *fourth* analyzes the three basic powers and their reciprocal relations (cf. D'Addio-Negri, 14-15). What is new about this work is that, despite the diverse interests of the authors, the *Federalist* shows a political conception, which the three thinkers have in common. Their starting point is, indeed, that of *identifying* what the *permanent* interests of the community are and, with true realism, how to achieve them. This aim remains fundamental in all of the writings even though, in some points, the specific interests of the various authors come out. For example, Jay emphasizes the primacy of foreign policy, hence the need for a State that devotes its attention to the permanent interests of politics, but also the general ones which might not be noticed by the various States of the Union (cf. D'Addio-Negri, 16). The bases of politics, which by their very nature require stability, can therefore not be left up to a popular assembly which, because of its continued succession of representatives, cannot only fail to guarantee objectivity, but cannot ensure that patient, meticulous and often continuing work of preparation which the great political actions require (cf. Federalist, nr 65), such as foreign policy or military alliances for example.

6.10 Suspicion of "assemblearism" and the desire to bring about a strong, mixed system also hide the fact that the Federalists have always felt the need to keep populist claims under control. For this reason, they claimed they would place as a counter balance to the Assembly a body, made up of respectable and balanced citizens, to limit those popular impulses which, if left to their own devices, would not be capable of setting a limit for themselves. Furthermore, demonstrating concerns that will also be shared by Tocqueville, the Federalists thought that increasing the number of representatives would, on the one hand, exalt the force of the passions over the calmness of reason and, on the other, facilitate election of representatives whose capacities are limited and who are not capable of reacting to the defects of populism (cf. Federalist, nr 63 and nr 58). The radical demands, present in some areas of the European Enlightenment, are expressly rejected here, as well as any equalitarian prospect. The intention is to recall that no assembly can consider itself infallible and all that turns out to be more easily understandable when one power encounters another one capable of limiting it (cf. Federalist, nr 37 and nr 65). Thus, the need to set up a second house arises: the Senate. This need comes from the fact that any single and large assembly tends to give in to the impulse of violent and sudden passions. Moreover, the Senate can often remind the other assembly what its real duties are towards its voters. It can, through legislative means, make people think of those aspects that an assembly too driven by popular passions may be unaware of. It can also adopt new lines of action and reflection which the other assembly had neglected or had not had enough strength to take into consideration. What is most important is that it can expeditiously make laws with a clarity which does not always emerge in popular assemblies (cf. Federalist, nr 62).

6.11 The Senate quite well reveals the role of the Federation, but an executive which can keep under control the excesses of popular demands, like those of the individual States shows itself to be important. A strong government, one which is capable of being a counterpart to the legislative, within the bounds of legality, makes possible the achievement of a great republic which would have been dispersed once the Revolution was over. The executive thus becomes a source of aggregation that can overcome the defects and limitations of the Confederation. Abandoning the idea of a federal government would lead the various States to establish a precarious offensive or defensive alliance which, in future, could also be changed, inducing the various States to become allies or enemies from time to time depending on the circumstances. If authority is not exercised by precise bodies capable of acting promptly, it is wise to give up dreams of creating a great Union. Here the crucial problem of politics comes out again, that of force. It is obviously posed in terms of legality, but of force, as well, all the more necessary when different, sovereign bodies with various interests in common are to be united. To do this it is necessary to "replace what is presently the shadow of a government" as efficiently as possible (cf. Federalist, nr 15).

6.12 The Federalists do not at all bow to utopian temptations. They well know that "if people were angels there would be no need for any government. If the angels governed men, any external or internal control over the government would become superfluous" but human vicissitudes are another matter. Thus, in setting up a government of people it is first necessary to put the government in a position to control those who govern it, then oblige it to govern itself. The authority of the people is surely a first system of control, but experience teaches us that other guarantees are necessary. For this reason, while a united republic has all powers vested in a single government, in a federal one like that of America the power is divided between two different constitutional systems within which the power is further divided into other sectors. It is to be recalled that American bicameralism is aimed at enabling the House of Representatives to be the expression of the people in their unity, while, in the Senate, to represent the various States on the basis of equality. This is because a republican regime must not only safeguard society from the possibility of a tyranny of those who govern, but also the position of any minorities from the tyranny of the majority (cf. Federalist, nr 51). The executive, like the legislative, comes up against precise limits to its action, but it also has an independence and autonomy which ensure real force in its functioning. Thus, every activity takes place within limits set by the Constitution and this represents a change, on the one hand, against the natural-law tradition and, on the other, against certain Enlightenment abstractions. The "rigid" Constitution confirms the primacy of law and justice over politics in the conviction that liberty, equality, and civil progress for the citizens has meaning only if achieved in respect of the rules (cf. D'Addio-Negri, 23). That classic relationship between law and politics reappears then, when society progresses and fulfils itself by means of the rules that it succeeds in giving itself: *ubi societas ibi ius*. Society is not something monolithic, but extremely intricate such that many facets within it, with diverging interests and categories of citizens, can act, feeling themselves protected by law even though they are minorities (cf. Federalist, nr 51).

6.13 The Constitution of the Union sets forth a rule which is to some extent a premise for understanding the functioning of politics: The people, as a collective unit, are precluded from participating directly in managing public affairs. They can do so through specific institutions. Here lies the enormous *difference between a direct and equalitarian democracy*, which, in the Federalists' opinion is in contrast to the nature of mankind, and *representative democracy* which finds expression in a republic with a mixed system. Only the latter can safeguard the diversities among individuals, diversity in abilities (the real premise for property law), differences in opinion, feelings and interests that then find expression in various parties (cf. Federalist, nr 63 and nr 10). Another difference concerning the latter, must be noted with the Europe of that time and the French revolutionary experience. While there was the conviction in France that factions, associations and parties could neutralize each other by submitting their areas of influence to that of the general will, in the *Federalist* it appears clear that a limited role is acknowledged for the various groups and parties, explicitly recognized in the institutional dynamics. Thanks to the definition of the roles, America ended up giving importance to the power of jurisdiction whereas in France, primacy was given to the power of legislation (cf. Compagna, OSC, 152-153).

6.14 Referring to the judiciary power the *Federalist* devotes considerable space to the procedure for appointing judges and all the characteristics of their terms starting with the duration, salaries and the measures to be taken to ensure their responsibility and independence. Going back to the classic suggestions of Montesquieu, it can be stated that if the judiciary power is not separated from the legislative as well as the executive ones liberty will be impossible; and, to guarantee that separation and independence, the fact that the judges cannot be removed must be a premise that cannot be relinquished. This is so because the very fact of being subject to periodic appointments would be fatal for the indispensible independence of the judges. Only this way will the judicial power be able to exercise a serious control over all legislative acts and declare those contrary to the Constitution null and void. The interpretation of the laws is a task specific to the legislative bodies. If such were not the case there might be the risk of preferring ordinary law to the Constitution. The autonomy of judges and superiority of the constitutional law constitute bulwarks for true protection of individual rights that could be put in jeopardy by "manoeuvres" "situations" or the "influence" of all those political components that tend to step beyond their limits and those set forth by the "rigid" Constitution.

C) *The government based on the Constitution: T. Paine*.

6.15 For Paine there is a substantial difference between the government of the people and the Constitution of the people. The latter precedes the government so that the government is limited in its action by the Constitution. If these limits are overstepped, they lead to power without law. This situation gives the people the right to resist (how this is done is not clarified). This right had greatly interested medieval minds and it becomes necessary since the power failed to respect the historical pact between the governed and those who govern. The government, in other words, comes out of the Constitution and must submit to it (cf. McIlwain, Ch I).

Thomas Paine was born in Great Britain in Thetford in 1736. He emigrated to America in 1774 and took part in the events of the revolution, becoming famous for two works published in '76: *Common Sense* and *The Crisis*. After the publication of the *Rights of Man*, in which he replied to Burke defending the French Revolution, he was obliged to flee to France. In Paris he became a member of the Convention until he was arrested in '93, because of being hostile to the Jacobins. In 1802 he returned to America where he died in New York in 1809. Among his writings *The Age of Reason* should be noted.

6.16 Paine took an active part in the debate on the two revolutions of the second half of the eighteenth century, and came to take overly radical positions. This is what perhaps discredited him in the eyes of those, especially among the Americans, who tended to accept the achievements that had come about and who wanted to ensure a period of stability. In *The Rights of Man* he argued strongly, and often rightly, against Burke and the "false" conclusions of his *Reflections* reaching the point of saying that he was "ignorant of the springs and principles of the French revolution (…) His book is a volume of outrage" (Paine, I, 60 and 69). It was all the product of a man who still followed metaphysical approaches. Rather than debate, each seemed to turn a deaf ear to the other where the former extolled the virtues of what the latter criticized. For Burke, everything came out of an abstract rationality, for Paine, that rationality was the very foundation of the revolution: "we see a revolution generated in the rational contemplation of the rights of man" (Paine, I, 62). For Paine the *Declaration* of the rights of man was the highest expression of the modern world so that only Burke was capable of disregarding the value of those rights obtained through great efforts. From these came the different way of understanding the government "*out* of the people, or *over* the people" and, hence, all political activity. The real point, however, was that of stating that "a constitution is a thing antecedent to a government, and a government is only the creature of a constitution" (Paine, I, 81). Here the conflict with the sense of tradition, privileges and history defended by Burke became sharp indeed. For Paine, English history was far from being a path towards liberty. It was only a long period of oppression (cf. Compagna, OSC, 175).

6.17 His considerations on the problem of representation are interesting. For Paine, the French National Assembly was an expression of the true social contract (cf. Compagna, OSC, 12), which is why people in France opposed bicameralism. The aristocracy, with all its privileges, hindered progress towards obtaining rights. The same applies to traditional religion which Paine the deist countered with the conviction that all religions possessed and defended the same moral principles. The monarchical principle gave rise to the same perplexity (cf. Paine, I, 95 ff.). Although Paine was an Anglo-American, he had acquired the totally French way of understanding not only representation, but the very concept of nation, as, for example Sieyès presented it. The conviction that one could manage the revolution departing from new foundations *ex novo* came from the French. It was to the effect that governments were invented and called for by reason alone. These governments, differently from past ones, could not be *mixed governments* which, among other things, are devoid of a real sense of responsibility. Mixed governments, like hereditary ones, were heading towards a decline just about everywhere, confirming the fact that virtue and wisdom are not qualities of one order or one class (cf. Paine, I, 138 and 143; II, 163).

6.18 The considerations in the second part of the *Rights of Man* that lead Paine to place the revolutions on both sides of the Atlantic on the same plane are questionable. However, his conviction that they have now set in motion a process that is unlikely to come to a halt is fundamental. So, it is natural to expect that other revolutions will break out (cf. Paine, II, 153). Consciences are involved and so upset by the course of events that revolutions will have their effects everywhere. On this subject, his considerations on the emerging bourgeois spirit are interesting: it involves capacities in every nation so that commerce takes on greater and greater importance even if it does not come "from the want of a government, but that government was itself the generating cause" (Paine, II, 157) because it consolidates the new mercantile society and protects it. For this reason, the *new governments* are induced to pursue the acquisition of benefits desired by society and, in view of these, ensure social peace. The modern world is moving more and more towards representational systems disdainfully rejecting the hereditary principles, convinced as it is that not even fathers like Homer or Euclid can guarantee intelligence and wisdom to their children (cf. Paine, II, 165-166). This conclusion, which seems to come out of Dante, brings out a classical principle even though Paine presents it as a new one: "The government of a free country, properly speaking, is not in the persons, but in the laws". Equally classical is the fact that the laws must consider the ends that make a government necessary, returning to the true sense of human *societas* (Paine, II, 173 and 185). Once again the Constitution is exalted as a fundamental rule for the wielding of power.

6.19 After returning to America Paine was greeted with hostility, because, among other things, of a violent criticism of Washington. The Americans had now accepted the constitutional premises and were thinking more about constructing than "arguing". Even the most convinced exponents of democracy had accepted the federal premises. The example of Thomas Jefferson (1743-1826), who was aided by Hamilton himself to become the second president of the United States, is a case in point. Although he had been in contact with French Enlightenment circles during his missions to Paris, once he returned to his country and also bound by events, he adopted the political approach of the federalists, showing great realism. Although driven by his "faith" in mankind and democracy, he took account of the American experience and accepted the constitutionalist liberalism of personalities like Hamilton, Adams and others as well.

7. The Consolidation of Liberalism. After the Revolution

A) *Reflections on the Revolution.*

7.1 There are certainly authors in the history of political thought like Gabriel Bonnot de Mably (1709-1785) the brother of Condillac, who, much to our surprise today, gained great renown in their time. Perhaps they offered subjects to public opinion which today seem to us devoid of originality. Mably's *Observations sur l'Histoire de la France* is a case in point. Its basic theme was the rights of the nation. This work reveals nostalgia for a sort of "democratic liberty" which did not survive after the rise to power of Charlemagne, despite the fact that the Estates General had grown up with the passage of time. It was quite close to a utopian sort of reasoning. Equally utopian for the time seems Mably's wish to implement a policy that can provide opposition to ambition and cupidity. To combat those passions he conceived of an enlightened model of legislation by means of which a Legislator, as Rousseau would have hypothesized, enables individuals to seek their own well-being within the common good. To make all that possible he thought of creating a mysterious *republican monarchy* capable of moderating the liberty sought by the bourgeoisie. Like Plato, for whom had had a fanatic admiration, Mably feared the caprices of democracy which, because of intriguers, ends up shunning any form of prudence and moderation. With all their contradictions, these conclusions show that in the Enlightenment analysis of history was aimed at prospects of models for the future rather than reconsideration of the past, even though they seemed, as in the case of the *republican monarchy* of Mably, little more than dreams of a growing constructivist mentality. That gave rise to the conviction that the social context, similar to a machine, could not only be designed, but also disassembled and re-assembled as one pleased according to the necessity of the moment. The marquis Marie Jean Antoine Nicolas Caritat de Condorcet (1743-1794) pursued the same thoughts, although with greater acumen and more concrete prospects. In his *Esquisse d'un tableau historique des progrès de l'esprit humain* the analysis of progress rises above commonplace observations. Emphasizing that the human race has worked to improve itself, the conviction that the path towards truth and happiness was possible to find gained support. It was possible to move towards a form of perfection for which nature has set no limit. It would be possible to give rise to growing comprehension among individuals facilitated by the adoption of a single, universal language, the abolition of wars thanks to the peaceful solution of conflicts, growing equality among peoples, a reasonable limitation on births and many other objectives. Science could make its contribution, too. Existence would be freed from the domination of chance and, as time passed, lengthen the average human lifespan. Some of these ideas had already been expressed by Anne Robert Jacques Turgot (1727-1781) above all in the *Plan de deux discours sur l'histoire universelle* where the coming together of various nations was perceived, thanks to commercial and political activities capable of uniting the diverse parts of the globe more and more and gradually ensuring greater and greater perfection. Turgot placed trust in a sort of set of inherent historical laws in human events. One of these came from the basically reasonable nature of man who, for this very reason, could be educated.

7.2 For two centuries the French Revolution had captured the interest of historians. Not a few, however, have examined it with a preconceived mentality coloured with precise political overtones, albeit in good faith. One need only recall Lenin who had referred to the Jacobin model after the division of the Russian social-democratic party (cf. Furet, 119) which ended up creating real confusion between two revolutionary conceptions in the conscience of Russian revolutionaries. The opposite was true for the thoughts of some great thinkers who examined it from an original, if at times questionable, point of view. Their thought was, however, set aside as reactionary. As Furet points out, one need only recall the position of Tocqueville who overturned the idea of the authors of the Revolution themselves, showing that rather than representing a radical break, the uprising, brought to a conclusion the bureaucratic centralization undertaken by the Kings of France. There was also Guizot for whom the Revolution is an outcome and not a principle, or Michelet for whom the Revolution cannot be understood without reviewing the entire history of France (cf. Furet, 116-117).

7.3 The revolutionary event was a truly curious thing. It was the watershed between two historical moments the first of which, the *Ancien Régime*, had an end but not a beginning (cf. Furet, 15-16). Things could not be otherwise: in the eyes of the revolutionaries, the *Ancien Régime* was lost in the night of the times, whereas the Revolution is a phenomenon which opened an era in which, upon closer examination, we see that we are still involved.

For one thing the French Revolution is the origin of those dynamics of equality which have stimulated the ideals of democracy and socialism (cf. Furet, 18), but also the source of those ideals of liberty to which much of liberal thought refers. Unfortunately, the fact of being the source of the revolutionary movement has not always been to the advantage of the French Revolution especially since, after 1917, the events in Russia were considered a derivation of the so-called bourgeois revolution. This ideological view has given rise to attitudes and lines of research that have, at times, been hardly objective and, in any case, partial so that it is possible to speak of histories of the French Revolution that are monarchical, liberal, Jacobin, anarchical, libertarian, and so on. Obviously, Marxism held the dominating position, and saw economic and social matters as the centre of gravity. They were overemphasized and the only result was that other ways of writing the history of the revolution, for example Tocqueville's, were neglected for a long time.

7.4 Up to now, studying the French Revolution has entailed a considerable risk. Furet rightly maintains that on the one hand, examining the causes of the revolutionary event has made people forget that discussion of the causes of the Revolution is not enough, on the other, that the revolutionary phenomenon ends up producing consequences of its own which, often enough, are not apparent to the protagonists of the moment themselves (cf. Furet, 39). The French Revolution has, furthermore, been seen by a very precise historiography as the birth and eventual victory of capitalism and the bourgeoisie, but that does not explain why there had been the need for a revolution only in France. As a consequence, the French revolution appears as a moment in which the dialogue between society and state led to the dominance of the former over the latter: from privileges, called for by a precise institutional structure, a need for equality was created. That explains why politics becomes the supreme means for the implementation of certain convictions.

7.5 It has been rightly said that the socio-cultural and political image of eighteenth-century France was characterized by intrigue. This is a very true image if one takes into account that, on the one hand, there was a literary world that created opinion, but failed to act or had no control over political action, on the other, there was a power that had no relationship with the new circles arising from the social body: enlightened opinion feared the plotting of the government or ministers, whereas the monarchical administration feared the plotting of intellectuals (cf. Furet, 60). This idea of plots and diffidence among the various conflicting groups appeared during the Revolution. Even in a period which could be called "institutional", when France had a constitution widely accepted by the main protagonists, who ended up thinking of eliminating rivals and groups different from themselves rather than uniting to recreate and stabilize national institutions, (cf. Furet, 71). A Revolution in the name of the rights of people, the nation and of equality seems to have ended up in mutual suspicion. "*Il s'agit de savoir* qui *représente le peuple, ou l'égalité, ou la nation*" (Furet, 72). What is meant by the people? That is not an easy question to answer even though a different *way of understanding* power, or rather the powers, comes out. This is the innovation from which a secularized version of the revolutionary ideology emerged: political action *drained away* the world of values, and so the sense of existence. Herein lay the need, more or less articulated, to create enemies to triumph over to bring about the triumph of ideology itself. These enemies had to be capable of weaving plots aimed at compromising the results of the Revolution. The "aristocratic plot" was to be the most typical because that could be set in opposition to the need for equalitarianism (cf. Furet, 77-81).

7.6 Understood in this sense, the Revolution, with Robespierre, can be said to have spoken "*son discours le plus tragique et le plus pur (...) Et que la Terreur fait partie de l'idéologie révolutionnaire*" (Furet, 87 and 90). In fact, in Cochin's opinion, it can be said that a sort of tendency towards Jacobinism had already been perceivable in '89, which manifested itself in almost "religious" form. "*Le culte du Social est en effet le produit naturel de la démocratie, valeur-substitut de la transcendance divine*" (Furet, 227). It all suggests the search for a mysterious "pure" democracy, and it seemed to seek justification in the will of the people in person upheld by the "*métaphysique égalitaire et moralisante de Robespierre (...) La guillotine est l'instrument du partage entre les bons et les méchants*" (Furet, 98). It all suggested to the people that a military career and glory were open to them as well as positions in the bureaucracy. This would not, however, be an essential fact: it can be said that rather than democracy's having been achieved, an equalitarian culture had spread, and in a manner that was not always clear. Out of this need would emerge that great debate on representation, however, that would be one of the most dazzling merits of the Revolution. The "positions" in the bureaucracy had contributed to "ennobling" exponents of the bourgeoisie; indeed, the monarchy, constantly assailed by financial demands, sold shareholdings, but also the old nobility was not standing still and was marrying its sons off to daughters of financiers. This is the greatest contradiction of the era. Absolute monarchy ended up being the compromise between the construction of a modern state and the conservation of social standards that had come from feudal society: thus, the *Ancien Régime* was too archaic in comparison to what there was in it that was modern, and too modern in comparison to what there was in it that was archaic (cf. Furet, 148). So a process of social mobilization was set off, which, at the same time was one of integration and disintegration, with which three different nobilities were created. Each had a different attitude towards modernization: a *Polish-type* nobility nostalgic for an idealized past, one contrary to the state that took away from it the former, local supremacy; another *Prussian-type* one that wanted to take advantage of modernization of the state monopolizing the crucial posts as well as the military structure; and finally an *English-type* one that pursued the ideal of a constitutional monarchy (cf. Furet, 150).

7.7 Now it can be understood why France was anything but lacking in change when the Revolution broke out. Indeed, she was completing economic and social transformations that had been under way for more than half a century. Those changes would, at times, be exasperated by the Revolution then exported through war which was suffered – more than wished for – by Europe whose crowned heads understood the danger of a way of conceiving politics that was spreading throughout the old continent. Furthermore, there was also the national feeling of the French, conscious of the newness of the revolution, who wanted to become models for other peoples. Out of this would come a sort of ideological messianism, the cause of long conflicts (cf. Furet, 165-166). Was it really something new? During those years in France there was a sort of love-hate feeling about the American Revolution considered by some to be a model to imitate and others, one to overcome. Suffice it to recall La Fayette for whom the "doctrine of constituent power (...) originated in America and was imported into France" (Compagna, OSC, 68). This position made it possible to take one's distance from Sieyès who emphasized that the constituent power had to come out of a representative system.

7.8 There remained attraction and diffidence often in the same individuals. Another example could be that of Rabaut Saint-Etienne. He "went to the point of hypothesizing that if the constituting members had wanted to find a model at all costs, the best would have been that of Pennsylvania, but immediately afterwards, he took pains to correct himself proclaiming: 'French Nation, you are not made to seek examples, but to give them!" (Compagna, OSC, 151). As Gauchet pointed out clearly the problem was to *surpasser l'Amérique.* So many voices were raised, manifesting this concern that the sharper minds felt the need of a distinction to be made. *La France n'est pas l'Amérique* maintained Lally-Tollendal bringing out the enormous differences between a nascent people and one with fourteen centuries of history, between a colonial people which breaks its ties with the mother country and a people which has a dynastic continuity of eight centuries, in short between a new people and *un people antique et immense* (cf. Gauchet, 49). America may have provided an example, but France had to show the *supériorité d'une legislation plus accomplice.* Furthermore, as Sieyès said, the criterion of giving the constitution a *forme populaire* had to be overcome, assuming one which aimed at a *forme raisonnée* (cf. Guachet, 55 and 51). This was not an easy task since, according to some such as La Revellière-Lepeaux, it was the time, in France also, to pursue *une liberté journalière* and thus certainly a more practical form, far from those metaphysical circles in which there was the risk that it would disappear (cf. Gauchet, 299).

7.9 Despite these praiseworthy intentions, abstract positions seemed almost to triumph. It could be said that the collapse of the monarchy and the incompetence of the aristocracy would open the way towards a vision of pure democracy, at least for a while, and this would lead to tyranny. De Ruggiero quite astutely observed this possibility when he saw that the Third Estate was represented in the Assembly by men of letters, lawyers and bankers without a trace of what "the English call the *natural landed interest* of the country. *Ability* prevails over property" (De Ruggiero, 78). That all seemed to be a natural response to views which were surely pro-aristocratic, like those of Henri de Boulainvilliers which traced the rights of the aristocrats back to the time of the Frankish conquest when the fundamental inequality between the conquerors and the conquered was established: the rights of the former had a historical basis, then, so that the king was the only person who could be recognized as *primus inter pares*. Jean-Baptiste Dubos opposed such a position. For him, on the contrary, the king and the people, the latter the heirs of the Gallo-Roman component and still supported by the *lex romana*, had entered into a sort of constitutional pact to oppose the privileges (cf. Compagna, 16). It is curious to note that, along with the idea of Dubos, "on the basis of the Roman-law provisions, absolute monarchy was legitimate. Its *maiestas* was traced back to that of Imperial Rome, and a potential parity of rights among all the French subjects was derived from it" (Compagna, 17). Even more curious is the fact that from Compagna's reflection it can be concluded that Sieyès' liberalism and Dubos' absolutism had a vigorous anti-aristocratic feeling as their point of departure.

B) *The Demands of the Bourgeoisie.*

7.10 The liberalism of Sieyès must be seen in the social and cultural prospective of France in his time. It was *social* because it aimed at overthrowing all those absurd preliminary questions as well as social and tax privileges of those "classes" that no longer counted in the real life of France; *cultural* because, in the light of natural equality and the anti-traditionalism of enlightenment culture, there were no longer any valid reasons for defending what the privileged members of the high clergy and aristocracy supported. Those two motivations became more acute in the light of the serious financial crisis which was gripping France. In this situation, side by side with those who were debating as to whether or not to imitate the English 'constitution' or the American model, an infinite number of proposals were being put forth and they animated the political scenario in those years. However, not everyone had the sure originality, clarity and prerequisites not to mention the power of argument of Sieyès, who not by chance became one of the points of reference in the political debate of those years.

Emmanuel-Joseph Sieyès was born in Fréjus in 1748, the fifth son in a bourgeois family. Sent to a seminary, he pursued ecclesiastical studies with little enthusiasm. He was attracted to Enlightenment culture, and, along with theology, he neglected history. Having become a priest then bishop's secretary, he devoted himself to public life and became a deputy of the diocese of Brittany. He frequented Parisian inner circles and after '87, as a deputy in the clergy list at the Orléans provincial assembly, he began his attacks against the privileged classes. He best known writings are from the two subsequent years: *Essai sur les privilèges* and, above all, *Qu'est-ce que le Tiers-État?* Then he was the inspiration for the most important decisions of the Constituent Assembly which he chaired in 1790. He was an ambassador in Berlin and, in 1799, accepted an invitation to be a member of the Directorate, fearing that the situation could degenerate into anarchy, and was a consul with Bonaparte and Roger-Ducos. During the Restoration, he went into exile in Brussels. He returned to Paris in 1830 where he died in 1836.

7.11 At the very beginning of *Qu'est-ce que le Tiers-Etat?* Sieyès asked three brief questions and already provided three cryptic answers to them: 1. What is the third estate? *Everything.* What has it been in the political system up to now? *Nothing.* 3. What is it asking for? *To become something.* This personal exchange, which, however, involved a large number of interlocutors, shows the character of a personality who tended to keep away from books and did not want to remain a theoretician. For this reason, it can be said that "the most significant part of Sieyès' work should be political action" (Cerroni, 13). This desire for action is confirmed by the words which immediately follow the three questions mentioned above; "We shall see if the answers are correct. Then we shall examine the measures which have been adopted and those that must be taken so that the Third Estate may actually become *something*". The title of the brief first chapter could already be called the motto inspiring the Revolution: *The Third Estate is the entire nation.* What is the justification for this? – simple: if it is private works and public functions that keep a nation alive and give it prosperity it is easy to see that the Third Estate performs "nineteen twentieths of these (…) Only the lucrative positions and posts of honour are occupied by members of the privileged order (…) If the privileged order were eliminated, the nation would not be something less, but something more" (Sieyès, 27-30). These are highly suggestive and strong statements and would be taken up by not a few intellectuals after the Revolution, too. What is striking in these very first pages is that sense of insurmountable limit that the bourgeoisie, whatever its particular abilities are, encounters along the way. The words "I shall arrive here and no further" resound like a warning, bearing witness to a setting of boundaries that is not only political, but cultural in the broadest sense of the term.

7.12 For this reason, the Third Estate has not counted at all. This is what emerges from the equally brief second chapter where it is pointed out that the Third Estate is deprived of liberty, because if it wants to obtain something it must form an association with a "personage" from the other two estates. As far as liberty is concerned, a difference between a democratic one, based on equality, and an aristocratic one, based on privileges comes out here. The latter are the backbone of the French state. Throughout the history of France it is clear that it is "the court, not the monarch which has reigned" (Sieyès, 36). In the end all that has shown that "one is not free by virtue of privileges, but by virtue of rights, which belong to everyone" (Sieyès, 32). Why does such a clear conclusion not take hold? ... simply because the Third Estate is condemned perennially to be in the minority, hence the requests unequivocally expressed in the first lines of the third chapter which can be summarized as follows: a) that the representatives of the Third Estate belong to its class; b) that they are equal in number to those of the other two orders taken together; c) that one uses one's head in voting – not in response to an order. It should be pointed out that Sieyès was writing things that most readers took for granted, but his intention was to convince the recalcitrant, that is, the aristocrats. For this reason, even though the matter of numbers might seem obvious, he was anxious to emphasize that it is not just a question of numbers, but also of value. The progress of the Third Estate reveals itself in every area and no-one can fail to be aware of it. That progress could be even greater if the veto power of the other orders did not exist. This veto must now be eliminated. "No-one can maintain that the law is an expression of the general will, that is of plurality, and at the same time claim that ten individual wills can counterbalance a thousand particular wills" (Sieyès, 44).

7.13 The rest of the work deals with subjects of major interest to a portion of the public opinion of that time. Why, for example, should we try to imitate England and not put ourselves forth as an example to imitate? To answer this question, another one must be resolved: has France a constitution or not? The answer can only come from extraordinary representatives, delegates, the nation, all of those authorized to find a solution. This is an important statement because it shows that Sieyès, unlike Rousseau, acknowledges the partial sovereignty of the representatives. This has led people to observe that "*Sieyès est opposé à la democratie directe, ou, comme on disait alors, à la démocratie tout court*" (Bastid, 369). It must also be kept in mind that when Sieyès speaks of nation, he does not refer to an abstract entity, but a concrete one which quite well explains why he was opposed to any idea of federalism, considered a danger to national unity (cf. Bastid, 377 ff.). The representatives are considered by the Third Estate not only an expression of that unity, but as true guardians of its will, qualified to decide for the entire nation, and they can even threaten to hold separate meetings. The force of numbers comes before any other logic and, naturally, that of tradition. The very idea of nation is far different here from what was to be formulated in a romantic context. For Sieyès only the Third Estate is a nation. This conviction is one of the basic premises of the Revolution and its outcomes will end up fleeing from the control of those supporting it.

7.14 The *Essai sur les privileges* was for less of a success, but it is no less important. Using the same dialogue style, it is aimed at dealing with the problem of privileges to show that these are groundless. Although they were admittedly based on the purest of origins, let us try to see what their effects have been. They have enslaved a large number of citizens preventing them from becoming aware of their true value as well as the chance to reach the point of revoking the bad laws which, in France, are so numerous. Can those laws which harm or are detrimental to others be called good? "If a law is good, it is binding on everyone; if not, the law must be abolished" (Sieyès, 3) otherwise it means that privileged people are allowed to commit wrongs which ordinary citizens are not allowed to do. No privilege, not even honorary ones can be saved. This does not mean that one should disregard the merits of those who serve the nation: "Let us not confuse things so different from one another as *privileges* and *rewards*" (Sieyès, 5). They can be called by various names, what counts is that they "last" as long as merit. Such is not the case with the system of aristocratic privileges which offend real talent and ridicule the virtues destroying that social progress which should indeed be encouraged. That does not happen because the ancient privileges are such that those who possess them look back to the past, live in vanity and consider themselves necessary when, on the contrary, this is useless. Indeed, acknowledgement of true merit opens our eyes to the future, encourage activity and modifies the criteria for sovereignty. As is evident, two different ways of viewing society, which give rise to two different social hierarchies, confront one another. That is not enough. "The two great driving forces of society are *money* and *honour*" (Sieyès, 18). How do the nobles acquire these? Certainly not through laborious efforts, but intrigue and begging. The economy of the nation is thereby mortified. The same must be said of the public administration, which remains in the hands of privileged people. They live in idleness, increase their incomes and all of this is at the expense of the third estate. The only result is that the privileged swallow up capital and impoverish those who work.

7.15 In this attack on privileges all of Sieyès anti-historicist arguments are evident. They are aimed at demolishing all that smacks of custom and that risks leading to the search for a constitution based on the English model. One must break completely with the past, and must deal with the future rights and duties of the nation. For this reason Sieyès believes, and he is the only one who does, that it is up to the Estates General to eliminate any pre-established power and create another one *ex novo*. If the other orders do not feel that they are capable of performing this historic duty: the initiative of creating new rules, a constitution in other words, it is up to the third estate, which represents the nation. At that point, privileges will have to be cancelled and account must be taken of the new forms of specialization that represent the new dimension of *citoyenneté* (cf. Compagna, OSC, 18-23). Here Sieyès dealt a definitive blow to the position of Necker for whom the Estates General had to provide an occasion for integration and not exclusion. No-one could say that he or she was "everything" or "nothing". Necker's position was of an English type since he wanted the better elements of the nation to undertake a process of reconciliation, as had happened in England a century earlier (cf. Compagna, OSC, 118-119). It was Sieyès who was really against a conclusion of that sort and who, indeed with the same force as he had exercised to keep his distance from any attempt to follow the English model, wanted to keep his distance both from the American one and the democratic standards of Rousseau. "Perhaps equality was a profound and sincere passion in Sieyès, but it was never an end in itself, or without control because, quite to the contrary, it seems dominated by a philosophy of rights and duties that was inherent in political liberalism and impermeable to social democracy" (Compagna, OSC, 50). In Sieyès' opinion, the more functions individuals succeed in delegating, the freer they are. Representation for him becomes a standard of modernity. It was the concentration of powers that led to absolutism not delegation: the latter is the *modern form of political participation* (cf. Compagna, 243-244).

C) *Representation and Liberty; B. Constant.*

7.16 The destinies of both Sieyès and Constant were curious indeed. They were "guilty of an incestuous union with Napoleon at a time interval of fifteen years from one another" (Compagna, OSC, 62). Sieyès performed the role of constitutional consultant during the rise of Bonaparte, and Constant, during the decline. It would be unfair, however, in order to nullify the liberalism of both, to overestimate the importance of these episodes. Besides being circumscribed in time, they perhaps bring out the need to safeguard the accomplishments of the revolution, which had now become uncertain. Perhaps Constant himself provides the key to understanding this in unequivocal terms: those who "have seen that a revolution had been something terrible and disastrous and thus conclude that a counter-revolution would be something fortunate, do not realize that this counter-revolution would be nothing but a new revolution (…) and take sides with a government which offers you peace and liberty and cannot collapse unless it is buried under its own ruins" (Constant, DLF, 38 and 46). The appeal was to take the side of peace and liberty avoiding, however, falling back into the *Ancien Régime* as the French monarchy demanded, incapable as it was of moving towards an English-style constitutional system.

Benjamin Constant was born in Lausanne in 1767 in a French aristocratic family. He studied in Germany and England. In 1794 he met Madame de Staël who encouraged the young man to engage himself more and more in French politics. From this experience come writings such as *De la force du gouvernmenent actuel de la France et de la nécessité de s'y rallier* in 1796, *Des réactions politiques* and *Des effets de la terreur* in 1797. After years of exile in Germany, where he met Goethe, Schiller and Friedrich Schlegel, he returned to France which he left briefly between 1813 and 1815, after the defeat of Napoleon in Leipzig. He became the leader of the liberal minority and in that capacity was elected deputy in 1819 and in 1824. He was one of the leaders of the July Revolution in 1830, the year of his death. Fundamental among his works are the *Principes de politique* to which he devoted himself for a long time as well as *De la religion considérée dans sa sources, ses formes et ses développements*, the first volume of which came out in 1824, *De l'esprit de conquête et de usurpation* in 1814 and the famous speech *De la liberté des anciens comparée à celle des modernes in 1819*. His writings on freedom of the press and the responsibility of ministers are also important.

7.17 Another of Constant's strategies was to retrieve a large number of intellectuals who had been traumatized by the experience of the terror. To gain them back meant to reactivate the ideas that constitute the real driving force of politics. Ideas and the spread of ideas make people truly free and make possible the creation of that society which, for Constant, precedes the State, and the State must guarantee their existence as well as the goals which individuals intend to pursue in freedom. All that means that an unbreakable bond must be formed between power and the opinion of citizens who must support it and recognize themselves in it: in short, between power and opinion (cf. De Luca, 10-12). Power must ensure stability and inspire credibility. Opinions must circulate freely. These are the guarantees of a liberal system which develops and consolidates its own institutions. They "*ne demandent que du temps, les opinions que de la liberté*" (Constant, DRP, 105). This relationship is more understandable if one keeps in mind that Constant conceives of the relationship between authority and liberty such that, if the first is eliminated, it puts any society in a condition to lose liberty itself. Liberty cannot coexist with absolute power, nor can it coexist without a power that defends and guarantees it (cf. De Luca, 14).

7.18 The need for a constitution comes from the need to set some political "rules of the game" within which liberty can be carried out. The State remains necessary to safeguard individual rights within recognized rules. It is therefore not coercion that distinguishes a liberal State from a despotic one, but the fact that the former exercises its force within the law. The Revolution indeed offered the prospect of a new liberal State, but it cannot become a political method for changing the rules. To perform those changes one must make use of the means provided for in the constitution (cf. De Luca, 15-21). If that does not happen, the inebriation of power leads to a sort of general inebriation which eliminates any limit and ends up causing the loss of liberty itself (cf. Constant, DEdlT, 166 ff.). For liberty to be kept within its just limits it must be recalled that the nature of freedom comes from religious feeling, present in every human being like the need for the infinite (cf. Constant, DLR, 51). No political situation can confine a person within the narrow limits of a power which, like absolute power, comes to consider itself unchangeable. This individual is entitled to an "open" political system, one capable of renewing itself continually. To be sure, Constant cannot be considered a believer in the traditional sense of the term, but a religious spirit which, not by chance, strongly opposed the atheists and materialists of his era (cf. Deguise, 266).

7.19 From this sense of religiosity comes the theory of responsibility of administrators and officials, which constitutes one of the most original aspects of his thought. Responsibility is seen in conformity with some rules within which all that is political must be contained. The revolution itself must be traced back to that "interweaving of principles" which governs political life (cf. Cerroni, 35 and 12-13). It is here perhaps where his most famous work finds its origin, the *Principes de politique,* in which modern liberty is analyzed on the basis of three fundamental guiding principles: "1) the priority of private happiness over public participation (civil liberty over politics), 2) the limitation of popular sovereignty, 3) a conception of the State as one merely guaranteeing 'individual freedom'" (Cerroni, 22). There is, however, a fourth point, perhaps the most important one with which the *Avant-propos* begins: the fact that the rules, like institutions must always be "open", in the sense that they can always *être améliorées.* There is only one way to improve them: establish and follow the rules. For Constant, who may be a bit simplistic here, only two powers exist: an illegitimate one, force in other words, and a legitimate one, the general will, which, however does not mean arbitrary will (cf. Constant, PP, 305 ff.). Indeed, he would write noteworthy pages against arbitrariness. Sovereignty exists, but in a limited fashion. There is a portion of human existence that always remains individual and independent, beyond any social jurisdiction and the universality of the citizens can never dispose of it. The consensus of the majority cannot, in all cases, legitimate any act whatsoever: there are some that cannot be justified in any way. This was the great mistake of Rousseau (cf. Constant, PP, 312-313). Unlimited sovereignty does not allow individuals to free themselves from the demands made by governments. In order not to have anything to fear, limits must be placed on both the possible despotism of individuals and that of assemblies (cf. Constant, PP, 321). These are the reflections of a man who experienced the Revolution in its every aspect and who wants to save certain accomplishments, yet eliminate certain methods forever.

7.20 In speaking of powers, Constant feels the need not only to separate and balance them, but also that of finding a "neutral" power which can be over and above the two powers and thus exercise a sort of impartiality. That neutral power is called real power. Aside from this, there must be the executive power, a lasting representative one, representative of opinion, and the judicial power (cf. Constant, PP, 324). The reference to the English situation is explicit because, among other things, the constitutional monarchy offers a perfect example of neutral power. The latter, being separate from the executive power, makes possible the exercise of the criterion of responsibility: indeed, in a constitutional monarchy the continuity of the crown with its stability and impartiality is kept intact, as well as the responsibility of the executive in performing its actions. That does not mean subjecting the monarchy to ridicule, because it retains noble prerogatives such as the right to grant grace, the right to confer forms of recognition on citizens who bring glory to the country, the right to some appointments, the right to distribute rewards and prerogatives and other things, as well as its ensuring the unity of the State and its public order (cf. Constant, PP, 333 and 336). Constant is most concerned about the two representative powers, however. Strong assemblies are indeed important and equally dangerous for freedom.

One need only think of the tendency to multiply the number of laws infinitely. This flatters legislators who feel the need to act and they take pleasure in being considered necessary. Hence the need, for assemblies, as well, to lay down some limits that cannot be surpassed. Among these there is also time. By dissolving assemblies the people can regain the possibility of exercising their basic rights since, where there is no freedom to elect, there is no representative system (cf. Constant, PP, 338-343, practically all of Ch. III). Alongside this house of representatives, Constant also examines a hereditary assembly for which he feels a need on the level of an English-style House of Lords or else, and it is curious that he does not say so, a Roman-style Senate. As in the case of the two institutions mentioned below, it is necessary that heredity not be the sole criterion for admission. Any simple citizen who distinguishes himself or herself with a particular merit may come to enjoy the same privileges as those enjoyed by the Peers. Indeed, if the latter were of a limited and pre-determined number, an overly strong aristocracy would be created, one capable of imposing itself on the monarchy and the citizens (cf. Constant, PP, 346-347).

7.21 What, then, are the conditions required for participation in the political life of the two assemblies? This has been considered one of the weakest points in Constant's analysis. Despite the fact that he claims not to like "*les fortes conditions de propriété pour l'exercice des fonctions politiques*", he goes so far as to state that it is preferable for the representative functions to be occupied "*par des hommes, sinon de la classe opulente, du moins dans l'aisance*" (Constant, PP, 364). The fact that only owners can be citizens has, in the past, unleashed Marxist critics and, more generally, democratic criticism against Constant: census suffrage doctrine is classist by nature. To be honest, however, we must make an observation relating above all to the historical context. As some point out, no-one proposed universal suffrage at that time. Furthermore, the census suffrage requirement was not an immutable principle, in short, the social "climb" had to be possible (cf. De Luca, 43-44). To facilitate matters Constant re-evaluates all those forms of political participation, contrary to what spirits more "open" than himself had maintained. He does so on a local, town and district level, too. Individuals are allowed not only to engage in political activities, but also to measure themselves against or oppose all other authorities who tend to go beyond the bounds of their own areas of action. One must *"introduire dans notre administration intérieure beaucoup de fédéralisme"* (Constant, PP, 427), but a true federalism, which binds people to their places, memories and habits and, at the same time, makes them feel like citizens of a great State, in the affairs of which it is always possible to participate and offer their own contribution.

7.22 The last part of the work is devoted to several principles which Constant considers inviolable. Property is the first subject dealt with and defence of property is the primary goal of a true liberal spirit. Curiously enough, Constant unwittingly repeats here one of the cornerstones of private law and the close connection that had already existed in Latin etymology between property and person. *"L'arbitraire sur la propriété est bientôt suivi de l'arbitraire sur les personnes"* (Constant, PP, 444). Having a piece of property taken away is, in a way, an attack against liberty. That is not the only problem: citizens eventually lose faith in the authority and the consequences are disastrous: any economic development is put in jeopardy. Where faith in public institutions is lacking it is as if the economies were condemned. After repeating his defence of freedom of the press, a problem which he had concerned himself with several times, Constant again underscores the importance of religious liberty. In highly romantic tones, he speaks of a feeling about which the State can have nothing to say. When it tries to do so, fatal forms of servitude are the result. If one only wishes to treat religion as if it were an opinion it must be admitted that, in such cases, the rights of the majority are the same as those of the minority (cf. Constant, PP, 462-463). The rights of the minority are the result of individual liberty. For this reason, no type of arbitrariness can be acceptable when it calls this liberty into question. To admit any arbitrariness whatsoever, as in the case of attacking individual liberty, means to eliminate the very reason for living in a society which lives under the aegis of laws and not caprice (cf. Constant, PP, 486-488). In order to safeguard the certainty of law Constant maintains that, in addition, naturally, to the fact that judges cannot be removed and to the uprightness of jurors, scrupulous and constant conservation of the judicial forms are necessary (cf. Constant, PP, 497).

7.23 Constant achieved fame before the general public for his *Discours* concerning the freedom of the ancients and the moderns. The underlying theme of this piece of writing comes out from the very start. The Revolution can be called a fortunate thing because it enables us to reap the benefits of a representative government, a truly new event in the modern world even though, and Constant himself admits it, there were some entities in Rome that *"avaient, jusqu'à un certain point, une mission représentative"* (Constant, DLL, 592). This admission is important because, in actual fact, when Constant speaks of the ancients, he speaks above all of the Greeks; one need only consider the fact that reference is being made to ancient republics closed within narrow boundaries. However, it is true that thanks to religion as well as moral and intellectual progress, the modern world has managed to increase commerce and exercise the freedom of professions (cf. Constant, DLL, 596 and 599). The relationship between peace and commerce is interesting, even though, curiously enough, it is not, as it had done in the past considered that both were guaranteed by a notable and original juridical instrument – one can think, for example, of the *pax romana* and the *pax Britannica*. For Constant, in any case, modern individual liberty finds a guarantee in political liberty even though moderns do not feel, as did the ancients, like making too many sacrifices of their individual liberties. All of this is seen by Constant as a possible hazard, however, because *when one is too taken up with one's own particular interests, the risk of giving up one's political liberties easily arises* (cf. Constant, DLL, 612 and 616).

7.24 Among the liberal spirits who recognized the merits of the French Revolution, but also perceived its limits, the personality of Humboldt stands out. He was able to see in the modern mechanism of the state, albeit created as a reaction to the absolutist conception, the risk of turning into a paternalistic expression of politics to the point of paralyzing the most noble energies of individuals.

William von Humboldt was born in Potsdam in 1767. After studying law at the University of Frankfurt and Göttingen, he made his first trip to France as the French Revolution broke out. After returning to his country he held political and administrative positions which, however, did not limit his multi-faceted interests. In 1792 he wrote one of his most fortunate works: *Ideas for a "Study of the limits of the activities of the State"* which, due to censorship, was published only partially before it came out, not until 1851, in complete form. He then took a series of trips to various parts of Europe until he was appointed Minister in 1821, and tried to give a constitutional and liberal direction to the Prussian monarchy. He died in Tegel in 1835 after having written numerous other works.

7.25 Humboldt is convinced that Kant's position is decidedly exaggerated and dangerous as well. For Kant, the State constitutes a mechanism that can also function in a situation of conflict in order to hold up under the tensions caused by a "people of devils". Furthermore, the proper functioning of the State cannot depend exclusively on laws, however clear they may be. This sort of argument is reduced to pure formalism and it is certainly not by chance that the Kant perspective seeks the most rigorous determination of the limits of freedom. For Humboldt the problem was precisely another, that is, that of assessing the limits of the activities of the State for the purposes of granting individuals the possibility that their best faculties and aspirations might coexist and develop in independence (cf. Carrano, 19-21). The State expresses the need for unity in commanding so that energies may be best channelled when there is a single will. Humboldt, however, places in opposition to the State, taken to be the area of subordination and mechanicalness, the nation seen as the sphere of independence, liberty, spontaneity and creativity. This distinction is possible when the State does not become involved in the citizens' achievement of well-being, but limits itself to being a factor of guaranteeing (cf. D'Addio, II, SDP, 108-109).

7.26 While exalting the French Revolution, Humboldt is nonetheless convinced that its limitation may be that of creating a state structure which reaches the point of reducing the hard-fought individual liberties. The risk seems confirmed by the fact that if people wish to create a constitution based solely on principles of reason and an entirely new one, they end up creating something lacking in vitality and forgetting reality in order to pursue abstract models. This explains why the importance of the constitution "lies more in its critical and polemic significance, than in its constructive and institutional one" (cf. Bedeschi, 124-126). What Humboldt intends to point out is that the true freedom of an individual can be achieved when the sphere of intervention of the State is more limited. This is true for property, true for the clearcut separation between the Church's prerogatives vis-à-vis those of the State, but it is also true for education which cannot be prescribed and dealt out by a central authority. In short, Humboldt has an unconditional faith in the individual and sees in his or her intimate creative energy the essence of progress as well as liberty.

D) *The Bourgeoisie Consolidates its Primacy: F. Guizot.*

7.27 Guizot's historical work is an expression of the century-long effort of the French middle classes, that Third Estate, which managed definitively to assert its primacy only after the Revolution. Perhaps the historical reflections are based on an overly Euro-centric vision, but it is true that for the first time in Europe, a bourgeois class rose to the forefront with its entrepreneurial and industrial initiatives, one that did not exist elsewhere. It has also been said that in Guizot there was that exaltation of France's leading role already proclaimed in the circle of "reactionary" Catholic thinkers such as De Maistre and De Bonald (cf. Pozzi, 14). Upon closer look, it seems to be a widespread feeling. How can we forget some of the writings of Cuoco and Gioberti in Italy or of Fichte and others in Germany? What is added in the pages of Guizot is not that optimistic faith to be found in the above-mentioned authors, but the fact that that faith lies "in the precision of the human sciences, *à propos* of which suggestions from the theses of Comte have been spoken of" (Pozzi, 16-17). This optimism is based on a careful analysis of the past. Expressing one of the convictions held in his era by way of example, Guizot exalts history and Medieval history in particular because without it, it is impossible to identify the seeds of modern society. In this respect he goes back to not a few masters of the previous century from Vico, from whom he derives the need once again to find the laws governing human action, to Montesquieu or Gibbon. Like them, he realizes that history cannot be seen merely from a civil point of view since the religious component in western civilisation cannot be considered a marginal element or one alien to society. It is, on the contrary, continually supplemented to the point of influencing the moral state of individuals and of society itself. On that subject, Guizot leaves no room for doubt: "*L'état social dérive (...) de l'état moral des peuples (...) les croyances, les sentiments, les idées, les mœurs précedent la condition extérieure, les relations sociales, les institutions politiques*" (Guizot, HCF, I, 33).

François Guizot was born in Nîmes in a Protestant family belonging to the middle bourgeoisie in 1787. After having carried on juridical and literary studies, he translated and annotated Gibbon's History, a work that earned him an appointment at the University of Paris as a professor of Modern History in 1812. During the Restoration he was one of the representatives of the doctrinaires until he became the leader of the liberal opposition. For a long period in the eighteen-twenties he kept his distance from politics and devised the famous lessons on *Histoire générale de la civilisation en Europe* and *Histoire de la civilisation en France*. After returning to politics he held many offices as the Minister of Education, Ambassador to London, Foreign Minister, until obliged to take refuge in England for a brief period after the events of 1848. He died in 1874 after writing numerous other works among which, in addition to some of the previous ones, can be recalled: *Quelques idées sur la liberté de la Presse* and *Sur le nouveau projet de loi relatif à la Presse* (1814), *Du gouvernement représentatif et de l'état actuel de la France* (1816), *De la peine de mort en matière politique* (1822), *De la démocratie en France* (1849), etc.

7.28 Somewhat like many other liberal spirits of the time, Constant for example, Guizot wishes to keep the most positive results of the revolution, justice, legality, liberty, etc., without accepting the revolutionary method (cf. Pozzi, 46). This is quite understandable when one thinks that the minds of the time were well aware of the distortions of the revolution, as well as the atrocities of the terror. There was also another reason: subscribing to the revolution *tout court* could mean cancelling out the entire past which, in the opinion of scholars such as Guizot, conserved the bases and spirit of civilization. Civilization consists basically of two elements: development of the *social state* and that of the *intellectual state*. On the one hand there was material or exterior development, on the other, the interior development of ideas. The two elements are integrated to such a point that it is impossible to conceive of material development without hypothesizing a corresponding moral one with the ideas that support and justify it (cf. Guizot, HCF, I, 6-7). These two aspects can always be revealed in historical analysis, but such is more the case in periods of transition, which are considered extremely important and the most instructive of all. They make it easier to look back at the past in order to see what of it has come through or has been transformed into the future (cf. Guizot, HCF, I, 175). Guizot's analysis shows a new relationship between facts and ideas, some have said between the real and the rational, never considered up to then. Facts had never carried so much weight in science, but the ideas themselves had never been seen in such a close relationship with facts. Out of this came an idea of the progress of society which consists in transforming mankind itself, enabling it to be free, that is, to govern itself by reason (cf. Guizot, HCF, I, 23-24 and 279-280).

7.29 France is the nation which best lends itself to being studied in relation to the entire civilization of the continent because the fundamental elements of European tradition come together here: 1) Roman civilization with its legality, 2) the new religious mentality which was highly original and took the best from the past, adapting it to the new exigencies and 3) barbarian individualism. As far as the first is concerned, making use of Savigny's reflections while criticizing them at times, Guizot comes to show that Roman law had always been present in western civilization, even in the darkest ages of the Medieval period when it helped to humanize laws, customs and institutions. Among these, it is worth mentioning that of the *defensor*, a particular magistrate present from the mid fourth century whom we could call a public defender today (cf. Guizot, HCF, I, 39 and 42). The soundness of Roman Law, and the consequent way of administering, is borne out by the fact that in Gaul, too, the imperial administration "*fut, à coup sûr, plus éclairée, plus impartiale, plus préoccupée de vues générales et d'intérêts vraiment publics, que n'avaient été les anciens gouvernements nationaux*" (Guizot, HCF, I, 49). Thus, the development of institutions and legislation is closely linked to that of society. Between society and legislation in general there is a close connection (cf. Guizot, HCF, II, 260), as Vico had already and amply pointed out. There is another element, however, almost never considered, which characterizes the presence of the Roman world on French territory quite remarkably: the fact that "industry" departs from the domestic dimension and creates a class of free artisans who work not for a proprietor, but for their own gain. How this came about is difficult to say but, at the beginning of the fifth century, the transformation had taken place. It was the beginning of those corporations, of that Third Estate, that bourgeoisie which would be behind the development of many European civilizations like that of France (cf. Gizot, HCF, I, 57-58). The *bourgeois* developed in the municipal administration, the true stronghold of Roman legality, where people learned to struggle against feudal barons to defend liberty (cf. Guizot, HCF, II, 443). The bourgeoisie had a fundamental feature due to its ability to change depending on the demands of the various moments in history. It was able to consolidate and defend its own achievements. For Guizot the class struggle, the real moving force in history, is not only a struggle of interests, but also of principles and institutions (cf. Guizot, HCE, 209-210). The French Revolution is the event that led to the conquest of power by the bourgeoisie.

7.30 The second element that characterizes European civilization is Christianity. Guizot's position, as is evident in the points at the end of the chapter devoted to Balmes, is that of a Protestant, but also that of a scholar who wishes to bring out the difference between western and eastern Christianity, one which not a few scholars had examined from the point of view of institutions, too. This difference can, in fact, be perceived from the beginning of Christianity, the rise of monasticism for example. Whereas the need for isolation was felt in the East, in the West the need for communal life prevailed and this necessitated forming communities to regain the security that had been lost, to shore up a civil society now in the grip of very dramatic disorders. Monasteries became civil centres around which not only spirituality flourished, but also agriculture, the crafts and labour in general (cf. Guizot, HCF, I, 122). This explains why the religious authority also became, as time passed, a moral, cultural and, finally, political one as well. It also explains why westerners sought in every way not to imitate the eastern mentality in which they saw not a few dangers of despotism as something inherent. All of these aspects were greatly emphasized in *Lesson XIV* of the first course, the one that deals with St Benedict. It is in this lights that one understands why *"le christianisme a été une révolution essentiellement pratique"* (Guizot, HCF, I, 152). The great interpreters of the political history of the Medieval period understood this. Charlemagne, for example, came to be an ally of the Church because he considered it *"la seule puissance capable d'enseigner et de prêcher alors la morale"* (Guizot, HCF, II, 167). It was the only force capable, of conveying the profound value of order and unity, because it was the only one over and above all the other, various ones. The most important feature of ecclesiastical history, however, is that the Church introduced that distinction between the spiritual and the temporal which is the real basis of the liberty of conscience (cf. Guizot, HCE, 57).

7.31 Arguing against those, like Dubos, who underestimated the influence of the Barbarians in the development of western civilization, Guizot tends to underscore the fact that among the German groups, there were three characteristics that could be considered no longer existing in Roman society. They were the *assemblies* of free men who debated all public initiatives, a hereditary or elected warrior *monarch,* and, finally, *aristocratic patronage* over fellow soldiers or colonists. Added to that is the spirit of individual freedom which, perhaps more than any other, would characterize the modern world (cf. Guizot, HCF, I, 213 and 228-229). That individualistic spirit would have to come to terms with the rules of Roman legality, if it were to yield true results. For one thing, being nomadic peoples, they began to understand the sense of property and need for laws only after the invasions. It should be recalled that many laws had been in part devised before the invasion, and that they had been written in Latin, as happened in the case of Salic law. Furthermore, they dealt more with criminal than with political law. Thus, the Barbarians came to understand that only Roman law could govern their social relations and make them last. That juridical certainty was what made the Roman world seem superior in the eyes of Barbarians (cf. Guizot, HCF, I, 309-311). *Lesson XI* is totally devoted to that subject. The Roman component merged with the Barbarian and, what is more, the "German-Romans" became the saviours of the Western world. They were able to resist the pressures from the North, from along the Rhine, and the Danube coming from new Germanic populations, Slavic especially, but they were also able to confront the Arabs who threatened the Mediterranean in the South and the Pyrenees, thereby saving a world which had recently been reorganized (cf. Guizot, HCF, II, 124). These dangers led to development of those social structures that had already formed subsequent to the first invasions and which would then be consolidated in the future world. There was the trend towards the development of the institution of the monarchy, the birth of a territorial aristocracy and the first form of municipal organization, "the vital remains of Roman society", within which that Third Estate would germinate and would be the backbone of French progress. Those municipalities, so important for French history, bore the marks of all the administrative components from that Roman tradition that would then give life to French cities, and this as early as the tenth century (cf. Guizot, HCF, I, 252-256, II, 405 and IV, 13-14).

7.32 Summing up, it can be said that Guizot's analysis, as emerges from his two fundamental works on history, is aimed at examining the thousand-year long path undertaken by France for the purpose of creating a society in the total sense of the word. The origins of this process can also be found in the early forms of feudalism which were coming into being around the tenth century, when the dichotomy came about, which then became dialectic between the *sovereign nation*, that is the owners of fiefs and the *nation possessed*, that is the oppressed people. From this conflict situation the energy and dignity of the individual would, however, emerge. The roles were to be redefined since *from the base* demands for liberty were manifesting themselves, and *from on high* calls for public order. Little by little these efforts were being governed from within a single system harmonized by the monarchy (cf. Furet, 178-179). This process became possible because the feudal aristocracy, lost in its own peculiarity, was never capable of giving itself a unified organization as happened in Rome, in Venice or in England where monarchy and feudalism came into being together. Thus, the French monarchy was the result of the aristocracy's inability to organize itself, but also the inability of local institutions to achieve forms of communal democracy (cf. Furet, 179-180). These inadequacies would lead to the Revolution which would present itself as a new unifying principle of society: the nobility and Third Estate would present themselves as rival groups when the monarchy would show itself to be incapable of resolving conflicts.

7.33 As the expression of the new and rising class, Guizot was convinced that absolute power corrupts any institution so that not only is a means of controlling it needed, but also one for limiting it. The sovereignty of law is the true basis of modern States (cf. Guizot, HCE, 405 ff.). Sovereignty is identified with reason, justice, and truth, which, in its essence, can only refer to God. This might seem a dogmatic statement hardly appropriate for a liberal spirit, but Guizot was convinced that only thus would it be possible to escape from the arbitrary and uncertainty, the real causes of despotism. It should not be forgotten either that society is not something purely voluntary and prearranged, but natural and necessary (cf. D'Addio, II, SDP, 215-217). The representational system presented itself as the best way to govern a society. Giving in to direct democracy meant creating different forms of constriction, basically similar to classic despotism. Representation, on the contrary, was an expression of the overall rationality of the society, and allowed the principle of inequality and that of equality to set in motion the dynamics of the life of the society. This was due to the fact that the *former* prevents stagnation and the *latter* does not allow privileges to become the source of domination and force (cf. Guizot, HOGR, 305-306). The need for representation, which has always gone hand in hand with the rise of bourgeois society, was expressed by the *philosophes,* even though intellectuals and bourgeois, who had always viewed one another with suspicion and diffidence because of the diverse roles they play in society, ended up by justifying one another albeit unwillingly (cf. Guizot, HCF, I, 171).

E) *Liberty and Equality: A. de Tocqueville.*

7.34 One of the most significant situations that made an impression on Tocqueville in the United States was the idea of progress. This idea was far closer to that of sixteenth-century travellers than to that of the *philosophes* and their heirs who, with their abstractions, had livened the French political debate (cf. Matteucci, I, 16). The American innovations made a new methodology necessary, but also completely renewed disciplines to analyze a fully achieved modern democracy. As an aristocrat, Tocqueville had the merit of dealing with the problem serenely and objectively, knowing that otherwise he could not make use of science. Examining liberty as a moral tension which develops and is carried out on concrete political terrain, he ends up overthrowing and completing the view of Constant on the liberty of the ancients and the moderns. The former, that is, the possibility of participating directly and collectively in the creation of the will of the State, is not in contradiction to the latter, but leads to and completes it. All of that keeps it free of the dangerous Rousseauian utopias and all those democratic convictions which, if actual brought into being, would threaten the very existence of liberty (cf. Matteucci, I, 37).

Alexis de Tocqueville was born in the castle of Verneuil, near Paris, in 1805. Coming from an aristocratic family, he was brought up to admire the Ancien Régime. A year after he received a law degree in 1826, he became a judge. After the events of 1830 he requested a leave of absence. Together with his friend Beaumont he went to the United States to study their penitentiary system. He remained almost two years on the American continent, returned to France and resigned from his post to devote himself to writing his most famous work *De la démocratie en Amérique*, of which the first part came out in 1835. Elected as a deputy in 1839, he published the second part of his study a year later. In the eighteen forties, he represented an openly liberal political position until Louis Napoleon came to power, because of whom he was arrested in 1851. He retired from political life and devoted himself entirely to his studies. He wrote the *Souvenirs, L'Ancien Régime et la Révolution* (1856), which, unfortunately was never finished because of his increasingly precarious health. His *Voyages* should be noted. He died in 1859.

7.35 Among the innovations that interested him the most during his stay in America was the equality of social condition. Tocqueville himself says this in the first lines of his most famous work. The path towards equality has now become part of the essence of western man to such an extent that it is inconceivable to imagine bringing it to a halt, as is the case for aspirations, culture and even religion. Even the political circles of the high clergy, those traditionally most conservative, are opening up to the rich as to the poor, to the plebeians as to the nobles. It can be said that equality is penetrating all the areas of society and even the government (cf. Tocqueville, DA, 4). All of history shows that this process has been under way for centuries so that it can be called a providential, and universal fact. Putting a stop to it not only means hindering the progress towards democracy, but almost "struggling against God himself". The main task of those who govern seems therefore to educate on behalf of democracy, regulate it, point out its hazards, but also its indubitable advantages. For this reason, a new political science has become necessary, one capable of analyzing those changes that democratic revolution brought about in society's material situation, in the area of laws and institutions (cf. Tocqueville, DA, 6-7). This, too, is a fundamental task: once the prestige of traditional power has disappeared as well as the sense of authority, one must have the courage to renew civil life. All the old and new forces must grasp the grandiose nature of this task. Christianity itself, which made all men equal before God, must help them to feel that they are all citizens equal before the law. This is no easy task for anyone and explains the great confusion that Tocqueville notes in the political debate over democracy and liberty, often opposed by those who should be defending it or, for self interest, exalted by those who should, logically speaking, oppose it (cf. Tocqueville, DA, 13-14). The best thing, however, in his opinion, is not to allow oneself to be drawn into party struggles and to examine such controversial problems as dispassionately as possible.

7.36 In order to understand a historical and political phenomenon like that of American democracy, it would be necessary, if possible, to go back to the original and constitutive elements of that society, returning to the era of the first migrations where it is already possible to see the seeds of free institutions, those of local governments and popular sovereignty which crossed the ocean during the Tudor period of monarchy. Psychological causes are more important, however. The émigrés left the mother country feeling no superiority over one another, convinced that to accomplish something good they had to work for it themselves and finally, sure that the freedom they sought had nothing aristocratic about it (cf. Tocqueville, DA, 31-32). The phenomenon that led to the creation of the American people was quite singular. There was no distinction between gentlemen or common people, rich or poor, just individuals, placed on a level of perfect *equality*, driven solely by exile and the austerity of life to bring about the triumph of the need for *freedom*. In America, the fundamental principles of modern constitutions would take concrete form over time: participation of the people in public affairs, a vote not bound by taxes, the accountability of those who govern, individual liberty and trial by jury (cf. Tocqueville, DA, 43). Above all, in America, there were two elements which modern Europe had ended up pitting one against the other: *the spirit of religion and spirit of liberty.* Religion, freed from the clutches of politics, feels all the more stable when it can count on its own strength. Liberty thereby ends up seeing in religion the companion in all of its struggles and triumphs as well as the divine source of all its rights (cf. Tocqueville, DA, 47-48). This relationship between religion and liberty is crucial because, in democracies, people end up loving equality without any sense of measure: at times it is possible to be resigned to suffering defeats in matters of freedom, whereas people prefer to die rather than lose equality. Thus, the religious spirit performs a great service to the democratic cause in the United States. All the religions support democratic institutions. The Catholics themselves, concludes Tocqueville with admiration, are continually increasing in number because they manage to be the most submissive of the faithful and the most independent citizens. It should, however, be said that even with the diversity of religions, each one finds a place in the great Christian unity, the moral of Christianity is the same everywhere (cf. Tocqueville, DA, 334-336).

7.37 To understand where this love for equality comes from, one must consider the principle of popular sovereignty which is, in actual fact, practically dogma in the United States. Its importance is equal to its effectiveness since it is not a sterile and abstract principle, as it seems in other nations, but recognized by customs and proclaimed by laws. Thus, one can say that American society "acts upon itself by itself", possesses all the powers and cannot even conceive of any other power outside of itself. The people participate in the making of the laws, choose their legislators and carry out the laws by electing the members of the executive. Popular sovereignty extends into the political sphere as God exercises his in the universe (cf. Tocqueville, DA, 60-63). This popular sovereignty departs from an institution which constitutes the force of free peoples: the local community. Here is where the individual begins to become accustomed to the spirit of liberty, understands its function and its limits, but also learns to protect himself or herself from the possible abuses of the despotism of the majority. Every citizen can perform the various functions that a community performs. These are compensated and thus enable the poor to devote their time to them. It should be recalled that this does not mean that the American system gives officials a set salary. Those who perform certain functions have a fee of their own for each act officially performed, thus they are remunerated in proportion to what they have done. Culture, wealth, origins, etc., do not distinguish individuals from one another. Each is considered equal to the others and, as far as reciprocal duties among citizens are concerned, has become subject to the laws that govern society. For that which does not concern others but individuals, they are free and answer only to God for their actions (cf. Tocqueville, DA, 69-70).

7.38 Communities enjoy genuine autonomy, but submit to the State when another, greater interest comes into the picture, and they share this with other bodies. To ensure further possibilities for participation and greater protection from a central power, the county was created, and it deals with purely administrative matters. It is the first judiciary centre and possesses a court of justice. County administrators have limited powers as well as exceptional ones which they apply in just a few cases which have been provided for and established. All of this leads to the conclusion that there is no State in the world in which the law has such absolute value and in which the right to carry it out is shared by so many hands (cf. Tocqueville, DA, 76-78). Public functions, in any case, always come about through election. Individuals choose their administrators amongst themselves and control them in the territory where they perform their functions and within the existing rules. After the communities and counties comes a legislative power of the State exercised by a legislative body divided into two branches. This conclusion was reached because the principle of the independence of the States triumphed in the formation of the Senate, that of national sovereignty in the composition of the House of Representatives (cf. Tocqueville, DA, 131). The Americans certainly did not wish to create a hereditary or aristocratic assembly but an elected, hence democratic one. Here, too, it was a practical necessity that led to distinguishing senators from representatives. Granting the former the possibility of being appointed for several years, the law sought to maintain some individuals among the legislators who were already experienced in performing certain functions hence capable of offering a positive contribution to the newly elected ones (cf. Tocqueville, DA, 93). From the base to the summit a decentralization was achieved, which no other State could accomplish without serious problems. The Americans, however, have fully understood the need for a central administration and, at the same time, that a central power, *"quelque éclairé, quelque savant qu'on l'imagine, ne peut embrasser à lui tous les détails de la vie d'un grand peuple"* (Tocqueville, DA, 100-101). The measure was dictated by the problem of political effectiveness. The Americans benefit from decentralization obtaining a series of advantages which they could not do without. Those advantages are often linked to individual liberty which no democracy could guarantee, without truly functioning local institutions.

7.39 The majority, which tends to become more and more absolute anywhere, did not increase the competences of the central power. It made it omnipotent in its sphere, but outside of this it placed precise limits on its action. The central executive body is extremely strong in its area, but the "jurist" is no less strong. Those who perform this duty on behalf of the people seem, in America, to be separated from it. In the United States a European-style aristocracy does not exist. Yet, if aristocratic principle were to be spoken of, this would not be found in terms of wealth or culture. The real American aristocrats are the jurists. This is a widespread body ranging from lawyers to judges and they constitute a true check and balance for democracy. The American judiciary can bring proceedings for a question of unconstitutionality, and thus it ends up having control over political matters (cf. Tocqueville, DA, 308-309). Jurists are not highly visible, hence not feared, yet they carry considerable weight. The picture is completed by the institution of the jury which seems really to place the direction of the society in the hands of the people, but, above all, the jury serves to form in the minds of all the citizens a portion of the practices of the judge, practices which help the people to be truly free. The practice of having juries infuses in everyone a respect for the case being judged, teaches the practice of equity and induces people not to shirk their own responsibilities; it can thus be considered as a sort of free school, always open, which teaches public spiritedness to the population (cf. Tocqueville, DA, 314-315): the most effective way to teach everyone to govern and to instil in them a sense of responsibility. It must have surprised European observers that the President of the Union was considered responsible for his deeds, whereas French law still maintained that the person of the King was inviolable.

7.40 Tocqueville's fear is that the majority may set up a tyranny of its own. The Americans had succeeded in avoiding this not only for the previously-mentioned reasons, but also because the majority of the United States is, in actual fact, made up of citizens who, whether out of interest or as an aspiration, wish for the well-being of their country above all. For this reason, they created parties and, in general, associated with one another (cf. Tocqueville, DA, 194). All of that determines the formation of American public opinion, the strong point of democracy. This public opinion does not know religious or class hatred, which exasperate Europe, and it concentrates on concrete problems, seeking possible solutions. Public opinion manifests itself thanks to a freedom of the press which, in Europe, is unthinkable. On this subject, too, Tocqueville shows considerable balance. Journalism, rhetoric and, we might say, political jargon worry him because of their superficiality. Political language, whether written or oral, tends to change continually in democracies. New words are introduced, even when they are not needed, because of a simple desire for novelty, but this does not always contribute to the clarity of ideas. Word meanings are multiplied and end up creating doubt. Tocqueville does not hesitate to say that he would prefer his own language with Chinese or Tartar words over vague French words (cf. Tocqueville, DA, 577-579). Despite this, he is convinced that a movement typical of democracy must necessarily affect the means of communication, too, as long is it does not become a form of abuse and so he ultimately accepts the freedom of the press. Although he is not entirely pleased with it, he maintains that he appreciates it "for the evils that it prevents, more than the good that it does". Furthermore, when everyone is granted a political right to exercise, the right of the person to be able to choose between the various opinions that disturb his or her contemporaries must be acknowledged. The sovereignty of the people and freedom of the press are two principles related to one another (cf. Tocqueville, DA, 202-204). A demonstration of this is the fact that there is not a town in the United States that does not have its own newspaper. It brings people together and makes it possible to develop another means of ensuring liberty: the tendency to form associations. The need for association is a typically American one for Tocqueville. From the day of birth, the inhabitant of the new world learns that he or she must count only on himself or herself and must not expect any aid from the political authority, except in the cases provided for. Thus, associations are formed to accomplish the goals of public safety, commerce, industry, morality, religion, purposes which can be more easily be attained through association. Freedom of the press offers considerable support to the formation of associations. It leads to the possibility of meeting and then, if there are political motivations, those who support an opinion they share can appoint those by whom they want to be represented in a central meeting (cf. Tocqueville, DA, 212-214). The possibility for forming associations, even for political purposes, is unlimited in the United States and constitutes yet another defence against the tyranny of the majority.

7.41 Many in Europe see a danger in this freedom of association, but anyone who reasons that way is inexpert in matters of freedom. Suffice it to realize that in America one can even associate when in a minority to thwart the moral domination of the majority and call any political argumentation of one's adversaries into question. Furthermore, what helps to moderate the violence of political associations in the United States is universal suffrage. Associations well know that they can never represent the majority, otherwise they would not need to associate to change the rules, hence they must be capable of respecting political adversaries and government which those rules guarantee. This is a case where extreme democracy prefigures the dangers of democracy (cf. Tocqueville, DA, 218-219). One of the negative sides of this way of participating in political affairs is that distinguished personalities rarely emerge. Charlatans know how to please the people and can keep themselves more in view, but knowing how to select people of merit is one of the abilities that seems to be lacking in democracies. The people seem to entertain little benevolence towards the upper classes or overly well educated people: "they do not fear the great minds, but they do not like them very much". Furthermore, it is not only the people who keep distinguished persons away from power, but the latter themselves shun political life in which they would have to make too many compromises (cf. Tocqueville, DA, 222-224). On this point, too, one exception: it is to be found in the Senate chamber. This can perhaps be explained by the difference in election method.

7.42 When democracy allows the concrete manifestation of individual liberties, an increasing well-being is usually the result. Liberty produces more benefits than it destroys and the same is true for the resources of the people which increase more quickly than taxes. This happens because governments have a different way of absorbing and spending. In aristocracies, money benefits the ruling class above all. Democracy, obviously that which defends and enhances liberty, gives little to the governing forces and a great deal to those governed. This sort of diversity is noticeable not only in internal politics, but also in foreign. However, Tocqueville maintains with a trace of aristocratic pride, the peoples who have most influenced the world, encouraged by great projects, from the Romans to the English, were led by an aristocracy (cf. Tocqueville, DA, 243 and 263). The democratic system, however, remains the preferable one because, if its defects are clear and visible to everyone, its qualities seem hidden and are revealed only with the passage of time, without considering the fact that the democratic system is certainly the one best adapted for bringing prosperity to society. More over, less honest and capable governors may operate in a democracy, but the citizens are better informed and more attentive. Power, that of magistrates too, may be misused, but those who hold it exercise it for a determined period of time and know that they can be removed. Finally, democracy may not favour the prosperity of everyone, but at least that of the majority (cf. Tocqueville, DA, 264-267).

7.43 Democracy must, then, be defended, but it must also be capable of maintaining its true prerogatives. This position is quite similar to that of Montesquieu. "After the idea of virtue, I know no other one more beautiful than that of rights". The two ideas seem to blend together so that the idea of rights is none other than that of virtue brought into the political world. As there are no great men without virtue, so there are no great peoples without the respect for rights. It is the latter that determine the limit beyond which people move towards license or tyranny (cf. Tocqueville, DA, 272). The reference to Montesquieu and to virtue implies a very close link between law and morality, understood in terms of custom, mentality, that which was called the *mos maiorum* in ancient times, and within which civil life took form. For this reason there is a grand idea of political rights in America, because they are the very raison d'être of civil life: the rights of others must be respected if one expects one's own to be. It is this awareness that activates both the individual and the civil society of a democratic State. Suffice it to move from a free State to one which is not, to go from activity to immobility, from prosperity to apathy (cf. Tocqueville, DA, 277). Truly democratic governments let things be done within the rules and never feel themselves to be omnipotent. The problem, Tocqueville seems to be saying, is to see to it that these rules are obeyed by everyone. There is no doubt that this is so for the population which has established itself freely on the new continent, but what about the other two races, native Americans and blacks? Can the same be said for them? The observations on the relationships that may occur in times to come among the future inhabitants of United States territory are extremely interesting (cf. Tocqueville, DA, 367 ff.).

7. 44 The second book of *De la démocratie en Amérique*, which came out in 1840, enabled Tocqueville to deepen his reflection – which we may describe as cultural in character – which examined the American nation as a whole. The renewed contact with France, reflection from a distance away from the United States and political duties that had arisen made possible that comparative analysis that make the work not only a classic of political thought, but a text in which points of interest to political studies, too, end up being intertwined with sociological, psychological and moral ones to the point of turning it into a sort of "encyclopaedic mirror" of the American situation at that moment. The French thinker attaches great importance to his thought on the cultural state of the time, even if the latter has not been adequately analyzed. A fall in cultural tension is a synonym of decadence. A sort of rather hazardous barbarity threatens us and we cannot believe that it is far off when there are peoples whose desire for knowledge weakens, and others who extinguish it (cf. Tocqueville, DA, 557-558). At the moment the love for the arts, science and culture in America is surely different from what the French demonstrate. It may be more pragmatic and utilitarian but, at least for the moment, it is present and vital. Tocqueville's concern is that aggressiveness and crudeness, often evident in the pioneering spirit, which judges everything solely in terms of money, may degenerate, compromising the total development of a people who, in order to be just that, must be harmonious. For the moment, this pragmatism is directed towards the public good and shows the need Americans have for one another, as if they felt a continual obligation to help one another. This is the origin of that need for association which, in democracies, gives rise to the sort of

set of intermediary bodies that equality alone would tend to eliminate (cf. Tocqueville, DA, 624). It is a way, along with federalism, to enable the individual not to depend directly on the central authority.

7.45 Tocqueville had *a new way of making history*. As Furet says, he introduced America to the Europeans not as the child of our continent, but as our future. This aim led him to analyze the past with a notable sensitivity to the present. The past serves to foresee. Thus, there is the close analysis of the three states of French society: next to a Church which has become a political body distant from the population, the analysis of a nobility precariously balanced between monarchy and the people – and incapable of opposing either one. Finally there is the *Third Estate* which, recalling Sieyès but not just him, can be said to be creating a new people, but *is giving rise to an aristocracy of its own*. What is the consequence on the political and institutional level? For Tocqueville there is an enormous one: as an aristocratic society tends towards local government, a democratic one, finding expression in the third estate, tends towards governmental centralization. This explains why the idea of common law was replacing that of privilege (cf. Furet, 173-177). Even the French Revolution did not seem to him so much a break, as a process. Reaching the point of abolishing not so much the aristocracy as the principle of aristocracy, the sole opportunity for social resistance to the centralized state, had been eliminated. The phenomenon had, in fact, begun at the time of Richelieu. Expansion of the centralized state had thus been accelerated, bringing out the predominance of administrative power over the communities and civil society (cf. Furet, 28-30). This is why it can be said that Tocqueville does not deal with a period, but rather a problem, that is, the fact that the Revolution is the logical continuation of the Ancien Régime (cf. Furet, 33). For this reason, the period studied by Tocqueville is quite extensive and gives considerable space to the reign of Louis XIV, even though it is, in general, a study of the entire pre-revolutionary society.

7.46 The study of French society up to 1789 departs from the *cahiers* drawn up by the three estates which, for Tocqueville constitute the testament of eighteenth-century France, the expression of its wishes, and manifestation of its will (cf. Tocqueville, ARR, 45). These *cahiers de doléance* were the memorials which the electors of the three Orders sent to their representatives at the Estates General when they met. From these came reports from the various districts that cast light on the real condition of the nation. This material explained why the revolution broke out "*chez nous plutôt qu'ailleurs*" and why the French once again took up part of what they had left behind, despite the first phase in which they had left the impression of wanting to destroy everything (cf. Tocqueville, ARR, 47). An extremely interesting picture of the situation emerges, one of instability for a considerable amount of time when everyone was gripped with the fear of losing ground and the mania of rising and making money. The relationship between the nobility and the bourgeoisie quite clearly shows these fears and manias. The collapse of the aristocracy, which had already been underway for some time, is one of the incontrovertible realities of modern France. Tocqueville, convinced of its inevitability but also the risks, witnessed this and described it. He did not do this in a spirit of nostalgia typical of those who want to maintain certain privileges. The French thinker was certain that all those societies who tend to destroy the aristocracy more than do others will have more trouble avoiding an absolute government: for a population, destroying the aristocracy means hurtling towards centralization (cf. Tocqueville, ARR, 50 and 131-132). This does not mean saving at all costs a class that has come down with "*une débilité sénile*", has not been able to change, and understand the changing times, as had happened in England. Rather, it means contemplating a renewed élite capable of experiencing democracy in such a way as to avoid the system's degeneration. Defeated by the Revolution, the aristocracy had no longer influenced France's political and juridical life for a long while, but kept awkward privileges and costly rights. The lost of functions performed in the past thus increased the burden of the privileges (cf. Tocqueville, ARR, 92-95).

7.47 One fact is remarkable, namely, for Tocqueville, the new administrative officials, almost all coming from the bourgeoisie, made up a sort of "*aristocratie de la société nouvelle*" already existing and ready to take the place of the old one. It was waiting only for the Revolution, to take the place of the old class. Herein lies the strength of the new bureaucrats convinced that they had acquired a power that was not likely to curtailed. It should not be forgotten that in France the government tolerates anything whatsoever. Any theory or religious principle can be discussed. Even the basic principles upon which a society is based can be attacked, even God can be called into question, as long as the smallest representative of the State, the lowest of its agents, is not censured (cf. Tocqueville, ARR, 136). The bourgeois acquired a new political importance which led them to separate from the people, as the aristocracy had once tried to distinguish itself from the bourgeoisie which now directed the political centralization of France. Upon closer look, however, this seems to be one of the ancient characteristics of all the French governments who have never imitated those executive figures who claim to want to be involved in everything and then navigate in the most apathetic sterility possible. On the contrary, in France the government wants to do everything, even what is above its capacity or what is out of the control of private individuals. For this reason one new rule follows another with such suddenness that even those who must apply them find it difficult to understand them. Even though the laws do not change, further evidence of the importance acquired by the bureaucracy, the ways in which they are applied do (cf. Tocqueville, ARR, 168-169 and 138-139). The nation thus moves towards a veritable worship of the state. As for the government "*ayant pris ainsi la place de la Providence, il est naturel que chacun l'invoque dans ses nécessités particulières*" (Tocqueville, ARR, 144). This form of centralization had got underway a long time ago in the *ancien regime* when all forms of municipal autonomy were gradually being eliminated. All that also explains why the French passion for "jobs" arose long before the Revolution and was continually increasing with the increasing prestige and force that was coming about as a result of those jobs (cf. Tocqueville, ARR, 170).

7.48 In his analysis of the United States, Tocqueville had already underscored the importance, albeit indirect, of religion even though he came to favour the strict separation of Church and State. Equally important are the considerations on the French Church about which a series of commonplaces circulated, as they still do. Tocqueville does not deny that eighteenth-century culture was irreligious, but he wishes to emphasize the fact that Christianity had given rise to criticism not so much as religious doctrine, but as a political institution. Priests were accused not so much of claiming the right to govern matters of the other world, but because they wanted to be the administrators and owners in this one. That explains why people saw "*graduellement la puissance de l'Eglise se relever dans les esprits et s'y raffermir*" as the clergy set aside all that concerned landed wealth and land agreements. This phenomenon is not just French since there is not a Christian church in Europe that did not flourish once again after the Revolution. This must not come as a surprise with Tocqueville because there is nothing in Christianity or in Catholicism that is contrary to democracy. Thus, believing that democratic societies are naturally hostile to religion "*est commettre une grande erreur*" (cf. Tocqueville, ARR, 63-64). His considerations on the clergy are quite valuable: more forcibly than others, they support the right of the nation to make laws and vote freely on taxes: he maintains that no-one should pay a tax that he or she themselves or a representative do not want. He calls for the free election of the Estates General, their annual convening, and wants assemblies of the three estates to be created in order to guarantee genuine decentralization, as happened in the ancient citizens' municipalities. Despite personal failings during the revolutionary crisis, the clergy possessed public virtues and an authentic spirit of faith, as the persecutions they underwent showed. Tocqueville was not afraid to admit that he began to study ancient society "*plein de préjugés contre lui; je l'ai finie, plein de respect*". Indeed, the only well educated person with a bit of culture who remained in contact, in all the senses of the word, with the peasant masses was not the philosopher but the curate (cf. Tocqueville, ARR, 198 and 210). The fact that Tocqueville, speaking of some of the characteristics of the clergy, ends up by making observations close to those of Balmes is curious.

7.49 The religious phenomenon must be viewed in terms of concrete matters. Concreteness was not always the motivation of the revolutionaries who, at times, considered *"le citoyen d'une façon abstraite, en dehors de toutes les sociétés particulières"* (Tocqueville, ARR, 71). Sooner or later this abstraction leads to delusion and unbelief. It is apparently one of the evils that came out of the modern world when, subsequent to criticism of official religion that drove not a few spirits away from Christianity gradually *"à l'hérésie avait succédé l'incrédulité"* (Tocqueville, ARR, 243). It was this abstractness, that encouraged that spasmodic need to create a sort of paradise on Earth, that led many to attack almost with fury the Christian religion, at times fanatically and in a true spirit of propagandizing. It is true that the Church was then, politically speaking, too, first among the powers and thus, the most detested of them, despite the fact that it was not the most oppressive, but it is also true that it was attacked because people had not yet understood that the religious phenomenon should be distinguished from the political one, as in the United States. Unfortunately in France, but in Europe in general, they were far from achieving what came out of the Revolution: the distinction between Church and State institutions, preventing the former from becoming the basis and model for the latter (cf. Tocqueville, ARR, 243-245). The hostility towards the ecclesiastical power can be explained by the fact that the latter controlled and censured all movements of thought from on high, from its moral authority. This was why the Church had to be opposed and also why the civil authority, at some time, felt almost authorized to replace it. Once, however, its temporal power had weakened, it regained that vigour and importance that the American population acknowledged it to have. First the nobility, then the bourgeoisie returned to their faith for a variety of reasons depending on the outcomes of the Revolution (cf. Tocqueville, ARR, 246-249).

7.50 Abstraction was prevalent in the French culture of the time which, for example, speaking of equality, was not capable of seeing it in its proper light. According to Tocqueville, France, even before the Revolution, was the country in which men had become most equal to one another (see Ch. VIII of Book II). To be sure, a series of corrections had to be made to make equality more effective, but without yielding to the charms of any sort of utopia. Otherwise, there was the risk of imitating some of those philosophers who, while intuiting the need for the Revolution, had no idea of the dangers that this could lead to (cf. Tocqueville, ARR, 232). Why was French political life driven by often abstract intellectuals more than down-to-earth people capable not only of managing public affairs, but also opinions and the political debate? The answer lies in the fact that the centralization that had been under way in France for some time, had deprived the French people of the ability to deal *journellement* with administration and practical matters, and, for this reason, they were easily incited by the writers' ideas (cf. Tocqueville, ARR, 233-234). Despite the many positive aspects of the Revolution, when one studies it, one realizes that it was carried on "*dans le même esprit qui a fait écrire tant de livres abstraits sur le gouvernement*", the same disdain for real facts counterbalanced by extreme faith in theory, the same desire to rewrite the constitution "*au lieu de chercher à l'amender dans ses parties*". This is a constructivist mentality, as we would call it today, which also contaminates political language filled with generic expressions as well as ambitious and unfeasible architectural forms (cf. Tocqueville, ARR, 240).

7.51 For Tocqueville, eighteenth-century French society gradually gained new advocates: the *philosophes* and people of letters. Literature took on a political function and writers became a political force, perhaps the most important one. Writers tended to replace the fact with right, the calculation of interests with assessment of the means, goals and values with power and action. What was the result? Quite simply, the French, deprived of concrete and true liberties, turned to abstract liberty. This was that illusion of politics that Marx would speak of (cf. Furet, 57-59). Furthermore for Tocqueville – and it would suffice to read the pages on the peasant situation – French eighteenth-century society had disintegrated considerably due to monarchical centralization and the development of individualism: the Revolution thus presented itself as a noteworthy process of social and cultural integration (cf. Furet, 134-135). This disintegration also affected the individual classes: the nobility itself, would be defeated, because it offered no social or economic homogeneity. Concerning the peasant situation, Tocqueville brings out a particular paradox. The peasant of the end of the eighteenth century had already become one of the nineteenth in many ways, that is, a landowner independent of his lord. This had happened for three quarters of the countryside long before the Revolution, and made the leftover feudalism all the more unbearable. This continued to involve part of the territory and explains why the administration of the Ancien Régime was so different and heterogeneous (cf. Furet, 185-186 and cf. Tocqueville, ARR, Ch. I of book II).

7.52 This difficult situation makes a serious reflection on what political language seeks to describe necessary. "What creates the greatest confusion in the mind is the use made of the words *democracy, democratic institutions, democratic government.* As long as we fail to arrive at a clear definition of those upon which we agree, we will be surrounded by an inextricable confusion of ideas, entirely to the advantage of demagogues and despots (...) The words *democracy, monarchy,* and *democratic government* can mean only one thing, however, in terms of the true meanings of the words: a government in which the people participate more or less on a broad scale in governing. Its meaning is closely linked to the idea of political liberty" (cf. Furet, 191-192, whom Tocqueville quotes). These words offer something quite new, as Furet rightly maintains, since democracy is not only examined on a social level based on the criterion of equality, but also on the political level based on liberty and participation in the management of power. In fact, democratic transformation was rendered possible by the inability of the upper classes to keep power or give rise to a new one (cf. Furet, 192-193). What comes out as clear in the aged Tocqueville is that centralization favoured the development and spread of the democratic mentality, but also customs. This lucid observation makes the author of the *Ancien Régime* far less optimistic than that of the *Democracy in America.* Indeed, one can speak of pessimism because (and here I do not think I am forcing the interpretation of Tocqueville who, in this respect, seems on the same wavelength as Rosmini, who indeed pursued a different path) the total elimination of limitations placed democracy on the road to a process of abstraction that could also end up embarking upon utopian or revolutionary itineraries in absurd and dangerous ways.

7.53 The dangers that democracy would degenerate are evident in a famous *Discours prononcé à l'Assemblée constituante dans la discussion du projet de constitution (12 septembre 1848) sur la question du droit au travail.* This text is understood and misunderstood in a variety of ways, but could be read in a context in which socialism, which the French thinker opposes, had not yet taken on those social-democratic traits even with liberal colours which we know today. For this reason, he is quite close to a statist conception, which is too ignorant of the sphere of the individual. In the words of the discourse, the concern for a more and more invasive State comes out. At the end, this state becomes the sole owner of everything and sole arbiter of salaries, production and organization of labour (cf. Tocqueville, D, 1140). Moreover, there is the primary concern that all the socialist schools, as had been shown up to then, insisted uniquely on the material passions of man. Secondly they attack the very assumptions behind private property. Finally, they show a form of disdain for the individual who is lost in himself, seeking every way he can to reduce, mutilate and hinder human freedom. The State wants to be the tutor of everyone and each one and actually ends up expressing a new form of slavery (cf. Tocqueville, D, 1142-1143). People thereby called into question even the glorious aspects of the Revolution such as liberty and property arriving at the point of determining a form of subjugation far more dangerous than that which had existed in the Ancien Régime. Going back to a principle which I have already discussed in the preceding volume, Tocqueville warns against the age-old mania that Robespierre intuited, of wanting to govern too much and, anticipating Owen, warns that that desire for statist socialism would be a society made up of animals. In several conclusions in this *Discourse* some of the critics have seen in the French thinker an aristocratic and liberal mentality. However, with the intention of defending that democracy that he had so exalted, Tocqueville rejects this accusation in a few lines. Democracy and socialism seem to have in common only love for equality, but democracy wants it in liberty, whereas socialism wants it in restriction and in slavery (cf. Tocqueville, D, 1145-1147).

F) *The Debate on Christianity and Liberty: J. Balmes.*

7.54 Balmes discussion of "Protestantism" departs from the fact that "the Christian religion, as the Protestants explain it, is an opinion and nothing more; (…) which places Christianity on the level of the philosophical schools" (Balmes, 49). From that position, it is a short step from secularization first and then de-Christinization. It is the latter that Balmes seeks to prevent. He indeed believes that he has detected a worm that eats from within the most intimate motivations of religiosity and carries along "with itself the ruin of all Christian truths" (Balmes, 48-49). This draining out and these crises of Christian truths lead to disarticulation of the entire society and elimination of the order on which it rests. In a view which we would call Augustinian, the social order disintegrates from within as those truths and values that constitute its foundation disappear. At this point, it is no longer possibly to save the social bond and not even the most erudite legislators and their perfect laws to which Rousseau abstractly refers are useful. Everything turns out to be useless for the well-being of the body when its spirit is weak and corrupted. A people thus reduced must absolutely regenerate, finding in religion not only its strength, but also its civil bond which only Catholicism can guarantee. The historical importance of the Catholic Church and the historical reason behind the temporal power of the Papacy can be appreciated when one thinks of the limitations which both place on the corruption of customs and ferocity of barbarians. All the peoples of Europe were taught respect for property, love of work, keenness of culture, purity of customs and hence respect for one's neighbour (cf. Casanovas, 181). The firmness demonstrated by the Church gave rise to faith and security, hence, the slow recovery of all those values on which life in common is based. Here the authority of the Church, that very authority that the Reformation had come to criticize, finds its justification. Contesting the religious and dogmatic role of the Church meant weakening the very role that it could play in creating proper consciences. Clashes in dogma and social disorders went hand in hand as French history amply demonstrates (cf. Balmes, 366). The result was absolutism and the consequent restriction, if not the very disappearance of liberty.

In his brief and intense life (1810-1848) **Jaime Balmes** was deeply involved in his mission and cultural activities. He had many interests and was a multi-faceted personality capable of moving from the most lofty theoretical analysis – for example, he studied and taught mathematics – to practical, everyday-life occupations. In addition to his scholarly activities he worked on, founded and directed several publications that were read in various parts of Europe. Along with *El Protestantismo comparado col el Catolicismo,* to which this analysis refers, other works should be recalled for which the year of publication does not always correspond to that of writing and of the conclusion. Among these are the *Filosofia fundamental*, the *Filosofia elemental*, *El Criterio* noteworthy for their pedagological and methodological innovations and which have been used to train entire generations of Spanish speakers. The *Pio IX* is a particularly noteworthy piece of writing, in which the future alignments of the twentieth century are almost prophetically suggested.

7.55 Balmes always stresses concreteness. Arguing against Enlightenment abstractionism, he ironically draws attention to the fact that the "enlightened" revolutionary France, through the hand of an executioner, burned the work of P. Mariana *De rege et regis institutione.* It had been published in Spain eleven years earlier without any hindrances and perhaps it re-discovered the innermost logic behind power and institutions (cf. Balmes, 561) as well as, for that matter, democracy. The latter can be better achieved when law and not the people governs. Europe certainly did not discover this principle with the modern world, since this was one of its first and most ancient accomplishments (cf. Balmes, 672). What the modern world has forgotten, most likely, is that laws govern only if they have a soul which is felt and respected by the citizens so that they come to identify with them. When that does not happen there is a dangerous conflict between visible and invisible society and a period of chaos and anarchy ensues, even when one has the illusion of being in a democracy. It is easy, however, for Balmes to recognize this false democracy. "Its basic dogma has always been that of denying the authority of any order, and that has the constant purpose of destroying it; a tendency whose origin is not difficult to discover in the heart of man" (Balmes, 674). This is further proof that everything comes from inner life. The step from anarchy to despotism is not only a short one, but also full of consequences. Like Burke, Balmes sees in the Restoration, and in the Terror before that as well as in the strength of the Napoleonic armies the physical outcome of revolutionary theories which, ignorant of the relationship between the visible and invisible society, have thought they could uproot everything by pursuing abstractions. "Order is the primary need of societies; ideas, customs and laws must bow to it" (Balmes, 699). All of that is perceived and understood in all its importance only when order itself disappears and it is certainly not a matter of curiosity that among the various reasons for this crisis of order, Balmes brings out a typically Augustinian one: the abundance of wealth and glory. Balmes is not to be misunderstood. He is certainly not opposed to progress, as we would call it today, economic as well, but he sees in wealth and glory a danger, above all of a psychological nature, that is, interior once again: there is the danger that contentment and happiness will numb intelligence (cf. Balmes, 698).

7.56 Balmes never misses the chance to criticize those who have, in various ways, justified those heresies which, in the final analysis, have never achieved the aim for which they had been created, but have only caused great damage to the Church and the unity of the faithful. This consideration is particularly applicable to Protestantism and all its multiplicity of sects. "This plainly shows what the real spirit of the sixteenth-century innovators was. Far from attempting to correct abuses, they set forth to intensify them" (Balmes, 32). In Balmes' opinion, a similar consideration can be deduced from Guizot's writings themselves. In *Lesson XII*, of his famous *Histoire générale de la civilisation en Europe* (*General History of European Civilization*), the latter criticizes those who claim that the Reformation was an attempt to rebuild the original Church, not to mention those who have attempted to give rise to a pure Church. In support of this point he quotes some statements of Erasmus according to whom "the Reformation ends up in the secularization of some monks, and in the marriage of some priests" (Erasmus' sentence is quoted by Balmes, 31). Still concerning Guizot, one of the most delicate points dealt with by Balmes is that of liberty. From the Protestant point of view the Church is accused of constricting the freedom of thought where faith is concerned. In this area everything must be submitted to the authority of the ecclesiastical teachers incarnated by the Church, which Guizot calls "stationary" in other words, static. For Balmes, who shows himself actually to be an apologist on this question, the problem is that of determining what is meant by *liberty* and, above all, what its *limits* are. When the Protestants speak of freedom, they do so concerning dogmas, but they forget that dogmas, like logical and mathematical truths, cannot be modified to one's liking without eliminating all the postulates upon which Christianity itself is built. These dogmas had been the spirit of all of Christianity up to the Reformation. After the Reformation, the Catholic Church remained firmly anchored in them. "In actual fact more than eighteen centuries have passed in which the Church can be called *stationary* in its dogmas; and this is unequivocal proof that it alone is in possession of the truth: because the truth is *invariable* because it is *one*" (Balmes, 32). What has the Protestant world produced? ... idealist philosophy which finds its ultimate pillar in the Ego, with all the risks that that entails, not only gnoseological but also the consequent moral ones. In this perspective, moral ideals are no longer a permanent and universal echo (cf. Minguijon, 206 and 244) of human nature reaching out towards God. On the contrary, they risk stumbling on the terrain of pure subjectivity, hence utilitarianism.

7.57 Another major point in the argumentation against Guizot is the basic contradiction that comes out in the Protestants' analysis of the Church between the fifteenth and sixteenth centuries. They reveal in the Church the maximum "intolerance, cruelty, the inability to leave the human spirit in peace" (Balmes, 34). Otherwise they reveal a worldly Church, which had come to terms with modernity, and Guizot himself says, "that the ecclesiastical government was not tyrannical in the sixteenth century, but *condescending, tolerant* and would itself have *left the human spirit in peace*" (Balmes, 34). The Reformation, for Balmes, is, upon closer look, a sort of ever latent danger in the Church and, in the period in which it took place, it would have come to pass in any case, even if the ecclesiastical authority had shown amenability towards the reformers (cf. Balmes, 37), because the causes that motivated them were of quite a different nature. Behind religious needs, often a cover, there emerged the political interests of rising States, of local Principalities, in other words, interests involved in a European political situation that was changing. All of that is proven by the fact that the religious intentions of the reformers were gradually fading away. Guizot himself supports this idea when he states, and Balmes quotes him, that "people were not able to reconcile all the rights and needs of tradition with the claims for freedom. This doubtless comes from *not having fully understood and accepted the reformation or its principles, or its effects*" (Balmes, 43). What remains of an operation of the sort on a religious level? ... only the social and political consequences and the start of a latent secularization.

7.58 Another source of disagreement with Guizot is the distinction between the individual and the citizen. It could briefly be said that for both scholars, the citizen is nothing other than a mature individual. For the Frenchman, however, the root lies in the barbarian sense of individuality which manifests itself in the uncontrolled love for independence. For the Spaniard, on the contrary, if one only stopped at this it would be impossible to understand how it had been possible to depart from that brutal individuality, "that savage feeling of independence, which could neither be reconciled with the well being, nor with the true dignity of the individual" (Balmes, 216). According to Balmes, it was the Church that opened up the true path towards "civilizing". It revitalized Roman law and converted the barbarian peoples. In speaking of the virtues of the barbarian peoples and comparing those virtues with those of the Romans, Guizot, in Balmes' opinion, not only makes an error, but forces the point historically speaking. The Romans of the time of the barbarian invasions were "those Romans so eager to satisfy themselves, and so consumed by that fever of which history has kept for us such dismal pictures" (Balmes, 219-220). Certainly they are not those described by Cicero, Virgil and Tacitus who "after nineteen centuries continue to make generous hearts tremble" (Balmes, 220). The sense of individuality manifested by that civilization was far more complete than that manifested by the Germans. The latter had a feeling that was often a craving; the Romans, on the contrary, had their sense of individuality protected not only by laws, but also by the role of the authority that these offered. Christianity developed all of that further. To the authority of the law it revealed the basis of that very law: the authority of God. "It was Christianity that impressed on the heart of man the fact that the individual has his duties to perform even when the entire world rises up against him" (Balmes, 231-232). It gave the individual the precision and clarity of his traits enriching his personality and controlling bestial impulses, which, because of possible anarchical outlets, would dissipate its notable wealth. Without those rules the barbarians could not have set up a civil society which, in Balmes' view, is constituted when the individual places limits on his action and, above all, knows that he cannot obey his conscience alone, since a public life exists as well as a private one. Only after awareness of the latter has come about "does our conscience tell us whether we have operated well or badly, excusing or condemning us, rewarding us with peacefulness of heart or tormenting us with remorse" (Balmes, 278). This, however, is not the first step to arrive at a realization of something far more important, that is "that the private conscience may be right or in error, just or lax, and the same is true for the public one" (Balmes, 278). This contribution came from Christianity alone and Protestantism, with its free self-examination without any sort of religious authority, has greatly jeopardized it. For Balmes, the Church is a source of security. The structures are, in the final analysis, instruments which, on not a few historical occasions, have been able to safeguard not only the true freedom of conscience of the individual, but also his physical safety since it constitutes the sole authentic bulwark against the abuses of secular power which, as the experiences of Protestant lands show, would not have an alternative capable of hindering it.

7.59 In 1848, Balmes and François René de Chateaubriand died just a few days apart from one another (Chateaubriand was born in 1768). He had experienced the most dramatic events in French history and had, after a critical period, ended up filling political positions of a certain prominence. His was a personality full of conflict and one worth recalling for political reasons, since he interpreted and summarized some aspirations of the era with originality, even though, at times, with contradictions. In his *Génie du christianisme* he sought to show that the Christian religion was more humane and more favourable to the development of freedom of the arts and sciences than any other. This way he arrived at aesthetic positions capable of emphasizing the important of feeling, typically in line with Romantic ideals. Freedom, *the greatest of goods and the foremost of human needs*, was inseparably bound to religion so that there cannot be a true religion without liberty nor a true liberty without religion (cf. Chateaubriand, 3). After the equalitarian manias of the revolution and the imbalances of the period of the Empire, this liberty seemed to have been recovered in the period of the Restoration. Hence there was that devotion to the past (cf. Chateaubriand, 317), rediscovered and renewed after the Congress of Vienna, which led people to forget that it was the legitimate monarchy that had been one of the causes of the revolution in the first place. However, that position showed the weariness which had spread over much of Europe and its better understanding. Like Chateaubriand, it was taking a new look at some of its overly radical positions of the past.

8. Religion and Liberty

8.1 A brief look at the past is necessary prior to a discussion of liberal thought. It will be immediately clear that it is inappropriate to speak of liberalism *tout court*, but more suitable to speak of various forms of this. The phenomenon had its origin in various parts of Europe after the era of absolutism. The desire was, first of all, to return to that concept of limits in politics that had accompanied much of classical and medieval thought. Secondly, it arose as an eudaemonological need in the sense that part of society was heading towards a more secular dimension, so that the need was felt to obtain complete satisfaction and no longer maintain an attitude of "after our time" but rather here, on Earth, as soon as possible and for a large number of individuals. This earthly view of happiness caused the most religious of spirits to reflect on eudaemonology as well. For them, the quest for happiness did not nullify – nor was it in opposition, if based on some assumptions, to – the Christian view of life and its eschatology. Perhaps the most characteristic case can be found in the thought of Rosmini. His reading of liberalism can be deduced basically from studies on the subject which have now become classics. Suffice it to realize that De Ruggiero finds in the nineteenth-century English religious movement a characteristic component of British liberalism in religious England, divided among Anglicans, dissidents, Catholics and exponents of *Dissent*, a sort of backbone of English liberalism (cf. Pezzimenti, PTLA, 11). This consideration seems to me also to come out of that uncompleted monument, the *History of Liberty* of Acton, in which liberalism is identified as a gradually obtained fruit of western history to which several theoreticians of political Catholicism have offered a determining contribution since medieval times. That conviction was to lead the overwhelming majority of the so-called liberal Catholics who remained sincerely faithful to their religion, were practicing and who entertained no doubts in religious matters, to be of the opinion that the Church had everything to gain from the new way of understanding political engagement. Engaged Catholics are also "convinced that representative orders, the parliamentary system, the various liberties, freedom of press above all, have triumphed, and that there is no reason to hope for a return to absolute regimes; and they believe that it is in the Church's interest to accept, reconcile, and not indulge in dangerous hopes for restorations" (Jemolo, CL, 417).

8.2 That conclusion was furthered by several events in the life of the Church of the first half of the nineteenth century, which seemed to justify the liberal Catholics. First of all, although the Roman Curia had been going through a very conservative period, for various reasons, it never supported the Holy Alliance seen as a dangerous expression of a total equalization of the various religions. Secondly, for the most varied reasons, the Church openly opposed the Holy Alliance to the point of taking a stand against it. One need only recall the difficult years 1830 and '31 when the Catholics, side by side with the liberals themselves, encouraged by the religious authorities, played a fundamental role in achieving the independence of Belgium. *This prudent assessment of liberalism by the Catholic hierarchy shows that every episode must be seen through different eyes and in consideration of the contingencies of time and place.* It is quite singular, in fact, that towards the end of the century,

Leo XIII, speaking of the situation of Polish Catholics under Russian domination, could maintain that everything had been complicated by the fact that the oppressors, in this case, were deprived of a man like Gladstone (cf. Pezzimenti, PTLA, 21). Was saying that the Russians were lacking a politician of that sort not the same as pointing out that in political matters nothing, not even the most genuinely liberal of intentions, can be invented *ex novo*? From the above comes a crucial point in understanding liberty from a Catholic point of view. It means that an interpretation of the liberal idea, for Catholics, cannot be performed from an Enlightenment point of view, that is, abstractly. Liberty cannot be spoken of, indeed, by taking it out of the historical context in which it grew up with its difficulties and contradictions, often not only national but also international. This means that from a Catholic point of view liberty is the fruit of a difficult historical journey which rests on the tradition of many centuries. The historical thought of liberal Catholics is not to be differentiated from Enlightenment abstractionism alone, but also from deterministic and dialectic historicism that has permeated European culture in the last two centuries. History – it would be sufficient to reread Acton, Newman, but also Rosmini – is not bound by any dialectic determinism, it has no pre-established earthly goals since it is the history of intelligence and liberty, hence it does not recognize any type of solution that can be called definitive. History thus understood is differentiated from historicism, which can be considered its most deleterious aspect. When, for Catholics, one speaks of history, one means then an analysis of reality which, as has already been said, cannot be considered in the abstract categories of the dialectical method, but must be understood as a constant moral effort typical of those societies which, in some way, have been affected by Christianity.

8.3 There is another aspect that is also worthy of consideration: liberalism itself, in its broadest meaning. It is a highly varied universe which often, because of some of its extremes, encounters difficulties in being accepted even in the most "open" of States. If, indeed, there is a liberalism which perfectly well realizes that there cannot be law if an authority capable of protecting it is lacking, there is also, on the contrary, a radical liberalism which is inclined to ignore the fact "that individuals do not always pursue the logic of their own interest with total coherence, and are, in fact, inclined to pursue poorly understood utility, in conflict with that of others, which, in the final analysis, is ruinous for their own interest, as well" (De Ruggiero, 99). It is to distinguish themselves from this liberalism that liberal Catholics insisted on a concept of liberty based on tradition, because, only that could guarantee a balance of liberty itself. Keeping a distance from radical liberalism meant, for many liberal nineteenth-century Catholics keeping a distance from the liberal conception that had come out of the French revolution, because the latter conceived of freedom in clear opposition not only to the past, but to religion, too. For Catholics all that seemed a contradiction in terms of both the historical and theoretical points of view. This is why when arguing, for example, against Enlightenment figures Catholics do not think that "man was born free, as Rousseau suggested, but must conquer liberty among all the contradictions of history and society, with an effort that involves every individual, including those whom the humanitarian philosophers had deemed insignificant" (Passerin D'Entrèves, OCL, 101). Equipped with that theoretical baggage, liberal Catholics faced the confrontation with history with the aid, depending on their culture of origin, of Vico, Herder or Burke, with more or less everyone going back to an approach towards a philosophy of history which is typically Augustinian (cf. Traniello, 151).

A) *The Multifaceted Patrimony of French Catholicism.*

8.4 For the entire century, France was, more than elsewhere, a flowering of movements, publications and original thoughts that influenced every other Catholic – and not just Catholic – state. French Catholicism, naturally more than any other liberal Catholic experience, found itself having to deal with the revolution of 1789 and its consequences. First, the so-called legitimist Catholicism manifested itself especially in the thought of Joseph de Maistre and Louis de Bonald, It saw Religion "as the foundation and constituting principle of every political order, in the light of a new conception of history, against the rationalism and philosophy of the revolution. Maistre and Bonald's criticisms were directed towards individualism promoted by the reform provisions of revolutionary legislators; the individual does not exist outside of society: considered as a single individual, in possession of his or her own rights to liberty and a new sovereign will, this is a mere abstraction" (D'Addio, SDP, II, 244). Individuals, outside the context in which they operate, act outside the tradition and culture which provide them with the language in which they expresses themselves, are reduced to an abstract conception that has no meaning. Thus that "debt" to history which is one of the bases of Catholic liberalism of every latitude comes out. Institutions cannot be invented *ex novo* because the values and principles from which they draw inspiration are the result of a slow and long process. Society, conceived of as unity-totality has its roots in the far distant and so greatly maligned Medieval period whose soul was to be found in Christianity and which enabled the modern age to offer the best of the fruits of liberty. It is only the Christian religion itself that keeps society together, guarantees its unity, identity and continuity. This explains why society must build the real foundation of the State (cf. D'Addio, SDP, II, 245). That view, defended several times by Maistre and Bonald, had its value on the level of doctrine, but, unfortunately, ended up identifying the cause of Catholicism with that of an Ancien Régime which called for monarchical legitimism. In this analysis there was not that serenity in viewing the past typical of Tocqueville's thought.

B) *Religion as the Basis of Liberty: F. R. de Lamenais.*

8.5 The events in Belgium, Poland then Ireland (keeping in mind the difficulty in the latter cases of settling emigrants on English territory) led not a few to take a fresh look at the relationship between religion and politics in an attempt to go beyond the rigid schemes of the Restoration. Without doubt, Lamennais (1782-1854) was the foremost of these. In his opinion, religion, as the legitimists would have it, loses all of its greatest spiritual energy, all its value, because it turns into supine resignation to the existing political order and stifles all of its innovative force. Furthermore, Lamennais believed that Christianity, in view of a cosmopolitan and universalist message (cf. Derré, 62-63), had to go beyond the narrow schemes of collaboration on a national level between the crown and forces, even if religious ones, of the Restoration. For this reason he claimed for the Church autonomy and independence from the State. In virtue of that autonomy, the Church could better understand, and also facilitate, that path towards democracy that the Restoration States, on the contrary, were hindering in every possible way, failing to realize the futility of their action. Democracy is, in fact, an inherent part of the historical process of modern Europe; seeking to ignore this or to bring it to a halt is an absurdity from which the Church has the obligation of disassociating itself. It will thereby succeed in preventing the State from interfering in the spiritual domain, in any case, that of the conscience, reminding the seat of power that its task solely involves juridical, political and administrative organization. However, the latter must not be unlimited, since it must also take account of the legitimate individual autonomies and natural centres of social aggregation (cf. D'Addio, SDP, II, 249-250).

8.6 The democratic process is inevitable because the peoples have now become the true protagonists of history. No-one can ignore this fact, Christianity included, and it has always been the true driving force of revolutions, "the driving force and the first cause" (Lamennais, 541) because the needs for liberty and equality came from Christianity. Aware of this relentless process, Lamennais is convinced that Christianity must fight to eliminate inequality, starting from practices of exploitation to abolishing any condition of privilege and monopoly (cf. D'Addio, SDP, II, 252).

8.7 Lamennais, de Maistre and Bonald had widely varying ideas, and this reflects how diversified the French Catholic world was. However, despite some conflicts, a sort of unity among most of its most representative personalities was maintained. It must be borne in mind that in France, more than in other countries, a liberal wing of Catholicism, side by side with a democratic one manifested itself. This is proven by the numerous publications which reflected the various ways of being Catholic in France: for example the *Correspondant, La Quinzaine* or *Le Bulletin de la Semaine* (cf. Gadille-Mayeur, 148-149). In addition to these forums, Catholics, with a typically French vivacity, debated in salons, in the country houses of some notables, in ecclesiastical circles and in universities as well. Obviously depending on where they were meeting, Catholics ended up in creating an identity. The legitimists very often met in the houses of notables, while liberals, not to mention the future democrats, went to less *à la page* locations (cf. Gadille-Mayeur, 152-155). The 1830-31 events in France and Belgium provided French Catholicism with new subjects for discussion and, above all, drew attention to the need or lack of need for autonomy of the Church from the State and to the relations between the State and the Holy See. The Belgian experience seemed to some a sign that it was also possible in Europe to create a free Church as in the United States. With Belgian independence, there were indications of a first surge of that Americanism that would be so important in Italy, too, several decades later. Returning to the events of 1830-31, it should be pointed out that, for French Catholics, the events of those years were reminiscent of some aspects of the French Revolution that liberal Catholics had always looked on with favour: the economic and social conceptions of liberalism as well as other forms of freedom, such as that of the press, of assembly, etc., in opposition to others who had reached the point of accepting division into classes as something that cannot be eliminated and, in a pessimistic view, something almost decreed by God himself. At this point a first conflict arises between those Catholics who oppose any intervention in the economy by the State and those who, appealing to more democratic and social ideals, called for it (cf. Gadille-Mayeur, 162). Among the former, the exponents of the School of Angers should be recalled, among the latter: Professors Jannet and Béchaux.

C) *The Difficult Existence of Italian Liberal Catholicism.*

8.8 In Italy, one of the best-known personalities in liberal Catholicism was certainly Manzoni (1785-1873). The need for his teaching is all "aimed at the interior person, inspired by an acute sense of the limitations of human action itself, as is shown in his *Osservazioni sulla morale cattolica* (1819) and by the calm irony of *I promessi sposi,* which made him view from a certain distance, if not open suspicion, the programmes of universal palingenesis, whatever their origins might be" (Gadille-Mayeur, 154). This is why, from a point of view that might be called Augustinian, Manzonian liberalism dampened the optimism of the radical liberals, who presented every achievement of liberty as the result of a long effort. In his historical investigations, furthermore, Manzoni revealed a "profound diffidence of any abuse of power, indeed a radical pessimism about the absolutization of power, even when it took on a democratic appearance. The concept of civil and political progress, which he did not reject, could not, therefore, be taken as a defence of the State" (Passerin D'Entrèves, P, 8). Thus, Manzoni bore witness to another constant in all Catholic liberalism: that of limiting the functions and intervention of the State. Conscience remains an insuperable limit not only for political power, but also for other authorities who might wish to exert religious pressures. "It is always the interior *dictamen* of the conscience that must lead the believer to accept Christian law which, moreover, is part of the order of grace and charity" (Passerin D'Entrèves, OCL, 100). Following the Gospel implies interior acceptance without which all is false. As has been properly observed, with his *Discorso sopra alcuni punti della storia longobardica,* Manzoni, following the example of Thierry and Guizot, was interested not only in conquered peoples, but also those classes from the high Medieval period to the seventeenth century who made up that Third Estate, that nascent bourgeoisie, which would be the fulcrum of future liberal society. In fact, it was the highly vilified Papacy that had been the sole defence against the harassment of the invaders on behalf of those classes, the conquered ones, who had been ignored for a long time. This conviction was again taken up and further developed by not a few other Catholics who, Tosti for example, went back still further in the past maintaining that, as early as the end of the Western Roman world, the universal vision of St Benedict managed to conserve, at Monte Cassino, the Roman code of liberty (cf. Croce, SCL, 122-123 and 141). Likewise Tosti, in Croce's opinion, had pointed out that only Catholicism could have kept the progress of civilisation on a moral basis with the solidity of its teachings.

8.9 The reflections on the French Revolution seem interesting, even if debatable in some ways. In this Manzoni does not distinguish "two times that were not at all different: the first with benevolent and knowledgeable intentions and generous efforts: the second with delirium and villainy". No, the first deviations, or rather usurpations, had taken place right from the beginning" (Giuliani, 8). In Manzoni, there is a concern that would be shared by not a few other liberal spirits. There is "the implicit rejection of Jacobinism and the permanent revolution" (Sanguinetti, 15) that could even put the highly just aspirations of the rebels in jeopardy. That is not only considered in bringing out the differences between the American and French Revolutions, but showing, in more than one writing, that the real problem of the latter was that it remained "in effect, without a true government, at least in name, and without opposition" (Manzoni, RF, 37). There are many passages that show that this was one of the real problems left unsolved by the revolution. The terror thus turned out to be inevitable, since no policy can be carried out without an authority, which may be different in nature, but, in itself cannot be eliminated. Any anarchical solution remains pure utopia. These considerations must be read in the light of a profound conviction of Manzoni's: in history, as in politics, a distinction must be made between the criteria of justice and utility. The former cannot be in contradiction with itself, while the latter, being a relative one, may be assessed in a variety of ways (cf. Manzoni, O, 273). In the case of the government, this means that the way it can operate is subject to discussion, but not the need for its existence. Existence virtually becomes a criterion of a moral nature and no exceptions can be made.

8.10 The "*Primato d'Italia* by Gioberti can be placed in the light of this. This book is a singular document testifying to the degree of exasperation that the national feeling had reached, furiously struggling against political oppression and moral shame" (Croce, SCL, 145). In fact, Croce brought out the merits of the historiographical investigation of the liberal Catholics who, after Vico, had explored events in Italian history that would otherwise have never come to light. However, he pointed at what, in his opinion, could be referred to as a certain bias (cf. Croce, SCL, 153-154 and 148), because the liberal Catholics remained within the most genuine orthodoxy above and beyond the choices made in common and, in any case, political ones.

D) *The Italian Renewal: V. Gioberti.*

8.11 Although the political action of Belgian Catholics represented a model for European liberal Catholicism, the results were not imitated in any tangible way. The reason is, unfortunately, very simple: elsewhere, in Italy especially, people failed to understand the importance of organizing the Catholic forces into a party. The most representative Italian intellectuals were, in part, hostile to the very idea of a party. "Gioberti considers parties as an element of weakness and dangerous division. Only after the crisis of Neo-Guelfism did Gioberti reach the point of intuiting the fruitfulness of civil struggles for which the parties are the protagonists" (Scoppola, 199). There was no other possibility: acceptance of Neo-Guelf ideas put those who subscribed to them in a universalistic perspective in clear-cut antithesis both to the ideals of the revolution and those of the reaction. It was the position of moderate Catholics who believed in a common and national Catholic policy inclined towards reforms such as freedom of the press, of assembly, and a policy of mediation among the various social classes (anticipating the popular and Christian-Democratic interclass collaboration) etc., capable of opposing the legitimist theories of the "reactionaries". The failure of those ideals was to bring about more careful consideration of positions that were more in line with prospects for creating parties.

Vincenzo Gioberti was born in Turin in 1801 in a family with a modest social background. He devoted himself to the study of theology, philosophy and letters. In 1826, a year after entering the priesthood, he was appointed Court Chaplain. In the years that followed, he had important encounters with the greatest exponents of Italian culture of that period such as Leopardi, Manzoni, and Rosmini. After having embraced Mazzinian ideals and supported several revolutionary uprisings, in 1833, he was released from his position as Court Chaplain, arrested and then exiled. After a long period of time in France and Belgium, he returned to Italy in 1848. It was practically a triumph for him in a country that was going through a period in which Pius IX spoke of "Catholic universalism", as if to confirm the political positions of Gioberti. After the reverses of 1849 he retired to private life in Paris where he died in 1852. Aside from the numerous works of noteworthy theoretical value, *Del primato morale e civile degli italiani* (1843) and *Del rinnovamento civile dell'Italia* (1851) merit attention here.

8.12 Especially when he was in contact with the French spirit, Gioberti took on their combative approach with the intention of defending religion from those who considered it to be in contrast with modern civilization. Gioberti went well beyond that. He sought to "bring science back to religion and bind it closely to it; refresh and reinvigorate religion, imbuing it with – and causing it to acknowledge the new, legitimate needs of the advanced human spirit" (Gentile, 753). In the light of this, there are those who have called Gioberti "one of the greatest reformers that the Church ever had in Italy" (Del Noce, 195). These reformist ideals sought to go far beyond the extremes of reactionary conservation or revolutionary innovation. The task was to reject two extreme positions both of which, however, had some aspects worthy of being seriously taken into consideration. This search for a balance between politically opposite positions can be called the true prerogative of Gioberti. One need only reflect on what he says about two forms of government upon which western man has always reflected. "Democracy and aristocracy, that is mediocrity and singularity of casts of mind are equally necessary to the life and purpose of the universe. The mediocre conserve; the great perfect and move forward. The mediocre popularize, carry on, perform; the great – invent. The former preserve the ancient, the latter discover the new (…) So the mediocre are useful, indeed necessary, as long as they do not stray beyond their circle, let them be satisfied with the role which nature has destined for them" (Gioberti, R, I, 416). There are those who, if only implicitly, are of the conviction that democracy and aristocracy can achieve the greatest goals only if they are integrated into a sort of *aristocratic republic* on the model suggested by Montesquieu in his "re-reading" of the ancient classics. The Piedmontese philosopher was to return to this subject in some significant pages of *Del rinnovamento civile d'Italia* (cf. Gioberti, R, Chs. IX, X, XI).

8.13 Italian renewal was not a utopian ideal in the eyes of Gioberti because the peninsula had been imbued with Christianity which, as a religion of the people and the community, did not make of a people a "simple aggregation (…) but a well organized body, in which each member has his or her prescribed duties and performs them taking part in the movement, the life, the duration of the entire machine" (Gioberti, P, 2, 391). To this "union" between the individual and the community corresponded, on the institutional level, that of the Papacy and the Crown, or to use the words from the *Primato*, between Rome and Piedmont (cf. Gioberti, P, 1, 125). Rome represents the idea of the primacy of the Pope which for Gioberti constitutes the only possible principle of union among the various Italian states since the Papacy has meant the only unifying element of the Italian people, its only moral guide, even in the dark periods of the barbarian and more recently, foreign invasions (cf. Negri, FR, 200-201). Piedmont represents historical necessity, the structure that can bring about the unity ideals which, otherwise, would remain in the realm of pure metaphysical abstractionism. In other words, political modernism combines here with the "philosophical and religious aspect. These, indeed, are the two historiographically relevant aspects for a Catholic culture that must free itself from abstract and rigid metaphysical deductivism, recognizing, with a new 'empirical and scientific consciousness' the structural changes, without become philosophically subordinated to them" (Vasale, 233).

E) *Political society and its rationality: A. Rosmini.*

8.14 Rosmini's thought, among the most lucid bodies of thought of his time, can be called one of the most constructive ones expressed at a time in which much political thought was devoted to criticizing and was incapable of producing concrete solutions. Worse yet, it pursued the path of revolutionary utopianism. Rosmini felt the need for a genuine change within the Church itself, as well. He clearly intuited the problems involved in bringing this about. He realized that the need for renewal was unlikely to be accepted immediately by the hierarchy, but this did not discourage him, convinced as he was that Catholic history has amply shown that a free and disinterested spirit has the duty to speak with the greatest possible forthrightness, while avoiding scandals or divisions, speaking out, but then submitting to the judgement not only of the authorities, but of God himself who operates within the history of the Church and who always agrees with those who are right. The expressions used on this subject are very beautiful: studying the matters of Christianity "a great many holy men presented themselves before my eyes, ones who had flourished in the Church in every century. Without being Bishops, like St Jerome, St Bernard, St Catherine and the like, they spoke and wrote with admirable liberty and straightforwardness of the ills that afflicted the Church in their times and of the need and way to find remedies for them" (Rosmini, CP, 46). This is further proof that, a Christian society operates alongside human society and it must be capable not only of stimulating people to pursue a precise path of perfectibility, but must also bear witness to that interiority of history, the fruit of acceptance of the truth of revelation (cf. Rosmini, NS, II, 587).

Antonio Rosmini-Serbati was born in Rovereto in 1797. After studying philosophy and theology he was ordained as a priest in 1821 despite family conflicts. His fervour led him to found the Institute of Charity, a new religious Order. During those years he concentrated on his intention, which he never abandoned, to renew Catholic culture in order to deal with the problems of modern man. His philosophical and literary production is monumental and multifaceted. Among his most significant works are the *Nuovo saggio sull'origine delle idee* (1830), *La filosofia morale. Storia comparativa e critica dei sistemi intorno al principio della morale* (1837), *Teodicea* (1845), *Delle cinque piaghe della Santa Chiesa* (1848), *Logica* (1854), as well, naturally, as the *Filosofia della politica* (1839) and some essays among which is *Comunismo e socialismo* (1848). His enthusiasm for *Risorgimento* ideals, some of his more audacious reflections and some enemies in the Roman Curia aroused hostility which, in 1888, led to condemnation by part of the Congregation of the Holy Office of some of his positions. He was a friend of and inspired writers such as Manzoni, Bonghi and Tommaseo. Reduced to isolation, he died in Stresa in 1855.

8.15 Perfectibility was opposed to perfectism because, for Rosmini, history, as well as politics, was characterized by a perennial conflict between evil and good. This made the achievement of a perfect society impossible. This Augustinian view was enhanced by all the speculation of Italian historicism from Machiavelli to Vico; a historicism which saw in the duality of history and politics the very essence of human being and becoming. "Consequently, politics is an activity aimed at the achievement of being in society (...) thus, the premise was established that politics is a substantially eudaemonological science" (D'Addio, I, 15-16). The primary goal of individuals in social life was, then, that of achieving their own happiness. "In any system, therefore, it will always be true that all exterior things can only be *means* whereby the desire of the soul is assuaged; thus these means would have no value if they did not reach the soul and did not contribute to offering it the desired satisfaction" (Rosmini, FP, 59). Politics, however, does not end in its action because the concrete dimension of individuals cannot satisfy the needs their being. This is why it is necessary, in political analysis, to distinguish the scientific moment from the philosophical one thereby proposing a dualism which would characterize all of Rosminian thought and his most important political works. If, indeed, politics is presented as the science aimed at the concrete satisfaction of human needs, philosophy is seen as wisdom because it tends to direct all means towards the ultimate and "highest" goals. This means that every person acts in a visible and material society, but also within an invisible and spiritual one since he or she is not only exteriority, but also interiority, body and soul. It is the latter, which gives life to what Leibniz called the republic of souls (cf. D'Addio, I, 21 and 23; Rosmini, FP, 57 and 176). Here too, it should be recalled that true transformations in society occur in the interior and in this, as St Augustine noted, commenting on Cicero, the crises are felt first, too. Who can deny that "internal, invisible society always perishes much earlier, since violence cannot operate on external society if the internal has not been annihilated much earlier. Thus, Cicero wisely said in his time: *Rempublicam specie quidem retinemus, re autem ipsa iam pridem amisimus*" (Rosmini, FP, 303. The meaning of the quotation is the same, but here Rosmini quotes from memory. The actual phrase is: *rem publicam verbo retinemus, re ipsa vero iam pridem amisimus*. From re pub., V, I of the Fragments).

8.16 Crises are also due to the conviction that society is the only component of human life. As had been the case for Vico, there is in Rosmini the certitude that absolutizing one principle only, or one aspect or only one part of society, brings about an irreversible crisis since, all that is human must be seen in its many facets and in its entirety. Any partial vision ends up being restrictive and hazardous. Like Vico, too, Rosmini is convinced that civil society comes from the family and the bonds of property as well as the dominion which manifests itself in the servant-master relationship, from which gradually come forms more and more worthy of man who must be considered as an end and not a means (cf. D'Addio, I, 26). All of that is the fruit of intelligence, which is what is characteristic of the human being. "Through pure intelligence humans may become aware of the relationships between entities and with the aid and guidance of their intelligence, as active beings, can be bound up with the various sorts of entities, depending on the various relationships they have with them, and that they have amongst themselves. There would, therefore, be neither *property* nor *society* if there were not intelligence; (…) *Dominion* then and *society* do not belong to irrational beings, but belong to the body possessing reason" (Rosmini, FP, 134). It is this rationality which is the foundation of civil life and it is also this rationality that finds its basis in "that highly general idea of being" which constitutes one of the cornerstones of Rosimini's metaphysics. Liberalism is based on this intelligence since without it, any suggestion of human improvement is impossible. Indeed, "with a turbid intelligence, almost devoid of any activity, society is impossible: then, if intelligence after having been spurred, is halted in its motion and becomes disorderly in everything, the society that has been formed dies out or tears itself to pieces" (Rosmini, FP, 258).

8.17 The totality of intelligence that succeeds in giving expression to a society comes from two different types of rationality: the *practical reason of the masses* and the *speculative reason of individuals*. "These two forces direct society. The practical reason of society, by which the masses are guided could also be called, albeit improperly, *social instinct* (…) The masses, then, have as the reason for their action present and immediate advantage". This practical reason has been and is of great importance above all in "non-Christian civil societies"; the other, on the contrary, the speculative reason of individuals, "concerns Christian societies more particularly" (Rosmini, FP, 93 and 98). The total improvement of the person and his or her interior acceptance of the religious message constitute an infinite drive and an eternal need for interior as well as exterior betterment, of which the societies not affected by Christianity are not aware. Religion does not only present the need to change by bettering itself, but also keeping all that is best that tradition has handed down. Conservation and innovation thereby become two components of that harmonious itinerary that is pursued within all those societies which guarantee that dialectical relationship between the two only apparently conflicting principles (cf. D'Addio, I, 29).

8.18 Two fundamental faculties can be identified in reason: *thought* and *abstraction*. Among the many differences in the two faculties we can say that "another function of the faculty of abstraction is: 'to provide us with the means to perform good works, that is, *goals* that the faculty of thinking presents to our soul'" (Rosmini, FP, 258). So, since thought must establish those goals to be achieved for which abstraction must seek the means, it is clear that "the two faculties are unlikely to progress together; the faculty of thought must be developed first, and that of abstraction must follow upon its heels" (Rosmini, FP, 258). If such is not the case, intelligence can no longer harmonize the two faculties; it places the means before the ends and everything is reduced to the spasmodic quest for tools capable of satisfying needs which present themselves to the individual in disorderly fashion without the individual's being able to make the best possible use of them in their just dimensions and designs. The means take the place of the end and artificial as well as extemporaneous need replaces actual need. All of the intelligence concentrates on the immediate flurry of needs, can no longer look beyond the present and, as a result, becomes sterile and incapable of being creative. The crisis of civilizations starts at this point or, at least, the process of regression. All that sustains intelligence, culture itself, does no more than "become a means for achieving purely utilitarian goals: reason no longer governs the social, but in turn becomes an obsequious functionary of the social" (D'Addio, I, 35) hence the conviction that it is sufficient to act on the social and the exterior to change all the political dimension and otherwise radically. So, one does not realize that it is possible "that while ways are studied to make this organization or totality somehow better, it will be harmed in some other, more essential part" (Rosmini, FP, 112). Concentrating solely on the real being, presumptuously sure that it can be changed is the real evil of perfectivism All those constructivist theories which exist under the illusion that the political entity is considered equivalent to a physical organism that can be studied, disassembled and reconstructed as if it were a machine outside of space and time are erroneous.

8.19 Rosmini devoted considerable energy to combating this utopian prejudice. His struggle was not only directed against those philosophies that put forth dangerous perfectivist dreams aimed at achieving a definitive earthly paradise. His intentions also had practical dimensions. He was concerned that some parties, especially those guided by utopian conceptions and, worse yet, perfectivist ones, could end up identifying themselves with the State thus denying any freedom to the individual. It can be recalled that he had occasion to write these prophetic works *à propos* of socialist utopia: "finally one is reduced to setting up an extremely rich, extremely powerful government, which is charged with the task of ordering and grouping all people in the most perfect possible way" (Rosmini, SCS, 61). A party driven by such a perfectivist prospect would shortly eliminate any purpose and any goal from human life (cf. Rosmini, SCS, 37) and would reduce political life to a sclerotic as well as repetitive mechanism from the electoral point of view, too. Rosmini's words leave no doubt: "How can there be an election where freedom is lacking, where individuals are reduced to the state of being machines or animals, to such a vile condition that neither Greek nor Roman slaves ever reached? Furthermore, who could govern in the new society if not the masters and chiefs of the sect?" (Rosmini, SCS, 86)The suspicion with which Rosmini viewed the parties thus seems justified especially when one thinks that those parties, appropriately enough, appeared to him inclined to create actual visions of the world which were all the more dangerous and utopian because they wanted to replace tradition and religion. In Rosmini's opinion: "anyone who ignores religion, hastily conceives a fallacious one to put in its place for fear of sliding into nothingness" (Rosmini, SCS, 91). As has been rightly observed (cf. Riva, 11), that does not negate the fact that Rosmini, convinced that Christianity had brought something good to every human movement, wanted to find out what there was of a valid nature in socialist demands.

8.20 Rosmini's anti-utopian balance can also be perceived in his reflection on the problem of Italian unity. The philosopher from Rovereto knew that there are two different ways of achieving the unity of Italy: the model of the French-style centralized State which the Savoy monarchy viewed with interest and in a spirit of emulation, or the Republican solution which saw in confederation the possibility of harmonizing the various traditions and expectations of the individual Italian States. The second possibility missed its appointment with history in 1848 when the various States sought to contribute to the unity plan. After the process of unification went over to the Piedmontese State, which was not only capable of handling international politics of those years, but also succeeded in taking over military direction of the Risorgimento movement (cf. D'Addio, RCI, 100) Rosmini was almost torn between the ideal and real since he knew that the Piedmontese hypothesis was surely the most feasible, but the other still enabled the Papacy to maintain a certain independence and autonomy in temporal power as well. However, politics is not the science of illusions. Now peoples were taking on a more and more determining role on the world scene and unity was offering prospects that were more and more difficult to control outside of the use of force. Certainly, on the ideal level, Rosmini was quite close to the central positions of the *Federalist*. Against the possible despotism of the rebellious majority and to defend not only traditions but also the various local minorities, he proposed legislative assemblies for each of the individual States for all those matters that did not have national import, thereby guaranteeing that autonomy that only a late-coming and often misunderstood regionalism would succeed in bringing about much later in Italy (cf. D'Addio, RCI, 136). Here, Rosmini referred to considerations typical of Tocqueville on American democracy, considerations which, unfortunately, would not find an audience in the Italy of that era.

8.21 At this point Rosmini offers a realistic consideration: in politics it is impossible to embark upon certain paths then pretend that everything is as it had been before. Pope Pius IX himself had opened up rays of hope in the first two years of his Papacy which had deceived the people who could not imagine that the appeal to certain Principles would make it possible to bring about a return to the previous situations. This, too, would have contributed to orient spirits towards those sovereigns who demonstrated that they did not want to interrupt the path undertaken. Upholding the Charter and maintaining the foreign policy against Austria gave new impulse to the aspirations of the Savoy. All of moderate Italy recognized itself in their designs and the Risorgimento took a more logical path, even though the federal one would have been more desirable. So the Papacy found itself dealing with a situation which it had, indeed, helped to create but now could no longer control and to which, in fact, it had to submit for the very reason that it resided in Rome. The nation wanted this city as its capital because, as Rosmini maintained, it could not imagine any other, more appropriate choice. In this conclusion to the discussion of Rosmini, it may seem paradoxical to recall a thinker like Cattaneo (1801-1869), but it must be said that he, above and beyond his embracing Republican federalism as opposed to the Mazzinian unity thesis, deemed it necessary to add, to the traditional factors of production, the intelligence that was not adequately assessed by the economists.

F) *Liberty and History: C. Balbo.*

8.22 One of the crucial convictions that Balbo expresses in his *Della monarchia rappresentative in Italy* is that, in view of the fact that the diversity of opinions is "inevitable and necessary: they turn into factions or sects if they cannot express and publicize themselves legally, they become parties when, on the contrary, they can manifest their presence freely" (Scoppola, 200). Attached to the English conception of representation, Balbo sees parties above all as instruments of Parliamentary debate even if this must not allow us to lose sight of the role they play in the defence of civil and political liberties, since they find their roots in that Christian tradition which is the foundation of human dignity.

Cesare Balbo was born in Turin in 1789 where he died in 1853. Engaged in thought as well as in political action, he wrote numerous works in which, as some feel, motives are expressed which are in conflict with one another. Those apparent conflicts reflect, however, an era full of conflicts in which Balbo actively participated. Among his main writings, *Meditazioni storiche* (1842-45), *Sperane d'Italia* (1844), *Sommario della Storia d'Italia* (1846) and, especially, *Della monarchia rappresentativa in Italia* (1857) are noteworthy.

8.23 The degree to which Balbo was bound to tradition and the English system is shown by the fact "that he always views the aristocrats as protagonists. Their role, virtuously correct, seems to him still prevalent in the nineteenth century" (Fubini Leuzzi, 17). In his opinion, this viewpoint made it easier to place those limits on government that are a true guarantee for political liberties. From tradition, of which the aristocracy was a component not to be ignored, came that law which, in a view similar to that of Montesquieu, seemed to him indissoluble from history. For this reason, he criticised the inadequacy of Italian studies of the past and the Medieval period in particular since the need was not felt to go back to the struggles and achievements on behalf of liberty typical, for example, of the Communal period. At that time the "secularization" of the concept of hard work, which practically constitutes the premise on which the utilitarian mentality is based was underway. "Utilitarianism, so deplored by intransigent Catholic sources, turned into hard work which developed the civilization of peoples and carried out the providential design of the perennial growth of Christianity in history" (Fubini Leuzzi, 31). This would make Italy one of the most advanced and civil societies.

8.24 In order to achieve all that, Christianity had to be a stimulus to hard work, to be, that is, moral support without being bound to the political structures. Convinced of the need to separate the temporal from the spiritual, he came to the point of writing that the Church and the State "are two powers, highly independent one of the other (Balbo, 491). This position drew him, as a Catholic, away from thinkers such as De Maistre.

9. *Liberty and Democracy from History to the Future.*

A) *The Economy between Liberty and Equality: J. Stuart Mill.*

9.1 In the wake of the Tocqueville experience, John Stuart Mill sought to integrate liberty and democracy to avoid having an exaggerated form of democracy lead to the despotism of the majority, a veritable tyranny guaranteed by the public authorities. Supported by consensus, tyrannies can go so far as to issue and carry out decrees either unjust or else dealing with subjects with which they should not be concerned. Protecting oneself from the tyranny of democratic administrators and magistrates is a duty, but that is not sufficient unless there is protection from the tyranny of public opinion as well. This, like everything in a democracy, must operate within certain rules. Thus, some limits must be set and these must be defended from any possible form of usurpation. Everything that has any value in our existence depends on the limitations that the action of others or of the State encounter when they perform the abuse of operating in a precise area where they have not been allowed to do so (cf. Stuart Mill, OL, 8-9). From the outset, in his famous *On Liberty*, Mill intends to explain his objectives on the subject: The only reason for allowing society to act in the area of individual liberty is to protect it, hence it is legitimate to make use of force against an individual only to prevent this person from harming others. Otherwise: *"Over himself, over his own body and mind, the individual is sovereign*" (Stuart Mill, OL, 14). This sovereignty underscores human liberty from three points of view. First of all, freedom of conscience which implies freedom of thought in every practical and speculative area. Secondly, the possibility of choosing preferences and occupations, that is, organize our lives according to our own inclinations. Finally, freedom of association, understood as the freedom to unite to accomplish any goal that does not cause harm to others (cf. Stuart Mill, OL, 16-17).

Son of the famous scholar James, **John Stuart Mill** was born in London in 1806 and rapidly showed his highly precocious genius and multiplicity of interests. He worked for a long time in the administration of the *East India Company* while continuing to pursue his philosophical, political economic and moral interests. He contributed to various journals, such as the *London Review* and *Edinburgh Review* for a long time. Among his most famous works, in addition to many writings on Bentham, Coleridge, Tocqueville, Michelet and Guizot, as well as the famous *System of Logic Ratiocinative and Inductive* (1843), *Principles of Political Economy* (1848), *On Liberty* (1859), *Utilitarianism* (1861), *Considerations on Representative Government* (1861), *The Subjection of Women* (1869) and *Chapters on Socialism*, all published posthumously must be mentioned. Shortly after his death in Avignon in 1873, his famous *Autobiography* was also published.

9.2 A society that genuinely respects individuals must constantly pursue the habit of correcting and revising its opinions, confronting them with those of others and ones that arise from time to time. In no way can it be presumed that a doctrine is true if it does not succeed in overcoming the many contestations that it may arouse. The freedom to contradict is indispensible as long as it comes from tangible assessments and does not take refuge in abstractions incapable of being upheld by a concrete reason which can stand on its own merit (cf. Stuart Mill, OL, 24-25). To escape abstractions we must not only take our own statements seriously but also those of people who contradict us, as Cicero did when he said that to reach the point of discovering the truth he realized that those who only know their own points of view do not know much. We may even have excellent reasons, but we must be convinced that these become so only after others have been allowed to contradict them. A truly liberal and democratic society should encourage *school disputations* as they existed in the Middle Ages. It is singular that a thinker like Mill ascribed to the Catholic Church the merit of having introduced the character of the devil's advocate, in beatification cases (cf. Stuart Mill, OL, 42-44 and 50). Anyone who wishes sincerely to question himself should take this figure seriously. On the other hand, why must at least two opposing parties capable of conflicting exist in a truly democratic system, within precise limits, to ensure the progress of a people? Both are free to express diverging opinions, to put forth their truths. Otherwise this truth would be biased and not only that, but it could not even be contested (cf. Stuart Mill, OL, 53-54).

9.3 Contrary to anarchical-type viewpoints, Mill was convinced that individual liberty must be circumscribed when it can cause harm to others. He was, however, likewise convinced that, in the modern world, the real danger does not come from individual exasperation, but from a society that is gaining greater and greater domination over the individual to the point that no longer the excess but the lack of individual initiative and responsibility is tending to become the characteristic of our time. Individuals seem to become the victims of conventions to which they will eventually conform, not having any possibility of reacting. They come to be reduced to the level of the mass and end up not even being aware of their own natural inclinations, losing their originality (cf. Stuart Mill, OL, 68). Thus, it is forgotten that individualism is the equivalent of development and only by cultivating individuality can it be put to use to better mankind. Education must aim not only at personal virtues, but social ones as well, since these are capable of obtaining advantages for one's neighbour, too (cf. Stuart Mill, OL, 71 and 84). Thus, it can be concluded that individuals cannot be responsible towards society when their actions involve their interests only, and that they can be considered responsible solely when their actions are detrimental to the interests of others. Otherwise, any government has only to take advantage of individual activities. The harm begins when rather than encouraging the activities of individuals or reawakening in them the need for action, the executive tends to replace their activities with its own. The State thereby tends to weaken individual capacities and limit their intellectual development (cf. Stuart Mill, OL, 104 and 127-128). The same thing happens when the State attempts exclusively to be the one director of education. State education tends to weaken the critical abilities of people and induce them to become conformists. Education controlled and established by the State alone should not even be accepted. Competition with private educational systems is fundamental. The government cannot even claim a monopoly over education when State teachers are on the average superior to private ones because, in this case as well, they cannot be containers of all knowledge. Having control over education would be despotic and the government would end up being granted the possibility of moulding the feelings and opinions of a people from early childhood on. The government may and must set up schools and universities, but it cannot prevent private individuals from doing so, too (cf. Stuart Mill, OL, 117-118 and PPE, 341-342).

9.4 The cultural problem is of greatest importance to the effective development of a people, because it makes it possible to cast light upon the true theory of utilitarianism which is not to be understood in a simplistic, or worse yet, vulgar fashion. The concept of utility is not just closely connected with that of pleasure, but also with improvement of the various faculties of individuals. It must be kept in mind that after selfishness, which does not make life easy comes the lack of culture. A lack of moral or simply human interests gives rise to indifferent spirits devoid of any sensitivity. Wealth and well-being should be used above all to increase needs for culture if it is true that poverty, which means suffering from any point of view, also means the lack of cultural opportunities (cf. Stuart Mill. U, 142 and 145-146). It is thus senseless to say that utilitarian morality does not ascribe value to sacrifice and only extols pleasure. What it says is that sacrifice cannot be an end in itself and that sacrifice can be considered useless and even wasted if "*it does not increase, or tend to increase, the sum total of happiness*" (Stuart Mill, U, 148). Happiness, therefore, cannot be understood merely as personal satisfaction, but satisfaction of all interests. If we do not accept this approach, we must reduce morality, as Kant said, merely to a sense of duty and we should condemn all those actions which, from day to day, each of us performs without being driven by a sense of duty. Rejection of the Kantian approach also comes from the fact that Mill does not believe that moral feelings are innate. Moral faculties are constructed little by little. With the passage of time they have then been codified and turned into law. For this reason it is considered unjust to take away from someone property as well as personal freedom or anything that legitimately belongs to a person. It follows that security is the most vital interest of every individual to such an extent that no-one can do without it (cf. Stuart Mill, U, 163 and 190).

9.5 That security is the result of order and it brings about progress. It is quite easy to define the latter. The definition of order, which, in its narrowest sense, means obedience – to a legitimate government – is more complicated naturally. In a wider sense, however, "*Order means the preservation of peace, by the cessation of private violence*" (Stuart Mill, CRG, 219). When this security does not exist, any distinction disappears and power itself ends up residing in one class exclusively, or in a group or élite which will come to dominate all the other expressions of social life. It is obvious that the classes excluded from the management of power will recognize that their interests are being neglected. For this reason, a political system capable of providing the broadest possible representation to the entire social body must be created. It can thus be said that the representative system is the best one since it can give the entire people, or at least a great many of them, the possibility of controlling the powers through periodic election of its representatives. This control must come about within very precise rules which, in the modern world, express themselves through constitutions (cf. Stuart Mill, CRG, 269-270). It is important that these "representative bodies" must not perform administrative activities. Popular assemblies are not fit for those tasks. Administrative acts require not only profound awareness and mature judgement, but also assessments that are possible only for those who function in a determined area, a minister, the director of a public service, for example. Due to the role they perform, they are invested with responsibilities which an assembly cannot assume. By its collective nature, it can, in many circumstances, escape the criterion of responsibility. Furthermore, the abilities of some individuals who will perform public-administration functions can more easily be assessed by specific persons than is the case for an assembly. For this reasons ministers or the head of government, for example, are controlled but not chosen and appointed by the Parliament, however, depending on the circumstances, by those who perform a role specific to that function (cf. Stuart Mill, CRG, 272-276).

9.6 Administrative ability, in the English philosopher's opinion, comes from aptitude in performing certain functions, and that comes from tradition. It has come about in the United Kingdom because, in the constitution, new elements are always taken into consideration, but they end up adapting to existing traditions. It is more or less what happened in the republics of Rome and Venice. English society had an aristocracy capable of running durable governments in accordance with immutable political principles, in which, however, continuous renewal took place. The Roman government like the English one, was the result of a constantly open aristocracy which, together with the Senate, governed, facing the risk of a terrible liability in case of failure. Thus, that mixture of collective politics developed, insofar as it was determined by the entire aristocracy with the support of the people, directed, however, by great statesmen, whom history has rewarded with praise, personally responsible for their acts. *Representation* and *responsibility* are both principles the characterize the truly great civilizations (cf. Stuart Mill, CRG, 282 and 288-289). The merit of Roman civilization was its concreteness, fundamental in politics. One should remember that governments must be created for people as they are or as they are really capable of becoming. They must reflect their degree of culture and their tradition, but must take into account their interests and rights. Even before government, the representational system itself should take all that into account to guarantee a real balance among the various interests, views and, above all, aspirations of individuals (cf. Stuart Mill, CRG, 298 and 301). A representative system that is biased in favour of one class or economic group can certainly not be called just. It is useful to recall that Mill was not very favourable to the creation of a second House which, in its way, would risk upsetting the balance of the representative system and would ascribe too much importance to a sort of caste. There were exceptions, however, like that of the *House of Lords* whose members not only made up of a traditional class and possessed their own wealth, but had no intention of putting democracy in bondage. Indeed, for the good of democracy, they could constitute a body *wisely* conservative capable of defending the fundamental premises. To do so, they should have imitated the *Roman Senate*, the best historical example of a political structure which succeeded in moderating and regulating the influences and excesses of democracy. A second House with the same intentions would certainly be desirable, but now, to create it, it would be necessary to find a number of representatives not cognizant of a portion of the class interests and prejudices of the majority and not at all hostile to democratic sentiments (cf. Stuart Mill, CRG, 388 and 391-392). In the modern world such a quest is certainly not easy.

9.7 A great problem aroused the interest of the English philosopher concerning the system of representation: its natural tendency to slide towards mediocrity. The American experience could confirm all that according to what Tocqueville had said. It would seem that everything, even the voting laws, works towards placing the various powers in the hands of people of little value without the greater intelligences being heard out. Putting aside the difficulties of the opponents of democracy, it must be provided that the minorities of educated individuals, spread out in the various voting districts, may unite to elect eminent individuals in proportion to their own numbers. Those people would always be a driving force among representatives because, in crucial moments in political life, the majority would find itself obliged to reply to the arguments of qualified people and people of experience. Thus, along with the legitimate numerical superiority, they would be a "qualitative superiority". *"This may be called the function of Antagonism"*. Obviously, qualified antagonism enlivens political life and gives new meaning to the relationships among forces. Antagonism or competition in ideas and opinions are the true essence of a democracy. Where a voice of opposition is suppressed and everything is made to conform to a unique model, not only does progress cease, but true decadence begins to invade the entire community, which closes up within itself (cf. Stuart Mill, CRG, 313-315). In a democracy, the educated minority may not have political influence in a numerical sense but it would have immense moral influence and could exert a real influence in any type of assembly.

9.8 Assembly debates involve not only the representatives, but also those who are represented and this can only improve democracy. Political discussion involves those who perform manual activities or other types of labour, and would be far from political problems, since these people are taken up solely with daily concerns. The members of a political community will end up developing their own opinions and will call their representatives into question. True democracy will come about. Indeed, it is absurd to oblige individuals to pay, to fight, hence to obey, then not provide them with the opportunity of responsibly manifesting their consensus or disapproval. Whether they know it or not, those individuals would not be respected and would not construct a democracy. Such participation in political life increases the need to know and to be informed and leads not a few individuals, left out of political life because of their ignorance, to feel the need to obtain an education (cf. Stuart Mill, CRG, 328-330). This explains why not only democracy, but the system of representation itself must be brought about gradually. The great danger of placing ignorance and science on the same plane is thereby eliminated. To be sure, the purpose of a democracy is to make all citizens equal, but in order to achieve true equality, errors and prejudices must be eliminated. Everyone must be given cultural tools to ensure real and stimulating individual progress. What has been said in general for the less well educated classes is supported by Mill on behalf of women. Not only in his famous *The Subjection of Women*, but also in other writings, Mill maintains that women are capable of making good use of the right to vote. Furthermore, saying that their family and social position make them incapable of understanding political life and taking part in it is a contradiction in terms. Most men who work in the field or workshops find themselves in the same positions, but they do not, for that reason, fail to desire to participate in the vote and conceive of it in a broader and broader way. Participation of women would qualitatively improve the vote. It would stimulate political debate in the family, too. All of that would contribute to greater political maturity on the part of women. Only when individuals are allowed to have their own opinions do they become true participants. Mill feels, ironically, that it is absurd that the English themselves, whose greatest sovereign was a woman, and who had had another enlightened female sovereign as the head of State, could not understand that it is not the sex that determines the difference in political attitudes and abilities, but the social, hence cultural situations in which woman are forced to live.

9.9 For a system to be truly representative there must be local representatives who deal with solving day to day or circumscribed problems which the central authorities cannot handle effectively, or with due safety, to a minimum extent. All too often, Parliaments, the English one included, albeit operating in the least centralized State in Europe, become lost in problems which they then solve badly because of a lack of competence; and all this to the detriment of other problems. Assemblies too, like governments, must encounter precise limits to their actions. On a local level, too, activities must be divided, as on a national level among several individuals if one wants problems not only to be faced, but also solved (cf. Stuart Mill, CRG, 411 and 416). In other words, to avoid an excess of power from central governments, Mill, too, is a supporter of federalism. For this to exist, however, it is necessary that there be sufficient bonds uniting the entire community and that there be language, traditions, and fundamental political institutions in common. There must then be, if necessary, a united defence without a considerable waste of resources among the various States that make up the Federation. The most important institutional task is to set forth the duties and functions of the central as well as the local government since citizens must never be cast into doubt, because they do not know which one to obey in significant circumstances. A Supreme Court must be set up to guide controversies that may arise and it must have supreme power over all governments, of individual as well as Federal States (cf. Stuart Mill, CRG, 435 and 439).

9.10 Mill's economic writings are quite new in their political implications, too. They seek to achieve a synthesis between the best of liberal tradition and the just demands arising from socialist thought. Mill anticipates subjects that would be debated only later, such as those of the distribution of wealth, which depends on the rules that every society intends to set forth for itself (cf. Stuart Mill, PPE, 6-7). Obviously, these rules cannot reach the point of denying private property if the wish is to keep a society operating under liberal principles. Showing extreme realism, Mill is convinced that Communist-type systems, despite the inevitable difficulties that they would encounter as they sought implementation, cannot, in principle, be called impracticable, because they arouse great fascination in the working masses, who live in extremely difficult conditions (cf. Stuart Mill, PPE 10 ff.). Rather than combating such illiberal approaches in theory, society must be reformed concretely. It must create well-being for those working masses, who will share in the advantages of capitalistic society, and give up revolutionary temptations.

9.11 With great honesty, the English scholar believes that, as is the case for those who defend the system of private property by presenting the future advantages that it can obtain for everyone rather than its limitations, when considering communism, one must not only consider its defects that are obvious to everyone but those prerogatives that a true democracy can take into serious consideration and implement. Mills is convinced that if there had been a tendency to favour the spread of wealth rather than its concentration, the principle of private property would not have aroused such hostility as was indeed the case. This means that *"property is only a means to an end, not itself the end"* (cf. Stuart Mill, PPE, 14-15 and 33). Property is the right of each person to make use of their faculties as they see fit and, thanks to these faculties, it can produce and then create an equitable market. The right to give what one possess to others is to be added, as well as the right of others to make use of it. For the property system to develop, there is a need for competition, but also custom and use, showing that the property mentality is one which comes from tradition and cannot in any way be improvised (cf. Stuart Mill, PPE, 28 and 50-51). Property must be guaranteed, but limitations may be placed on it, too. Furthermore, a better society goes through universal education which can, above all, enable everyone to understand how population growth can be contained. Then, it is necessary to make the best possible use of the individualistic system while exploring the best forms of socialism, as well. We still know far too little about both systems. It is certain, however, that once the means of achieving true subsistence are ensured, needs for liberty will increase, whatever form the government takes. For this possibility to be ensured, public opinion must be kept genuinely free to avoid the uniformity of thought and conformism that lead to tyranny (cf. Stuart Mill, PPE, 16-17).

9.12 It is the traditional categories of income that guarantee growth of national wealth. What is new is the fact that workers, wage-earners, land owners, private-income earners and capitalists living from profits go beyond the traditional static aspect of an economy aimed at reaching ideal balances based on natural models. Much of Book IV of the *Principles of Political Economy*, beginning with the first chapter *General Characteristics of a Progressive State of Wealth*, show us that economic science, aside from the static aspect, must be seen in its dynamism due to the evolution and interconnection of several variables such as capital, population and technology. The former is the fruit of saving which not only is not a sacrifice, but ensures the accumulation of capital hence economic progress. The population will sooner or later begin to decrease because of increasing awareness on the part of the poorest classes, and this will enable wages to increase from the bare subsistence level, and to thus guarantee an increasing standard of living to the working class. Improvement of technology is the result of a particular political action aimed at improving an ever growing level of education, assisting research, encouraging people of science, ensuring social peace, and attracting intellectuals, including foreign ones, etc. As these variables evolve with the consequences that come from this, at times unexpected, a change takes place in some things accomplished which classical economics considered stable: aside from the concept of price, that of value must be considered. As a result a veritable change in the customs of society is brought about, because concepts such as those of profit, income, even rents undergo change. They had seemed to have been fixed once and for all, but instead, they end up varying as market and political conditions change. Book V of the *Principles of Political Economy* quite effectively points out the limits that governmental activity encounters as it takes economic action as well as taking on those activities that it cannot avoid initiating. The author confutes the erroneous theories claiming that the government should interfere in areas with which it had no concern, but he strongly criticizes the limitations of *laissez-faire* which, for many, had become almost a fatal justification for everything that happened in economics, a science, for Mill, continually evolving and on which it *was never possible to pronounce a definitive judgment*.

B) *Religion and Politics: Lord Acton.*

9.13 From the Christian point of view, history is a process that is never satisfied with itself. What is new in Christianity, historically speaking, comes out of this perennial impulse to improve, always present because God, who reveals himself at every moment, in history, too, but not only in history, sees to it that mankind is never fully satisfied and so, carries along a discontent that encourages human beings to go further and further in the quest for a perfection that history will never offer it. History, with all its political events, becomes philosophy of history with outcomes that are surely meta-historical, unknown and unimaginable to us. It is thus clear why Acton considered Saint Augustine to be the one who had "*the deepest influence of one mind in the Church*" (Fasnacht, APP, 144) because he devised the first philosophy of history and Aquinas, because he maintained that it was the right of peoples to elect and remove sovereigns, hence he "*devised Whiggism to prop religious absolutism*" (Fasnacht, APP, 144) and reached the point of basing political freedom on the freedom of conscience. This discovery was to come out most clearly in Tocqueville, who saw religious awareness as one of the pillars of freedom. Also, thanks to a deeply rooted religious awareness, he saw freedom as something capable of defending itself from the "*omnipotence of a majority*". Tocqueville was also admired because he seemed almost to have maintained that "*liberty, too, must be limited in order to be possessed*" (Mathew, 93). Elimination of the limits of freedom is tantamount to elimination of freedom itself. The teaching of the sense of "the limit", in a legal sense as well, is one of the great teachings of Christian tradition which neither philosophy nor modern politics can do without.

Lord John E. E. Acton born in Naples in 1834 can be called a true European intellectual because of his education and culture. Thanks to his diverse family origins he spoke and read several languages: English with his son, German with his wife born in Bavaria, French with his sister-in-law and Italian with his mother-in-law. All of that enabled him to read books from various disciplines in the original and meet the most prominent personalities in European Catholicism, in France Mons. F. Dupanloup, in England Wiseman and Germany J. I. von Döllinger. He also had friends such as Simpson and Capes who, in the eyes of the *old Catholics,* seemed like representatives of the *Catholic Left.* He met and worked with personalities such as Newman, travelled a great deal in Europe and overseas, and wrote for several journals, such as *The Rambler* and *The Home and Foreign Review,* with which he held various jobs. For many years a rumour circulated that Acton was working on a sort of *magnum opus* that would have almost universal dimensions. It was a sort of evolution of humanity in the form of *The History of Liberty,* called by some "the most famous unwritten book". Material from the most diverse periods was gathered for this work and individual essays were also written which came out in various collections after his death at Tegernsee in 1902.

9.14 As far as Acton was concerned, democracy had to be reconciled with religion and it was necessary to realize that only the nations having a true religious spirit were capable of governing themselves and were fit to enjoy freedom. Without this ability to govern themselves, who would be able to avoid the dangers of centralization towards which all democracies tend when they cannot avoid degeneration? (cf. Fasnacht, APP, 197). Thus, putting our faith in history, always seen as open and subject to improvement, we must not create for ourselves the illusion that any historical solution will lead to perfection as if a Hegelian trick of reason would enable everything, finally, to fit within a predetermined logic. Acton felt that Hegel was the most serious of all the enemies of religion because he reasoned not only in abstract but also deterministic terms and because he did not recognize the true nature of religion which he sacrificed in a sterile religiosity. Furthermore dialectics relieved history of any prospective metaphysical possibility and this resulted in creating a vacuum in mankind as well as pessimism without any avenue of escape. Acton's interest in history gives rise to the conviction that the duo liberalism and democracy on which Catholicism conferred vitality was the natural outcome of western history. It was natural, but not to be taken for granted: indeed, if the democratic component risked suffocating the liberal one, the desire for religion in the political dimension would be eliminated. At this point a not insignificant question arises: "How can a portion of liberty be saved in the new society whose democratic exigencies are so apparent?" (Alatri, IA, L). To answer this question it must be kept in mind that Acton's liberalism can be called "historical liberalism", that is, based on tradition and, therefore, together with liberty, aimed at defending from the emerging revolutionary logics, all those guarantees that it had achieved in time through great efforts. This also explains why Christianity above all has the duty of safeguarding that sphere of interior liberty from which all the other forms of liberty arise (cf. Gasquet, 254). Practically speaking, this means the division of Church and State. Their historical contrast was due to the fact that neither one was willing to leave individuals at the mercy of the other. When the rigorous distinction is not observed it is almost impossible to avoid various forms of absolutism (cf. Acton, HFOE, 205).

9.15 When he speaks of *Christian Democracy* Acton tends to oppose two different types of democracy, both of which are a threat to liberty. On the one hand, he opposes those that our century has called *popular democracies* which, given their nature, have a tendency to become powerful and sclerotic. On the other hand, there is that sort of *democracy of the Caesar*, that is, those *populist democracies* which had arisen, for example, in France. It mattered little that the first were the fruits of revolutionary ideals and the others, of counter-revolutionary intentions. Both ended up stifling individual desires. If *Christian democracy* was based upon the concept of responsibility, the others paradoxically made the individual irresponsible. The anonymity of the structures, of the community or the nation ended up stifling personal responsibility and, indeed, stifled every form of authentic liberalism (cf. Pezzimenti, PTLA, 193-194). Liberalism can survive only in a *Christian democracy* since there is no liberalism that cannot be called Christian, since the first and most important liberty is that of the conscience. The others are built on this. The extreme forms of democracy had a defect, a cultural – even before a political – one. They pursued philosophies which, when analyzing history, examined *only* the facts, neglecting their interiority. The latter is the element that links the various historical vicissitudes together, otherwise, the latter would be reduced to pure accidents as from the positivist and Enlightenment points of view. Both positions are incapable of considering the moral striving of individuals, since a merely factual approach does not take into consideration interior tensions and the cost of overcoming them. Consensus itself, the real premise of liberalism, had been misunderstood. Its necessity had, indeed, been brought out by all those thinkers who, while not yet being aware of liberal politics, cherished liberty. It is possible to go back to Cicero, to look at all the medieval theoreticians and come to Locke, Jefferson, Hamilton and Mill. Without consensus, even the laws are not valid.

9.16 When speaking of "limits", other than those imposed by tradition, we can also see what we could call institutional ones. Among these, what seems most successful in preventing the tyranny of the majority is federalism. Acton, who borrows this thought from Tocqueville, considers federalism a limitation not only on forms of democratic degeneration but also against the absurdity of nationalism which was becoming more and more threatening. On this subject the English historian is lapidary: The true and natural check on an absolute democracy is the federal system, which limits the central government by means of restricted powers, and state governments by means of powers which they have relinquished. This is the immortal contribution of America to political science (cf. Acton, ELIH, 393). Federalism is also one of the ripest fruits of Christianity which, already in the Middle Ages, inspired all those local governments, communes and maritime republics, which are at the heart of modern liberty. This is why the federalist idea could not come from Asia, a continent only marginally influenced by Christianity. It developed in the United States instead, and was the *logical and best possible continuation of European history* which, in the modern era, had lost its consistency often compromising the conquests of liberty. The *Federalist* as the basic text of *Conservative Democracy* is the result. In the adjective *Conservative*, which is not to be associated with parties as in present-day usage, lie all those basic features which are not only found in democracy but also defend it, safeguarding it from dangers. In other words they "conserve" it. Another strong conviction of Acton is present in the *Federalist*: "There is the rejection of equalitarian democracy and the profound conviction that only a republican democracy, which mediates the popular will thanks to the representative system, is capable of guaranteeing civil, religious and political liberty as well as the interests of individuals and the community" (D'Addio-Negri, 24). Then, federalism represents a check on a nascent danger inherent in modern states: nationalism. Acton was not unaware of the just aspirations to unit of some peoples, but succeeded in distinguishing between nationality and nationalism, reaching the point of predicting how a national State might give way to a nationalistic policy based on force and centralization. This explains why, on the one hand, he admired a multi-national State such as Austria in some respects, and on the other, criticized Prussian nationalistic policy (cf. Mathew, 77). Certainly a phenomenon like national unity did not carry with it solely negative effects. Indeed, it was capable of remediating a series of glaring errors committed by the great European monarchies. The Polish case is an example. The partition of Poland was an act of cynical violence. For the first time in modern history a great State was eliminated, and an entire nation was divided up among its enemies (cf. Acton, EFP, 146). Events like this gave rise to national feeling, which, if kept within proper limits, would be a legitimate aspiration.

9.17 Why is Acton so concerned with limits? Because the crisis of a civilization is always due to the disappearance of its limits, leading to the crisis of rationality and the unleashing of instincts. In those critical situations, political life is dominated by a paradox: all energy is concentrated on the needs of the moment and on contingencies. Everything ends up being sacrificed to contingencies, even freedom and the elementary forms of justice. Who is to keep democracy within its proper limits to avoid its dangerous forms of degeneration? According to Acton the middle class must do this, a class which, in France, drew inspiration from liberal principles and then sought to contain the cravings for "populist" democracy. It failed in this because it used the lower classes to bring down the aristocracy, thereby encouraging the equalitarian dreams of the people. Once the nobility was eliminated, the people did not accept the idea of allowing the bourgeoisie to establish a new form of inequality on its own behalf and thought to fight that bourgeoisie, since it had not kept its promises.

9.18 However strange it may seem, Acton thought that in future, socialism, born of democratic ideals, could survive like democracy, by reinstating some fundamental premises of liberalism. Socialism, dangerous as it is when it presents itself as a new religion to the point of introducing a new *Weltanschauung*, is too important to be ignored. Acton was a keen reader of some works of Marx and Engels. His copy of *For a Critique of Political Economy* of Marx, which he left at the University of Cambridge, was annotated with great care. *Das Kapital* was considered an engrossing and decisive work so that the English historian recommended reading it to Gladstone, and was surprised when Gladstone replied that he did not have time to do so (cf. Fasnacht, APP, 117). *Das Kapital* was called a sort of *Koran* for the new socialists (cf. Fasnacht, FS, 21). If, on the one hand, this definition expressed the force and novelty of Marxism, on the other, it implied that there were dangers. Acton seems to be saying that it is a sort of disguised religion, where there is no distinction between Church and State, and where individuals are crushed by the totality. The fact remains, however that Marx was the spokesman for a new message of "liberation" with intentions that were practical above all. The hazards of Marxism do not come from its intentions, but from its method. Acton associates the followers of Hegelianism with those of Marxism. He calls them, *Monistic philosophers* (cf. Kochan, 94) all, more or less consciously the children of Hegel. Marxism seemed like the concrete possibility of overcoming Hegelian dualism involving the bad conscience, and of reuniting political and religious aspirations on a par with the Moslem religion. Herein lies the lucidity of Acton's judgment of Marxism: if it is impossible to accept it because of the prospects it holds out, the fact remains that its practical and political importance is noteworthy, but cultural as well, one could add, because it drew many scholars away from the idyllic temptations of classical economists. Acton grants Marxism the merit of having led to demolition of the contradictions of classical economics and of having revealed the wretched living conditions of some individuals. Marx's dialectics seemed too simplistic and one might say Manichean, however. Furthermore, having been an avid reader of Mill, Acton was convinced that the distinction between public and private was fundamental not only for civil liberties, but also for that liberty of conscience, without which a political system worthy of mankind cannot exist (cf. Himmelfarb, 48). Acton had considered Mill one of the greatest defenders of liberalism because he made that conception depend not only on political premises, but economic and moral ones as well. Indeed, the latter became authentic premises for politics and economy to the point that "*Mill treats political economy as a deductive science*" (Fasnacht, APP, 69). It was *deductive* because it was based on those ethical values which, in turn, come from religious ones. If they are eliminated, it is impossible to bring about a liberal economy.

9.19 Socialism is not just Marxism. Acton followed the evolution of the socialist phenomenon and surely thought that it would evolve in a way similar to that of democracy. The theoreticians of democracy themselves had abandoned the most radical positions that would have run the risk of leading to the so-greatly feared tyranny of the majority. Indeed, proportional representation had been proposed and put into effect. This was profoundly democratic, since it increased the influence of the masses that would otherwise not have had any voice in the government. It also brought people closer to a condition of equality, enabling every voter to send a deputy to Parliament who would be the expression of his or her opinions. Preference for the proportional system is due to the fact that it ensures the only possible balance between liberty and equality. If these terms are taken to their extreme conclusions, they end up excluding one another. When certain examples of intransigence were abandoned, socialism would make "moderate democracy" possible. It would be a *partial Socialism* in which the English historian was interested, which depended on some starting assumptions: 1) private enterprise had failed to solve the problem of distribution; 2) what the poor needed first of all were the *comforts* and security; 3) the division of power is the condition for liberty; 4) the right to self-government is inherent to all the corporations and associations. For those reasons, the State must not control all economic life (cf. Fasnacht, FS, 27). Acton can thus be considered a precursor of liberal-socialism and a true prophet. He was favourable to everything in socialism that was compatible with true liberty and a standard of economic responsibility. He believed that the spread of wealth was one of those paths the State could follow to offer real, albeit indirect, aid to the individual (cf. Fasnacht, FS, 29).

C) *Liberty, Democracy and the Industrial Society: H. Spencer.*

9.20 Spencer's thought is based on the conviction that a holistic principle presides over all the evolutionary processes in nature, which is understood to be a living totality. In nature, aside from inorganic natter, there are principles and laws governing the various phenomena. Those principles and laws act on natural, but also on social phenomena. Thus, society is the result of a long process of evolution, especially when it reaches the point of becoming a structure of various organisms capable of acting in complementary ways, each performing its own function and strictly interdependent at the same time, and each differentiated. It is understandable that Spencer sees in society a process of continued and growing aggregation such that it is possible to speak of simple, complex and doubly complex societies (cf. D'Addio, SDP, II, 354-355). This holistic conception avoids, at least partly, however, constructivist temptations typical of Comte because there is concern for "single, autonomous and self-sufficient individuals, whom Spencer always took care to rescue from State interference" (Ferrarotti, 39). One of the most stimulating motifs in Spencer's thought is this changing relationship between the individual and society with its institutions.

Herbert Spencer was born in 1820 at Derby in an independently-minded and non-conformist family. He pursued scientific and philosophical studies, which were of great importance to him, practically speaking as well. He had, in fact, worked for several years in a railway company until he became the assistant-editor of the *Economist*. He then directed his already multi-faceted interests towards social studies. In the last decades of his century he rose to considerable fame, on an internal level too, because of some writings that led to the cultural and political debate of the time. He died at Brighton in 1903. The year after, he famous *An Autobiography* came out. Among his other writings, *The Principles of Psychology* (1872), *First Principles* (1886) can be recalled. *The Principles of Sociology* in which Part V, *Political Institutions* (1882), should be recalled above all, as well as the various parts making up *The Principles of Ethics* and *The Man versus the State*, appearing in 1884 in *Social Statics*.

9.21 One type of society that could be called archaic is of the military type, which is in opposition to a more advanced society – the industrial type. This distinction would be too simplistic if it did not take account of the fact that both, each in its own way, can reappear in the various periods of history. Furthermore, it should be recalled that the two functions characteristic of these societies, defence and the betterment of individuals, are typical of every human community, but can also become ones that characterize it, when they become the motives that inspire civil life. At that point the relationship between commanding and obeying, the social organization, the ethic and religious objects as well as every other aspect of living in the community take on a particular form (cf. Spencer, PS, 259-261; *hereafter, the numbers always refer to the paragraphs*). The organization of labour also reflects the type of political system on which it is founded. Industrial society, with increasing specialization and an increasing division of labour are expressions of an artificial system of regulation which contrasts with the natural one. It is competition, which sets these modifications in motion. Fighting against competition means reintroducing primitive societies where the military component once again predominates, even if it is brought up to date. One need only consider the fact that communistic forms and organizations of life, where the warrior aspect was fundamental, had already existed in primitive societies. In fact, a society that wants to defend itself against hostile forces, finds its first condition to be that of military action. Only when the real or presumed danger abates does the military component tend to weaken (cf. Spencer, PI, 562-563). This is indeed the present position of communism which feels the need to defend itself from within from the reawakening of individualistic temptations and externally from the States that have not yet carried out the revolution thereby offering value and an infinite existence to the military component.

9.22 Logically, the private action of the individual is placed within narrow and very precise limits, which tend to become more and more restrictive. On the contrary, the individuality of citizens in an industrial system tends more and more to be protected by society, which has as its prime goal that of defending the individuality of each person.

Protecting them becomes the basic function of the State. This is a tangible protection, which concerns life in all its expressions, starting, obviously, from liberty and property. The fundamental duty of the government is thus to ensure all the conditions required on behalf of the best possible expression of individual life. Departing from this premise, the government must avoid all the communistic forms of distribution which *tend to equalize the lives of good and bad, idle and diligent* (cf. Spencer, PI, 564 and 567). Private action encounters highly precise limits, and these are set forth by law. Individuals know what they can or cannot do and nothing is left up to arbitrariness. Within the rules, the spaces for action are left up to the inventiveness of individuals who are inclined to widen their spheres of action more and more. For this reason, public organizations shrink more and more while private ones expand to a greater and greater degree. There is a sort of law: *"The spheres left vacant by the one are filled by the other"* (Spencer, PI, 570). There seems to be here a recollection of Tocqueville's conviction that what private individuals do not do, the State does. This action of individuals and their quest to improve life means a continual transformation of society and its order. The fact remains, however, that the fundamental feature of this society is that it is based on the consensus of individuals upon whom the authorities cannot impose basic choices that operate against the will of fellow members of the society. This solution, typical of advanced societies, came about thanks to long periods of peace which give rise to stability, thereby favouring economic development. As long as hostile relations between neighbouring societies prevail, insecurity reigns and economic activities are sacrificed to other necessities. When, however, peaceful relations are established, industrial activities tend to break down barriers of all sorts. The prejudices of nationalism are overcome. Individual State organizations show themselves to be insufficient and a federation, at least, of governments becomes necessary, to overcome the goals of a single government (cf. Spencer, PI, 572).

9.23 Federalism and decentralization are the ripened fruits of an authentic industrial society. As a result, private life becomes less and less controlled and disciplined by the governmental sphere which withdraws to perform specific and limited functions. But not everything appears to be positive in the development of this society. Some drawbacks tend to sacrifice some individuals who must bear up under the weight of this development. Many workers do not have the freedom of labour. They are obliged to accept any type of work, if they are to survive. Those workers sacrifice themselves to guarantee the development of the entire society and to see to it that liberty is not lost. However, Spencer is not resigned to those injustices. He knows that eliminating economic freedom brings about very serious disadvantages, however, he does not accept excessive capitalist power, either. He expresses the wish that workers can improve their condition and encourages organizations, such as the *Trade Unions*, who can oppose the unbridled force of those who are the leaders of industrial society.

9.24 The elements of hardship cannot simply be material. Others, of a moral nature prevent many from enjoying the advantages, not to mention privileges, of industrial society. More fortunate citizens cannot withdraw within themselves selfishly without grave dangers arising: indeed, the objective of earning for the sake of earning emerges on the horizon and selfishness takes precedence over any form of "solidarity" among individuals. This is why the moral problem is important. Spencer believes that ethical principles play a determining role in directing human life towards effective improvement, and he does not always accept the extreme utilitarianism of some of his contemporaries. He seeks a sort of rational utilitarianism which attempts to reconcile selfishness with altruism (cf. Spencer, PE, Part I, Ch. XI and XII). This reconciliation is made possible by the laws of evolution themselves to which everything must eventually submit, even the moral laws and the principles governing them. Those moral principles have accumulated in the experience of history and they are the *a priori* morality of every person, even though they are an *a posteriori* for the human species, inescapable fundamentals which actually become obligations.

9.25 This social evolution has succeeded in gathering up what is best in human activities, even ones that have not come about and developed in a preordained fashion, but spontaneously, thanks to the initiatives of individuals, such as many of the economic activities generated within a liberal society. The modern world has not always been able to understand and defend such activities. Communist theories, like nationalistic ones too, have provided for the total rationalizing of the economic sphere, in fact curbing the intelligence and action of individuals. The outcome has been only to reintroduce archaic, military societies in which various forms of civil control and consequent domination have been legitimized. *Totalitarianism and militarism* are the ghosts which float about in the nebulous future of European industrial societies, ghosts *which Spencer warned against when no-one had been able to foresee them.* He called for the need for a limited state authority, but saw a modern "Leviathan" taking clear and clearer form, which, with its many tentacles, was strangling individuals. A true *liberal*, he intuited the madness of the arms races which would only give rise to destruction and barbarity, and he tried to counter them not with a romantic vision of peace, but a pacifism based on reason and upheld by a scientific position based on analysis of the conditions which had favoured the development of humanity, together with a condemnation of those which, in various eras, had hindered it. Pacifism he saw as a political solution, sustained by that "federation of governments" which revealed the need for an international organisation to operate above all the barriers created by the various manifestations of national selfishness. Despite the moment in history, Spencer was optimistic about the future. Indeed, he belongs to that group of philosophers who believe that now the logic of progress has become a "law" of nature which cannot be eliminated (cf. Muller, 281). The verb to believe is not, in this case, exaggerated if it is true that some believe that for Spencer "faith in individuals is the faith in the third estate which creates its own self, as long as its path is not blocked by feudal privileges, State bureaucracy, too many regulations, in other words, provided that one is left 'free' to 'do', to 'enjoy'" (Ferrarotti, 40). There is no doubt that his confidence is one of a class which is about to enjoy its triumph, but to reduce Spencer to this perspective would mean to underrate him. He possesses a sincere desire for liberty and the conviction that it must be defended from the monstrous political mechanisms which the twentieth century has created against it. In this respect, the English philosopher has succeeded in showing the spheres within which power must be restrained to avoid allowing it to overflow, invading the areas which are the exclusive domains of people.

10. Socialism and the Open Society.

10.1 I realize that many people will find it strange that a chapter on socialism is included in a study of open societies. Yet, I am convinced that if it is possible to step aside from all the Communist, statist, or generally monocratic deviations that the contemporary world has inflicted on us, it will be easy to acknowledge the contributions that some authors in this area, too, have offered to the development of democratic ideals and practices. Who can deny that the struggles, debates and proposals of so many innovators, who had nothing in common with dialectic absurdities, have contributed to improving, in England for example, workers' conditions which, as several investigating commissions have shown, shocked even the most imperturbable conservatives? Among the large number of texts one by Maurice Niveau comes to mind: *Histoire des faits économiques contemporains* (cf. Ch. V of the first section). Here it is pointed out that Parliament even had to note cases of child torture in factories to the dismay of all. Workers were induced to create movements which then became part of the democratic arena and obliged politicians to face the subject of reform seriously.

10.2 The difficulty encountered in recognizing, I would say in recalling, these and other numerous episodes that, once resolved, contributed not a little to democracy, surely comes from the fact that socialism has almost always been considered a universal category for which, as Cole points out at the very beginning of his basic work, it has been possible to give a definition. Paraphrasing Plotinus, we could say, *ad escludendum*, that with two centuries of history behind us, it is easier to perceive the genuine nature of thought which had from the start alerted us to the dangerous centralist positions that ended up turning humanity to ridicule, although the intention had been to redeem it. Who can deny that a rereading of Proudhon can enable us to perceive all the future contradictions of the twentieth century? How can anyone forget Bernstein? Even before names, however, how can we forget what Cole recalls in this *Introduction* and which I try briefly to summarize: without socialism people would, in any case, have hastened to devote attention to that sense of limitations to be placed on certain types of action and economic interests, and typical of every liberal-democratic society, given the predominating tendency to exalt of the rights of the individual? It is no accident that the adjective social was created to be placed in opposition to individual. The first was not intended to destroy the second, as real socialism or communism wanted to do, but to place it in relation to the first. That certain socialists were "different" from those that history more vividly revealed to us later, is proven by the fact that they were criticized by the advocates of scientific socialism, for being diffident towards politics and, even worse, towards the revolution that they did not view as the solution to the ills of society.

10.3 Among the outstanding features which the humanist socialists, along with other popular forces, contributed to consolidating, there is such an interest in education that a good education is considered a fundamental right of mankind. Like other achievements, this one, as Cole constantly reminds us in his dense *Introduction,* had to come about outside of the class struggle, a system of confrontation repudiated by most people. It was the advent of the Communist ideal that took attention away from the efforts of those who, on the level of reforms, attempted to change society with methods of democratic struggle. It must certainly be recalled that many of these authors who opposed any utopian dream, were, in turn, misrepresented by their own followers. Furthermore just as not all Marxists place themselves along the orthodox Marxist line, the same can be said for the Saintsimonians and Saint-Simon or for the Proudhonians and Proudhon.

A) *A Precursor, Saint-Simon.*

10.4 Saint-Simon (1760-1825) certainly could not be called a socialist and he put forth quite debatable ideas in many cases, but he had several fortunate insights on the social and political level, not to mention the dream, shared by many thinkers of his time, of compiling all the universal scientific knowledge in a new Encyclopaedia, which would be of use in changing society. Without this tool, everything would have been more arduous since it is not at all true that history always proceeds in a progression. Constructive phases correspond to critical phases or ones that are actually regressive if institutions turn out not to be fit for progress in science and economy. Like other French men of his era, he offered a highly positive judgment of the medieval Church because it possessed indubitable moral authority, which it had exercised, and so had been a pillar of social stability, and had also played a great role as an educator. Saint-Simon was little concerned by the fact that the institutions of the past had not been very democratic or democratic at all. For him, the concern of an organized society had to remain that of creating well-being then perhaps the rest would follow on its own. It is true that he did not have faith in the masses, but because he worried that ignorance might prevail over knowledge. Only the latter would end up improving the lives of all by increasing the purchasing power of the masses and favouring the further development of industries (cf. Cole, I, 39-43). To accomplish all of this, French society had to be substantially changed. It had remained unchanged since the time of Louis XIV. The king had given power and a role to the aristocracy which the French Revolution had just succeeded in undermining. Industrialists, scientists and the bourgeoisie in general had seen their dreams of a Restoration frustrated, having again conferred on the old class the governing of society.

10.5 Saint-Simon was not a pessimist, however. He was convinced that the industrial phenomenon, with its guarantees of wealth and prosperity and its increasing specialization in the various professions, had become an orientation which future society could not reverse. Growing rationality, not abstract as in the past, but based on rigorous scientific methods, would make possible a new approach to the various social realities and would bring about more rigorous organization of political life. We have not yet arrived at Comte, but the possibility could already be perceived – and this was an impulse towards modern constructivism – of actually considering society a social body whose vital principle was, it can be said, conferred on it by industry. An adequate political system was needed, one continually evolving as modern exigencies required. One might not agree with Saint-Simon's methodologies, but there is not doubt that he strongly felt the need for reforms that would prevent dangerous conflicts, and indeed foresee and resolve them. History was to see the progressive consolidation of the industrial class, which, perhaps, would lead to a new aristocracy based, however, on tangible and easily verifiable merits. A new command-obedience relationship would thus be created, established no longer by force, but by science:

commands would become directions and the new leaders would no longer be military or politicians, but industrialists. Decisions themselves would no longer come about as the result of extemporaneous improvisations, but would be the result of scientific demonstrations. Liberty itself, no longer able to ignore them, would have to turn into the science of liberty. In other words, politics would be scientific. Despite all the dangers, the wish was to change the dependency relationship to carry out decisions that would be the result of competence (cf. D'Addio, SDP, II, 177-179). To accomplish this, a constitutional reformed would be needed, providing for three different houses in each of which there would be engineers, physicists and mathematicians, in other words, components of the various branches of production.

10.6 Industry, with its new culture, would found a new bond of solidarity among humans, bring about a new religion in order to solve problems of poverty and moral wretchedness. It had to be based on a new social ethic turning on a strong faith in God, but it had to be a religion without theology: this is the aim of the *Nouveau Christianisme*. This work had been laid out just as the author died. He had managed to write just the introductory part in which all his intentions are indicated. The conviction that reveals itself in these few pages is that of those figures of his time, such as Condorcet, who were convinced of the perfectibility, at times even of perfection, of future humanity. What is most important, however, is that Saint-Simon seemed concerned –and the same would be true of Comte – about giving back to the western world that unity of intentions which had been lost after the Reformation. In his opening remarks, he says: "In those cases where the Church has leaders more capable of directing the forces of society towards the divine goal, I believe that it can be considered infallible, without problems, and that society will act wisely if it allows itself to be guided by it". It is a new infallibility, based on science, which, in accordance with the intentions of Saint-Simon would avoid useless conflicts with the consequent waste of time and useful energies.

B) *Evil as a Social Problem: R. Owen.*

10.7 Robert Owen's (1771-1858) works contain not a few innovations. More a man of Acton than of thought, Owen, in his writings, too, could shock public opinion and force it to take into consideration social problems caused by rapid industrialization. To overcome them, he undertook a "policy" of reforms that were at the heart of the co-operative movement. If he attacked *laissez-faire,* he did so because he felt that it was the cause of poverty and moral decay among workers. The horrendous "existential" conditions in which they were forced to live were what unleashed alcoholism, prostitution, theft and other evils towards which many of the wretched poor were thrust. That led him to what is perhaps the greatest and most hotly debated conviction that would then be one of the pillars of Marxism: the character of individuals is a function of the society in which they live. Evil, therefore, has social roots. If it is to be fought, society must be changed. This is what comes out from his very first essays assembled under the title *A new view of Society and other Writings*. However, the expression society still seemed too vague: the rude character of a worker was the result of his life in the factory because that was the world for workers. This was to be the point of departure to re-educate, then educate the future generations.

10.8 An errand boy who had become an entrepreneur, Owen understood the factory not only in terms of the way of working, already inhuman in itself, but, in view of the fact that workers spent almost all their time at work. He understood it in terms of the way of eating, conversing, spending one's own free time, in other words, living. For this reason, serious reform should not only involve working hours, but also would have to deal with the canteens, recreation facilities, study environments, play and the physical development of children. Implied in the reform of the factory was that of the small world in which entire families and human beings of all ages operated. Modifying the working environment was the most effective way to mould the characters of the future generations. The pedagogical problem thus became crucial for this purpose. Owen did more than just incite, he sought to apply his aims in Lanark County. Later, he attempted to carry out this aim in the United States as well, in the New Harmony community where he quickly failed, having certainly not been aided but also subverted by various opportunists. The idea was quite simple, in any case, but perhaps it was not yet ripe. This was the co-operativist conception: basically that of giving birth to farming or industrial villages that would be self-sufficient.

10.9 It may seem strange but, as Cole justly observed, Owen's judgments on nascent capitalism were not displeasing to many highly-placed circles of old Tories who detested the nouveaux riches from the manufacturing industry. Among other things, these people were taking labour away from the countryside. If Owen had avoided casting his darts against the Anglican Church and religion in general he would have had those conservatives on his side. The same reason was perhaps behind the failure of the American venture. There, while the Owenites sought to create "modern" communities that would be capable of preventing the harmful effects of industrialism, the American communities had arrived in the new lands mostly to flee religious persecution and it was on the basis of these principles that they wished to organize the new settlements (cf. Cole, I, 93-97). The relationship between religion and socialism was one of the great problems in the history of the left and of democracy in the nineteenth century. Had they not created an abyss and had they tried to find a form of cooperation based on mutual respect, the workers' movement might have obtained greater success and it would also have avoided the absurd forms of radicalizing that we are all familiar with. Moreover, thinkers such as Philippe-Joseph-Benjamin Buchez (1796-1865) or Constantin Pecqueur (1801-1887) could surely have had more influence in circles which, feeling themselves under attack, ended up even refusing dialogue. For the most part, they were personalities who saw aid to workers as one of the fundamental missions of the Church, which, however, had to protect itself from those who wanted to fight a just battle in the name of atheism and materialism.

C) *The first Denunciation of the Communist* Weltanschauung: *P.J. Proudhon.*

10.10 Proudhon has a place of his own among those who understood the danger of communistic State-controlled economies. He found certain conceptions almost repulsive. Radical positions never fascinated him because, in his view, they were the fruit of intellectuals who had no relationship with the daily lives of common people. Indeed, the more they kept their distance from the tangible problems of the people, the more they ended up building utopian systems that could not be achieved in any way. Proudhon was a sincere lover of equality, but he always understood that it could not be turned into an absolute. It had to co-exist with justice and liberty. These had to constitute the limit and foundation for any social organization. Thus, one can speak of positive anarchy just as one can call the French thinker a socialist, as he liked to call himself, on the understanding that for him socialism did not imply a specific control of the State and its central organization. Furthermore, he always rejected the idea of a State that ultimately imposed itself on the people in any way whatsoever.

Pierre-Joseph Proudhon was born in Besançon in 1809 of a modest family that could not aid him in his studies. With the help of student aid he studied in the *collège* of his city of birth for several years, up to 1827. He devoted himself to various jobs until he began to run a typography in 1836, and again took up his studies. He began to work out his thoughts on social reform which also led him to have problems with the legal authorities, who, in any case, absolved him. In 1844 he met Marx, Bakunin and other political refugees led by Herzen in Paris. After publishing *Qu'est-ce que la propriété?* (1840), in 1847 he published one of his most important works *Système des contradictions économiques ou Philosophie de la misère*. This was sharply criticized by Marx in the *Misère de la philosophie*. He took part in the February Revolution of 1848 and was elected as deputy to the Constituent Assembly. In this period he thought of setting up a People's Bank to provide free credit. Among the many works he wrote, the *Idée générale de la révolution du XXe siècle* (1851), *La justice dans la révolution et dans l'église* (1858), *De la capacité des classes ouvrières* (1865) and other writings on the federation principle are worth mentioning. He died at Passy in 1865.

10.11 In Proudhon's opinion, post-revolutionary systems that appealed to liberal and democratic principles were not, in some respects, very different from *Ancien-Régime* monarchies. In any case, the criterion of property, even if based on different premises, was defended without any concern for how it might exist alongside that of justice. For Proudhon, property cannot be defended on the basis of natural right because it would end up denying the right to equality. If this consideration applies for real estate, it must apply for personal property all the more, especially when they are the tools of human labour. Those who work have the right to own what they produce. If anyone wishes to maintain that by paying wages the owner compensates the worker for a day's labour, that person forgets that the product realized is not only the fruit of the individual's efforts, but also the result of co-ordination and merging of several labour forces that turn out not to be paid, in their entirety, by the owner. This is what leads to the dependency of workers who become mere instruments of production and have no further possibility of manifesting their liberty (cf. D'Addio, SDP, II, 295-297). On the contrary, the moment of labour should be that of the highest expression of the personality because it is in their labour that people fulfil and express themselves. Suffice it to analyze the way labour is organized in a society to understand how it – and the various social classes – are organized. For this reason, Proudhon did not want to replace capitalistic management of industry with a political system that would manage it bureaucratically. In both cases it would be an offense against individual liberty. This liberty could be defended only by competition capable of avoiding total standardization of the economy, which, in turn, would lead to a new form of despotism. A monopoly of the economy, but also of ideas, would result. Proudhon can be said to have been the first to identify the tendency, typical of Marxism, to turn ideas into unquestionable dogmas (cf. Pellicani, MM, 84 and 103). This is why he was opposed to the excessive power of the specialists (which separated him from the Saintsimonians) and bureaucratic officials (cf. Cole, I, 204-205).

10.12 Proudhon counted on societies based on the individual in the family rather than on the State. The family was seen as a principle of social co-operation. Solidarity between the various families and their antagonism were the driving force of society and the incentive to improve. The State could only perform a limiting function, that of keeping watch over justice in financial relations. It had to see to it that the contract itself, certainly not the one of Rousseau's distorted vision, could be freely implemented. Every person must be free to make the agreements he or she wants with others. Everyone must, therefore, be capable of negotiating freely and taking personal responsibility (cf. Cole, I, 205-206 and 209-210). If, for that reason, he opposed the State of politics, Proudhon wanted a State in the sense of an arbiter which had to guarantee security, ensure the defence of the weak and support the working classes against the excessive power of capital, but also from any economic form capable of tending towards monopoly. Defending workers meant seeing to it that they became protagonists in the production system making sure that the distribution of wealth, carried out on the basis of the principle of mutual aid, would make possible equality and liberty for all those associated. To do so Proudhon proposed the creation of "workers companies", sorts of joint-stock companies, whose shares were held only by those who worked and were called upon to manage their own activities thanks to facilitations granted through the liberalization of credit (cf. D'Addio, SDP, II, 301). Anything that smacked of centralization had to be abolished because in those cases the State became the major organizer of the economy. Thus, ministries and their areas of competence had to be abolished, and these were to be delegated to local administrations under the full autonomy of the workers. Only those central offices dealing with statistics were to be conserved. This was the seed of the federal system which, among other things, also had the task of moderating the excesses of nationalism which, for Proudhon, degenerates into imperialism.

10.13 Federalism eliminates the worst ill of the modern State: centralization. In this case, as in the state as Rousseau and the Jacobins conceived of it, not only does the citizen give up sovereignty ("*se démet de sa souveraineté*") but towns and all associated bodies end up being absorbed into the State. The consequences become apparent to everyone quite soon: citizens and towns are deprived of all their dignity and forms of State interference multiply. Moreover, taxpayers' burdens "*croissent en proportion*" (cf. Proudhon, PF, 143-144). It is understandable why Proudhon's federal organization, which must expand from France to all of Europe, is one of communes and cities. When cities realize that there is no longer work for the various groups and associations, they must consider themselves saturated and encourage the creation and expansion of other cities. In this action, the medium bourgeoisie, with its organizational and entrepreneurial ability, could perform a highly important duty, practically as important as what a completely renewed school could do. Proudhon suggests that the school operate hand in hand with needs and job prospects and that it be based on the apprenticeship system to place people more easily in the system of production.

D) *The* Sozialdemokratie: *E. Bernstein.*

Eduard Bernstein was born in Berlin in 1850 in a Jewish family of Polish origin. At a very young age, he embraced Marxism and became a leading figure in the German socialist movement. He came into contact with Marx and Engels when the periodical *Zukunft* was founded. He held important positions in the movement in Germany even when Bismarck's antisocialist laws were in effect, and in exile in Zurich and London. His writings on the history of socialism and autobiographical notes are numerous. The monthly periodical *Dokumente des Sozialismus* is important for the bibliography on the socialist movement. He was the editor between 1901 and 1905. His renown is, in any case, related to *Die Voraussetzungen des Sozialismus und die Aufgaben* *der Sozialdemokratie*, in which he included articles from *Neue Zeit*, published first in 1899, revised several times, and translated into various languages. He died in isolation in 1932, in Berlin.

10.14 As the century drew to a close, and social-democratic ideals arose, the Marxist view and its ability to change the industrial world for the better was definitively condemned. In a series of articles which came out in the journal *Neue Zeit*, starting in 1896, Bernstein accused Marxist socialism of utopianism, showing that the idea that capitalistic society was then on the brink of destruction was absurd, and that this would mean that the working class could effectively obtain tangible advantages. That meant the inability of Marxism to read the future and the impossibility of correcting society by means of socialistic measures if the revolutionary method were accepted. Rather than sudden events, socialism would need reforms, legality and gradual change, precisely what the Maximalists and the Marxist orthodoxy rejected. Needless to say, that rejection involved all of dialectical materialism and its absurd scientific claims.

10.15 The critique of "historical necessity" struck at the heart of all the Marxist framework. Bernstein did not limit himself to this criticism, however. He cast doubt on the validity of the concept of surplus value on which the entire economic theory of the author of *Das Kapital* was based. He did not acknowledge the tendency towards concentration of capital in the way, and, especially, the period of time set forth by Marx. He wondered whether workers were really plunged effectively into a condition of growing poverty or whether the opposite did not take place, right where capitalism continued to develop. It should be added that capital was not being concentrated in the hands of a smaller and smaller number of individuals due to the birth and growth of joint-stock companies and that, as a consequence, the middle class would assert itself in new forms instead of disappearing (cf. Cole III/1, 281-283). That all implied a radical change not only in theoretical analysis, but especially in socialist practice. In a new conception of history that rejects the dialectical method as being scientific, and thus grants history only the possibility of effective improvement and not the certainty of achieving a perfect society, liberalism was no longer seen as an obstacle to be eliminated but a great ideal movement, which socialism had to inherit to allow greater possibilities for reform.

10.16 The subjects dealt with by Bernstein along with others of a more strictly economic nature such as the development of cartels and trusts, socialization of production and democratization of capital were also treated by other thinkers of the time. Rudolf Hilferding (cf. Colletti, XXVI) is an example. Bernstein, however, introduced that political content that others had not been able to offer. Going back to some later points of Engels he maintained with extreme clarity that "the doubt concerns the premises themselves. All indications say that a political revolution that might bring a bourgeois-radical party into power, is now something of the past in the advanced countries of Europe" (Bernstein, 68). While Engels, however, seemed to be airing the prospects for a new way of bringing about revolution, in Bernstein's thought there was a radical change in the direction of embracing the methods of parliamentary democracy once and for all. Not doing this meant failing to take into account the creativity of the individual mind or, worse yet, mortifying it. Close analysis of the situation showed that "it as a truth no less consolidated that in an entire series of branches of industry, side by side with the large companies, the smaller and medium ones gave signs of an incontestable vitality" (Bernstein, 98). The crisis, leaving the market, surrendering to the competition of some company gave way to the immediate rise of others, with other products and new ideas. This was the actual driving force of a society that was always open and the socialists also had to accept it. "Socialism does not want to create a new, closed system, of any sort. The individual must be free – not in a metaphysical sense that anarchists dream of, that is, free of any obligation towards the community, – but free of any economic constriction in its movements and professional choices" (Bernstein, 188).

SECOND PART

11. From Absolutism...

11.1 In the modern era, the political question presents itself in new and dramatic ways, which do not necessarily mean innovation. Whatever judgment one may place on it, the new era offers new artistic and scientific achievements, but also a true paradox. A culture focused on human beings, their greatness and nobility, politically speaking, witnesses not only the triumph but also the exaltation of absolutism. Everyone accepts and justifies reforms as something willed by God. Even some exponents from the Catholic world, Bossuet for example, consider it the political system that best conforms to the Holy Scriptures and they ignore all the limitations devised by the theoreticians of the medieval period. The right to resist, the exercise of power under the law are not only empty words, but dangerous artifices capable of placing the ever growing role of the sovereign in jeopardy. Absolutism becomes the unopposed master of the political scene and its theoreticians the most highly considered and most widely read authors.

A) *The Need for Power and the Problem of Security at the Time of the Reformation.*

11.2. Luther's thought (1483-1546) came into being in one of the most tormented ages in German history. As far as political analysis is concerned, it seems "almost guided only by occasional polemic contingencies" in a plight which "had split up the centuries-old identity of religion and morality"

(Firpo, 5-6). Luther's political conceptions can be divided into three periods: one which precedes the moment of open rebellion and in which the attempt to give life to an ethic of solidarity fails; the other starting in 1520, which aims to claim the freedom of Christians in opposing spiritual questions, the total submission to centuries-old authority in political matters; finally, in his later years, to ensure for himself useful support for the Reformation, he even justifies the intervention of the Princes in religious matters, formulating what can be called a sort of *lay absolutism.* In this perspective all the medieval speculations on the legitimizing of power disappear and spiritual is confused with political authority. Absurdly enough, both are seen as one, even when they govern in the most despotic way, as if this were willed by God. The faithful are given no opportunity to rebel. Their liberty of faith is only interior. Subject such as those pertaining to the justification of tyranicide seem almost to come from another planet (cf. Firpo, 6-7).

11.3 To be sure, the Reformation gained a foothold due to a series of concomitant causes that cannot be ignored. Limiting ourselves here, too, to those that are not of a religious nature, we must recall the serious German economic crisis, the crumbling of the imperial political structures now reduced to fragile schemes and, not the least, the invention of the press which was put to use opportunely. Symptomatic is the fact that an Augustinian renounced the separation between the two cities proposing their complete identification to the point of considering disobedience, civil as well, one of the most serious sins, indeed, extremely serious. Power, in its every manifestation, must be submitted to passively. Luther's thought thus comes as a "tendentious apology of absolutism and ends up by freeing secular power from any bond: the sovereign is free from every law, deaf to any advice, unaware of any right (...) indignant at the excesses of the rebellious. Luther dictates the libellous pamphlet *Against the impious and villainous bands of peasants*, abandoning himself to unheard-of verbal excesses, in a true excess of cruel rage: the rebels, he proclaims, are street marauders" (Firpo, 11) and any restrictive measure against them is, obviously, admissible. It should not be forgotten that, after the terrible and unheard-of massacre at Frankenhausen, he went so far as to be joyful because, too, a certain Münzer, whom he considered a false prophet, had died. The peasants were possessed by the devil and thus committed only diabolical acts. On these occasions Luther took upon himself the task of teaching the consciences of the secular authorities who, without any pity whatsoever, had to beat the rebels into submission. They had forgotten to swear fidelity and obedience and they did not practice the latter. It is a sensational fact that this recalls that whoever is "accused of sedition is already under Papal prohibition (...) For that reason, anyone who can, must strike, slaughter, massacre publicly or in secret". The peasants have no right to protest. Their protests are due to the demons who no longer exist down in hell, but have all come up among the peasants. So, it is not only a right, but also a duty to punish them. It almost seems as if "God perhaps stirred the demon to punish the entire German nation". This is why the time of ire and the sword must replace the time of grace. A prince, more than a prayer can procure himself a place in heaven by shedding blood (cf. Luther, XVIII, 335-343).

11.4 Not only is Luther's concept of politics, as Firpo continues, reduced to "shabbiness without hope", but it gives rise to one of the most closed societies that have been theorized in the modern era, since it is completely static. Political authority, which people had sought to contain with the defences typical of the middle ages and the concern for law of the classical world, no longer encounters any type of barrier, since the dualism between the spiritual and the temporal, the source of many battles for liberty, has disappeared. Luther had created a sort of pluralism within the Church. Now he was bringing about a sort of State Church. Contrary to the variety of opinions, he maintained that heresy must be repressed by using all means (cf. Firpo, 14-16) even though such had not been the case for his own, obviously. There was a return to a sort of mosaic of theocracy which cast aside that drive carried on in the west to secularize power. As a result not only were intellectuals or the people removed from the task of managing the state, but also people became indifferent to the desires and sufferings of the humblest layers of the population which, because of sin, always had to be disciplined and controlled in all of their manifestations. Luther clearly distinguishes the state of liberty from that of captivity. In his famous *On the Liberty of the Christian*, he clearly maintains that the former is exercised only spiritually, whereas the latter manifests itself in practical life (cf. Lutero, VII, 12-39).

11.5 What characterizes all absolutists, from whatever cultural environment, is their acute pessimism. Calvin (1509-1564) does not escape this either. He has been described to us as a dark, frigid, joyless personality "who flees, hides, steeped in chasteness and reserve, who writes a great deal, like all of his contemporaries, but does not speak of himself (...). His profession of faith (...) in Chapters VII-IX of Book III of the *Institutio*, is also expressed objectively" (Tourn, 16 and 20). This objectivity permeates all of Calvin's works, by and large. Indeed, he has been called the one who has regularized, what could be called the Lutheran reform. He was able to put ideas in order with a sense of structure, understanding that the force of the Church, which had nonetheless been fought, was organization. This is why, approaching Calvin, one realizes that the political aspect of the religious question cannot be forgotten. Indeed, the political dimension involved everything and everyone so that Geneva would become the "Stronghold of the Reformation". Like it or not, all of its economic, professional, commercial, fair and recreational life would be transformed in terms of all-absorbing religion, which would now be called totalitarian (cf. Tourn, 23-25). Thus, Calvin cannot be called an innovator; his conception of society is absolutely traditional and not at all tolerant, even of those reformed fringes, such as the Anabaptists, who had also been the fruit of contestation in the Church.

11.6 The means of repressing freedom of conscience and thought were the same as those for which the world of the Counter-Reformation or Catholic Reformation would be reproached. The *Consistoire,* a juridical body made up of ministers and a set number of lay people, an actual City-Church, was set up in Geneva. Its activity was essentially disciplinary, to the point of warning and excommunicating, and, where necessary, burning people at the stake. Even the simple "curious minds" or "spiritual libertines" were the objects of suspicion and considered as dangerous as the Pope (cf. Tourn, 33 and 46). It seems an aristocratic form worthy of Platonist governors, to whom he often refers. But all that finds a justification from on high, in what for Calvin must be the reason for being of the civil government, against which "barbarous and mad people are encountered, who would like to overthrow any authority whatsoever, whether or not established by God (…) The purpose of this temporal government is, on the contrary, to ensure and maintain the service of God in its external form, the pure doctrine, religion" (Calvin, IV, 20°, 1-2). A feeling of "reverence" towards authority and towards one's superiors must constantly be maintained". "There is no doubt that one must submit to anyone who has been granted superiority. When the Lord raises someone to power he tells us his will is that that person reign. The Scriptures as a whole bear witness to this fact" (Calvin, IV, 20°, 28). To be sure, superiors and subjects have duties in common, but this cannot be an excuse to drive anyone to disobedience. Even fathers have obligations towards their children but, if the children do not absolve him, they cannot be disobedient in any case. "If anyone wished to deduce from this that obedience is owed only to a just person, they would be reasoning perversely (…). It is not up to us to remedy these evils but all that can be done is to beg for help from God" (Calvin, IV, 20°. 29). Where has the *right to resistance* gone? It had been the crucial premise for civil disobedience.

11.7 As Plato would have said, the magistrates will also perform an action typical of censorship: "will they have the courage to tolerate the presence of some iniquity in their office when they realize that it is the throne of the living God?" (Calvin, IV, 20°, 6). The continued references to Moses must not deceive us. Even if the "reminder" to avoid evil surely has value religiously speaking, here, that task is carried on by civil magistrates. The confusion between the spiritual and the temporal moment is a further prelude to the implementation of a theocratic view which denies every form of division of powers and, thus, of liberty. To disobey – and this is paradoxical in the reformers of all religions, means to rise to the level of judges. What, however, has become of the freedom of conscience and that very consent which, without the faculty of judging, is pure submission? Furthermore, why should everyone except the reformers obey?

B) *The Birth of the State and the Need for Absolutism: J. Bodin.*

11.8 The wars of religion heightened the climate of insecurity and out of this came the theoretical and practical justification of absolutism. Particularly in France, the need arose to face the problem of the unity of the State. Bodin reflected on this subject and, despite the fact that he offered an original analysis of the fundamental concept of sovereignty, he did not free himself from the absolutist mentality. Indeed he became one of it's main supporters. The modern "constitutional" State can be said to have originated officially with Bodin, because he claimed for the State a particular independence from all the religions, but this also led him to fight all those "parties" which, in some way, could threaten the monolithic unity of the State. He remained tied to the relationship of law and politics, which had meant a great deal in the Italian thought that had gone before. However, he rejected not a few and basic contributions from tradition and the very ones that spoke of liberty: he was harsh towards theoreticians of the right to resist because they viewed the political authority as dependent on the consensus of those associated. This was an element of weakness for the State (cf. D'Addio, SDP, II, 347-348).

Jean Bodin was born in Angers in 1529 in a modest family who sent him to the Carmelites to study. Free from his vows at the age of twenty, he went to Toulouse where he taught for about a decade. These were also years of law and political study which led to his being elected in 1561 as an attorney to the Parliament of Paris where he kept up closely with a dramatic period in French politics. In 1566 he published the *Methodus ad facilem historiarum cognitionem.* Along with *Les six livres de la République* published in 1576, this work gained him an important place in French politics. The years that followed were marked by variable political fortunes until he decided to interrupt his political activity and withdraw to Laon where he died in 1596. His writings on juridical, and also religious matters are numerous as far as the relationships among the various religions are concerned.

11.9 Bodin, like few others, perceived the economic innovations of his century even as he dealt with some crucial themes such as sovereignty. He seemed to pursue the widest variety of subjects in an encyclopaedic way almost always failing to synthesize his results. The reference to the Republic is strange. It had almost always had quite a different meaning from that which Bodin used. For him, it represented a just government of several family units and what they had in common. All was guaranteed by the sovereign power (cf. Bodin, I, 2) a true bond capable of creating a single body from several nuclei. The government was just, well defined, well ordered, and it operated legally in the sense that it had to have its legitimization. Anticipating themes which would be developed by Vico in another manner, he considered the family as an essential cell in the political whole because it manifested the goal of happiness, to obtain which, order was necessary. The family also gave rise to the need for a sovereign power considered almost a natural thing without which the political community would not exist. Hence the conclusion: the Republic is the *sovereign* power, because it is just and natural, *perpetual*, because this sovereignty is exercised for life, and *absolute*, because the monarch who wields that power is freed, *absolutus* (cf. Bodin, I, 8) from the laws themselves whether they are expressions of the will of his predecessors or his own, since he can change them at will. Thus, he cannot feel limited in any way.

11.10 The novelty of the concept of sovereignty again became bogged down in the problems of the time. A sovereign had to become omnipotent; indeed, this was the only way, in Bodin's view, to guarantee national unity. This meant complete concentration which denied any idea of political division, a dangerous legacy of feudalism. Unity and national independence led Bodin to prefer monarchy although it did not exclude sovereignty for other forms of government. Obviously, Bodin was taking a stand against the Estates General which, for him, were the old expression of division in medieval France. He was equally hostile towards a mixed government, a deceiving regime, not only because it guaranteed the presence of other sources of power, but because any form of dissent could arise. Dissent is a great danger for the unity of the State. Here the nature of one contrary to any form of openness is revealed. Through law, the State manifests its will. When humans act law offers that certainty that reaches its highest point when human law integrates with divine and natural law. Both, finally, are the only limits which sovereign power encounters as it acts and from which a wise prince should not deviate in any way.

11.11 Monarchy is the best form of government because it is closest to nature itself. Observing nature, one realizes that everything justifies this form of government. Suffice it to look at the family, the sky, the world, etc. A monarchy, guided by natural law, ensures that the subjects may freely enjoy their property. It offers greater guarantees of choice, in matters of State, of wise and capable people because the sovereign is free to choose them (cf. Bodin, VI, 4). Then, it is the form of government that ensures *a longer lasting government and greater stability.* This is so because, for Bodin, true monarchy is harmonious in the sense that it can keep the various components together in harmony. For this reason, it succeeds in avoiding extreme discontent and revolutions. To accomplish this it periodically consults various bodies, listens to and gives credence to the intermediary bodies so that even if the final decision is up to the sovereign, that monarchy can be called absolute but not arbitrary. It is practically surrounded by a halo of holiness so that one can suppose that it is willed by God, and this will be the supposition in future.

C) *Absolute Power and the Catholic Reform: J. B. Bossuet.*

11.12 Bossuet's position in justifying absolutism seems even more paradoxical (1627-1704). His *Politique tirée des propres paroles de l'Ecriture Sainte* sounds even more absurd than the writings of the Protestant Reformers. The latter had abandoned the path opened up during the middle ages, and did not know about the various theories on resistance or the role of laws in the control of political power. Bossuet, however, is even more responsible for having ignored the classics, which go from John of Salisbury to Aquinas, and he should have taken them into account. Perhaps the only justification for him can be the climate of insecurity in which he lived. It drove him, like Hobbes, from whom came translations dedicated to the king, in France as well, to take refuge in absolutism and, in any case, take a step backwards in political thought. He would provide material for all that current of opinion that we would call the "reactionary Catholics". Bossuet wrote with the precise intention of having God speak through the Holy Scriptures, attempting to show the future king of France that the Providence of God supports him and that he must do all he can not to stray from them. It was a book for a single reader then, and written in the form of an easy-to-consult manual, clear, with divisions and subdivisions as if it were meant to be memorized easily. Out of this came the celebration of a divine sort of absolutism, of a prince willed by God. If it is true that humans are naturally sociable, it is also true that they are born in original sin, so they need a strong government which is capable of keeping them united only by subjugating them completely. Everyone gains from this subjection, because, to paraphrase Hobbes, it my be said that either absolutism is instilled or chaos will reign.

11.13 The superiority of the monarchy is evident and this is written in the nature of things. It is, after all, the most ancient, most common and hence the most natural form. It can already be seen in the creation of the family which constitutes further confirmation of the fact that all individuals are born as subjects and need an authority (cf. Bossuet, II, 1-7). This point of view is almost functionalist, as well as utilitarian: this form of power experiences no divisions because, for one thing, it is carried on directly through the male line. God is the God of peace and peace, like order, is achieved by following the government of one's own country. This is a further confirmation of Bossuet's conservative view. For him, the problem of order is quite far from that of consensus and, hence, legality. The *characteristics of monarchy* are simple: it is *holy* in the sense that monarchs are like ministers of God to whom they must answer for how power has been used. At the same time it is *paternal* because the sovereigns interpret the designs of God the Father. Thus it is *religious*, otherwise there would be no reason to obey, on the assumption, of course, that religion cannot be other than that of the sovereign. It follows that it is *just* because it seeks to bring about divine justice. Then, it is *absolute* insofar as the orders, for the very reason that they are legitimate, are obligatory (cf. Bossuet, IV, 1-3). Such absoluteness confers a form of rationality on it. The sovereign is aware of all that concerns life and what is better for the subjects and for France. As far as France is concerned, it is easy to see that Bossuet's religiosity has a certain Gallican flavour to it, this too, capable of influencing not a few currents in French Catholic thought. This Gallicanism justifies absolutism, which can be hindered only if it operates manifestly against the word of God and the laws of nature created by Him.

D) *The Aberrations of Absolutism: the Leviathan.*

11.14 The most disparate observations have been made concerning Hobbes. People have gone so far as to say that he was the first theoretician of the possessive individualism that would be characteristic of modern bourgeois and capitalistic societies (cf. Macpherson, 52). All the suppositions that place Hobbes outside of the category of absolutism and authoritarianism must be rejected, however, because there is nothing in his writings that could represent a defence of that area of laws which are the crucial point for identifying an open society, as far as this work is concerned. Moreover, as has been unequivocally shown, the realization of which can be called market societies "presupposes the institutionalization of a 'protected area' (…) In other words, it presupposes the separation between sovereignty (public) and property (private) and thus the rigorous setting of limits to the circle of power of the State" (Pellicani, HSB, 3, which contains an observation by J. R. Commons). It is a division of two areas, coming from Latin tradition, which is unknown to theoreticians of absolutism and which was later to be ignored by those of totalitarianism who, with Hegel in the lead, wished to bring back that synthesis of the public and the private typical, according to their interpretation, of the Greek dimension. For Hobbes, there is no other bulwark that can defend the individual from action by the absolute authority, aside from the right to personal safety. Nor is it possible to accept the position of Bobbio according to whom Hobbes ruthlessly presents a political form of unification to overcome medieval dissolution (cf. Pellicani, HSB, 4). It cannot be accepted because there is a lack of awareness of the other attempts which did not move in that direction.

Thomas Hobbes was born in Malmesbury in 1588. He received a degree at Oxford, became the tutor in the family of the Baron, then Earl of Cavendish. His primary interests were humanistic in nature and, in 1629, he published the English translation of the *Stories* from Thucydides. He made several trips to France and Italy and had an opportunity to meet Descartes and Galileo as well. Perhaps it was they who eventually oriented him towards scientific and philosophical studies, which led him to publish the *Elements of Law Natural and Politic*. Later, he took refuge in France, because of the English political situation, and remained there until 1652. It was in this period that he wrote *De Cive* (1642) and the *Leviathan* (1651). After returning to his country, he found protection in the house of the Earl of Devonshire, his former disciple, at Harwicke, where he died in 1679. Here he wrote many other works among which the following should be recalled in order to become familiar with his philosophical system: *De Corpore* (1655) and *De Homine* (1658). To understand how he viewed his times, it is important to read *Behemot. The History of the Causes of the Civil Wars of England*. In his old age, he even translated the *Iliad* and the *Odyssey* into English, completing them when he was close to the age of ninety.

11.15 Hobbes' century was tragic for English political life, but also for absolutism and its representatives. It was the century of revolutions, of civil and religious wars. It is an extremely tempestuous period, lacking in legal certainties and security. The glorious outcome of the Revolution of 1689 would not be seen by Hobbes who lived through the drama of his era with an extreme sense of participation, emotional as well. His political thought developed in the age of Cromwell, but was also influenced by the European cultural climate. Open criticism of Descartes could be sensed in the conviction that a reform of politics is possible only if accompanied by a serious reform of thought. The latter had to attain the rigour of Euclidian geometry. Only that way could philosophy and consequently politics become an irrefutable science, because it was based on the principles of nature.

11.16 It has been said that Hobbes' political thought was born of the antithesis between anarchy and unity (cf. Bobbio, TH, 30). That is doubtless true, but it cannot be forgotten that one must become familiar with the scientific philosophy of his time, and bring out the gnoseological motivation on which all of his political thought is based. If Machiavelli's anthropological considerations are based on an analysis of history, those of Hobbes, which certainly do not disregard them, are intended to have scientific objectiveness, derived, as well, from an analysis of nature. The premises on which Hobbes' natural philosophy are based are quite simple and self-evident like the body and the motion from which come the first fundamental concepts of space and time. For Hobbes, Descartes' distinction between thought and extension does not exist because *sensation,* any sensation, departs from a mechanical and materialistic conception which finds motion to be the prime cause of everything. The bodies, with their movement, trigger the brain leading to a *fantasy* or mental representation. When the object disappears, the representation remains and this determines a past sensation, the repetition of which triggers the memory, from which comes the possibility of comparing the present images with the past ones. The conventional use of words arises from the need to fix images, which are gradually repeated: "*the most noble and profitable invention of all other, was that of Speech, consisting of Names or Appellation and their Connection*" (Hobbes, L, 100). The name is a sort of *momentum* that is a sign that calls back to mind a memorized image. Simple ideas, which are at the heart of our awareness, group together and break up as do atoms depending on circumstances. This gives rise to logical discourse. Thus, logic is the consequence of a group of compositions and decompositions quite similar to mathematical operations.

11.17 The same must be said for morality which is affected by the process of attraction and repulsion, present in all of nature. All passions, not only those that are felt in the broad spectrum of pleasure and pain, are, in the ideal of Epicurus, to be ascribed to questions of movement and are aimed at a single tangible end: the self-preservation of the subject who might otherwise be the victim of various dangers due to nature in general and human nature in particular. In the midst of so many hazards, due to change and to human ill will, how is the survival possibility determined? Here, the question of the natural, which has become the moral, comes into play. It involves politics which, in Hobbes, means the need to leave the relative and the uncertain in order to attain the certain, the absolute, to the greatest degree possible, that is to absolutism. The problem, then, is that of security, closely tied to that of certainty. Politics must be given that same logic that operates in the sciences in order to make it certain in its action and goals. It is a bit like geometry considered the only science whose conclusions have become irrefutable at this point. Politics, too, must become irrefutable, which means not only a methodological revision of action, but even before that the very principles of knowing. "If the main cause of the ills that afflict civil society is philosophical in nature, the remedy can only come from philosophy... but what philosophy?" (Bobbio, TH, 33). Here that constructivist vision which inspires all of Hobbes' works, from the very start, is clear. The Leviathan is defined as an *Artificial Man*. To accomplish his goal, Hobbes must fight not a few adversaries, first, Aristotle, for whom "ethic and politics were not awareness of the certain, but of the probable"; secondly, against all those who "base their theories not on reason and experimentation but on the authority of precedents"; finally and thirdly, against those who confuse "their fantasies with truths revealed by God", that is the fanatics, the utopians and the visionaries of various sorts who abounded in the time of the reforms and, generally in periods of crisis (cf. Bobbio, TH, 34-35).

11.18 It is easy to construct the artificial man, as long as the mechanism of nature is identified. To imitate: this is the secret capable of giving artificial structures, the *artificium*, the precision and efficiency of the natural machine. Without such a plan, a continuous state of conflicts reigns among people, a free for all, due to the maximum liberty that each can exercise towards the others and which, sooner or later, also puts the strongest in the condition of undergoing the reactions of the weakest. There is equality between liberty and insecurity so that if one increases, so does the other. Liberty and insecurity are characteristic of the state of nature (Hobbes expresses this, for example, in Ch. I of his *Elements of Law Natural and Politic*). Here the faculties of human nature are explained and can be reduced to four types: physical force, experience, reason and passions. To that are to be added the desire for equality and the mutual desire to do harm to one another which lead to growing fear in the human soul. This fear increases in the conflicts and disagreements that come from the diversity of opinions, giving rise in each person to the conviction that he or she can rise to the position of judge in his or her controversies. Human beings almost feel tempted to live along, but they know that they cannot do so. They know that they are not up to supporting an isolated existence, because some advantage comes from the others, although the price is high. Living together with others means seeing in the other a competitor and all this increases mutual distrust. Hobbes does not, as some do, see a component of progress in competition. The positive values that come from the reasons behind the competition are inferior to the negative ones. The anxieties and expectations that it causes are added to those that religion already creates to such a degree that desires and expectations could even become unmanageable. All of that leads to a continual state of war, hardly appropriate for the preservation of the species and property. It increases fear more and more (of which Hobbes said that he was born a twin), and this leads to the need for a certain and irresistible power, capable of obtaining and maintaining peace (cf. Hobbes, E, Ch. I).

11.19 If peace is to be achieved, the rules capable of protecting it must be obeyed by everyone and, in the state of nature, that does not happen, because if anyone violates them, there is no-one strong enough to be able to oblige them to obey. It follows that the need to set up a strong power capable of binding those who disobey the rules, is a useful conclusion, and advantageous for everyone (cf. Bobbio, TH, 46). The setting up of civil society and its rules respond to the utilitarian principle that inspires all of Hobbes' thought. However, those rules are not the fruit of tradition nor are they improved by the difficult achievements of humanity, as happened in the open societies, but arise from a pact established at a precise moment in history. That pact does not require consensus in the future, but submission, unless, the one who makes it binding is incapable of keeping the peace and protecting the safety of individuals. If such were the case, there would be a return to the insecurity that is characteristic of the state of nature preceding the drawing up of the contract. Once the contract is stipulated, it constitutes the final criterion for judgment and the laws from which it comes differentiate the just from the unjust. Furthermore, in a state of war involving everyone against the other, there can not be any criterion for justice. This is the state of nature: *"The notions of Right and Wrong, Justice and Injustice have there no place. Where there is no common Power, there is no Law"* (Hobbes, L, 188). After the contract, everything is personalized in the power of the sovereign, since to realize those conditions of life, it has been necessary for all people to give up their own power to transfer it to another. The result is to "attribute to an impartial third party all the power that each has in the state of nature" (Bobbio, TH, 50). Here there is the complete denial, not only of any limitation of power, but even the impossibility of opposing any possible abuse of power. There is also irony against the effectiveness of possible mixed governments or constitutions capable only of giving rise to continual disorders from which only a climate of growing fear can come about.

11.20 The reason why people give up their liberty, *the final cause* for which they agree to introduce precise rules governing their behaviour, is to obtain a *particular security* which cannot be encountered in any state of nature. The Leviathan, comes out of this. He is a sort of *"Mortall God, to which we owe under the Immortal God, our peace and defence"*. That Leviathan must not only ensure peace internally, but also against foreign enemies and is called a Sovereign because he holds the *Soveraigne Power* to which everyone must submit. That absolute power is determined in two ways: either on the basis of the *Naturall force* possessed by an extraordinary personality, especially in case of war, to dominate all others when, *voluntarily*, all submit to a third power which can express itself in various ways but which must be in the hands of one and only one if it is to be effective (cf. Hobbes, L, 227-228). Once the agreement is reached, every form of protest against the Sovereign must be considered an injustice since no-one can, in any way, accuse those who keep us alive and ensure peace. No other form of government can do better. Although other forms of government may exist, monarchy turns out to be the one closest to perfection. Thus, it can be said that Hobbes, with his absolutist conception, brought together those two contracts which the Middle Ages had succeeded in keeping distinct: the *Pactum unionis* or *societatis* and the *Pactum subjectionis*. Power became absolute because there was an absolute renunciation. Without this transfer, the state of struggle would continue. For this reason, that transfer must be *absolute*, but must also be *definitive*: all people even divest themselves of the right to judge. The fact of being definitive is obviously conditioned by several objectives, which are not only those of maintaining peace and security of individuals and goods. The Sovereign must be capable of being the law, himself. Representing the only possible legislative body, he can make and abrogate laws as he wishes, and encounters no limits in natural law, either. The sovereign is the law because he the repository of good and evil. For this reason, divine right itself is not an effective law form. The limits on the power of the Sovereign are political rather than legal: aside from the fact that he must obey the laws that he himself makes until he makes others, which gives an effective force to the laws, the sovereign must avoid defeats in what Machiavelli called a logical and indispensable search for success. The Sovereign's political defeats give rise to mistrust in the social body and, soon or later, thrust it back into that state of insecurity that had preceded the agreement. It is true that absolute power is the most efficacious, the most rapid and in so many ways the most "moral" (the absolute monarch must not argue with anyone, he is not obliged to request advice and, above all, being the head of everything, is not subject to pressures of any sort), but it is also true that the efficaciousness, rapidity and rigour must be real, otherwise the actual force of power diminishes and its existence deteriorates.

11.21 Under the authority of the "mortal god" there is that certainty of law that no other form can ensure. The Leviathan practically becomes the personification of civil law to such a degree that it can be said to have been born with him, and without him, there would be an abrupt return to the brutality of the state of nature. "*Take away the Civil Law, and no man knows what it is own, and what another mans*" (Hobbes, L, 296). Does it follow that property is something granted by the Sovereign, and, if otherwise, who could enjoy it? This is why the Leviathan is necessary, because the true justification of power resides in the well-being and security of the people. *Salus populi* is the prime criterion of politics and the only one on the basis on which power can be judged. Already stated in the Introduction, this is clearly repeated several times: "*A good Law is that, which is Needfull, for the Good of People, and withall Perspicuous*" (Hobbes, L, 388). Religion can be said to be seen exclusively in terms of its civil value which involves an absolute identity between spiritual and material government. Two truly alarming conclusions come from this: first of all, what is of interest is certainly not tolerance, but sheer conformity, and secondly, that the Sovereign could do everything in the area of religion if he had time, even administer the sacraments.

11.22 In this sense religion cannot be something private. It must depend on the laws of the political community and the sovereign who personifies it above all because, without the authorization of that sovereign, the faithful have no right even to assemble, whatever their form of Christianity may be. The criterion of good and evil itself cannot be left up to the discretionary power of the conscience, but must be submitted to civil law, since the conscience may be mistaken (cf. Hobbes, L, 498 and 365-366). To achieve salvation, Hobbes reminds us that faith alone is not enough. Obedience is required. This is possible only if one is convinced that there can be no contradiction of any sort between the laws of God and civil laws (cf. Hobbes, L, 622-625). Religion cannot be a philosophical matter either, hence, subject to reasoning, otherwise it would lead to infinite disputes. It must be the object of law in every civil community (cf. Hobbes, DH, XIV, 4). Therefore, Hobbes has taken a stand against all the established Churches, and this reveals an obstinate anticlerical spirit on the part of one who supports an intransigent, radically secularist position, aimed entirely at combating any exterior manifestation of religion (cf. Bobbio, TH, 77). Religion is thus presented as another civil bond which, as would happen later in Hegel, is aimed at repairing the schism in Christianity and between public and private in Roman law even before that. The German philosopher considered that division absent in the Greek world.

12. ...to Totalitarianism

12.1 In Germany, the bond between religion and philosophy and then between religion and politics that existed throughout the early nineteenth century, is nothing more than the further development and investigation of subjects already taken up by the Enlightenment. One need only recall that people actually maintained that with "the French constitution, religion gained something" (Merker, OIT, 61) because it regained its integrity. Furthermore, the alliance between Christianity and revolution was propagandized just about everywhere in those years. Proof of this is, for example, is Hoffmann's writing *The Catechism of the Aristocrats*, which supported the idea of the alliance. Then, how could Lessing's work be forgotten? It was the Lutheran Pastor Goeze who, in his writings, "immediately pointed out the connection between Biblical criticism and contestation of the constituted order" (Merker, IL, 11). This shows that religion was starting to be considered, little by little, no longer as a subject for pure contemplation and simple action that always had its metaphysical connotations, but as a sure guide capable of transforming the human situation. It was also with Lessing that the relationship between revealed and reasoned truth was beginning to be considered in a new light (cf. Merker, IL, 37) which bore witness to the growing interest in practicing it.

A) *The Defence of God the Person.*

12.2. That such an approach to the religious question risked forcing religion into cladding itself in the *instrumento regni* of politics or, in any case, in veritable immanentism, could certainly not escape the attention of those who wanted to safeguard the transcendental aspect of Christianity. It was Jacobi who had a clear view of this transformation. He immediately understood that the new approach aimed at distorting the relationship between faith and religion, giving the latter a pre-eminent role (cf. Bobbio, IJ, XI-XII). Faith thereby ended up being the supreme form of knowing in order to become a necessary support of practice. In this immanentism, now delineated, what function could the traditional *God the Creator* have? Certainly none, and it was for that very reason that Jacobi, with his anthropomorphism, fought on behalf of attribution "to God of the personality as well as liberty and providentiality together" (cf. Bobbio, IJ, XV). Jacobi understood quite well that giving up the idea of God the person meant *deifying humanity* and all it does in view of a future and totally earthly liberation. Bringing God into the realm of the visible and the existing and circumscribing Him meant confusing Him with nature and ascribing the characteristics of omnipotence to nature (cf. Jacobi, VdgD, 117-118).

12.3 It was logical that Jacobi should view works like those of Lessing with suspicion, for example *Die Erziehung des Menschengeschlechts* (*The Education of the Human Race*), in which it was maintained that certain religious positions of the past had exclusively pedagogical value. Finally, when humans were not capable of being arbiters of their own actions they had called for other laws (or alleged laws) which could now be definitively abandoned. Jacobi was uncompromising on this point. He personally told Lessing that their bases of believing were totally different, since Lessing was a Spinozan in the final analysis, he believed "in an intelligent and personal cause of the world" (Jacobi,

ULS, 20). It can be stated with a reasonable degree of confidence that Jacobi's position as opposed to Lessing's is similar to Kierkegaard's in relation to the materialists of his time. According to Jacobi, Lessing "wanted everything to be explained naturally, that there could not be a natural philosophy of the supernatural, and that both evidently existed (natural and supernatural)" (Jacobi, ULS, 31). The existence of these two dimensions guaranteed Jacobi the existence of a personal God and this was exactly what Lessing rejected since "he could not tolerate the idea of a personal being, absolutely infinite, in the immutable enjoyment of his supreme perfection. He related that to an idea of an infinite boredom, which, for him, was a source of anxiety and pain" (Jacobi, ULS, 34). Every reality, even religious, was beginning to be set aside, and was being consumed in its immobility. All that exists is subject to the *becoming*, even *truth* as Hegel would say.

12.4 Jacobi was troubled by another concern: he had actually foreseen that setting forth the problem as Lessing did, in terms of immanentism, not only involved integrating two entities, the natural and the supernatural, which in themselves had to remain distinct from one another, and this meant irremediably confusing them. The questions raised risked distorting the religious perspective. For example, Jacobi wondered: "how it is possible for a single and same essence, that is the spirit of the world, to be an internal and external religion, a principle and cause, at the same time?" (Jacobi, ULS, 188). This question was certainly not without meaning for those, as Bobbio maintains, who speak of Christianity in apologetic tones. To bring God into the world not only meant denying his existence as the creative and personal principle, but, especially, posing the problem of *salvation* in *earthly terms*, changing every eschatological perspective. The realm of God could no longer be outside of time since God had now been included in it and the realization of such a realm could no longer be postponed infinitely. On the contrary, it could be approached and hastened by a decisive and serious involvement of human beings.

B) *The realization of truth.*

12.5 A religion brought down to reality is a religion which is historicized. It is a faith which finds tangibility in an ethical and civil reality. In other words, religion takes on the consistency of a something which is "destined to be explained in a more or less distant future" (Olivetti, FR, 16) thereby abandoning that approach according to which the realization of the future Kingdom is subject to interminable postponement. However, it was not yet time for a systematic definition of the problem. The time would be ripe only in the romantic and idealistic context and would then be fully formulated in Hegelian thought. Hegel would be able to gather together and synthesize all the Enlightenment and Romantic contributions to which Herder had given a decisive contribution as far as the religious problems themselves were concerned (cf. Olivetti, FR, 74-85). Hegel embraced the dignity of Christianity as greater than that of the other religions, as this idea emerged in the romantic period. He was critical of traditional theology because it had never succeeded in moving from the prospect to the realization of the Kingdom of God (cf. Hegel, B, 29-33). A God which becomes tangible in the world which, in turn, becomes the concrete totality in which divinity is incarnated, is thus brought "to completion as an historical whole in which the 'truth', which is also the 'whole', has been fully explained. The real totality does not take form in an indefinite and infinite process, but in such a way that, in the end, one can take account of its beginning (…) The model of this manifestation of the absolute in the history of the world is the Christian faith of the revelation of God in the history of humanity" (Löwith, DHL, 8-9).

Georg Wilhelm Friedrich Hegel was born in 1770 in Stuttgart in a middle-class family. He studied theology at Tübingen University together with Hölderlin and Schelling. Between 1793 and 1800 he worked as a tutor. In 1801 he began his university career at Jena. For years he wrote about politics and theology and these writings were published posthumously. He then taught at Heidelberg and, finally, in Berlin. *Die Fhänomenologie des Geistes*, (*The Phenomenology of Spirit*) (1807) was the work that made him famous. Then the *Wissenschaft der Logik* (*Science of Logic*) appeared in two volumes (1812-16), the *Enzyclopädie der philosophischen Wissenschaften im Grundisse*, (*Encyclopaedia of the Philosophical Sciences in Outline*) (1817), which came out in several later editions, and *Grundlinien der Philosophie des Rechts* (*Elements of the Philosophy of Right*) (1812). He died suddenly in 1831. His lessons were published posthumously: *Vorlesungen über die Philosophie der Geschichte*, (*Lessons on the Philosophy of History*), *Aesthetics, Vorlesungen über die Philosophie der Religion*, (*Lessons on the Philosophy of Religion*) and *Vorlesungen über die Geschichte der Philosophie*, (*Lessons on the History of Philosophy*).

12.6 In Hegel, the need is felt to place faith in history, in human deeds, because this historical process is guided by an intrinsic theological reason and is certainly not left up to chance. The *succession* of events in Hegel is not only temporal, but also *logical*. For this reason, philosophy deals with history for the very reason that here it finds a rational perspective. Placing faith in reason is, indeed, operating in conformity with an end which is the true driving force of history. That an end governs history is proven by the fact that history allows itself to be *intuited* in a finalistic, theological, rational sense. This is what Hegel meant by philosophy: explaining reality rationally, that is, understanding the historical process as the expression and fruit of human reason.

12.7 This Hegelian perspective further brought the religious perspective into reality, even though the terms and tools of analysis of the historical and social world remained theological in character. It has been seen, in fact, that history keeps its finality and the very approach of all of the history of philosophy is affected by a sort of organicistic prejudice in the sense that its various moments constitute a corresponding number of stages on the way to manifestation of the totality. Furthermore, it is this trip down the historical and philosophical path that determines the achievement of truth. The *truth* for Hegel cannot be given once and for all, as certain religions claim; on the contrary, the truth matures in history and it can be said to have been acquired only when a certain period is completed (needless to say such a position greatly influenced all the nineteenth-century thinkers). Hegel takes for granted that truth proceeds at the same pace as philosophy which is being historicized. His statements leave no room for doubt: "Philosophy is the objective science of truth" (Hegel, VGP, 30). Since truth can only be rational, the aim has been to "make Christianity rational" (Hegel, VGP, 31). As in the religious perspective "the instinct of reason has the invincible feeling, or Faith, that there is only one truth" (Hegel, VGP, 36). This truth is unique, temporal, finite and, above all, implemented in so far as this "unique truth is not a simple and empty thought, but determined by itself" (Hegel, VGP, 39).

12.8 At this point, it is easy to intuit that truth is not an entity given in itself to which the individual must conform. Truth is a realization, which, in certain particular moments, humanity achieves. Only thus can one understand why philosophy is superior to religion and indeed replaces it, in so far as only philosophy can render that truth tangible which, according to Hegel, religion keeps in a veritable abstractness, since it is crystallized and is outside the world. Philosophy does not eliminate religion. It revitalizes it, integrating it with reason, so that, according to Hegel, it is absurd to speak of atheist philosophy. At the most one can speak (here, strangely enough, he takes up a statement of Jacobi's) of pantheism in philosophy (cf. Hegel, E, 380-381). Philosophy cannot be a-religious because its main purpose is to present and implement the truth. Certainly one problem did not escape Hegel's attention. It was easy to call into question all of his construction bringing up a doubt not easy to resolve. "How is it possible that philosophy, which seeks the one and eternal truth, is fragmented into a temporal plurality of philosophies"? (Löwith, DHL, 8). The answer came to Hegel as natural "in the sense that truth already has in itself the tendency to occur in the course of time" (Löwith, DHL, 8). The manifestation of a plurality of philosophies has represented nothing other than the process of attaining the truth.

12.9 In the road taken by mankind, faith becomes tangible, a "faith" in history which (as Löwith reminds us) Croce himself called "the last religion of civilized man". Croce would leave this subject on an aristocratic level and only the Communist movement would bring it down to the level of the masses. For Hegel, the truth to attain through the processes of human history actually follows a chronological *procedure* in the sense that not all the stages are necessary, but, above all, every stage is strictly bound by its era and cannot, in any way, attain anything more than the truth of its times. For Hegel it is "an idle hypothesis, that of thinking that some philosopher in an era of the far distant past can have been considerably closer to the truth of the world, than the philosophers who followed one upon the other in that age which, from time to time, is called the present" (Löwith, DHL, 8). Thus, truth is acquired in history. It is now a prospect within the reach of humanity.

12.10 The image of God seems once again to be humanized and definitively this time: it would, however, be better to say that humanity is acquiring divine features. The Absolute abandons transcendent reality to become objectivised in human becoming. It was not easy, to be sure, to spread this idea among people, but Hegel did not have the slightest doubt that sooner or later that conception would come into its own. It would be sufficient to prepare the minds. In him, as would be the case in Marxism (one could also think of Gramsci), there is the conviction that this new faith of humanity must follow a secure pedagogical path and without hesitation. Religion had always influenced ethical relations among individuals and this was precisely what had to be aimed at (the new way of presenting and evaluating them) if the new theodicy was to succeed. Hegel was extremely convinced of this; in the final analysis "religion holds for him, as for Kant in fact, an unquestionable educational value, and it is especially from this point of view that he observes it" (Mirri, 14). Worship itself had great importance for Hegel since it succeeded in bringing humanity back to the foundations of religion. He kept this conception firmly in mind when it became a matter of setting forth the requisites for a new, popular religiosity. Hegel "observed that doctrines must be founded to be sure on universal reason, so that on the one hand every person senses it and senses its obligatory nature, on the other that they do not lead to an attack from the intellect, to which doctrine ascertained only by faith is necessarily subject" (Mirri, 15-16). It almost seems as if the German philosopher foresaw a necessary period of transition from the phase of traditional religion to that of rationality, a transition period that many of his successors would consider something now out of date.

12.11 Hegel thus proposed abandonment of a prejudice for good: that of seeing religion as something exclusively personal which is fulfilled in the intimate relationship which every individual can have with God. Thus "it must be pointed out above all that religion is insistently seen by Hegel as supreme objectivity and thus appreciated in so far as it is something positive and not understood as abstract interiority, everything from the subject's point of view" (Oberti, 25). A religion that was limited to the moment of subjectivity would certainly not be useful to Hegel for two reasons: the first lay in the fact that if religion were limited to the subjective sphere, it could never be the basis of a universal reason; the second (inferred directly from the first) is that in the area of subjectivity religion dissipated in its immobility and could never undertake the path towards truth, a journey which Hegel eventually identified with religion in its authenticity. "This process of religion is the true theodicy; it shows the need for all of what the spirit produces, of every form of its self-awareness, because the spirit is life, it is thought, it is the urge to delve deeper and deeper into self-awareness through the series of its phenomena, that is, to arrive at the whole truth" (Hegel, VPR, 88). Hegel was convinced that human reason was actually giving life to a process of liberation, a sort of exodus which would culminate in abandonment of the old mental patterns surrounding religion and that it would bring about an authentic Realm of Liberty in the fullness of the truth.

12.12 The reason for that can be found in the dialectic of the spirit and that of the objective spirit in particular. The subjective spirit comes into contact with other free spirits when it reaches the point of manifesting itself as a free spirit, and finds in the law the first moment of the objective spirit, the opportunity to govern external relationships among individuals. The counterpart of *law*, the moment of *confirmation* of dialectics, is *morality*, the moment of *negation*, which "regulates" the moments of interior life among individuals. *Ethicality* constitutes the moment of synthesis, or of *negation of negation*, which in turn becomes dialectical in the family, civil society and the State. The *family* is the prime and basic form of ethical totality. *Civil society* is built on the period of necessities and to meet these necessities, work appears to be a necessary condition. Civil society is constructed to coordinate the various activities. It thus gives rise to corporations which defend their autonomy within society and lay down the premises for recognition of private property, the expression of the various attitudes and liberties of individuals. As for Smith, the various activities, three in particular (farmers, land-owners, industrialists and here, especially in Hegel, we should recall the administrators as well) actually acquire an ethical dimension. Families and civil society find their synthesis in the *State*. The latter cannot be founded *ex novo*, but is the result of the historical process. It finds its reason for being in history and, as Montesquieu would say, expresses the maximum of its rationality in the constitution. Hegel is not very original on the political system of this State. He speaks of constitutional monarchy and refers to a model quite similar to the English one.

12.13 In certain respects, this progress towards truth in Hegel remains an élite phenomenon; despite its indubitably political implications it has not yet acquired totalitarian characteristics. In his view "the more religion is intensely confirmed, the more energetically it serves to bring about the philosophical dimension and overcoming of itself in this" (Oberti, 43). This is quite an important operation since religion, permeated with philosophy, divests itself of all of its specious arbitrary aspects, in short, it divests itself of its irrationalism and is saved by the rationality of philosophy itself. As Hegel said in a famous passage, philosophy cannot imagine that it will edify the spirits, this is the duty of preaching, but it must conceive of the spiritual progress of humanity, turn it to reason, because only by delving into the most intimate reasons for this process can the destiny of mankind and the ways of bringing it about be foreseen. Only this signifies implementing the truth of the spirit (cf. Hegel, VPR, 14). Thanks to philosophy, religion acquires new light because this union offers the possibility of making that conception of the world tangible, a conception which traditional religion presents but without suggesting the actual means by which it can be achieved on earth. Philosophy enables that synthesis between the individual and the world which would otherwise be impossible. Indeed outside philosophical consciousness religion and the rest of awareness are conceived of in mutual isolation. The source of alienation of the original religious impulse can be seen in that, and it is the duty of philosophy to prepare meditation upon and reconciliation of the two separate terms (cf. Hegel, VPR, 15). Philosophy revitalizes religion, therefore. It offers it completeness, but does not eliminate it at all because philosophy would not be possible without religion or, at least, that absolute philosophy which obtains its basic terms and terms of reference from religion would not be possible. Actually, the terms are the same, truth, absoluteness, the Kingdom of the Spirit and yet others, only that in the religious area they remain in their abstractness whereas in the philosophical ones they become tangible.

12.14 Traditional faith had dried up then because, in Hegel's opinion, it rested on static assumptions and thus had no vitality. That was not enough, however. The real drama was due to the fact that there seemed to be no way to close the gap, or more precisely, the break between the spirit and the real world. The introductory pages of the *Science of Logic* are revealing on this subject. One need only remember Hegel's position against formal logic which by its very nature is excluded from real truth and is the considered and interpreted as a step in preparation of a truly scientific knowledge or as a methodological premise, too (cf. on this subject the interesting introduction by Leo Lugarini to G.W.F. Hegel, *Scienza della logica,* Bari, 1974).

12.15 Upon closer look, however the reason Hegel considers Christianity to be an *idea-force* can be sought in the fact that it has always aspired to attain a perfect city, even though it has never done so. The model is unattainable but incontestably human. The city offered an anticipation of that idea of a world placed in a transcendent perspective. Hegel could never do without this urge to seek perfection. There was a sort of inner need in him, a religious desire not at all extinguished, that could only be concretized in his philosophical approach. Hegel thereby provides a philosophical justification for all those aspirations towards cosmopolitanism which, confusedly at times, had been formulated by the Enlightenment. One could refer, for example, to the idea expressing faith in progress which culminates in the Kantian conception of a cosmopolitan society. This is shown by the fact that there existed, in the mentality of that time (free of religious approaches, but with legacies from religion) the firm conviction that humanity was now moving towards a period of social peace, perfect and universal cohesion. For Hegel, to paraphrase his philosophical language, it can be said that the realization of the Kingdom constitutes the full revelation of God in history. The so-notorious *God is with us* is equivalent here to *God is in us* or rather *We are God*. In this journey mankind has not only rediscovered reason, but truth, too, because truth and reason cannot be separated. Thus Hegel's enlightening statements can be understood. They are in the preface to his *Phenomenology of the Spirit*: "The real form which truth takes, can only be the scientific system of truth. Cooperating to bring philosophy closer to the form of science – half-achieved which can replace the name of *love* of *knowledge* with *true knowledge*, – this is what I have set forth for myself" (Hegel, P, 14). This is tantamount to saying that truth must be entirely submitted to the control of mankind because only human reason can know it. The new universality rested on a new *Theologia civilis*, which filled the void created by the crisis of medieval theology. A new, totally earthly belief constituted the new fundamental law of society. Rebelling against it meant no more and no less than being an atheist in the Middle Ages. One can think of Rousseau's civil religion as an example. This could not operate differently in Hegel, either, since stating that thinking dialectically meant thinking *sub specie temporis*, he brought everything down into the world of becoming. Even God *became* in this system where there was no longer any room for immobility. The divinity itself had to advance towards perfection.

C) *The Road to Salvation.*

12.16 With this secularization of the Christian faith or, as Hegel would have it, with this realization of the spirit, he believed that he had remained faithful to the spirit of Christianity and was bringing about the Kingdom of God on earth. Since he brought Christian expectations of a final fulfilment down to the historical process as such, he considered the history of the world as something which was self-justifying (cf. Löwith, MiH, 57-58). What remains most Christian in Hegel, as in all the thought coming out of Hegelianism, is the conviction that the Christian expectation of the earthly paradise is about to be achieved in its entirety. It seems as if we are experiencing once again in philosophy, that magic moment of early Christianity, when there was the certitude among believers of an immediate Second Coming of the Lord. There is no mystery about the fact that anyone who asks questions, from Hegel to Lenin, believe, whatever their aims may be, that the achievement of the new era is only a question of time and that it cannot be long before it happens.

12.17 In the light of what has been said, Hegel is the first to conceive of a history of philosophy which reflects the spiritual history of humanity. For him, the history of philosophy can be identified with the philosophy of history, where this latter expression "is used to mean a systematic interpretation of universal history in accordance with a principle by which historical events and successions are unified and directed toward an ultimate meaning" (Löwith, MiH, 1). It is easy to see why a theological background practically based on the ancient Biblical conception of the exodus and retained in Christian apocalyptic expectations can be perceived in the Hegelian conception of history. It is based on this eschatological future that must be experienced, because this alone constitutes the ultimate term of reference, the key to interpreting or rather analyzing, that is taking apart then reassembling, all of history. Adopting this approach one comes to the paradox or, if one likes, the contradiction of giving life to a *history Christian in its premises and anti-Christian in its conclusions*. This seemed inevitable in fact, since "even replacing the faith in a divine Providence with faith in the progress of humanity, or faith in the fulfilment of the spirit of the world or in the advent of a classless society, the philosophy of history has retained a theological mark, and has remained tied to an eschatological perspective" (Rossi, 13). Incredibly enough, just when one seeks to free oneself from the Christian religion, criticizing it in every possible way, one accepts its basic requisite which is that of representing a "way to liberation" in view of a better world.

D) *Humanity is made Divine and is Reconciled (Interpreters of Hegel)*.

12.18 Why, despite Hegel's efforts, was the universality he had foreseen fulfilled only in logic and had not become part of daily practice? "An investigation of this sort must never lose sight of how backward Germany was at that time, socially and economically, as well as politically" (Lukács, 24). The relationship between religion, philosophy and politics thus had to be integrated with another category, the economic one, in view of the inevitable capitalistic transformation awaiting Germany as well as the rest of continental Europe (England was already in a more advanced phase). This is why the close relationship in Hegel between religion and philosophy was gradually placed in the service of Germany's political situation and then "in the service of the universal historical moment of more extreme socialism" (Löwith, DHL, 7). This socialism cannot be anything but the "scientific" version promoted by Marx, scientific because it takes its origin from the Hegelian science of history, although revised for Marx's purposes, which constitutes the only sure source of discovering and knowing. This conviction precedes all the historical approach culminating in *The Manifesto*. The starting model still remains the conviction and need for "the absolute to manifest itself in this history of the world" (Löwith, DHL, 9), an absolute which frees itself from idealistic premises, and seeks to come closer to reality.

12.19 After the death of Hegel the problem was that of whether or not to investigate the theological aspect of his philosophy. More precisely speaking "the dispute centred around the atheistic or theistic interpretation of the philosophy of religion; whether or not, that is, the absolute had its real existence in a God become mankind or just in humanity" (Löwith, DHL, 15). It had to be established whether or not God was merely a projection of mankind and, therefore, it was mankind's task to *fulfil* all those requisites which, in the past, had been attributed, transferred, given away in an "abstract" dimension. If that were the case, those who called themselves the legitimate heirs of Hegel were right in proclaiming that a revolution for a Kingdom of mankind was imminent, since mankind had overcome all the traces of the past. Those who had no interest in a change in society, those who feared the loss of advantages clearly appealed to that past: the bourgeoisie, that is. This the *identification* and contraposition on the one hand between the bourgeoisie and Jewish as well as Protestant religions and, on the other, between the anti-bourgeois and supporters of a new world comes into play. It is logical, then, that "the passage from a self-sufficient philosophical theory to historical praxis consists above all in criticism of the existing bourgeois State and the Christian religion; the goal of this criticism is a radical upheaval" (Löwith, DHL, 17).

12.20 The "new" Hegelians did not give up, indeed they retained an essential requisite for the Hegelian philosophical and theological approach. They believed that the future world would be one of peace because it would bring about a real *conciliation* between the universal and the single, between humanity and the individual which, in actual fact, was nothing but the conciliation between God and mankind foreseen by Christianity and then theorized by Hegel, a conciliation which was, however, to be accomplished in history. Here lies the point of transition from Hegel and to his followers of the left because the master himself had underscored the fact that history was exclusively the doing of humans. This extreme humanization of thought, already brought out by Hegel, was taken up in all the German circles. As early as 1831, with Strauss, a fundamental questioning of matters surrounding the philosophy of Hegel was undertaken. Did Christ have to be deemed the sole manifestation of the Absolute or did he not risk becoming one of the many historical manifestations of the Absolute itself? It is clear that this questioning definitively compromised the balance of the Hegelian system at a crucial point, that is, the relationship between philosophy and religion and it is also clear that the way chosen was that of going beyond traditional religion giving other Absolutes (*the proletariat*) the possibility of manifesting themselves in history. Bauer, in turn, carried the matter to extreme consequences, referring to the concrete political problems of a Germany of the era in which the old aristocratic and feudal structures, closely connected to the interests and basic premises of the Protestant Church, still had their importance... So a complete secularization and autonomy was eventually claimed for the State (and for the efforts being made to construct it) vis-à-vis the Church: in short, a more decided practical and political involvement.

12. 21 Now it seems clear why the point is reached at which "with Feuerbach, it is believed that the religious world is only a shell surrounding the earthly nucleus of the human world (...) therefore Feuerbach had wanted to discover only the earthly nucleus of religion (...) from an historical analysis of earthly life relations, what wretchedness and what contradictions in the relationships of this world make religion possible and necessary" (Löwith, VHzN, 376). Philosophy has the duty of explaining the anthropological foundation of positive religions. Traditional religion is nothing but a projection of mankind; God therefore dies and "the new human, the human-humanity is born". But what human is it? The one who has finally understood that "he does not arrive at a knowledge of the universe except through knowledge of his own kind. Thus man is the God of man (...) without other humans nothing can be, physically or spiritually (...) isolated human strength is limited, united it has no limits" (Feuerbach, 242-243). Statements of this sort leave no more room for doubt: the true divinity becomes human totality and its action acquires, practically, the social requisite for a religious mission. History becomes, above all, *history and politics* and "the true religion cannot be other than a paradise on earth, an earthly Kingdom of political liberty and social justice" (Löwith, DHL, 32). In this Kingdom those initial mistakes already taken into consideration by Rousseau as he examined the causes of inequality will finally be eliminated. In this new approach of history politics takes the place of religion keeping its premises, however, and becoming, indeed, a religion in itself. Feuerbach says this clearly: "*Politics* must become our *religion* – but it can become that only if we, in our conception, have a supreme value which makes of politics our religion" (Feuerbach in Löwith, DHL, 228). This is not enough, however: the arena, the training ground, in

which human political activity is carried out, becomes the providential ground for mankind. The true absolute is the dimension, the structure which this path guarantees, in one word, the State, according to Feuerbach, is the real absolute. The totalitarian conception is at hand, "the State is unlimited, infinite, authentic, perfect, divine mankind. Only the State is mankind, mankind which determines itself, which finds its satisfaction in itself, absolute mankind" (Feuerbach in Löwith, DHL, 228). One need only replace the word *state* with the word *party* to understand where a root, at least, of Lenin's party approach and its intransigence finds inspiration. The philosophy of religion intrinsic in idealism has completely become a worldly thing and history has become the only source of knowledge because it draws on the real and active action of mankind. This is why, "as soon as this process of active life is represented, history ceases to be a collection of lifeless events, as in the empiricists who are themselves abstract, or an imaginary action of imaginary subjects, as in the idealists" (Marx, DdI, 27). Knowledge, or rather science of history, thereby officially becomes the only true science which is in direct opposition to classical German philosophy "which comes down from heaven to earth, here it rises from the earth to heaven. That is, it does not begin with what people say (…) but begins from people, who are actually doing, and, on the basis of the real process of their lives, the development of the reflections and ideological echoes of this life process are also explained" (Marx, DdI, 26). It almost seems, as Löwith appropriately sees, that in Marx there is non-philosophical confidence placed in historical thought in the name of a practice which becomes a new and veritable dogma. In truth, it must be said, however, that this aspect is not typical of Marx alone but of all those, who, referring in some way or another to the Hegelian approach, ultimately weigh the historical and political dimension of mankind, a dimension which thus becomes all-embracing and capable of all.

E) *Towards the Idea of the God as All: the Liberation of Humanity.*

12.22 With Marx we are no longer in the idealistic sphere which views mankind in its abstractness nor are we in the area of classical political economy which views humans merely as simple workers. These two prospects are rejected by Marx because "both are unaware of the total humanity of sensitive and natural man" (Löwith, VHzN, 299). The two positions are brought together in the sense that one becomes the explanation of the other. Only thus can there by a complete synthesis of the phenomenon humanity and, thanks to this insight, it is possible to move on to a phase of liberation desired by those, too, who had had ideas that could not always be applied and thus "utopian" ones about the future Realm. An example could be the *Nouveau Christianisme* of Saint Simon, the French thinker's will and testament. Perhaps it is unnecessary to recall the fact that, what Marx criticizes in Saint-Simon and others, too, is not the desire for a better society, but the fact that this desire simply remains a dream, since the instruments and means for fulfilling it have not been foreseen. Marx believes that he possesses these instruments for what is needed, the Hegelian dialectic method which, if stripped of its abstractness, retains scientific rigour.

Karl Marx was born in Trier in 1818 of a middle-bourgeois family of Jewish tradition, although his father had converted to Christianity in order to carry on with his career in the administration. After undertaking legal and literary studies in Bonn, he studied philosophy in Berlin, and studied the thought of Hegel. He was involved in various vicissitudes, as an exile first in France then in Belgium, and participated in the publication of several journals, together with other German exiles. He produced writings that were not published for a long time, and met **Friedrich Engels** (1820-1895) with whom he would be associated all his life. Together they created the *Manifest der kommunistischen Partei*, (*Communist Manifesto*) (1848). Earlier, Marx had written *Zur Kritik der Hegelschen Rechtsphilosophie* (1843), *Oekonomisch-philosophische Manuskripte* (1844), *Die heilige Familie, oder Kritik der kritischen Kritik, The Holy Family, Critique of Critical Criticism* (1845) and *Die deutsche Ideologie. Kritik der neuesten deutschen Philosophie,* (*The German Ideology*) (1845-46). In 1849 he fled to London after a brief return to Paris. After a period of difficulties, he also delved further into his economic studies and his political engagement. This gave rise to the International Association of Workers. In 1859 he published *Zur Kritik der politischen Oekonomie,* (*For a Criticism of Political Economy*) seen as practically an introduction to his basic work *Das Kapital* the first volume of which came out in 1867. The other two volumes appeared after his death, in 1883, where were edited by Engels in 1885 and 1894. The latter, whose originality was gradually discovered, is famous for many other works among which should be mentioned: *Antidüring, The Origins of the Family, Private Property, and the State* (1884) and *The Dialectics of Nature* published posthumously in 1930. His activity as an organizer was considerable. He was a point of reference for the workers and Marxist intellectuals' movement. Engels again published and disseminated various works of Marx as well as his own.

12.23 In Marx there is the tacit conviction, as Rousseau had said, that the laws upon which political theories had been based had to be overthrown. Like the Genevan, Marx, too, was convinced that the ultimate sources of evil and conflicts must be found in history and not in human nature, a nature which, contrary to what some people maintained, was not in itself bad. The idea that evil has social origins and cannot be uprooted unless society is changed is taken up again, and given justification in dialectics. Marx thus carried Hegel's argumentation to the extreme as he had done for that of Rousseau, Owen and still others. *Material equality* is the basic criterion that must be followed for the sake of reconstruction, whether or not this is to the detriment of liberty, because the sole and real evil in the world is inequality itself. All "that an individual as such has that is more than what others have is now a product of society at the same time and must be established as a privilege" (Marx, DdI, 422). It is these privileges that must be abolished if equality is to be reconstructed. Finally, the *moment* of *synthesis* appears: the individual, separated from the rest of humanity because of his or her "privileges", returns to the human totality, in universality, in the world of peace far from conflicts. Here there is an identification between mankind and the community which virtually corresponds to the *identification* between the individual and mystical Body of Christian tradition. This ultimate community set forth by Marx is, in fact, the classless society which finds its initial moment and prophetic phase in the proletariat. "Marx's philosophy has found its natural weapon in the proletariat (...) whereas the proletariat possesses in Marxism its spiritual arm" (Löwith, VHzN, 338). It is thanks to this arm that the liberation of humanity is being attained and the reason why the proletariat is taking on worldwide dimensions; it would almost seem that the divinity, the Hegelian spirit which guarantees history, has found its reincarnation. After a reading of Strauss, we have a *new* revelation of the Absolute, but final and definitive. According to Marx, the proletariat is the universal class and it is this prerogative that guarantees that it will obtain its own liberation.

12.24 The bourgeois world will be eliminated because it is based on a false form of life, hypocrisy that forces the larger number (the proletariat) to live in an alienating situation opposing the true solution of problems. This is why Hegelian philosophy, which is the mirror of that society, is far, despite its aims, from attaining the truth which it is necessary to change society. It is necessary to revolutionize it. Revolution is the sole instrument of truth. "Revolution for Marx is the implementation of philosophy and (...) elimination of capitalistic alienation" (Coppellotti, 12). Lenin, too, will emphasize this aspect as well as others who have called upon the theory of revolution based on the premises of dialectical materialism. Perhaps it is superfluous to recall at this point that if revolution were not proposed, history would fall into a period of immobility from which, according to Marx, no contradiction taken in itself could free it. Indeed, "it must not be forgotten that in contradiction, the driving force is not contradiction itself, but the movement to free oneself from it" (Monnerot, 172). Being content with the situation as it is – is, therefore, not to consider history because history can only be understood in a dynamic sense. History is such only when it seeks to contradict all that has already happened, which, in other words, it is not content with itself. That discontent comes out in the proletariat. The bourgeoisie is opposed to it and indeed has a fear of revolution because it constitutes the end of that class. The bourgeoisie views the future proletarian society with growing concern so that Marx and Engels, predicting that future, did not hesitate to make use of images that had a certain Biblical and prophetic tone. "A spectre is hovering about Europe – the spectre of Communism. All the powers of old Europe (...) have allied in a holy and ruthless crusade against this spectre" (Marx-Engels, M, 461). They have formed an alliance because, to paraphrase Marx, for them history has reached its culmination and they intend to exclude the proletariat, the overwhelming majority of humanity, from it.

12.25 This exclusion is the point of departure for the great egalitarian claim which is in opposition to economic individualism and personal profit and finds its full expression in *The Manifesto*. The work is full of radical judgments, some think that they are Manichaean, and proposes to bring about the complete transformation of society. The writing is full of propagandistic force, and can offer two levels of explanation, hence ways of being read. A simple reading is possible, but not a simplistic one. This is intended to appeal to those exploited by their social condition, who seek a way to achieve liberation. Then, there is a more complex reading that can be undertaken by those who read *The Manifesto* and who have a Hegelian preparation, and find in dialectical materialism, which is the inspiration behind the entire work, the conviction, an almost scientific one, that a new realm is coming. Yet, *The Manifesto* opens with a *First Part* concerning the relations between bourgeois and proletarians (*Bourgeois und Proletarier*) in which praise of the bourgeois is offered, as a class which had its revolution and transformed the world. Here lies the key to reading the *Second Part* (*Proletarier und Kommunisten*) in which not only is the position of the Communist vis-à-vis the workers and peasants (always viewed by the Communists with suspicion) is set forth as a whole, but the necessity for the Communists to be able to organize themselves in terms of their particularity, in terms of that new awareness that will be the battle cry of world Communism. The need for and defence of this particularity appear clear in the sarcasm of the *Third Part* (*Sozialistische und Kommunistische Literatur*) towards all those socialist views that have not accepted the dialectical method, thereby reaching the point of denying scientific socialism and remaining tied to useless utopian dreams. The *Fourth Part* is quite short but no less important. Considering the need concretely to set forth the way in which revolutionary Acton will be carried out, it outlines the possibility that the Communists may take a position in relation to the other opposition parties which in some way are moving in the direction of changing the system.

12.26 That philosophy had turned into action alone was now clear. This is clearly pointed out in the *Thesen über Feuerbach* (*Theses on Feuerbach*) as proof once again of the need to make every religious idea of mankind more immanent removing all that had been metaphysical in the past. "The human essence is not something abstract and immanent in the single individual. In its reality it is the totality of social relations" (Marx, TüF, 6). Taking away all that is metaphysical and, as can be seen, reducing everything to pure immanentism remains static and cannot be made operative within social relations, in actual practice: a true way towards truth and liberation. "In practice humans must test the truth, that is, reality and power, the immanent character of their thought" (Marx, TüF, 5). The idealistic approach is thus overthrown even if the tools used, once they have been refined, continue to be valid. Perhaps no writing is more enlightening, for an understanding of this upheaval, than that which Marx devoted to the critique of the philosophy of right of Hegel. In these pages certain "concrete points" of Hegelian thought are directly attacked in their abstractness and, on the contrary, other entities neglected by Hegel are placed on the level of protagonists. Here too, Marx is quite clear and concise. He speaks and writes in the tones of an inquisitor: "The State is an abstraction. Only the people are something tangible. It is noteworthy that Hegel ascribes to the concrete only with hesitation and reservation a living quality such as that of sovereignty" (Marx, KHR, 229). In this there is a polemical reference to laws which, seen in their abstractness, claim requisites which they do not and cannot have since they, too, are the fruit of human action. The selection is symptomatic, however, because it is an expression of that reversal of the Hegelian approach which characterized not only Marx, but an entire philosophy going up to Lenin and beyond, as well. It may seem paradoxical, but Marx summarizes, almost, the historical and political prospective in extremely clear-cut and simple terms. The bourgeoisie and the proletariat engage in a struggle between the *faithful* and the *infidels* towards progress which, in any case and almost as if it were a *divinity*, will prevail, corroborating those who, with force and decision, have believed in the advent of the coming Realm and have implemented it with their force. Lenin will operate on the same terrain since "Leninism is nothing but the precise political application of this new force of moral Manichaeism which leads one to conceive of reality in rigidly dichotomous terms: on the one hand the army of progress (the world Communist movement) and on the other, that of reaction (all the forces that do not accept the revolutionary alternative)" (Pellicani, G, 61).

F) *"Rigorousness" of the Dialectical Method (Historical Materialism)*.

12.27 The most paradoxical aspect of post-Hegelian historicism is that the dissolution of the Judeo-Christian approach is declared on the one hand, and on the other, people attempt in every way to convince themselves of the fact that another, sole explanation of the world and history can exist: a Marxist one. This view, using, as luck would have it, the scientific tools that the previous century made available, seeks to explain all of what we call existential problems and which have always been at the heart of any religious investigation. A logical explanation of the origin of man, society, history and the aim of history is sought, in other words. It is difficult to provide convincing reasons for all of these aspects, even if the claim is made that they represent the true situation. The result is a new dogmatism of which the system put forth by Lenin is the most logical and inevitable conclusion. It is this latent dogmatism along with a scientific rigour which characterizes Marx's actual thought. "He is, on the one hand, tied to the eschatological prospect of the advent of a classless society, but on the other – to the degree to which he departs from Hegel – constitutes a considerably more important effort to understand the historical process at the heart of the real needs of human beings and their actual condition of existence" (Rossi, 16). In other words, Marx wavers between a rigorous observation of the facts and a covert dream of a better world. What really counts in his thought is this duality in actual fact, which was well received, even though it wavered between rigour and dreams. Scientific rigorousness represented the necessary premise for truth to emerge as far as his followers were concerned, while the eschatological prospect constituted a real stimulus.

12.28 Here, too, concerning the scientific nature of the method, a typically Hegelian requisite reappears: universality. The method is scientific only if its canons are accepted and recognized by the entire universe of humans. It could also be said that the method is scientific for the very reason that that is the approach, in the sense that it does not admit contradictions, and is self-evident like every statement backed by scientific rigour. A refusal to accept it means being irrational, uneducated in a certain way of understanding the matters of the world, being totally incapable of reading history. Not a few dissidents have undergone this fate. There is only one possibility for these people, that of educating themselves. Following this path, everything is allowed as long as the end is conserved, that of freeing and transforming humanity. This phase can be marked by a reconstruction which, to use the fortunate expressions of Marcuse, arrives at the greatest depth of the institutional structure of mankind, the "changes in morality" can penetrate "the biological dimensions and modify organic behavior" (Marcuse, 10-11). This, furthermore, was Marx's intention when he "was preparing to publish *Capital*, in which all history is absorbed into an economic process moving toward a final world revolution and world renovation" (Löwith, MiH, 33). This is why Marx's philosophy can be said to have achieved the union and merging of hope and reason in reality. The hope is that of creating a new human being and the certainty is based on the fact that history is marching towards such a goal. Marx does not have the least doubt: "But we recognize in this antagonism the clever spirit (Hegel's 'cunning of reason') which keenly proceeds in working out all these contradictions. We know that the new form of social production, to achieve the good life, needs only (!) *new men*"(Marx in Löwith, MIH, 36). People must be recreated, then, however it is no longer God who recreates them but humanity itself which, having acquired and taken over all the requisites of the divinity, also has the ability to regenerate, or better yet, renew the human race. This is why the secret history of the *Communist Manifesto* is not its conscious materialism and what Marx thinks of it, but the religious spirit of prophetism. The *Communist Manifesto* is, above all a prophetic document, a verdict and an invitation to take action, but it is absolutely not a purely scientific analysis based on empirical data. Even though Marx wishes to explain the fact of exploitation with the theory of surplus value, exploitation remains a moral judgment in any case; it is something absolutely unjust, if measured against a determined idea of justice (cf. Löwith, MIH, 43). The proletariat is, therefore, actually God incarnated in the totality of human beings because, like the Judeo-Christian God, it is the *guardian* of *justice*. In Marx, although he denies it, there is the Jewish need for a chosen people and a promised land which he reutilizes for the earthly prospect.

12.29 Christianity must be eliminated because it nullifies, makes impossible, the earthly realization of the Kingdom. With Christianity the world is estranged from itself. "The fact that the earthly foundation becomes detached from itself and constructs for itself the haze of a fixed realm, can be explained only through dissociation from oneself and the self-contradictory nature of this earthly basis" (Marx – rephrased by Engels –, TüF, 534). The classless society eliminates this detachment, the proletariat is the true instrument of *redemption* because it recreates the world in its true dimension eliminating, as Hegel had said, the fracture created by the Christian religion. This fracture is counterproductive and harmful because it is capable of creating only confusion and useless delays. As is evident, the basic thesis in Lessing's thought reappears: the Christian religion is nothing but a stage in the history of humanity. Marx goes beyond Lessing, however, and in this surmounting nullifies what there was of an individualistic and bourgeois nature in the German Enlightenment. Lessing, in fact, in the criticism of religion, occupies a position typical of the intellectual satisfied with himself and who is not yet concerned about the huge numbers of people in the lower classes. His is a personal atheism which, at times, he seeks to camouflage. The same cannot be said for Marx. With him and Engels, after various presuppositions of the Hegelian left, atheism becomes a social matter with collective dimensions for the first time. This, too, is a sign of the desire of the two founders of dialectical materialism to recreate mankind *ab imis*.

G) *Labour and Revolution.*

12.30 Religion is an illusion and all the promises of liberation it holds are illusions; human beings created them when they saw no other tangible roads to salvation. For Marx, clearly and strongly influenced by Feuerbach, there are no alibis: "man creates religion, and not religion man. Religion is the consciousness of oneself and the feeling of self in human beings that have not yet conquered themselves or have lost themselves (...) Religion is the sigh of the oppressed creature, the feeling of a heartless world, as well as the spirit of a spiritless condition. It is the opiate of the people" (Marx, KHRE, 378). That is not all. Marx is convinced that there is no point in eliminating religion if that world which gave rise to it and continues to be its expression, is not eliminated. The struggle against religion thus becomes the struggle against that world, of which religion is the experience. Religious misery is, in fact, both the expression of misery and the protest against the real misery together. Now that this protest is taking on more tangible and valid forms, the religious world of the bourgeoisie is shaking and the early, illusory and counterproductive one of the proletariat has been replaced by a new view of the world, which has become scientific, hence realizable.

12.31 This new *Weltanschauung* can be achieved since human beings have finally re-acquired the tools that can enable them to regain possession of the world. This repossession has been made possible because humanity, organizing itself into a proletariat, can be the owner of its own labour and the property produced by it. Taking possession once again of one's own labour and its fruits means really becoming masters, not only of oneself, but of the entire world and its history. Indeed, "all of the so-called universal history is simply the generation of mankind by means of human labour, the becoming of nature for mankind, so that it has evident and irresistible proof of its having been born of itself, from its original process"(Marx, OPM, 546). Examining the world of labour is thus re-examining history from the economic point of view which establishes all human relations. Labour, with all its related or resulting problems, becomes the soul of every vital process, a soul which has come totally down to reality and which eliminates every illusory metaphysical premise from history. In the final analysis Marx sees history itself as being invested with new tasks thanks to which Hegelian idealism, the real *leit motiv* of dialectical materialism, is overthrown. Marx is extremely clear on this point and it is worth underscoring the consciousness of this upheaval by using his own statements. "Once the afterlife of truth has disappeared, it is then the task of history to re-establish the truth of this life. Above all, it is the duty of philosophy, which is in the service of history, and once the sacred countenance of human self-alienation has been unmasked, to unmask self-alienation in its profane figures. Thus, criticism of heaven turns into criticism of the earth, criticism of religion into criticism of right, criticism of theology into criticism of politics" (Marx, KHRE, 378-379). Mankind thereby recovers itself, frees itself from its true original sin which is that of not being the master of himself and, indeed, being alienated from himself.

12.32 That revolution for Marx is a transitory phase is beyond any doubt. Revolution serves only to eliminate, as Marcuse clearly states, a *bellum omnium contra omnes* that has become civilized, in which happiness for some "must coexist with the suffering of the others" (Marcuse, 14). Revolution makes it possible to overcome this situation characterized by an ever growing number of exploited people since capitalism reproduces itself by transforming itself and this transformation operates mainly for improvement in exploitation (cf. Marcuse, 13). Thus, revolution brings these conflicts to an end, eliminates them and creates that phase of "perpetual peace" which, after the teachings of Kant, constituted the dream of a great many German intellectuals in the nineteenth century. Marx's approach, however, deserves closer attention. According to him, with revolution, every type of conflict will be eliminated since the primary reason for every conflict has been eliminated: capitalistic society. Marx did not in the least imagine that conflicts can exist that do not have economic sources. For him, ideological disputes or disputes over values are the result of superstructures and will surely be eliminated once the existing economic structure has been brought down. This, basically, is the *ultimate truth* of Marxism. So it is easy to intuit why, once Communist society has been established, it will be impossible to imagine any type of conflict and dissent.

12.33 Marxism seems innately to have two faces: progressivism up to a certain era, immobility after that. "Let us not label Marx a counter-revolutionary, that would not have any sense, any more than it would have made any sense to consider him as eternally a revolutionary or still a revolutionary (...) The truth – a sacrilege for the Marxists – is that European thought did not come to a halt after Marx, just as philosophy and history did not come to a halt after Hegel" (Monnerot, 188 and 195). From the Marxist side, two replies: either the bearers of those conflicts are incapable of interpreting the evolution of history or, as a consequence, the authentic Communist society has not yet come to pass and the phase of passage to a world without classes is in the process of becoming a reality. This latter hypothesis, that developed all in the western countries, is the result of that theory of the establishment of Communism over a *long period* that began to gain ground between the two world wars and of which Gramsci was the main creator.

H) *Constructivism as a Social Theory: A. Comte.*

12.34 The speculation of Comte (1798-1857) had not a little influence on the possibility, conceived of in Marxist thought, of actually bringing about a new political order capable of eliminating injustices and contradictions. Comte was the author, among other things, of the *Cours de philosophie positive* and a *Système de politique positive* both published in several volumes. In Comte's opinion, thanks to the contribution offered by sociology, it would be easier to make a systematic design of society in order scientifically to solve the problems of society itself. It is quite true that Comte shows noteworthy differences from Marxism. For one thing, he foresees an alliance among philosopher-scientists and the proletariat in order to guarantee a new social order. It is equally true, however, that this, according to the French thinker, is achievable thanks to a new scientific methodology which is not the one provided by Hegelian dialectics. Furthermore, Comte is convinced that that the evolutionary movement is inevitable, and the scientific spirit offers it a noteworthy contribution (cf. Comte, IV, 195). He is also convinced of the possibility of predicting its outcome. All this leads him to be certain that political science can formulate hypotheses on a par with the other sciences of nature, that can be verified, or better yet, be implemented (cf. D'Addio, SDP, II, 185-186). From this comes a mentality which is not only deterministic, but also constructivistic, so that the task of politics is to carry out all those provisions aimed at transforming society.

12.35 There is, to some extent, a dialectic in Comte, since the new social science is divided into two sectors that continually interact: *Social Statics* that analyzes the laws of coexistence of social phenomena and considers that of order as the crucial problem and *Social Dynamics* which analyzes the laws pertaining to the connections between social phenomena and takes them into consideration on the level of progress. These two different moments have always been present in history and have characterized its various phases which Comte examines, making distinctions between the famous three "stages" which mark the progress of civilization: theological-military, metaphysical-revolutionary and positive. The French philosopher concentrates on the latter, obviously, because it will be in this period that a new, homogeneous society is achieved, upheld by institutions open to all the classes, on a par with what happened in the Middle Ages thanks to the Church. The gradual dissolution over centuries of the theological and feudal system opened the way to what would become the French Revolution; this was the metaphysical phase which showed the inability of the revolutionary assembly system to obtain a new political stability, thereby demonstrating the emptiness and lack of concreteness of the concept of sovereignty that had come out of the most diverse utopias. The consequence is that people are living in *profonds désordres* which can be overcome by creating a science capable of bringing about a *prévision rationelle* in order to act effectively on the social situation (cf. Comte, IV, 214).

12.36 Comte puts forth the need to arrive at a "sociocratic" constitution which will have to take into account that natural hierarchy, of a material, moral and intellectual nature, which comes out of the "social economy" and which the latter establishes and helps to progress. He further distinguishes between productive and distributive industrial activity. In favouring the latter, he eventually speaks of "social individualism" criticizing Communism because it mortifies the differences that are an essential component of progress. Furthermore, Communism has not understood the uselessness of the fight against private industry because only industrial expansion can solve the problems of the proletariat (cf. D'Addio, SDP, II, 191-193). Industry, progress and the sociocratic constitution will give way to a new spiritual homogeneity and will fill the gap left by the Medieval Church with new content. A new religion of Humanity will thereby be achieved, a positive religion capable of facing and solving tangible problems in solidarity and without conflicts. The radical criticism of the society of the time, already embarked upon by personalities such as Charles Fourier (1772-1837), thus finds a tool for renewing the world in its entirety through social physics, later called sociology.

THIRD PART

13. Utopia or the Need for a Different World.

13.1 Utopians could be included among enemies of the open society, because they are caught up in constructivist ideals. However, differently from the latter, they are fully aware of the fact that they are introducing plans outside of reality. Furthermore, what ennobles their descriptions is that craving for justice and renewal of the politics of their times seemed to have lost sight of. There are numerous writers who fall in the area of the multifaceted utopian school. A great many belong to this area, even thinkers from Machiavelli to Marx, some others that range from Savonarola to Erasmus. Here, the preference has been given to discussing those others in different chapters because they have, in the final analysis, played a different role which, not seldom, has strongly influenced practice, despite the fact that they have utopian traits.

13.2. *De Hominis Dignitate* by Giovanni Pico della Mirandola (1463-1494) may be considered not only the manifesto of humanistic and Renaissance *humanitas*, but, in some ways, the utopian dream par excellence of future humanity. It was a new dream which, like all genuine new experiences, summarized the best of past culture and projected it towards fascinating and hope-inspiring objectives which aroused the fervour of contemporaries not a little. Vittore Branca has shown this quite well (cf. *L'Intesa*). He was able to grasp not only the yearning, but also the cultural upbringing of Pico, who became part of those noble spirits of his time and answer to the name of Savonarola, More, Erasmus, etc. They were able to synthesize the rediscovery of the classics and the tradition of the Church, carrying on that task which had already been initiated by the Church fathers. It can therefore be said that Pico, "taking up a principle of the Ciceronian Jerome and yet more of Augustine, defends scholastic Latin, so that barbarous is not he who writes badly, but who thinks badly" (Carena, L). Thus, he is defending a model of culture which is also a model of society over which he sees menacing clouds forming. His generous ideal can be summarized in his aspiring to attain the "marvellous felicity of mankind! To mankind is given what he desires and to be what he wants" (Pico, 9). For this reason he is to be distinguished from the brutes that have neither free will nor creativity. This was the expressed divine will when it was said to Adam: "The other beings have an indefinite and closed nature within terms and laws established by me. You, not closed within narrow confines, according to your free will, which I bestowed upon you, will determine your nature" (Pico, 8). This dream was destined to be shattered all over Europe, which was marching briskly towards different forms of absolutism.

A) *The Island of Utopia T. More.*

13.3 Utopias are all a bit alike because they show the same yearning for perfection, static "order", justice and morality, in both the governing and the governed. This all reveals an unquestionable state of discontent with the present. The work of Thomas More does not elude these considerations, although his writing presents some ideas that are to be found only in his "utopian republic". Suffice it to consider that all the ideal cities are against private property and its determining cause which, in More, is the family: More refers more or les explicitly to the earliest stages of Christianity. Property in common does not imply abolition of the family which indeed constitutes the essence of the ideal State.

Thomas More was born in London in 1478. After having begun classical studies, then, subsequently jurisprudence, he pursued the career of magistrate. He met Erasmus in 1499 and their friendship was to last his entire life. In those same years, he studied the political thought of St Augustine. In 1504 he was elected to the House of Commons where he distinguished himself for his opposition to the tax demands of Henry VIII. He succeeded in obtaining tax reductions. From that time to 1529 he occupied the most prestigious political and diplomatic positions culminating in that of Lord Chancellor of England, the top government post. It should be pointed out that when he was appointed Speaker of the House of Commons he asked that the sovereign guarantee complete freedom of expression to the representatives. However, a difficult period ensued. In 1534 he did not want to subscribe to the king's ecclesiastical policy. He was imprisoned and his property confiscated. Placed on trial for having denied the king the title of head of the English Church, he demonstrated that the accusations had no foundation. False testimony had to be used to obtain the death sentence, carried out on 6 July of 1535. In 1516, *Utopia* was published by Erasmus. There are numerous other humanistic writings, among which we mention the *Latin Epigrammes* (1518-1520), and the translations, such as those of Lucian's *Dialogues*, undertaken together with Erasmus or of the *Life of John Picus, the Earl of Mirandola*. His historical as well as theological and religious writings are noteworthy. Among these the *Responsio ad Convitia Martini Lutheri* (1523).

13.4 Many are the remarks that suggest to readers that More, on many occasions, felt the need to free his republic from an imaginary vision and place it in the area of the concrete, but all that remained on the level of intentions. He well knew that only few, amidst many experiences and serious dangers, were capable of acquiring that sense of reality which, once learned in that world, are never again forgotten.

He knew equally well that certain punishments, like those inflicted on thieves, not only worked against justice, hence were for the good of no-one, but they were even counter-productive when it would be better to provide them with some means of survival, so that no-one might be forced by necessity first to steal and then to die (cf. More, 61). In this respect utopia seems to have a prophetic sense since some of these appeals did not represent a vague need to flee from a determined reality with proposals that would be never carried out, but which would provide reasons in advance for some social reforms of our time. In this case, as Mannheim maintained, utopia brings about an actual change in reality because it gives rise to new values capable of being not only components of ferment, but also transformation, even if not immediate.

13.5 As had already been the case in Plato, the need for justice is closely linked to the pedagogical problem for the purpose of avoiding that up to the most tender of ages, the mores [of the citizens] be corrupted in order to punish them, then, necessarily, when they have become adults, they commit those crimes which they had given indications they would commit from the time of their childhood (cf. More, 71). Curiously enough, at this point More shows signs of a mixture of concreteness and idealism. Speaking of delinquents, he says that they must be punished in any case, that one must reason as the Romans had done, highly expert as they were in the administration of the State: they sentenced those guilty of major crimes to work although, a few pages later, he claimed that as Plato had taught, politicians must pursue other ideals of perfection. Suffice it to think that if the kings had not personally dedicated themselves to philosophy, it never would have happened that they totally approved the advice of philosophers, because they were immersed in false ideas from childhood on (cf. More, 75 and 87). The need to build reality on models which only a few can attain and others must simply follow came to replace a school, which spoke of justice based on tradition and experience.

13.6 All of the last part of the first book seems to bring out another contradiction. More emphasizes the fact that well-being, more specifically wealth, and liberty are not willing to tolerate hard and unjust impositions and so they fortify the mind, whereas he maintains that poverty and need weaken it and cause it to become resigned. Then, however, exalting Plato's Republic, he sings its praises especially because, as in Utopia, there is no private property (cf. More, 95 and 101). The latter leads one to measure every aspect of life in terms of money so that happiness and even justice are thus compromised. This is so because not only are they in the hands of very few people, but also and quite often of the worst. There is no alternative but to abolish property and establish the equality of assets. This situation eliminates continual sources of discontent and the perpetual possibility of revolutions (cf. More, 103-107). The second book opens with the description of the Island of Utopia from which it is immediately inferred that even the configuration recalls the Platonic ideal of geometrical perfection since the outer limits seem traced out with a compass. The island practically transposes the myth of the Demiurge, and has been ordered according to the ideals of Utopus, the mythical conqueror, whose name it bears and who laid out the ideal map of the city. Immobility and ideal perfection are expressed by the cities all spacious and magnificent: language, costumes, institutions and laws coincide. The structure is identical and the appearance is similar, the capital, since it is in the centre, I would say, of that land, is the most suitable position for all the ambassadors that must meet there. In Utopia, if you know one city you know them all (cf. More, 113 and 117). It is a purely agricultural plan and, in some points, reminds one of some Maoistic suggestions. It is governed by several magistrates as well as the inhabitants, and, above all, farmers, where and when circumstances dictate. At times, they are even chosen by lot. All clothing is the same and everyone must be content with only one toga for more than two years. Working hours are precise and limited because the State, which also governs culture, wants the citizens to have a broad education and to be able to carry on other activities, convinced as it is that that contributes to making them happy. Those who can learn the various scientific disciplines might be allowed to abstain from their work for an indefinite period of time. However, if they do not show that they deserve the trust that has been placed in them, they are returned to the world of the crafts to take up once again the duties to which they had originally been assigned. The future magistrates, priests and ambassadors are selected among the meritorious (cf. More, 127 ff.).

13.7 Characteristic of Utopia is continuous control. The cities may not become depopulated or crowded beyond measure. The same is true for the family components. The most numerous families are transferred. Control is even more minute, however, and also concerns the world of labour. For one thing, with a statement that would find considerable agreement today, there is concern, for example, that highly expert doctors always be present in the hospitals (cf. More, 135-137 and 141). To these acceptable controls are added other, truly asphyxiating ones. For example, it is impossible to travel even within Utopia without the Authority's permission. To travel, "a letter" is needed that certifies the granting of the travel permit and sets the date of return. Anyone who takes it upon himself to go beyond the confines of his city and is caught without the authorization of the magistrate in charge is treated harshly and brought back home like a deserter with the exception of the very few who have gone abroad for a valid reason (cf. More, 145-147 and 155). If he does it a second time, he is actually condemned to slavery. Those who can remain idle do not exist and there is not even any pretext for wasting time in the city where, as Owen would say, there is no inn, tavern, brothel or chance to be corrupted. At this point, the pedagogical programme is introduced and it has clear references to Plato's. In Utopia care is willingly given to beauty, physical strength, agility, as specific and agreeable gifts of nature; then the Greek language is studied, to such an extent, says the narrator, that I have a suspicion that those people are of Greek origin, since they judge Latin to be important only for poetry and history (cf. More, 177 and 181). This shows that anyone who associates himself with a utopia not only imitates Plato's plan (it is certainly no accident that all utopias are basically alike), but ultimately ignores law and, in particular, private law. This position is upheld with great clarity since in Utopia, where the private does not exists, the public interest is truly served. When that does not happen, anticipating a Marxist-style reflection, "a plot of the rich" is implemented who, shielded by the name of the State, carry on their business (cf. More, 237-239 and 241). The author knows that where a utopia is involved, not a few of the subjects dealt with in this tale, in which he plays the passive role of listener, may seem strange and absurd, but he does not take a position above and beyond general observation. Given his times, just one consideration, it seems to me, should be underscored: reason alone is weak in the quest for true happiness and cannot achieve convincing results (cf. More, 161).

B) *The* Nova Atlantis: *F. Bacon*.

13.8 Although the *Nova Atlantis (The New Atlantis)* of Bacon follows the lines of the other utopias as far as political organization is concerned, it has a certain singularity. It predicts many of the achievements of science that would come about in future centuries. It must be said, however, that in the way of dealing with science to arrive at the innovations desired by all, the centralized model returns, which is at the heart of all utopian ones. That is, the ancient Platonic dream returns, confirming that well before Popper, Plato, considered the main "author" for utopians (cf. Bacon, 377), was a point of reference for those who placed their hopes in a well-prepared and capable political class that could carry out and manage the public good, this in the name of the totality of citizens aiming at performing the duties assigned to them.

Francis Bacon was born in London in 1561. His was a privileged youth and well-educated, since he was the son of Sir Nicholas Lord the Minister of Justice of Queen Elizabeth. He studied at Cambridge, at the famous Trinity College, where he began to fall out of love with the philosophy of Aristotle. After carrying on law studies, necessary to enter political life, he left for France with the ambassador Sir Amias Paulet. Disenchanted with France, but also because of his father's death, he returned to his country seeking, with alternating fortunes, to devote himself to political life. Success came as he reached the top of his political career, only after 1603, when King James I, who loved culture and was a protector of intellectuals became king. In 1620, he published his most famous work the *Novum Organum* with which he intended to replace the Aristotelian perspective. The book was to be the second part of a more ambitious work: the *Instauratio Magna* whose introduction and general outline were published the same year. In 1621 he was accused of corruption and condemned, although the sentence was never carried out. Bacon continued to devote himself to his studies, although he could no longer occupy political office, and did so until his death on Easter day in 1626. He wrote many other works among which, for the purposes of this book, we recall the *Nova Atlantis* which, however, was never completed.

13.9 As the friend and secretary of Bacon, W. Rawley, reminds us, the beginnings of the *Nova Atlantis* review the dream of all the utopias and all the philosophers from the Greek world, that is, they discuss the laws, or the best possible structure of States (cf. Bacon, 357). The ideal is that of a perfect society where honesty and progress prevail, since everyone receives "a salary from the State for his work" and thus has no need to give in to any corruption. The State provides for the expenses of all the guests who have come to those remote lands, but, in exchange, regulates everything, even the possibility of moving about on the island (cf. Bacon, 364 and 368). The laws do not come from tradition and are not perfected over time. They are set down once and for all by mythical legislators. The Lycurgus of the moment is called Salomana. Among his fundamental laws, there are many on prohibition of entry to foreigners. In the case of trade, this was due to the fear of the new. Our trips abroad, too, legislators took care to eliminate absolutely. Naturally, those authorized for the purpose of gaining knowledge, hence those of public utility, too, are excepted when there is the commission to give us information on the realities and situations of the places we reach, above all on the sciences, arts, mills and inventions of the entire world, and also to bring us books, tools, samples of every sort (cf. Bacon, 381-382). The purpose of these trips must only be cultural and the acquisition of things must also be for this purpose. All other trade for the sake of personal wealth, must be banned. Prosperity, even that of the family, is a matter of State. Celebrations and family legislation are demonstrations of this. Celebrations are described in their every detail and are carried on in the presence of a magistrate. One consults on marriages and the most appropriate marital status for each person. Their marriage legislation is abundant, certainly very sensible and decorous (cf. Bacon, 386 and 394) further proof that the state intends to control the life of each individual even the feelings.

13.10 The final part of the *Nova Atlantis* is quite different (cf. Bacon, 398 ff.). Conclusions that smack of prophecy are hypothesized here and have driven critics and philosophers mad in their attempts to characterize the English philosopher in different ways. Science placed at the service of mankind leads to the curing of unknown illnesses; never-before seen tools make possible the long-term conservation of foods and modification of flavours; farming techniques offer ways of obtaining harvests out of season and several times within a year; acoustical devices enable the capture of the most diverse sounds modifying their volume and intensity as one likes; artificial mines provide previously unknown alloys and metals stronger than traditional ones; perspective chambers capture light and can propagate it where and how anyone likes, and so forth, for the thousands of other wonders prophesied. It has been said, appropriately, that the utopia in all that consists in the fact that this happens outside of the conflicts and contradictions that govern human life, because one has definitively broken away from all the *idola* that dominate in our world where, even traditional science now prevents one from making progress (cf. Cacciari, XVII). It is only a change in social conditions that leads to progress, hence the need for a *perfect state*, which also means the ability to keep everything under control. It is a State with infinite possibilities that "gathers all and sees all", with a univocal direction using individual members as its trusted tentacles (cf. Cacciari, XXIII-XXIX). This situation continues as long as that order reigns which goes back to the natural order, obtained not out of interest, but thanks to a scientific knowledge which seems almost to be an end in itself. This is why the utopian aspect of Marxism seems to be anticipated, "only one science is lacking in Utopia, and it is political economy (…) *Ou-topia* is modern science without a modern market (…) The modern technical and scientific project *works* since, among other things, it is capable of imagining itself to be autonomous or neutral compared to the mercantile and political orders" (cf. Cacciari, XXXVI-XXXVIII). In fact, here is the eternal utopian dream that gives rise to the belief that progress can be had in the absence of political or economic struggle. In order to fulfil this expectation a transformation of human nature becomes necessary, confirmed by the importance of religion in this long and remote island where being religious is not a reason for conflict, but a driving force on behalf of progress.

C) *The* Civitas Solis: *T. Campanella.*

13.11 The *Civitas Solis* (*The City of the* Sun) also goes back to the Platonic idea of perfection. "The political, social and cultural environment surrounding the tormented life of Campanella is, then, basically the characteristic of Italian regression (…) and from here, Campanella's anti-Machiavellianism takes its form, as well as his constant criticism of the 'raison d'état'" (Seroni, 8 and 24). The Italian regression, both a cause and effect of political decadence, relegated the peninsula to carrying on a secondary political role in future. Italy was a victim of those great forms of absolutism that were gaining more and more ground in western Europe. Anti-Machiavellianism manifests itself in the fact that for Campanella, from what has come down from the classic and scholastic tradition, power and force are not considered as ends of politics, but it is still maintained that politics must bring about a solid community life to enable not only a peaceful conservation of the human species, but a real pursuit of that happiness for which human beings were created. What harms this aim is the clear holistic view, typical of all utopias, which goes back to the ideals of Plato. The *Civitas Solis* is a place where one is taught to "concern oneself above all with life in its entirety, then with the individual parts" (Campanella, 70).

Tommaso Campanella was born in 1568 in Calabria, at Stilo. He entered the Dominican Order at a very young age, had occasion to travel a lot, perhaps even to avoid conflict with his superiors. In Padua, where he met Galileo Galilei, he was accused of heresy and sent to Rome in 1594. Up to the end of the century he was put on trial several times and managed to be released although he was ordered to return to Calabria. In those same years he wrote his most significant works such as *Philosophia sensibus demonstrata* (1591) where the influence of Bernardino Telesio is felt, *De monarchia christianorum* and *De regimine Ecclesiae* both in 1593), *Dialogo politico contro Luterani, Calvinisti e altri eretici* (1595). In 1600 he headed a conspiracy which should have reconstructed the political and religious order of all of Europe, starting from southern Italy. A new egalitarian and Communistic system would be the means of realizing this. He was arrested for an attempt at insurrection. To escape the death penalty, he feigned madness and was condemned to life imprisonment. After a harsh period in prison he was then treated gently and found a way to write, receive friends and carry on correspondence. From this period come the *Aforismi politici* (1601) and *Civitas solis* (1602), which came out in various editions. Definitively freed in 1626 by Urban VIII he went to Rome. In 1633 he took refuge in France after being accused by one of his disciples of having taken part in a plot against the Spanish. In France, received by Richelieu himself and by Louis XIII, the King, he wrote more political works. He died in Paris in 1639. Among the other, numerous works the *Metafisica*, rewritten in Latin in 1608 after the Italian edition of a few years prior had been lost, is worth mentioning.

13.12 "The supreme prince (...) we would say 'Metaphysician' (...) with one sole book for everyone (...) read to the people, according to the Pythagorean method" (Campanella, 9 and 11) are expressions which make clear from the opening lines, that the *Civitas Solis*, too, refers to a model which has its profound inspiration in Plato. It has, in fact, a political vision which finds the "ruler-philosophers" the inventors and planners of everything since they are in possession of the truth. The Dominican Father's words leave no doubt: "it is the Metaphysician who speaks of all that with the three principal magistrates; but without him, nothing can be done. All the affairs of State pass through the hands of these four, but everyone bows before the preferences of the Metaphysician" (Campanella, 17). Obviously in this political model as well, property is opposed, since it is not only an expression of injustice, but also a cause of diversity. In order to exist, the same family requires separate domiciles, the certainty of offspring and so, the exclusivity of wives. From this comes the aspiration to power, wealth, honour, in a word the birth of that pride which opposes love of the community. As a result, some people have too much and many do not have the basic necessities. In the *Civitas Solis*, no-one is lacking in necessities (cf. Campanella, 18-19). As in Plato, the pedagogical problem is fundamental, here too not free, but managed by the "kings". "The inclination of each person" has to be examined to direct the youngest towards what will be the most useful for the community. The control reaches every aspect of the life of the State through the appointments for the individual posts which must be held by officials "elected from those first four". The matter of educating those who aspire to the highest positions and for those few who will be able to replace the four at the head of the city is far more complex. For those, an extraordinary capacity for metaphysics and theology, a far-reaching knowledge of the basics and fundamentals, and examinations in all the arts and sciences are needed" because they will have to have a view "of the totality" (cf. Campanella, 22-25). It must be said that males and females may perform the same tasks, when account has been taken of their natural differences, while their services are performed in shifts, as if they were in barracks.

13.13 The central political leadership decides absolutely everything, even on matters pertaining to eating and dressing. Centralism goes even further, however. It involves not only education, but also the union between males and females, who have a date set in advance for their first relations and procreation for which they must "however, request permission from the First Master of Procreation". This person establishes not only the moment of mating but also those who must mate following rigorous criteria of eugenics. To arrive at those assessments, the characters, intellectual inclinations, physical aspects, etc., are considered. This is a crucial aspect because of the conviction that from this comes "a great and persistent harmony in the State". For this, the "great doctor in medicine, employee of *Amor*, one of the triumvirates" exists. Not even feelings are left up to individuals. Politics invade every area of life. Liberty remains a simple illusion which, however, must be safeguarded, because it seems that one cannot do without it. Hence, a stratagem is used. "In Plato's judgment it is appropriate that distribution be made by lot, (…) those who do not deserve to inseminate the most beautiful women should even be deceived (…) But (…) this is not necessary for the inhabitants of the City of the Sun since ugliness does not exist among them". It can be said that the use of a selection methodology has eliminated that (cf. Campanella, 31-43). All those games, too, like dice, which make people lazy and dissolute are eliminated. Those which fortify the body and make people active and laborious are, on the contrary, encouraged. One is thus useful to others and always ready for any circumstance such as war. Persuaded that the political message of the city is the best "they must fight, they say, solely to improve the conquered, not to exterminate them (...) They are convinced that the entire world will one day live following their systems; thus they continually investigate whether or not there is a people that might live in a more highly recommendable and excellent way than they themselves" (Campanella, 62 and 69).

13.14 It is clear that in this presumption of being the best in everything, there is nothing useful to be obtained from others. "Trade has little use" (Campanella, 64). Nothing good can come from abroad, so that the integrity of the State must be safeguarded. Attacks to institutions and the State itself are to be considered as if they were against God and must be punished by death. One may be more clement in cases of guilt due to weakness or ignorance, but "political" crimes cannot be tolerated even if attempts are made to understand the motives. In this perfection, governed by a few, clear laws, it is thought that the sole changes can be due to reforms carried out by exceptional prophets who will be capable of renewing everything without causing harm (cf. Campanella, 82 and 108).

D) The Commonwealth of Oceana: *J. Harrington.*

13.15 The need for equality and, above all, justice characteristic of all utopian dreams comes out in *The Commonwealth of Oceana* by James Harrington, as well. This work, like many others from the same period, does not come out of academic circles, but commercial ones and from the artisan class, an expression of those new and rising social layers that were able victoriously to support the Parliament in the struggle against the Crown. The idea of Oceana brings out that necessity, common in many other writings of the time and, fortunately, not always utopian, to seek in the popular will the original component of any State even if this presents itself as an authoritarian system. Hence there is the need to make comparisons with ancient republics that existed more or less concretely, or with other modern ones still and actually functioning like Venice, for example. The desire was to show that this republic, at the very time when the projects of "Cromwell the usurper" were manifesting their presence, was possible in England, too (cf. Schiavone, 15-16).

James Harrington was born at Upton in 1611. He educated himself especially by means of his important trips in Europe among which, one to Venice, which deserves special mention. The institutions of Venice aroused his enthusiasm. He took active part in the events surrounding the English Civil War. Indeed, after the Restoration came, he was imprisoned for a short time, having been accused of conspiracy. His best known work, *The Commonwealth of Oceana*, was for a brief period "kidnapped" by Cromwell, himself. He died at Westminster in 1677.

13.16 What is characteristic of this utopian plan, as of the others, is its constructivist and so centralistic vision. Another Plato-like holism is proposed and it presents the analogy between the body politic and the human body, comparing the study of politics with that of anatomy. The objective of social and political stability is attainable only thanks to a solid State power capable of eliminating continual conflict among the various groups (cf. Schiavone, 32-33). Naturally, this conflict is not seen as an element of progress. This need to create a State with solid and strong institutions brings Harrington's thought closer to that of Machiavelli who, in some ways, can also be thought of as a utopian thinker. Much more important, however, are the suggestions due to Plato: the possibility of carrying out the project begins with a pedagogical approach, managed by the State, which allows "conscious participation" in political activities. Another Platonic element is that of egalitarian distribution of wealth in the conviction that economic events have a too great influence on political ones (cf. Schiavone, 36 and 39). If it is true that a fundamental cause of revolutions is the need to bring about a balance in the distribution of property, and here there is the echo of a typically Aristotelian approach, it is obvious that the first important reform to implement is agrarian (cf. Harrinton, § 5 of *The Commonwealth of Oceana*). In fact, the importance of agriculture, to which Roman statesmen also devoted their attention, is underscored throughout, starting from the Introduction of the work.

13.17 The constructivist component which recalls Plato most of all comes from the fact that the elements that qualify power are authority and wisdom. "Those who have so much wisdom that they can arouse the general interest are often few, however (…) in virtue and in merits acquired through actions on behalf of the common good, like the philosopher-kings of Plato (…) Once again we find the Platonic suggestion of the philosophical virtue of power" (Schiavone, 45-46 and 53). From this comes a vision where not only are politics capable of everything, but where the unity of the State is seen as something monolithic which does not permit particular differentiations of any sort. Religion itself cannot be thought of as an autonomous reality because it would give rise to a dangerous dualism in the consciences. It becomes a part of the State, as Hobbes himself wished, tied to its destiny and its fortunes.

FOURTH PART

14. The Republican Ideal confronting the Raison d'État.

14.1 Machiavelli is surely the most representative personality of his time. The duality brilliance-ambiguity applies to him more than to any other person. Even thinkers very different in their approaches, Maritain for example, consider him the greatest interpreter of one of the most highly disputed ages in history. On the one hand, he gathers the classical and medieval heritage, of which his republican mentality is an expression, even where this has been reinterpreted to meet contemporary needs, on the other hand, he devised the first theory of modern absolutism, the result of his own personal observations.

Nicolò Machiavelli was born in Florence in 1469 in a family of merchants. Although their financial situation was modest, they had participated in governing the city. In 1498 he was appointed the secretary of the second Chancellery, which enabled him to observe Italian and European politics from a close vantage point. Years of travel and encounters followed and these inspired various political writings as well as the future *Portraits*. His observations made in this period on military matters and army organization are very penetrating. The eclipse of the Florentine Republic caused him to experience one of the bitterest periods in his life, the two-year period – 1512-1513. However, it was then that he began to reflect on his works, whose influence would be great, first and foremost, the *Discorsi sopra la prima deca di Tito Livio* (*Discourses on the First Decade of Titus Livius*) interrupted in December 1513, so that he could write all of *Il Principe* (*The Prince*). Between 1518 and 1520 he wrote *L'arte della guerra* (*The Art of War*), the *Mandragola* (*Mandrake*), and *La vita di Castruccio Castracani*

(*The Life of Castruccio Castracani*), after which he devoted himself to the *Istorie fiorentine* (*Florentine Histories*) for a long period of time. The alternating fortunes of Florence, between new attempts to form republics and the returns of the Medici, cast a pall on the last years of his life which came to an end in 1527, when the fate of the peninsula was now definitively compromised. In addition to the works cited, he left behind numerous other writings of a literary and historical nature, as well as a highly interesting collection of correspondence.

14.2 In a Europe which, following the ending of past universalisms, was outlining the roles of future powers were becoming better defined, and Machiavelli, through his travels among other things, felt the need to confer on Italy a modern State structure to make her capable of competing with the new and powerful countries. This need was what probably led to a fascinating body of thought. It can be called not only political but philosophical as well, since it is supported on a serious anthropological conception, with which, however, one may not always agree. As in Hobbes, whose premises, of course, are different, there is a certain way of understanding nature and history, which then results in a precise political view. Human nature is selfish and disagreeable. People desire good in a disordered way and become "fed up" with good once they have attained it, after having enjoyed it for a while. They are attached to their own property to such an extent that "they more readily forget the loss of their father than the loss of their property". Even after a lot of time has passed, they wish to regain possession of it because it is "truly a very natural and ordinary thing to wish for gain". They are so superficial that "in universal matters men judge more from their eyes than their hands; because it is for everyone to see, and few to hear: everyone sees what you appear to be, and few hear what you are". They are eager for novelties then they fear them, so that one must take into account the "incredulity of men, and those who in truth do not believe new things, unless a solid experience arises from them". They are not capable of forgiving so that those who "believe that great personalities and new benefits make one forget old injustices are deceived" (Machiavelli, P, 163, 125, 166, 132, 139). This lesson in extreme realism must be transposed into politics where necessary "to seek the effective truth of the matter rather than imagine it. And many have imagined republics and princedoms which have never been seen nor have they been known in their true essence" (Machiavelli, P, 159).

14.3 Like Guicciardini and unlike the Italian politicians of the time, Machiavelli understood the momentous transition underway, but both thinkers failed to convey to those upon whom the fates of the individual states depended a sense of the urgent need to adapt to the new exigencies. This lack of comprehension further increased bitterness due to a highly contradictory situation, because a people at the height of its Renaissance splendour but incapable of giving expression to its needs found itself face to face with inept politicians. Machiavelli's expressions, as always, were concise and totally clear: "But let us return to the Italians, who, not having had wise princes, have not taken good orders, and, because they have not had that need which the Spanish had, they have not taken them for themselves; so that they remain the disgrace of the world. However, the peoples are not guilty of that, but the princes themselves; who have been castigated, and have not been properly punished for their ignorance ignominiously losing the state, and without any example of virtue" (Machiavelli, AG, 687). What Italian politicians have not been aware of first of all, and which is one of the basic points in Machiavellian thought, is that politics cannot be practiced without adequate force. Indeed, "anyone who has observed the changes in realms, the ruin of the provinces and of the cities, has not seen them caused by other than the lack of arms and judgment" (Machiavelli, PSP, 12). These highly effective expressions show that force as an end in itself must not be sought, even though it has more often than not been interpreted in this way, but force accompanied by a knowledge and awareness, of possible future events that make of the politician a person of science and not an improviser.

14.4 Political action is not easy to carry on nor can in be performed by all in Machiavelli's view. "So anyone who does not recognize evils when they arise in a princedom, is not truly judicious: this is the gift of few" (Machiavelli, P, 156). This is why, as with other activities, it requires intuition and creativity, typical of artists, as well as knowledge and ability to view the whole along with the particular, which are characteristic of scientists. That politics is science, and science autonomous for its divergence from ethics differently from what Aristotle maintained, is well known to all. It is the particular aspects of political science that must be examined, because they constitute that synthesis between the ancient and the modern which is one of the premises upon which the thought of the Florentine secretary is based. It all finds expression in the famous letter to Francesco Vettori of 10 December 1513. In the hours of the day when "I enter the ancient courts of the ancient men (...) and for 4 hours of time feel no boredom, forget any woe, do not fear poverty, am not awestruck by death: I transfer myself to them. And since Dante says that he does not perform science without believing he has understood it, I have written down (...) and composed a work *De Principatipus,* where I delve as best I can in the knowledge of this subject, debating what princes are, of what species they are, how they are procured, how they are maintained, why they go astray" (Machiavelli, L, 296). The summary is concise as always, in this case, of a text destined to become part of history. The science is not theoretical, however, but practical, to return "to having a stone rolled", that is to act since, in politics it is the results by which the capacity of people is measured. In other words, the past cannot be proud ostentation, but preparation to interpret the present more seriously and operate in it.

14.5 Princedoms can be hereditary, new, mixed or ecclesiastical, unlike the republic which he will deal with in the *Discourses*. The ecclesiastical ones arouse only the irony of one convinced of the extreme difficulty involved in carrying on political activity based on Christian principles. Mixed republics deserve separate consideration in certain respects. Machiavelli's attention is drawn above all to the hereditary and new ones. It should be recalled that, when speaking of forms of government, in addition to the republic, the monarchical system, which it seems more appropriate to call despotic here, and the aristocratic one can be singled out. The distinction is a functional one in particular since for the former, it can be said that if it is created with difficulty, it is certainly more easily maintained. The precise contrary is true for the latter. Returning, however to hereditary and new princedoms, Machiavelli's attention is devoted to the latter, because here it is possible to bring out the true qualities of a prince, whereas "in the hereditary states accustomed to the blood of their prince, there is far less difficulty in maintaining them than in new ones" (Machiavelli, P, 120). It is difficult, and in some ways almost impossible to create a new princedom in which live a people accustomed to enjoying liberty, even when it is disordered. So "he who becomes the head of a city used to living free, and does not dismantle it, expects to be undone by it: because he always has as a refuge in a rebellion the name of liberty and of his ancient orders, and that is never forgotten for length of time and for benefits" (Machiavelli, P, 130). Here it is easy to see as in not a few circumstances, that politics requires clear and timely choices because delays could be the cause of ruin. The problem of force returns and this seems to reaffirm the fact that power is not a question of right. There is, however, also a practical necessity behind this conclusion. "I shall only conclude that it is necessary for a prince to have the people on his side, otherwise he has no remedy in adversity". So, it is necessary for men "always and in every quality of time, to have need for the state and for him; and then they will always be faithful to him" (Machiavelli, P, 144-145 and 146). In other words, when every other policy is destined to fail, force is needed. It must be an *extrema ratio* to be used above all with those who, when a wrong has been suffered, might have the strength to take vengeance, which men always want to do. So it is necessary to take care to assess the enemy carefully before "offending him". If he is too strong, one must be resolute in destroying him, otherwise it is better not to provoke him.

14.6 The question of force obviously leads back to that of the army whose corps can be its own or mercenaries or a mixture of the two. Mercenaries offer only "infelicity" especially because the "mercenary captains are either excellent men, or not; if they are you cannot trust them, because they always aspire to their own glory (…) but if the captain is not virtuous, he ruins you for simple things" (Machiavelli, P, 151). Thus, the prince must himself deal with commanding "the arms" and seeking, in these, "to send his citizens". Machiavelli has little faith in auxiliary armies, too. At times they can even be useful, "but for him who calls upon them, they are almost always harmful: because they are crushed when they lose; when they win, they are his prison". While mercenaries are dangerous in one respect, auxiliaries are in another. "In short, slothfulness is what is most dangerous about mercenaries, in the auxiliaries it is virtue" (Machiavelli, P, 154-155). This word is fundamental for the Florentine secretary who brings out the capacity, courage and perspicacity of rare personalities. They must be armed with their own weapons which are the best and must not imitate the unarmed prophets who easily "spoil". This is all more the case if they govern princedoms, "since between an armed one and a disarmed one there is no proportion at all, and it is not reasonable that those who are willingly armed to obey those who are disarmed, and that the disarmed one is safe among armed servants" (Machiavelli, P, 157).

14.7 Concerning virtue it can be said that it characterizes that side of politics that brings it closer to art than to science, even though the latter constitutes the support. Advice can be useful here, but the ability to take it is a sort of innate gift, which one either has or does not have. Having said this, discussion can begin on whether a prince must "desire to be deemed compassionate and not cruel: nonetheless he must take care not to use this pity badly" (Machiavelli, P, 162), hence the famous dispute as to whether it is better to be feared or loved. The range of possibilities is enormous and depends on the valour of those who command. In any case, if it were necessary to choose between extremes, it is preferable to be feared because "men have less respect for offending one who makes himself loved, than one who makes himself feared, because love has a bond of obligation, which, since men are sad, is broken by considerations of one's own advantage, but fear is upheld by a fear of punishment that never leaves you". It is an extreme to be sure. The prince must seek never to make himself hated but be respected "because being feared and not being hated can go quite well together" (Machiavelli, P, 163). Given the circumstances, he must understand two fundamental things: the *first* is that every political choice leads to consequences that one must be able to foresee, the *second* that, should those consequences show themselves to be too dire, it is even preferable not to keep his word and promises. In such cases would it be "laudable for a prince to keep his word"? To cope in such situations, which are certainly not easy, "a prince needs to know how to make proper use of the beast and the man (…) to capture the fox and the lion" (Machiavelli, P, 165). Bestial behaviour is not easy always to display and is not advisable either, but one must make it understood that this is possible when necessary. Now comes one of the most controversial passages in Machiavellian absolutism: the possibility of simulating and dissembling. "Therefore, a prince need not have all the aforementioned qualities in actual fact, but it is highly necessary to appear to have them; indeed, I shall venture to say this: that if he has them and always observes them, they are harmful, and if he seems to have them, they are useful" (Machiavelli, P, 166). Everything is functional for the conquest and keeping of power, this is why *to command is to make believe*.

14.8 The ability of the politician is measured by how he wields power. Cynically but unequivocally Machiavelli develops the theory of political success. This depends on a series of reasons and circumstance by which a true prince cannot allow himself to be destroyed. Fortune itself, understood as blind force can and must be overcome by the "virtue" of the prince. It suffices to understand, foresee and utilize it. "However he must have a spirit willing to be directed as the winds of fortune and variations in matters command him; and, as I said above, not to take leave of the good; but to be able to partake of evil, if necessary" (Machiavelli, P, 166). But fortune must not be considered merely in the conquest of power, otherwise it is unlikely to be stable, it must be considered and foreseen at every moment. The comparison between fortune and a catastrophic natural event is highly appropriate: (fortune) is a swollen river that leads to a flood and, if it does not find embankments already set up to control it, it is unstoppable and destructive. On this subject, Chapter XXV is highly enlightening. One must know how to conquer fortune and seek to dominate it. Anyone who does not succeed cannot blame misfortune, but rather his own slothfulness. "I deem this to be good, that it is better to be impetuous than respectful: because fortune is a woman and it is necessary to beat and strike her, to keep her under control. And it is clear that she allows herself to be defeated more by this one, than by those who proceed calmly; yet always, like a woman, it is a friend of youths, since they are less respectful, more vicious and more bold and command her" (Machiavelli, P, 189). The relationship between youth and force will be one of the crucial themes throughout the work of Machiavelli. One can think of his theatrical compositions where, as in the *Mandrake*, the aforementioned relationship is seen in contrast with that of old age and weakness accompanied by the *insania mentis* of the declining years. These themes will be taken up by other authors, in some of Goldoni's plays, to site one example.

14.9 In seeking to conquer fortune thereby to maintain power and success, the prince faces a dilemma: is it more difficult to handle the relationship with the "great men", other princes from whom some help has perhaps been obtained, or with the people? Here, Machiavelli offers one of his most subtle analyses, one which is not always brought out by critics. His point of departure is clear: "I conclude that a prince must have esteem for the great, but not make himself hated by the people" (Machiavelli, P, 170). Again it is emphasized that the prince, not always being able to make himself be loved, must make himself be feared and must never reach the point of making himself hated by the people. Moreover, without the support of the people, in the long run, it is impossible to govern: thus the powers and princedoms granted by the great and guaranteed by their support are fragile, like the ecclesiastical ones. It almost seems as if the Florentine secretary is returning to one of the themes most dear and determining of that Roman republic that he studied in such depth: consent. The need not to make oneself hated comes back and, indeed, one must gain support. "However, the greatest fortress that exists is that of not being hated by the people; because, although you have the fortresses and the people hate you, these do not save you: because there is no lack of people who have weapons, of foreigners who sustain them" (Machiavelli, P, 178). Here the realism is based on a republican awareness that brings out the real paradox of Machiavelli's mind: whether because of absolutist necessity, or republican upbringing it is, in any case, a mind in pain and torment. At this point, one can agree with the analysis of those who consider *The Prince* a work, which is the fruit of a period of crisis and, thus, a study of the means to get out of this crisis and disorder. This is the origin of that realism, bitter to be sure, which anticipates, as Chevallier pointed out, that duality of the rational and the real typical of Hegel's thought. It is certainly no accident that the German philosopher will reconsider the problem of force and will make it one of the premises of the German Renaissance (cf. Chevallier, Ch. I).

14.10 Machiavelli's upbringing, based on prudence, characteristic of those who examine history in its antilogies, comes out many times in the prince. In addition to the problem of consensus, it is brought out on what we can call the training of the prince, without which, no politician can hope to succeed and govern properly. It is clear why "as far as the exercise of the mind is concerned, the prince must read the histories and in those consider the actions of excellent men, see how they conducted themselves in wars, examine the causes of their victories and their defeats, in order to escape the latter and imitate the former" (Machiavelli, P, 158). Politics are again seen as a difficult form of discipline, backed by serious training capable of avoiding facile illusions or forms of utopia in facing "effectual" reality. Now, the relationship to fortune can also be better understood. Not only can the politician face and foresee fortune effectively when he is well trained, but he knows that he cannot totally depend on it. "Becoming, from private life, a prince, presupposes either virtue or fortune, it seems the one or the other of these two things mitigates many difficulties in part; nonetheless, he who has been less on fortune has maintained himself better" (Machiavelli, P, 131). That *who has been less on fortune* means has trusted it less, has based himself less on fortune. In other words, improvisation is the most deleterious vice of politics and the one which risks causing irreparable damage.

14.11 Is the writing of *The Prince* a chance occurrence? It is difficult to say even though it would seem so, when one reads entire passages of the *Discourses*. In the opening lines of the other great work, where Aeneas is spoken of, he writes as follows: "whose virtue is recognized in two ways: the first is in the selection of the site; the other in the ordering of the laws" (Machiavelli, D, 200). Admiration for the latter brings him back to his homeland. If *The Prince* arises from admiration and concern for dawning foreign states, the *Discourses* return to admiration for the past and for Roman tradition, but also that of Italian republics such as the Florentine to which he had sought to give worthy service. The institutions of these republics must defend liberty which rests on precise ethical substance. Indeed, as he says clearly in the title of Ch. XVII of the First Book, "A corrupt people, having gained liberty, can be kept free with very great difficulty". To keep this corruption at bay the prince with his virtue is not enough. It is the entire people who must be virtuous and this virtue must come from tradition. In these republics, most men "will never agree to a new law that concerns a new order for the city, if they are not shown a need to do so" (Machiavelli, D, 203). Otherwise, individual citizens, aware of the greatness of their order, do not worry about changing their political system. They trust the administration of justice which "is performed without private forces, and without foreign forces, which are those that ruin a life of freedom, but it is performed with public forces and orders, which have their own particular terms, and do not descend to what can ruin the republic" (Machiavelli, D, 218). From this sentence arises a classical type of republican conviction, one which gave rise to the mixed constitution in Rome. Having *terms* means having precise limits which no public body (*public orders*) can overstep.

14.12 A mixed republic finds its strength not only in the division of powers, but also in the activities of independent judges backed by precise rules. This means that "a republic must establish before the law what every citizen can be accused of, without any fear and without any respect; and when this is done, and well enforced, it must punish slanderers severely who cannot complain when they are punished" (Machiavelli, D, 221). This is the certainty of law accompanied by true equality before the law, true discernment between serious accusations and calumny "because when accusations are useful to republics, calumny emerges; (...) calumny needs neither witnesses nor any other particular proof (...) since accusations need real proof and circumstances which demonstrate the truth of the accusation" (Machiavelli, D, 221). On the same page it is possible to see one of the many comparative political-history approaches of which the Florentine secretary always makes use. Rome managed to "order itself" for a long time this way, differently from Florence, thus the Roman Republic prospered in stability, the Florentine one foundered in disorder. The sovereignty of law, in some cases, went beyond the republic in Rome so that there were emperors who lived in the observation of the laws differently from some contemporary princes who operated against the most basic traditions of their princedoms. When the law, which in Rome was much more than a simple set of provisions but a custom, a mentality and history, was overstepped, the civil religion was destroyed, the stability of the republic dissipated and the utility and honour of the people were compromised favouring the ignorant, impious and the "worthless" (cf. Machiavelli, D, 225 ff.).

14.13 Concerning the civil religion, Machiavelli can be said to have anticipated one of the crucial subjects in contemporary political thought. Rome was great due to the fact that its laws had greater-than-human value, from tradition came their strength and their spirit and these were capable of infusing a super-human value in them. Anyone who studies the history "of the Romans will see for themselves that those citizens much more greatly feared breaking the oath than violating the laws, which stimulated the power of God more than that of men" (Machiavelli,

D, 229). The comparison with the Christian religion is striking. Despite Christianity's unquestionable values, it cannot be thought of as a "civil" religion. From Christian Pietism only resignation can come in Machiavelli's opinion and he even adds that commiseration, pardon, magnanimity and so many other manifestations of the Christian spirit such as renunciation, are hardly suitable in politics. The civil religion arouses something quite different. "And it is seen: he who carefully considers Roman history, how much religion served to command armies, to stimulate the common people, and keep people under control, to put kings to shame (…) where there is religion, it is easy to bring in weapons and where there are weapons and not religion, it is difficult to introduce it" (Machiavelli, D, 229-230). In other words, religion was among the major causes of the greatness of Rome because, among other things, it did not imply a longing for transcendence, but served a raison d'état to which, in rare cases of conflict, it had to give way. As for the Romans "when reason showed them that something had to be done, even though the auspices were adverse, they did it in any case; but they did so with such apt terms and manners, that it did not seem that they were doing it with disrespect for religion" (Machiavelli, D, 237). The dignity of religion was not in any way to be compromised.

14.14 The absence of religion brings about a lack of fear of God and this gives rise to a lack of civil commitment and of the obligation to obey laws. Civil religion, in other words, determines the fortune and successes of a republic and leads it forward to perform great feats. A lack of religion is replaced, sooner or later, by the fear of a prince if people do not want the civil fabric to disintegrate entirely (cf. Machiavelli, D, 230). However, even the best of politicians can only be a momentary device to ensure the fortune of a political order. "It is not, therefore, the salvation of a republic or a kingdom to have a prince who governs wisely while he is alive, but one who governs it in such a way that, when he dies, it maintains itself" (Machiavelli, D, 231). How far we are from the solutions of the prince! Here, even the greatest of men, can mean a momentary solution and certain one that does not resolve matters, since he is unlikely to revive the civic spirit in people's consciences in a short time. When these civic "virtues" do not exist, even liberty ends up being compromised and people are no longer accustomed to it. Contrary to what is maintained in *The Prince* and what Hobbes himself will say, most men "desire liberty to live in safety" but this liberty is based on the respect for the orders which a civil religion alone can guarantee. *If a people is corrupt*, as comes out of Ch. XVII of the book, it is unlikely to keep itself free, because *liberty does not possess bases of any sort*. The relationship between ethics and the political order cannot be called into question: "just as decent behaviour requires laws, if it is to be maintained; laws, if they are to be obeyed, require good behaviour". How can those good laws, which a republic, at the start of its life makes, still be valid, if the morality that led to them dies? Failure is also certain because the new laws, in such cases obviously, are the fruit of corruption (cf. Machiavelli, D, 240-246). Concerning what I maintained at the beginning of the chapter on Machiavelli's philosophical thought, it could be said that here, from what Hegel's point of view will be, law and morality tend to merge into ethicality.

14.15 To confirm the ties between laws and civil religion, which lead to the possibility that free institutions can survive, it must be pointed out that the best laws are incapable of solving the political problems if they are not inspired by a spirit operating in society. This is why there is no point in renewing the "orders of the state, which, in corruption, were no longer good," since "those laws, which are renewed, were not enough to keep men good" (Machiavelli, D, 246). This all compromises the election or appointment to the highest offices which are no longer obtained thanks to the great integrity in the behaviour of men, but out of favouritism or corruption. The laws are no longer able to correct or to govern, and so other "forces" come along which can restrain the instincts of men. At this point, what was to become the predictions of Hobbes comes to pass, a head upon whom "force" has been bestowed should do what the laws are no longer capable of doing. The political system and its roles become sclerotic. There would no longer be that mobility in the possibility of occupying the various positions which is typical of a republic and where it is not an affront for a citizen among the most distinguished, who has held high positions, to end up holding lesser ones, in certain periods, none at all. The rotation of offices is one of the great premises on which the life of a republic is based (cf. Machiavelli, D, I, Ch. XXXVI) and the laws first of all must be concerned with this. These laws in this circumstance too, demonstrate their ability to express a sense of civic religion because they must suggest a sense of limitations to the citizens, which, then, is the sense of duty. "If closely examined, it will cause those who make the laws of republics or kingdoms more prepared to restrain human appetites, and take from them the hope of being able to move as they wish with impunity" (Machiavelli, D, 289). The laws must therefore be equipped with the force necessary for them to be obeyed: only in such a way will men seek not to err. "Because I do not believe that there is a worse example in a republic then that of making a law and not obeying it, and worse yet, when it is not obeyed by those who made it" (Machiavelli, D, 292). In conclusion, as can be read in the final chapters of the first book of the *Discourses*, the duration of republics depends on good laws and on the fact that they are observed.

14.16 The sacredness of civil laws in the Roman republic is so important that the Romans left their laws and even the fundamental aspects of their administrations to all the peoples with whom they came into contact, except in very rare cases, that is "they kept them in their state and dignity", only "they obliged them under some conditions, which being observed, kept them in their state and dignity". These in fact were the bases of the Italic federation (cf. Machiavelli, D, 383 ff.). The duties of the central power were few, such as defence, and "foreign" policy, as well as some financial prerogatives, then there was decentralization for all other matters. The duration of the republican government was due to the fact that it governed little. In other words, if the republic lasted longer than many other forms of government this is due to the fact that it was highly decentralized and thus could "better adapt to the diversity of temporal matters depending on the diversity of citizens", something which a centralized government cannot do. For those who are far away from the problems, it is difficult to understand them, especially if there is not representation, as in the republics, but they are alone as in the princedom (cf. Machiavelli, D, 449-450). With time, centralization leads to the impoverishment of the people. The people become corrupted and lose faith in the laws. The only goal that remains is to imitate the rich and their standard of living and, for this reason, people are ready to do anything. This is precisely what was happening in the Florence of his time: "those who were impoverished, found ways of prevailing over those who were less powerful then themselves (…)

In confirmation of this condemnation, Lorenzo de' Medici says: *And what the Ruler does, many do, / All eyes are pointed towards the Ruler*" (Machiavelli, D, 490). Losing the civic religion, therefore, is the source of the corruption and decadence of institutions up to their inevitable crisis.

15. Politics and Holy Scripture in Spinoza.

15.1 Spinoza's political thought became widely known at quite a specific historical moment: it concerned Holland in the mid-seventeenth century, when the conflicts of the emerging Dutch State, its divisions and disputes required not simply theoretical thinking from the minds of that era, but what might offer a tangible response to the problems of the time. Among other things, the extensive conflicts existing between those who intransigently defended Calvinism and those, on the contrary, who looked forward to the ideals of tolerance had to be resolved. This point is generally accepted that Spinoza was in favour of the latter, but in such a way as to embrace the ideals of reason, rejecting those of the faith of his ancestors, who, in his opinion, were in conflict with the political notions that he was developing.

Born in Amsterdam in 1632 in a modest family of merchants of Iberian origin, **Benedict Spinoza** was educated in the Jewish tradition until he met Franciscus van dem Enden. His interest then expanded into the humanistic, scientific and juridical areas, which he analyzed often in contrast with his religious faith. Indeed, he was expelled from the Jewish community in 1656 because of being considered heretical. Persecutions followed and he abandoned Amsterdam, taking refuge at Rijnsburg. A period of critiques of Cartesian ideals got under way and culminated in the *Principia philosophiae Cartesianae,* as well as the *Cogitata metaphisica* published in 1663. In 1670, with painful efforts, he published the *Tractatus Theologico-Politicus* anonymously. A difficult period began, due to the killing of the De Witt brothers and the defeat of the democratic party. Both episodes cost Spinoza the security that he had enjoyed and his works had to be published posthumously, the same year as his death, his famous *Ethics* (*Ethica ordine geometrico demonstrata*) in 1677, after he had witnessed condemnation by the Dutch Courts, of his *Tractatus* in 1674 for its theories contrary to the State religion.

15.2 For the aforementioned reason, it has been said, appropriately, that "the God of Spinoza, as can be seen transparently throughout his works, from the *Short Treatise* up to the *Political Treatise*, through the great central stages of the *Tractatus Theologico-Politicus* and the *Ethics*, is not the God of transcendence and miracles, of prophecies and the mystery, but a God who manifests and expresses himself in the clear language of reason, in the great laws of nature and society" (Cantoni, 20). These laws of nature and laws of God have nothing to do with the Kaballah. Whether or not real atheism is involved is a matter of debate, but there is no doubt that tradition, which has often been used solely to increase superstition, seems inadequate. If Spinoza's Judaism is not yet atheism (and this has yet to be fully proven), it is certainly an abstract Judaism without roots. Without traditions, what is left of Judaism, and in fact, of any religion? This is why all the points of view are true for Spinoza to the extent to which all are considered as *fantasies* or fictions, inventions or creations of the mind (cf. Cantoni, 41). That combating intolerance is a virtue is unquestionable, but when all that reduces faith, its Object, and interior searching to partial and ephemeral forms can we say that religion and faith keep their actual meaning? Are they not deprived of their nature?

15.3 If this interpretation were a distortion, those who, for more than two centuries, have maintained that the philosophy of Spinoza is not merely a synonym of atheism, but also of free thinking or a libertine way of living (which, in eighteenth-century terminology is not at all different) should be considered biased and even ridiculous. Jacobi's famous work on Spinoza's teaching (*Uber die Lehre des Spinoza in Briefen an den Herrn Moses Mendelssohn*) is an example. Furthermore, it is certainly no accident that Jacobi, in the *Preface* to the third edition, revealing the "free" spirit in the thought of his time, writes that "without morality there is no religious faith whatsoever". Not by chance Jacobi, who was the last to arouse the sarcasm of Hegel, in the *Preface* to the second edition, writes of the pantheism of Giordano Bruno, explaining, in my opinion, that a narrow thread of thought brings together Bruno, Spinoza and Hegel, a line of thought that Marx would find it natural to pursue. Why should we be surprised at a conclusion of that sort? If, as has been observed in our time, the man of Spinoza is the *homo homini utilissimus* (cf. Cantoni, 47), what use is there for transcendence? There is no longer any distance between God and man: the latter is identified with reality, as religion and politics are identified with the State. This is the key to understanding the *Tractatus Theologico-Politicus.*

15.4 It is a firm conviction of Spinoza's that the Bible should be read and interpreted in accordance with rigorous scientific criteria, typical of the modern exegesis, in order to arrive at a thorough intellectual knowledge of God which is fitting for the "wise" man "that is he who is aware of the autonomy of reason" (D'Addio, I, SDP, 456), and who thereby understands God differently from how he is understood by the masses. The same distinction between the wise man and the masses which is evident in the area of religion is also brought out in the context of politics. Indeed, "since most men seek to pursue that which is useful to them without concerning themselves in any way with the precepts of religion, to found and maintain society, a coercive power must be set up" (D'Addio, SDP,I, 456). That power must be wielded in the name of that very reason which, extends beyond the limits of the totality of individuals who are not capable of pursuing other than their own interest, is capable of understanding everything, and seeking well-being for all. In the name of that reason, capable of understanding the interest of all, religion and politics are closely connected, and religion thus becomes an instrument of the State. On this subject, Spinoza's words are, in actual fact, quite clear. We need only recall what he wrote in reference to the Pharisees: "who believed that he who obeyed the laws of the State, that is the law of Moses, led a happy life. I repeat, however, that that law concerned only the State and did not serve in the moral teaching of the Jews, but rather a constriction of them" (Spinoza, TTP, 146). Spinoza's conclusion is truly paradoxical: "It is thus beyond doubt that when the State no longer existed the Judaeans were not bound by the law of Moses any more than they had been before their political community was set up" (Spinoza, TTP, 148). Religion thereby becomes a mere instrument of cohesion and obedience, typical of the theocratic societies of every era; when the political power no longer recognizes it, its reason for being is lost. What sense is there, however, in speaking of a spirit of tolerance? Logically speaking, this is practiced only and exclusively towards those religions that appeal to civic ethics and which, in the outer manifestations of piety, adhere to the precepts sanctioned by positive laws. For the rest, every individual is free to interpret the word of God, but only in the private sphere.

15.5 We must not be surprised by these conclusions. Spinoza's immanentism reduces everything to a terrestrial level. The question of the virtues, too, neglecting the intimate desire for transcendence, is reduced, as happened previously with Hobbes, to the context of the simplest accounting typical of the rising bourgeois society of which Holland was the most notable example. We need only recall what Spinoza wrote, on this subject, in his *Ethics*: "virtue is nothing but action in accordance with the laws of one's own nature, and no-one strives to conserve his own being except according to the laws of one's own nature, hence it is to be inferred first of all that the basis of virtue is the very effort to conserve one's own being" (Spinoza, E, 196). However, does that not perhaps mean that all those who, in the Old Testament as well, renounced their own natural interest to oppose power are nothing but mad? What should the three youths of the Story of Daniel have said? What, in concrete terms, does it mean to wonder what sense there is (if any) in speaking of dissent in a society such as the once conceived of by Spinoza?

15.6 Chapter XVII of the *Tractatus Theologico-Politicus* is an explicit confirmation of that: the masses must be moulded by those who hold power, with the goal of making them capable of carrying out all their duties towards the authority, since it is assumed that only those who wield power, as the highest expression of "true" reason, know what is just and what is useful. In fact the masses, or rather the multitudes (as Spinoza writes in the preceding chapter, XVI), are incapable of distinguishing between good and evil, the just and the unjust, the useful and the harmful.

15.7 At this point, it would be possible to state that Spinoza's position is quite close to that of Hobbes, but, in actual fact, one arrives at far worse conclusions. Hobbes still operates within Judaeo-Christian ontology so that he places theology above philosophy albeit in the limited area of the immortality of the soul and, in the final analysis, leaves up to the *Scriptures* judgement of the final questions concerning man's destiny (cf. Di Vona, 34 and Chapter IV). Spinoza, on the contrary, subordinates religion to reason and so subordinates the man of faith to the philosopher. The State that comes out of such a way of thinking may actually be democratic, but it is a democracy whose nature is exclusively aristocratic, in so far as it is directed by philosopher-kings, as in Plato's polis. Here we are not dealing with a reason which recognizes its own limits, but rather reason raised to the level of a system. Furthermore, whereas the pessimism of the English thinker gives rise to a rigid authoritarianism, the supposed optimism of reason characteristic of Spinoza leads to a society which is democratic and tolerant only in appearance. I emphasize *in appearance*, because only those who are equal through privilege enjoy it, even intellectual privilege, precisely as in the modern societies based on democratic centralism. These people, *via* Marx, are the direct heirs of Spinoza and Hegel's thought. For this reason, Spinoza's political thought does not represent a step forward, but rather a considerable step backward since "it does not recognize the legitimacy of the right to active resistance to tyrannical power: the subject cannot oppose an unjust command by using force" (D'Addio, SDP, I, 459-460). Yet this had been one of the most proudly defended conquests of western civilization, even in the Middle Ages, in so far as it had been obtained at a high price.

15.8 It would be unjust to fail to recognize that, for Spinoza, liberty is the true intent of political society and the State, at least since he clearly points out in Chapter XX, concluding the *Tractatus Theologico-Politicus* that the State that denies freedom of thought ends up denying itself. However, upon closer examination, it shows that the question is one of pure philosophical freedom, that is the freedom of few and, in any case, that of those who are allowed to practice it. Likewise at the end of the *Tractatus Theologico-Politicus* it is again stated that everyone is obliged to take the greatest care not to expose the sovereign authority to any danger, since that would be tantamount to calling into question the real security of the political community. Religion, too, must keep from being an element of disruption in criticizing the State which, among other things, has full authority over everything, even the sacred (cf. Spinoza, TTP, Ch. XIX). Thus, if the dualism religion and politics ceases to exist, the bases for authentic liberty cease to exist as well.

16. The Abstract Society of the Just.

16.1 Despite the civic engagement of not a few exponents of Enlightenment culture, Voltaire or Diderot for example, Rousseau's theoretical approach has lent itself to a variety of interpretations, and reveals not a few contradictions. Among the most highly discussed people who have contributed to the rise of the democratic conception, Rousseau is enormously perceptive but paradoxical in some ways. The considerations he expressed about government, and the problem of teaching and morality are examples. The latter evolves in society, or rather in institutions, as a result of the political engagement aimed at changing the social situation. Yet, Rousseau does not avoid a sort of *a priori* assumption, set forth at the beginning and outside of history: this is the state of nature, a metaphysical hypothesis similar to what had been seen earlier with the happy golden age and what Biblical tradition identified in a paradise lost as a result of original sin. A sort of original sin is also present in Rousseau's thought initial thought, and his political thought was developed for the very purpose of cancelling that "sin".

A restless and vagabond spirit, **Jean Jacques Rousseau** was born in Geneva in 1712. His family was one of modest means, but Rousseau was able to receive an education thanks to Madame de Warens who assisted him up until he reached the age of thirty. He also had experience as a secretary in the French embassy in Venice. In Paris, with advice from Diderot, he took part in a contest at the Academy of Dijon in 1749 on a subject that would be fundamental for him: "Has the restoration of the sciences and the arts contributed to refining moral practices?". He obtained considerable fame from the prize awarded to him by the Academy. His most significant works come from this period, as well as the *Discours sur les Sciences et les Arts,* the *Discours sur l'origine de l'inégalité parmi les hommes* of 1753, the famous *Lettre à M. d'Alembert* of 1755, then the *Contrat Social ou Principes du droit politique* of 1762, which was supposed to be a far more imposing work, but whose initial plan was abandoned. Worth noting among the other, numerous works are *Considérations sur le Gouvernement de Pologne et sur sa réformation projetée en avril 1772, Emile, Les Confessions* and *Julie ou la nouvelle Héloïse.* He met the greatest minds of his time. In England, he was the guest of Hume in the Castle of Wootton, but, perhaps because of his intransigence, he was always forced to wander from place to place. He died in 1778 in the Castle of Ermenonville where he had been the guest of the Marquis de Girardin.

16.2 From his earliest writings on, Rousseau suggested that the problem of mankind, its origins, its destiny and how to determine this were fundamental to his thought (cf. Alatri, IR, 27). This would become of crucial importance in the subsequent century for Hegel and Marx to cite two examples. In addition to being political, it would become moral since it would lead the citizen of Geneva to set forth a new way of conceiving of good and evil. Hence, there was a need for another regeneration aimed at eliminating injustice by returning to the original happiness. That a simple goal, and with its dramatic results, conditioned the contemporary world is clear to everyone. For Rousseau, problems such as those of good and evil depend on human beings. They are the cause and can also be the solution, finding, for example, a new way of considering progress, making a *tabula rasa* of all that signifies social and civic corruption which risk compromising what in progress can be found that is truly useful for a genuine development of humanity (cf. Alatri, IR, 35-37). Thus, as Rousseau seeks to safeguard the democratic approach, he must think of a particular management of power which leads individuals to take their place in the totality to the point that the criterion of equality almost eliminates that of liberty. Liberty not only prevents a return to the state of nature, but it also complicates the realization of a perfect society which, in the find analysis, is the great dream of the Genevan. It is certainly no accident that Rousseau has been considered the father of modern democracy by those thinkers who witnessed his anticipation of the dreams of Communist equalitarianism. This subject arises again in the consideration of the relationship between religion and politics, if one thinks that the religiosity of the population can continue to exist but the State which does not profess it must teach a sort of civic religion that offers a sense of belonging to the political community, thereby becoming the basis of every truth. This line of thought going from Rousseau to Marx seems confirmed by the fact that nineteenth-century liberalism, from Constant on, has always spoken of the State of law intentionally leaving Rousseau out of the discussion (cf. Alatri, IR, 65-67).

16.3 The state of nature hypothesized by Rousseau builds a sort of working hypothesis in order to answer the question behind his first discourse "Has the restoration of the sciences and the arts contributed to refining moral practices?" If it is true that governments and laws should provide for the safety and well-being of the citizens, can science, letters and the arts "put men in chains", suffocate their feeling for the liberty in which that were born to the point of leading them to a state of slavery? It would almost seem that *"le besoin éleva les trônes, les sciences et les arts les ont affermis"* (cf. Rousseau, DSA, 2-4). This is a strong and terse statement and it seems to set Rousseau in opposition to not a few Enlightenment circles who saw progress as a fundamental component of the modern world. For the citizen of Geneva the role played by the arts and sciences led to a distortion of human nature and its moral tension. It eliminated mutual trust, esteem and friendship. It disseminated coldness and fear among men giving rise to hatred, betrayal and inequality of various sorts: what were once considered vices could also be called virtues (cf. Rousseau, DSA, 5). Abuses of every sort occur in such a society built more on empty phrases than on good action so that fatuous spirits are rewarded and virtues that always remain without honours are not acknowledged (cf. Rousseau, DSA, 19-20). This moralistic and pessimistic Rousseau has already suggested in this first *Discourse* that bringing about a "perfect society" is an urgent matter.

16.4 In the second *Discourse* the problem is again taken up and further developed from the very first lines in which Rousseau, dreaming of a political entity where no-one could be said to be above the laws and where one can live and die free, reveals to us that he would wish to have been born in a country *"où le souverain et les peuples ne pussent avoir qu'un seul et même intérêt"*. Can a recently constituted republic, however, fulfil such a desire? It is not easy to accomplish. Perhaps in history only the Roman people achieved *"ce modèle de tous les peuples libres"*, and this encourages Rousseau to maintain that a happy republic of this sort should have highly ancient origins, severity and pride in moral practices which, through long experience, have accustomed the citizens to be free and independent (cf. Rousseau, DOI, 26-27). These extremely ancient origins and the long experience show us that in Rousseau the relationship with natural origins was crucial for safeguarding liberty and equality. There is no doubt that the latter has vanished due to the degeneration of natural man and, to regain it, a hermeneutic study of the disappearance of the natural society is needed. It must be understood how man lived in it in order to understand the reasons for its decline. Rousseau's examination is not that of a reactionary thinker who wants to return to the state of nature as it had been. He has no intention of relinquishing the achievements of progress. However, he wants all men to enjoy them in a state of perfect equality as it existed in the natural society. The inequality that Rousseau is eager to eliminate is obviously civil because the nature, for which one is shorter or fatter, etc., is a given and it is useless to contest or investigate it (cf. Rousseau, DOI, 35 and 39). Except in rare cases, natural inequalities are accepted. The others, on the contrary, make civil life difficult and so Rousseau wonders which, between civil and natural life, "*est la plus sujette à devenir insupportable*", because bondage is based on the dependency of some on others because of certain needs, and exists only in the civil state whereas in the natural one there is no situation of dependency. This latter has caused the race to decline and deprived it of its initial state of liberty and happiness (cf. Rousseau, DOI, 56 and 65).

16.5 When indeed was civil society founded? The answer is a simple one: when private property was established. When the first man fenced off his land and said this is mine and found those who, failing to understand, believed him, civil society was born. Property has not just civil and political importance, and it cannot be interpreted merely in economic terms, either. For Rousseau it has a moral importance because crimes, homicides and conflicts of various sorts have been justified in its name. Only after it was established did a sense of morality begin to find its way into human actions. This was the start of laws because earlier, every human being was the sole judge and the only one to take revenge for offenses suffered. Punishments became harsher and more certain and it was thought that laws could be a deterrent to crime. Natural compassion was gradually altered. As equality disappeared, property gained in importance. Labour became a necessary fact, the natural environment was transformed and, very soon, as slavery arose, the poverty of many spread (cf. Rousseau, DOI, 66 and 72-73). This thought was simply a working hypothesis, but it was important. It visualized a transformation from interiority to exteriority for mankind as it left the state of nature. Conscience and nature changed, in Rousseau's view, and they degenerated. As time went by inequality became worse and worse because the development of propriety had increased, and circumstances made the differences more noticeable and lasting. That situation was to remain precarious for a long time until rules were established in order to eliminate the uncertainty: they were those laws that led to the creation of civil society. The reading of this moment, certainly not seen through the eyes of Locke, further accentuated inequalities which lay obstacles before the poor and give new force to the rich destroying liberty and encouraging usurpation by the few from the many. Societies spread over all the earth and civil law became the rule for all citizens, but it guaranteed rights only for a few. The more intense the conflicts became the more necessary and oppressive were the laws. It would perhaps have been more just to make them less strict and take away the moral causes that led to certain crimes (cf. Rousseau, DOI, 79 and 61).

16.6 With such an approach, it is clear that Rousseau cannot help mocking the other ideas of contracts set forth to justify the limitation and often the relinquishing of liberty. Relinquishing means acting in such a way that the property I possess becomes completely alienated from me: but is it possible to deprive oneself of the basic characteristics of human nature, degenerating to the point of nullifying one's own being despite the fact that it is maintained by scholars such as Pufendorf? That means that governments which justify such a hypothesis are the result of a process which has somehow betrayed the initial conditions and which has given rise to inequality, as well as to the loss of liberty (cf. Rousseau, DOI, 84). This is why the various forms of government were created in accordance with the actual forms of inequality existing among human beings. Only time will tell which of these forms could be the most advantageous. Where wealth did not prevail preference was given to merit and judgeships were elected positions. As inequality grew power went from being legitimate to being arbitrary. The first division between rich and poor became one between master and slave. This was the origin of civil then political distinctions. When all this came to pass the difference between the savage and civilized man came about, so that happiness for the one was despair for the other (cf. Rousseau, DOI, 86-87 and 91). Projection of the civil dimension into the political one is a fundamental statement for future thought. It immediately recalls what Marx was to sustain concerning civil society on which and for which the political dimension is created.

16.7 From the very beginning of *Du Contrat Social ou Principes du droit politique* Rousseau seeks to investigate the possibility of not separating justice from utility in order to overcome the most inhuman paradox that exists: "*l'homme est né libre, et partout il est dans les fers*". How could all that have happened and why is it now considered legitimate? The Genevan believes that he can answer these questions. One's liberty must be regained just as it had been lost and, if this is fair, it means that it was not legitimate for anyone to relinquish it or allow it to be relinquished. Upon careful reading of these first lines of the classic it seems clear that the author's real concern is for justice, the sole condition for achieving order "*l'ordre social est un droit sacré qui sert de base à tous ôter*" (cf. Rousseau, CS, 235-236). Somewhat like Plato, Rousseau writes driven by this motivation with the conviction that extirpating evil, and everything that it has caused, is possible and proper once the cause has been identified, a task already undertaken and resolved in the two preceding discourses. As for Plato, likewise, the causes of evil are all earthly ones and, to eliminate them, a new "city" must be brought into being in which totality prevails over individuality and all that the latter implies, starting with property. As has been seen, property is a sort of original sin which has sullied all of human history, but it can be eliminated with a regeneration capable of returning mankind to a state of original good. This is why the two immediate consequences of what can be called a sort of degeneration are examined in Chapters III and IV of Book I: a) the illegitimate affirmation of the right of the strongest, b) the consequent rise of slavery, which could be affirmed thanks, also, to the excuse that it ensured the supposed tranquillity of the subjects.

16.8 Rousseau maintains that one must always go back to an original agreement thanks to which, as Grotius says, a people may confer upon itself a king, but this means that the people have indeed constituted themselves as one before giving themselves a king, and this is done by public deliberation. A society is, therefore, not founded as the power has determined, but by the act that that power determines. This point is reached because when men are convinced that the original state can no longer exist without endangering the very existence of the human race, they come to formulate a pact to protect each of those associated while continuing to safeguard the liberty which they had originally enjoyed. To understand the actual provisions of this pact, it can be said that these are reduced to only one: all those who have associated, surrender themselves and all their rights on behalf of the entire community. Since each individual surrenders all, conditions are equal for everyone and it is not in anyone's interest to make them more burdensome. Furthermore, with this relinquishing, the most perfect possible union comes about, and no-one has any more need to make claims. In this union, the relinquishments have been equal for everyone, and what had been lost is regained on a level of perfect equality. The act of association automatically gives rise to a collective body which replaces the individual contracting party: the individual "ego" becomes a *common ego* (cf. Rousseau, CS, 242-244). The act or social pact comes from the *sovereign body*. A crucial chapter is devoted to this subject from which it is inferred that that sovereign or political body can never be bound by something that departs from the original act or contract, considered sacred, because that would mean transferring another part of oneself to another sovereign body which, in actual fact, does not exist. Since the sovereign body is made up of all the individuals, there is no-one who can consider himself excluded from this. Fidelity to that body is due to the fact that it defends the common interest. Anyone who does not behave in conformity with that fidelity is to be considered a dangerous, selfish person because that person would like to enjoy all the rights of citizens without carrying out the duties of a subject. This is why "*quiconque refusera d'obéir à la volonté générale, y sera contraint par tout le corps*". All that is already totalitarian democracy seen *in nuce*, and means that the individual is obliged to be free (*qu'on le forcera à être libre*). This means that the duties of a citizen are legitimated, but, behind this lie great dangers for the individual that Rousseau seems not to see. Indeed, taken up by the need to create a just society, he maintains that the transition from the state of nature to the civil state signifies a crucial change for mankind "*en substituent dans sa conduite la justice à l'instinct*" conferring upon his acts that morality that had not existed heretofore. It is a transfer from natural to civil liberty. The former finds a limit in the individual efforts of the individual, whereas the limit of the latter comes out of the general will. In this environment, resulting from the civil state, moral liberty is also encountered and it enables man really to be in command of himself (cf. Rousseau, CS, 245-247).

16.9 The most important consequence is that only the general will can direct the forces of the new political entity so that it will come out of the agreement of the various private interests which have made possible the founding of the society. At the heart of the society and the reason why it must be governed is the integration of the various interests, aimed at creating an interest in common. Hence, the general will represents the essence of sovereignty and explains why that sovereignty can never be renounced. Similarly, it cannot be divided for the same reason, since the will is either general or it is not. It is therefore logical that only when it is, the manifestation of the general will becomes law. When that happens no-one can doubt its justice and the fact that it is always for the public good. Due to this, it cannot err: it is the truth and deserves to be obeyed. History has shown the degree to which these considerations, expressed in the first three chapters of Book II of the *Contract*, were taken seriously. One need only recall that *Pravda*, the Soviet Communist Party organ founded by Lenin, means the *truth*. In the light of this it is understandable why the sovereign power, however absolute, sacred and inviolable it may be, never goes beyond its limits. If all the people decide on behalf of all the people they can only make decrees governing themselves. At this point the questions on which they deliberate are general as is the will which establishes them. This is what *"j'appelle une loi"*, one which can act on a large number of matters, even on establishing a royal government or all that concerns the well-being of the community. It is thus ridiculous to wonder whose responsibility it is to make the laws because these are acts of the general will and are simply recordings of the general will. This can be called a true republic. However it is governed, it can be said that the public interest prevails and it alone governs. At this point another of the many paradoxes of Rousseau comes into play: despite the fact that the people always want that which is good, they do not always recognize it on their own. Their will may always be correct, but their judgment not always enlightened. At this point some profiles of wise legislators emerge and give voice to the general will. These are personalities such as Lycurgus, Solon, the decemviri, etc., who, however, can only formulate the laws according to what the general will should be (cf. Rousseau, CS, 258-262). This is the only way the main goals of the legislative power, liberty and equality, can be kept intact, and one cannot exist without the other.

16.10 In every body politic we can recognize force and the will: the latter finds expression in the legislative power, the former in the executive. The legislative certainly belongs to the people who, however, cannot exercise the latter. The government is a body set up to carry out the laws and maintain civil as well as political liberty. It exercises these functions by means of an assignment, a mandate which sets it up as a simple functionary of the sovereign power. This is a legitimate exercise, therefore, because it enforces the orders which it gives to the people (cf. Rousseau, CS, 272-273). There are various possibilities for being governed and one directly exercised by the people is surely not advisable. It is incredible that Rousseau can reach such a conclusion, yet it all has a logic, indeed, a people which always acts properly, should not need to be governed, hence, the famous conclusion that if there were a people of gods, the latter would govern themselves democratically, but such a perfect form of government is not fit for human beings (cf. Rousseau, CS, 280-281). Only the aristocracy and the monarchy are left. The former may be of various types, but it requires the moderation of the rich and the ability of the poor to be content, in any case. As far as the monarchy is concerned it should be said that it is the government which has the greatest vigour. There is no other which can govern with greater ease. Any form of government, however, has some disadvantages along with its advantages and it should be added that not every form of government, as Montesquieu said, is fit for all countries. Liberty itself is not within the reach of all peoples (cf. Rousseau, CS, 282-284 and 289). The best way of judging a government seems to be an empirical one: a government under which the population increases and improves its living conditions is good. It is worse when a people diminishes in size and withers away. The fact remains, in any case, that when the people are brought together to exercise the legislative function, any government jurisdiction, even the most legitimate, ceases. The executive power is suspended because the legislative can decide to change any law and also thwart some of the existing ones (cf. Rousseau, CS, 294 and 300).

16.11 Rousseau does not believe in representation and says so clearly in Ch. XV of Book III. Sovereignty cannot be represented for the same reasons that it cannot be relinquished: either the will is general or it is not. There is no middle course. Any law that is not ratified is null and void. The idea of representatives coming from the feudal world is not original. Hence, legitimate governments are only those which observe the general will. The latter can modify any provision, because no basic law exists in the State. Even the social pact could be abrogated, if all the citizens so desired (cf. Rousseau, CS, 307). The general will clearly presents itself as something sacred. It has within itself a particular religious quality, entirely of a civil nature, obviously. Rousseau devotes all of the long Ch. VIII of Book IV to religion. For him, three different types of religion exist: the *first* is the religion of man which is limited purely to the inner worship of God, without times and ceremonies, it is "*le vrai théisme*", it is that natural religion described, for example, in *Emile*. There is a *second* religion, judged to be bizarre, which can be called that of the priest. It is undoubtedly to be criticized since it leads to a sort of dualism that destroys social unity and places man in contradiction with himself. Finally, there is a *third* form of religion which is a civil one, typical of many ancient peoples. The purely civil profession of faith allows the sovereign body to set forth the articles of faith without which there can be no good citizens and faithful subjects. Those who fail to conform to what is established may be banished from the State in so far as they are impious and anti-social, incapable of loving the laws and justice. Anyone who claims to recognize these dogmas, then fails to behave in conformity with them, must be punished with death for having committed the worst of crimes, because they compromise the unity of the social body (cf. Rousseau, CS, 331-336).

16.12 The idea that all citizens who are part of the sovereign body must obey the law they have set forth for themselves has led some justly to feel that Rousseau ended up not distinguishing between the rights of individuals and those of society, a distinction which constitutes a crucial guarantee for liberty (cf. De Luca, 36). That may have led Rousseau, who, nonetheless, was an astute critic of absolutism, to take, in the perceptive judgment of Denis Richet, a hostile position towards individualism as well, so that his opposition to liberalism found expression more on the level of sovereignty than on that of legality. Indeed, rightly criticizing absolutism for tyrannical connotations he perhaps unwillingly constructed another tyranny that was no less violent (cf. Di Donato, XXIV). All these concerns were clearly intuited by Constant at the beginning of the nineteenth century when, in open criticism of the government, he reached the point of maintaining that a majority can certainly not be sufficient to legitimize any act since, in certain cases, there are acts that no majority can legitimize. On the contrary, collective sovereignty has often encouraged the most disastrous pretexts to thwart liberty. Rousseau's mistake, which Constant views as magnified by the Abbot Mably, is that of having confused the authority of the social body with liberty. Rousseau thereby assumed an almost metaphysical position in which he acknowledged on behalf of the social body idyllic abilities to defend liberty by itself, forgetting that it must be defended with laws so austere that the community does not always succeed in following them without adequate controls (cf. Constant, DLL, 604-608). It would almost seem that the social contract has exceptional thaumaturgical capacities succeeding not only in conveying mankind back to his original state of goodness, but also keeping it in its original state of innocence free of that malice which can harm others.

17. The Individual, Society and the State.

A) *Formal and Substantial Law: I. Kant.*

17.1. Some have, appropriately enough, pointed out that in Kant "politics cannot be separated from reason" provided that "the powers and the limits" of reason are defined. At the same time, it must not be forgotten that reason "in so far as it is activity that produces awareness, is removed from the determinism of nature (…); it is therefore constitutively free". The ability to know represents the foundation of liberty, the idea of which constitutes "the transition point from pure to practical reason" (cf. D'Addio, SDP, II, 92-93). Among the duties of reason there is the pursuit of moral good which for Kant must not only be distinct from happiness, but must have unquestionable priority over it. Furthermore, morality is distinct from law: whereas the former refers to an interior determination, the latter only governs external action. For this very reason, law exists thanks to constraint. This is useless for morality because the will is free only if "it adapts entirely to the principle according to which it must be determined". Only will, in so far as it can perform an action or not, is free to choose (cf. LD'Addio, SDP, II, 95). This conviction is a prelude to the dialectics of the objective spirit in Hegel.

Immanuel Kant's entire life was devoted to study. Kant was born in Könisberg in 1724, and carried out his university studies in his town of birth. After receiving his diploma, he was a tutor among the wealthiest families in Könisberg where he obtained the chair in Logic and Metaphysics in 1770. In 1781 he published the *Kritik der reinen Vernunft* (*Critique of Pure Reason*), and seven years later the *Kritik der praktischen Vernunft* (*Critique of Practical Reason*) and, in 1790, *Kritik der Urteilskraft*. Three years after that, he encountered problems with censorship because of *Die Religion innerhalb der Grenzen der blossen Vernunft* (*Religion within the Limits of Reason Alone*). From 1795 on, when *Zum ewigen Frieden. Ein philosophischer Entwurt* (*For Perpetual Peace*) was published, he wrote numerous political, juridical, historical and anthropological works such as the *Die Methaphysik der Sitten* (*Metaphysics of Morals*) in 1797. He died in 1804 in the city of his birth.

17.2 Kant takes the basic features of his political thought from the letters of Montesquieu from whom he adopts the classical division of powers acknowledging that the sovereign power lies in the legislative branch. Only thus, as other contemporaries had also seen, can liberty, equality and the independence of individuals be ensured. Individuals have total freedom on the level of religion, as well. The State cannot intervene on matters of conscience and worship, it must only take care that nothing conflicts with the laws in effect (this is quite a delicate subject and it implies the appropriateness of taking exception. I shall return to this subject subsequently). The State which knows better than any other how to achieve the division of powers, having, at the same time the force and the authority necessary to pursue the desired goals and to coerce, is a republic whose constitution "is the only one which is perfectly adapted to the law of humans", even though some maintain (here there is a critical reference to Rousseau) that they would have to be angels (cf. Kant, ZeF, 233-234). A republican constitution is a better guarantee than any other of liberty, equality and the independence of individuals. He takes his distance from Montesquieu when he rejects the relationship between tradition and privileges since he does not grant the aristocracy any prerogative. This had happened in the United Kingdom, which recognized for all social classes, but the bourgeoisie in particular, equal opportunities to occupy positions or take office. Indeed, "no inequality can arise in legal status no submission to coercive laws, that are not those which the individual, as a subject of the single supreme legislative power, has in common with every other one (…) no innate privilege can exist for a member of the civil community" (Kant, ÜdG, 148). This statement must be read, above all, with the eyes of those who have before them a feudal state structure which must be reformed. The State must reform landed property that is still tied to atavistic schemes and must have it at its disposition in order to accomplish public goals.

17.3 One of the basic perplexities to which Kant's thought gives rise, and which produces not a few corollaries, concerns the supreme postulate of law: "Only in the State does law become peremptory, and the conditions are found for it to be realized (…) The State is the idea of law implemented". It being understood that the State confers on law that force of coercion without which one would only remain on the level of good intentions, the limits of this force and the very basis of law leave us with more than a few perplexities. It can be a waste of energy to seek the empirical basis of law. The original contract is basically an idea originating in reason which is not necessarily formed on the basis of consent, but more likely on violence (it is truly curious that Kant, who uses an infinity of expressions taken from classical law, omits the expression *consensus iuris* itself, at least with the meaning that it took on from Cicero and thereafter. Cicero himself had taken it from tradition). The contract, finally, "is a necessary idea of reason" which lays the foundation for the legitimacy of the State with which each person identifies himself or herself (cf. Solari, 14), otherwise, there is the danger of actually losing liberty. Kant does not seem to have an optimistic conception of liberty at all, since he does not have faith "in enlightened selfishness governed by reason", as Locke maintains. Nor does he have faith in the "authority of reason against the excesses of selfishness", as Leibniz believed. He seems, in fact, to share the pessimism of Machiavelli and Hobbes to a greater degree than people may think (cf. Solari, 18). Those who do not think so should recall the considerations against the right to resist preconstituted power, a right which, in Kant's view cannot in any way be admitted. It gives rise to a dangerous state-worship in which the "State for Kant is not only the keeper and defender of law, but it personifies the needs of life associated, contemplated *sub specie aeterni*" (Solari, 19).

17.4 Law, for Kant, must have universal value, but while it should be an aspect of legality, albeit fundamental, it becomes something exclusive for him. Solari rightly points out that "in practice law and the State are transcendental concepts for Kant, which draw upon intelligible reality and can only be constructed *a priori* outside of any experience. Only that which is *a priori* has objective, universal validity" (Solari, 23-24). Forgetting that law is also the prize of arduous achievements means forgetting its deep relationship to morality and it means taking refuge in a conservatism which ignores legitimate aspirations upon which Latin and British juridical greatness are based. Not only that, when the objective validity of certain rights is called into question by the State, how can they be regained in a practical sense if not only resistance to established power is not allowed, but a body of law cannot be conceived unless it is capable of being constructed *a priori* outside of any experience? I do not believe that it is far-fetched to feel that Kant reaches these conclusions because he considers individuals the logical premise of the State, yet he considers them almost in conflict with society. The history of the best juridical experiences, however, tells us that individuals set up law, although they bring some *a priori* to bear, only if they create a society that guarantees the development of law; if anything, the problem is to see how to remain faithful to certain premises, keeping in mind, though, that society is the dynamic aspect of the coexistence of individuals.

17.5 Considering individuals the logical premise for the State does not mean for Kant that this is the expression simply of the sum total of the wills of individuals, but that it constitutes and represents a unified whole, a sort of general will of the sort that Rousseau sought. Hence there is "the objective need for the State rationally to organize life in common". The wills of individuals must acknowledge a unifying will above them to which they must submit (cf. Solari, 28-29). This interpretation cannot be considered far-fetched. Kant's words leave no room for doubt: to achieve a "civil" consensus, "the will of all men *individually committed* to living in accordance with the principles of liberty in a legal constitution (that is that there be a unity distributive of the duty of *all*) is not enough. *Everyone together* must want this state (that is, that there be the *collective* unity of united wills" (Kant, ZeF, 230-231). The people are sovereign in so far as they are a collective entity and fatally (I would call it blindly) they must obey this rational need for unity. This is not an extemporaneous idea of Kant, but a conviction that runs throughout his thought. In *The Critique of Judgement*, speaking of the entire body of the State, he points out that every member "while contributing to the possibility of the whole, is in turn determined by the idea of the whole, in relation to his place and function" (Kant, KdU, 323 note). It is now understandable why it has been said that if law expresses particular wills or even the sum total of the various wills it can be called unjust, "whereas even the harshest of laws is just when it comes out of the unified will" (Solari, 31), and because it is indeed an expression of this law, the State virtually becomes a moral person to whose development everyone not only can, but must contribute.

17.6 At this point it is quite understandable why Kant, departing from such a conception of the State, could not offer any possibility for the right to resist. As for Rousseau to some extent, disobeying the State is disobeying ourselves. Worse yet, the State aims at a Platonic sort of perfection which remains a constant point of reference, even though it can never be attained. *A propos* of the Platonic republic (never has a word been more inappropriate), in *The Critique of Pure Reason*, he expresses himself as follows: "although this latter case can never come to pass *(that is, achieving a perfect republic)*, nonetheless the idea that sets forth this *maximum* as an archetype is totally correct, so that in the legal constitution of men, observing it one may come closer and closer to the greatest possible perfection" (Kant, KrV, 324, italics mine). This *"nonetheless the idea is totally correct"* cannot be ignored. Above all, who decides how correct the idea is? It can only be the State and obviously those who are qualified to do so on its behalf. Then, saying that no-one knows "the highest point, at which humanity must stop" does not solve the problem because, depending on the times, the various philosopher-kings of the moment, who interpret the various States, can design various models. This is so because, among other things, philosophers are masters at relating their ideas, political and moral, to the reality surrounding them. Thus, Kant hastens to say that "concerning nature herself Plato correctly sees manifest proof of its origin in ideas" (Kant, KrV, 325-326). In Kant, this nature anticipates the deterministic model of Hegel, otherwise how could certain statements be interpreted? "Nature still wants humanity to be obliged to implement on its own these like all the other goals to which it is destined (...) only by performing and completing that task can it achieve all its other goals concerning our species" (Kant, Ize, 39). In other words, knowing the truth brings about the obligation, I would also say moral, to implement it. It is no accident that Kant calls this Platonic ideal a *respublic noumenon*, which is certainly not a senseless chimera, but a point of reference for an organized civil society, a *respublic phaenomenon*, which "can only be achieved laboriously through numerous wars and conflicts" (Kant, DSdF, 364).

17.7 Machiavelli's conception, based on the idea of political success, was mentioned above. It ultimately justifies any political event that prevails, thus Kant is in agreement with the Florentine secretary. While being opposed to any form of rebellion against the constituted power (even when not a few earlier theoreticians had suggested that various forms of resistance were lawful) and thus being opposed to any type of revolution that might lead to the conquest of power, however it was carried out and whatever the reason for it was, it must ultimately be justified. It follows that "the illegal nature of its origin and the way in which it has been established cannot free the subjects, as good citizens, from the obligation to adapt to the new order of things, nor can they refuse honestly to obey the authority which currently holds the power" (Kant, DMdS, 442). This means that it will be necessary honestly to obey Hitler or Stalin who, in the "new order of things", represent the "authority which presently holds the power". The justification is even more paradoxical because if anyone dared resist, "this resistance would take place according to a maxim which, made universal, would destroy any civil constitution, so that the only state in which people can in general be in possession of their rights would be destroyed" (Kant, ÜdG, 156). Even if the dissident were right, and it seems to me that history has shown this not a few times, resistance cannot be acceptable because, not being able to decide on which side the true right exists, in Kant's opinion, the would-be dissident would always end up "being the judge in his own suit. There would have to be a second sovereign above the sovereign, to decide between the latter and the people: which is a contradiction" (Kant, ÜdG, 156). Such a figure does not exist and thus the right of necessity cannot be appealed to, only the obligation of submission exists, even if the sovereign were the worst of humans. The highly moral Kant is unaware of the moral obligation which so many of those who have fought in the name of liberty have felt, from Cicero to John of Salisbury and up to the present. The appropriateness of tyranicide does not cross his mind either because "the people have no right to coerce their own sovereign, since it is only through the sovereign that the people legally can apply constraint (...) a right (of resistance in words or in acts) to coerce the head of state can never belong to the people" (Kant, ÜdG, 159-160). This is not merely a matter of principle as some people maintain. What has been said applies on a practical as well as a theoretical level. The head of state is also responsible for deciding what degree of well-being to attain and how to achieve it, setting forth which "provisions contribute to the prosperity of the State" (Kant, ÜdG, 155).

17.8 Kant reaches these conclusion because of an erroneous approach to the moral problem. His deontology is perhaps based on a misinterpretation. He believes that "duty in itself is in fact nothing but the *limitation* of a will" (Kant, ÜdG, 132-133). At best, that maxim is questionable. Sartre and most existentialists would say that duty, too, must be desired if it is to be performed, hence the performance of duty is the affirmation of the will itself rather than its limitation. Even considering duty the consequence of the principle of universal reason, its implementation always requires the free acceptance of the subject hence a full manifestation of the will. The problem is that Kant confers on reason requisites of absoluteness and truth which can only be denied *a posteriori*. "Reason cannot err (*Die Vernunft kann nicht irren*): every force has its path laid out. The condemnation that reason lays on itself does not take place when it is judged, but only afterwards, when one is in another position or when greater knowledge has been acquired" (Kant, R, 774). Aside from the fact that here too, Hegelian rationality and "truth" can be perceived, not the slightest doubt arises for Kant when taking a decision that it can be erroneous or, at least, incomplete. However that "duty in itself is none other than the *limitation* of the will" brings forth another holistic meaning in Kant which, taken to its most extreme consequences, is ultimately totalitarian. *I do not think that this conclusion can be considered too far-fetched.* Implicitly and even explicitly at times, Kant admits this. When he says that "each one in the state considers the body in common the maternal womb from which each obtained life" (Kant, ÜdG, 146), in contradiction with the inalienability and universality of rights, he means that only the State is the source of right and no substantial right can be acknowledged for the person in himself or herself. So the State may apply the death penalty and even maternal infanticide. "The baby that has come into the world outside of marriage is outside the law (because marriage is the law), and it is thus not under the protection of the law. It has, so to speak, insinuated itself into civil society (like forbidden merchandise), so that it cannot fail to be aware of its existence and, as a result, its destruction, as well" (Kant, DMdS, 458). Statements of that sort must not astonish people if one thinks that it is "the maternal womb" of the State that is the sole source of right and not the human being. Here lies the clear difference between those who recognize the formality of law and those, on the contrary, who, not acknowledging that the state can be the sole and incontrovertible source of law, speak of the substantiality of law (I hope to treat this aspect of the subject in another work).

17.9 The concept of the person understood in that sense is obviously not exhaustive. Kant is clear in his definition. "The *Person* is that subject whose actions can be imputed" (Kant, DMdS, 329). The principle of responsibility is undoubtedly a fundamental characteristic of persons, but it is nonetheless restrictive, because, among other things, it is enough that "someone" not recognize them as responsible, or, they are not so for medical reasons. Any horror whatsoever may be perpetrated on a person. Someone, Kant himself for example, could speak of "the incompetence of the slave" setting history one dangerous step backwards, almost into prehistory more than into the ancient world, because many of his considerations on slavery had already been overcome by Roman law which itself is part of Kantian culture. Suffice it to reflect on the fact that at the end of his juridical work, perhaps his most important one, he states that "the best constitution is one in which power is not in people, but in the laws" (Kant, DMdS, 479), it is the latter that make us free. This was already Cicero's conviction when he maintained that in his republic the laws governed and not the kings as in Plato's, laws which protect our liberty because "legum servi sumus ut liberi esse possimus" (cf. the first volume Ch. I and II).

17.10 As far as the death penalty is concerned it should be recalled that Kant accepts it in full. This cannot be justified by speaking of an era which had not yet reached maturity. It cannot because Kant participates in the debate of the most enlightened spirits of his time who were against the death penalty almost ridiculing it, ultimately. The book *On Crimes and Punishments* was the centre of a European debate. Kant maintains, however, that "Because of a pretentious humanitarian sentimentalism (*compassibilitas*) Marquis Beccaria maintains that every death sentence constitutes an *injustice*: This could indeed not be included in the original civil contract, because every individual among the people would have to consent to losing his or her life in case he or she had to kill another (among the people)" (Kant, DMdS, 457). For Kant this reasoning is a sophism and denatures law because *no-one can decide on his life* (!?). In the original agreement or social contract "there is no promise to allow oneself to be punished thereby having the power to decide on one's own life. Indeed, if the right to punish were to be based on a *promise* of the guilty party to *allow himself* to be punished, he would also have to be allowed the faculty of himself declaring whether or not he deserves the punishment" (Kant, DMdS, 457-458). Rather than commenting on this statement, we should recall that the death penalty could also fall upon an innocent person who, not being allowed the right to resist or disobey an unjust verdict, must passively submit to the death penalty. Universal reason calls for this and the law of the State constitutes the source of law.

17.11 On a juridical level, the individual is not the one who has the "right to the truth", an expression which for Kant is senseless, but all of humanity. Nonetheless the lack of truth, speaking on the juridical level obviously, directly harms whoever is primarily and tangibly the victim of a lie. "Lies therefore (...) always harm another, not a determined person, but rather humanity in general, since they contaminate the source of law itself" (Kant, ÜevR, 638). We find ourselves face to face with the typical abstraction of formal law. It is certain that lies can harm all of humanity, but one who is directly affected is harmed in a different way. A lie which harms all of humanity calls into question the very foundation of law which is its certainty, but some of those directly involved immediately suffer an injustice and, not infrequently, a punishment as well.

17.12 One of the innovations in Kant's juridical and political thought is erroneously thought to be the division between public and private law. Not that this division is not important, but it is certainly nothing new in western tradition. Kant himself cannot help but recall that "this division can easily be made according to Ulpian" whom he credits with having created formulas that "make it possible to develop and introduce" modern innovations. When these basic points are dealt with several contradictions arise which are not of a secondary nature. When speaking of the division of law, Kant rightly maintains that equality must be considered innate because it rests on the original independence so that one cannot "be constrained by others to anything more than we can constrain them mutually". However, since this principle may, at times, be called into question, why should human beings be prevented from defending this principle by having recourse to the various forms of resistance? This is still Kantian formalism which universally sets forth a principle that can then, in practice, also be disregarded. This formalism also comes out when Kant speaks of the social and civil states. Regarding these the juridical terms used must be clarified otherwise great confusion will result. Maintaining that "there can certainly be a society in the state of nature, but not a civil society" merits a not inconsiderable explanation if one has used Ulpian as a starting point, and has also referred to Cicero. For classical law, referring to civil society is a useless tautology because, etymologically speaking, society is either civil or it is not. Departing from the concept that *ubi societas ibi ius*, the Kantian distinction is not only useless, but also dangerous. It is no accident that the Hegel and Marx's concept of civil society will be based on that distinction with all the consequences that we are familiar with. In other words law is either the basis of society or it becomes *uniquely* its superstructure.

17.13 Keeping in mind the classic concept of society, Kantian unsociable sociability, which the classics had examined departing from different premises, becomes more understandable. Saying that man seeks harmony because nature, almost as if thanks to an arcane mystery, calls for discord, and can be dangerous because the mystery of uncontrollable forces among people is included. Kant, almost recalling Spinoza, is the one who uses these nebulous words: "*Nature* the great craftsman, from whose mechanical course, the goal of drawing people away from discord, harmony as well, even against their will, becomes evident." It is as if this goal were "called *destiny*" (cf. Kant, ZeF, 217). For classical jurists there is no destiny, nature, understood to be the Great Craftsman, has no better knowledge of what is good. Individuals know that together they can pursue their own tangible interests but they also know that they must control their selfishness, which is capable of various abominations. They therefore agree, while realizing that they do not have pure hearts. This is why Lucanus reminds us that his contemporaries were already speaking of *Concordia discors* (cf. the first volume II.24).

17.14 Society, understood as a group of members who, abiding by a set of rules, pursue their objectives is the environment in which a certain *modus vivendi* is to be established, one which guarantees security and stability or, perhaps, the salvation and prosperity of those associated. I spoke of salvation because the word from the classical authors which Kant uses is *salus* taken from the *De legibus* of Cicero. However, the quotation is not accurate. Kant takes the maxim *salus publica suprema civitas lex est* which he acknowledges to have "unchanged validity and authority" forgetting that in Cicero and the classical authors, a different word is used. The second word is not *publica* but *populi*. It is not an oversight typical of those who quote from memory nor is it a misunderstood term. Kant wishes to express another thing. For him "the public safety, which is to be taken into consideration *first and foremost*, is precisely that legal constitution that guarantees each person liberty through law" (Kant, ÜdG, 154-155). Certainly the word *populi* implies all that, but makes a concrete reference which removes law from its formalism. I do not think that this specification is a hair-splitting one, otherwise it would not be possible to explain why, in ancient times, the evil-doer, who, however, enjoyed the right of citizenship, that is, belonged to the people, was to receive forms of punishment that could not go beyond a certain limit, for example crucifixion unworthy of the *civis*, because he belonged to the *populus*. For Kant, such is no longer the case and he wonders if "the respect due to humanity in the person of the ill-doer" must still be taken into consideration. One cannot wonder at the fact that he goes so far as to state: "I consider that as far as the form is concerned, the *ius talionis*, is the only idea that can determine the principle of criminal law *a priori*" (Kant, DMdS, 487). What about where the law of retaliation is not possible, for example, in cases of rape and pederasty? Kant does not hesitate to maintain, in the subsequent sentence, that guilt of that sort must be punished with castration and exile "*ad perpetuum* from civil society". It is a bit like Rousseau when he returned to the idea of excommunication, so greatly vilified.

B) *The Regulating State: J. G. Fichte.*

17.15 If for Kant politics had been an aspect of philosophical thought, which, however, had an ample relationship to morality and law, in Fichte it becomes the centre of philosophical reflection so that the other interests of speculation relate to this. It is perhaps not an exaggeration to say that, thanks to politics, Fichte overcomes Kantian dualism. Theory and politics, speculation and action, pure reason and practical reason find in the action of the ego in society that synthesis that resolved one of the heretofore troublesome dichotomies of philosophical reflection.

Johann Gottlieb Fichte was born in Rammenau in 1762 and was of humble origin. Supported by the Baron Ernest Haubold de Miltiz, who had intuited Ficht's keen intelligence and propensity towards study, he completed university studies in theology before becoming a tutor in a Swiss family in Zurich where he came into contact with French culture, and, in particular, Montesquieu and Rousseau. After returning to Germany he had the opportunity to meet Kant and show him his *Versuch einer Kritik aller Offenbarung* (*Attempt at a Critique of All Revelation*), a work which was eventually very successful. In 1793 he published, anonymously at first, *Beitrag zur Berichtigung der Urtheile des Publikums über die französische Revolution* (*Contribution to* *the Rectification of the Public's Judgment of the French Revolution*), which was followed by other political writings. Perhaps his most important theoretical work followed in 1796: *Grundlage der gesamten Wissenschaftlehre (The General Science of Knowledge)*, which went into several editions. This was followed by *Der Geschlossene Handelsstaat (The State according to Reason, The Closed Commercial State)* (1800) and other works such as *Einige Vorlesungen über die Bestimmung des Gelehrten (The Mission of the Scholar)* (1805), even though these were based on lessons held years earlier and the famous *Reden an die deutsche Nation (Addresses to the German Nation)* (1808). He died while still young in Berlin in 1814.

17.16 Individual liberty finds expression in action and brings about the obligation to examine the political context in which one operates, in order not to accept it passively, but to formulate all the changes that become necessary. Nothing, therefore, can be considered immutable on the political level, including the traditional privileges that the French revolution has now shown to be untenable (cf. D'Addio, SDP, II, 117-118). Fichte's critique operates on various levels, but first of all it criticizes liberty understood in a formal sense, then it attacks the aristocratic and ecclesiastical orders reiterating the idea that there is no social structure that can be considered immutable. Those orders are the expression of a way of conceiving of property itself which must be overcome and which we could call passive. On the contrary, property must be understood as the expression of the authentic personality of the individual. It is a juridical sign of human activity which tends to modify all that with which it enters into a relationship. "This modification of things by our own force (education) is the real basis of the right of property". Property is thus seen in a dynamic sense, as the result of human action. This is why the rational nature of man "is the source of the right of property. We undoubtedly possess something purely on the basis of natural law and we can legitimately exclude all others from possession of the thing itself". Fichte's revolutionary liberalism induces him, in this case, to maintain, appropriately, that that right is acquired "entirely independently of the State" (Fichte, BzB, 267 and 273).

17.17 It is understandable why Fichte, anticipating some of Hegel's conclusions and criticizing Rousseau's idea concerning the happiness typical of the state of nature, comes to consider civil society the result of a relentless historical evolution. Civil society is considered superior to the State, almost reduced, in this analysis, to a mere instrument of society itself. It is in this that each person must exercise his or her liberty, which finds its highest expression in work. If, on the one hand, law sets forth the limits within which liberty is made to operate, on the other, it is only work which, with its retribution, that provides the means to avoid having liberty remain an abstract aspiration. From this come two tasks of the State: it must guarantee observance of the law and, at the same time, provide everyone with the opportunity for employment. Concerning the first point, Fichte maintains that the best constitution should be democratic (and in this he overcomes not a few Kantian perplexities) and representative, but he also maintains that the State, through law, expresses a certain type of rationality which leads it to manage, on behalf of individuals, activities that partial rationality could deal with only incompletely. At this point Fichte's liberalism encounters socialism then nationalism.

17.18 The handling of financial matters must be controlled by the State because, as a "rationally constituted State" it is aware of what individual citizens in the sense of entrepreneurs may not be aware of. Just as the State handles the application of the laws and justice by full right within its borders, so it has the right to accomplish the commercial balance which would fail if private individuals could have an influence and if that influence on the aforesaid balance were not subject to its laws. The possibility of that influence must therefore be taken away (cf. Fichte, GH, 128 ff.). It is no accident that here too, behind the need for stability, there lies concealed suspicion of the class of merchants, a suspicion which goes back at least as far as ancient times, with Plato and Aristotle. On a par with other classes, merchants must make up a number established and controlled by the government which has the right to make provisions as it likes "to keep every class within established limits". The State must also place trade limits on that class and punish those who go beyond the limits. The limits concern not only the goods bought and sold but also the quantity, times and the modes of trade (cf. Fichte, GH, 117 ff.). To avoid possible international upsets and conditioning, the State has the right to plan economic life and orient the various productive activities. It should not be forgotten, however, that State control of the economy is based on the conviction that it is possible to organize economic activity through rational deduction from philosophically and scientifically incontestable schemes.

17.19 These convictions must not seem extravagant and the result of a reflection in itself. They are in line with much of Fichte's speculation and, anticipating the conception of the organic intellectual that Gramsci would be fond of, he seems almost to recognize that "intellectuals would be the designers of future society and thus guide humanity" (Merker, IF, XXV). Albeit with some romantic grandiloquence Fichte underscores all of this: "I am called to this duty, to bear witness to the truth (…) and am a priest for the truth; I am at its service; I have pledged to do, dare and suffer anything in its name" (Fichte, EV, 58). Such words will be echoed, dramatically, more than a century later from Moscow to Berlin. How can one not see behind Fichte's words the justification of those revolutionary guides who would dedicate themselves so much to a project to the point of become its charismatic and irreplaceable professionals? "The idea of a largely social function for intellectuals combines, in the final analysis, with an aristocratic and elitist view of their *modus operandi*" (Merker, IF, XXIV).

17.20 The problem of education becomes the central theme of the famous *Reden an die deutsche Nation*, a work that certainly reflects the spirit of the age, since other, similar ones were coming out in those years everywhere, including in Italy. In Fichte, however, it has characteristics of its own which are closely related to his idea of the State. This education will make the German people different from others because the purpose of this new culture will be that of delving into the intimate being of humans not only to change social life broadly speaking but also mental life. This will be possible because Germans, differently from the other European peoples, have remained rooted in their original authenticity, like their language which, as it happens, is the least Latinized one. As Mann will do more than a century later, Fichte strongly opposes those Germans who want to imitate what is foreign at all costs. The German people have their own qualities which have led to their greatness and which cannot be forgotten. Among these, how could one forget Luther "the German par excellence", the one who first set off on the path of reconciling philosophy and religion? This is the road – he seems to be echoing Plato – which will lead to the setting up of the perfect State through the education of the perfect man. *Language, religion, education* flow together in history and in the *tradition* of a people which has been able to defend its identity against all others, starting with the universalistic demands of the Roman Empire. Although this is a recurring point in German nationalism, suffice it in this case, too, to look at Mann among so many. Here Fichte aroused the irony of those who reminded him that while he was speaking of the merit of German arms, outside the classroom where he was delivering his *Reden* there were French occupation troops who were checking to see that all of this remained on a theoretical level.

Works cited

ABBONDANTI W., GHIRINGHELLI R., *Appunti sul pensiero politico inglese. Da Bacone alla rivoluzione industriale*, Cisalpino-Goliardica, Milano, 1978.

ACTON J. E. D., *History of Freedom and other Essays*, London, 1907.

ACTON J. E. D., *The Influence of America*, in *Essays in the Liberal Interpretation of History; selected Papers*, Ed, by W. H. MCNEILL, Classical European Historians, Chicago, 1967.

ACTON J. E. D., *Essays on Freedom and Power*, New York, 1955.

ACUTIS C., *Introduzione* a BARTOLOMÉ DE LAS CASAS, *Brevissima relazione della distruzione delle Indie*, Arnoldo Mondadori Editore, Milano, 1987.

ADAMS J., *A Defense of the Constitutions of Government of the United States of America against the attack of M. Turgot, in his letter to Dr. Price, dated the twenty-second of March, 1978*, in *The Works of John Adams*, edited by CHARLES F. ADAMS, Little and Brown, Boston, 1951.
The quotations are from Vol. IV and VI.

ALATRI P., *Introduzione* a J. E. D. ACTON, *Cattolicesimo liberale. Saggi storici*, Firenze, 1950.

ALATRI P., *Introduzione* a J. J. ROUSSEAU, *Scritti politici*, UTET, Torino, 1970.

ALBERTONI E. A., *Storia delle dottrine politiche in Italia*, vol. I, Edizioni di Comunità, Milano, 1990.

ALTHUSIUS J., *Politica metodice digesta atque exemplis sacris et profanis illustrata*, Herborn, 1614.
The date refers to the third edition, which is more complete. The references are to the chapter and the paragraph.

ALTHUSSER L., *Montesquieu, la politica e la storia*, Roma, manifestolibri, 1995.

AMERIO F., *Introduzione allo studio di G. B. Vico*, S.E.I., Torino, 1947.

ANTISERI D., *Premessa alla seconda edizione italiana* di K. R. POPPER, *La società aperta e i suoi amici. Platone totalitario*, vol. I, Armando Editore, Roma, 1996.

BACON F., *Nova Atlantis, New Atlantis*, in *The Works of F. Bacon*, volume V, Brown and Taggard, MDCCCLXII.

BADALONI N., *Sul vichiano diritto naturale delle genti, Introduzione* a G.B. VICO, *Opere giuridiche*, Sansoni, Firenze, 1974.

BALBO C., *Sommario della storia d'Italia*, in *Storia d'Italia e altri scritti editi e inediti*, UTET, Torino, 1984.

BALMES J., *El Protestantismo comparado con el Catolicismo*, in *Obras completas*, vol. IV, BAC, Madrid, 1949.

BASTID P., *Sieyès et sa pensée*, Librairie Hachette, Paris, 1970.

BECCARIA C., *Dei delitti e delle pene*, Rizzoli Editore, Milano, 1980.

BEDESCHI G., *Storia del pensiero liberale*, Editori Laterza, Roma-Bari, 1990.

BELLARMINO R., *Scritti politici*, a cura di C. Giacon, Editore Zanichelli, Bologna, 1950.

BELLARMINO R., *De laicis sive saecularibus*, in *Secunda controversia generalis, de membris ecclesiae miltantis tribus libris explicata*, Liber tertius, in *Disputationum* Roberti Bellarmini Politiani S. J., *De controversiis christianae fidei adversus huius temporis haereticos*, Tomus secundus, Neapoli, apud Josephum Giuliano Editorem, 1837.

BENTHAM J., *Defence of Usury*, in *Economic Writings*, ed. by Werner Stark, vol. I, London, 1952.

BENTHAM J., *An Introduction to the Principles of Morals and Legislation*, Methuen, London-New York, 1982.

BENTHAM J., *A Fragment on Government*, Cambridge University Press, 1988.

BERLIN I., *The Crooked Timber of Humanity. Chapters in the History of Ideas*, Alfred A. Knopf, New York, 1991.

BERNSTEIN E., *Die Voraussetzungen des Sozialismus und die Aufgaben der Sozialdemokratie*, Dietz, Stuttgart, 1920.

BIEN D. D., *Aristocrazia*, in F. FURET-M. OZOUF, *Dizionario critico della rivoluzione francese*, Nuova edizione, Bompiani, Milano, 1994, vol. II, pp. 717-729.

BOBBIO N., *Thomas Hobbes*, Einaudi, Torino, 1989.

BOBBIO N., *Introduzione* a F. H. JACOBI, *Idealismo e realismo*, Francesco De Silva Editore, Torino, 1948.

BODIN J., *Les six livres de la République*, Paris, 1583.
The quotations refer to the book and the chapter.

BOLINGBROKE H. S. J. de, *Fragments or minutes of essays*, in *Works*, Volume IV, London, MDCCLIV.

BOSSUET J. B., *Politique tirée des propres paroles de l'Ecriture Sainte*, Paris, 1709.

BOTERO G., *Della ragion di Stato*, Donzelli Editore, Roma, 1997.

BRANCA V., *L'intesa Pico-Poliziano e una lezione comune sulla dignità e la libera coscienza dell'uomo*, in PICO DELLA MIRANDOLA G., *De Hominis Dignitate*, S. Berlusconi Editore, Milano, 1995.

BRYCE J, *Flexible and Rigid Constitutions*, in *Studies in History and Jurisprudence*, vol. I, pp. 145-252, Clarendon Press, Oxford, 1901.

BUCCILLI N., GUIDI M., *Introduzione* a J. BENTHAM, *Difesa dell'usura*, Liberilibri, Macerata, 1996.

BURGIO A., *Un'apologia della storia. Con Montesquieu tra Ancien Régime e modernizzazione*, Introduzione a Louis Althusser, *Montesquieu, la politica e la storia*, Roma, manifestolibri, 1995.

BURKE E., *Reflections on the Revolution in France, and on the Proceedings in Certain Societies in London relative to that Event*, Penguin Books Ltd, 1981.

BURKE E., *Speech on Moving Resolutions for Conciliation with the Colonies*, in *Select Works* of Edmund Burke, vol. I, Liberty Fund, Inc., Indianapolis, 1999.

BURKE E., *An Appeal from the New to the Old Whigs*, in *Further Reflections on the Revolution in France*, Liberty Fund, Inc., Indianapolis, 1992.

BURNS J.H., HART H.L.A., *Introduction* to J. BENTHAM, *An Introduction to the Principles of Morals and Legislation*, Methuen, London-New York, 1982.

CACCIARI M., *Disincantata utopia*, in BACON F., *Nova Atlantis*, S. Berlusconi Editore, Milano, 1996.

CALVIN J., *Institutio christianae religionis nunc vere demum suo titulo respondens*, tr. it., *Istituzione della religione cristiana*, UTET, Torino, 1971.
The quotations refer to the book, the chapter, and the paragraph.

CAMPANELLA T., *Civitas Solis*, S. Berlusconi Editore, Milano, 1998.

CANTONI R., *Introduzione* a B. SPINOZA, *Etica e Trattato Teologico-politico*, UTET, Torino, 1972.

Cantù F., *Bartolomé de Las Casas nel quadro del suo tempo*, in *I diritti dell'uomo e la pace nel pensiero di Francisco de Victoria e Bartolomé de las Casas*, Studia Universitas S. Thomae in Urbe, Massimo, Milano, 1988.

Capozzi E., *Introduzione* a H. S. J. Visconte di Bolingbroke, *Sul Governo*, A. Guida Editore, Napoli, 1997.

Carena C., *Il significato dell'orazione sulla dignità dell'uomo*, in Pico della Mirandola G., *De Hominis Dignitate*, S. Berlusconi Editore, Milano, 1995.

Carletti G., *Melchiorre Delfico. Riforme politiche e riflessione teorica di un moderato meridionale*, Edizioni ETS, Pisa, 1996.

Carpenter W. S., *Introduction* to John Locke, *Two Treatises of Government*, Dent & Sons Ltd, London, 1975.

Carrano A., *Introduzione* a W. von Humboldt, *Il secolo XVIII*, A. Guida Editore, Napoli, 1998.

Casanovas I., *Balmes. La seva vida. El seu temps. Les seves obres*, vol. II, Barcelona, MCMXXXII.

Cassirer E., *Die Philosophie der Aufklärung*, Verlag Von J. C. B. Mohr (Paul Siebeck), Tübingen, 1932.

Castaño J.F., *Il diritto internazionale da Francisco de Victoria a oggi*, in *I diritti dell'uomo e la pace nel pensiero di Francisco de Victoria e Bartolomé de las Casas*, Studia Universitas S. Thomae in Urbe, Massimo, Milano, 1988.

CATERINA DA SIENA (CATHERINE OF SIENA ST), *Epistolario*, Edizioni Paoline, Roma, 1979.
The letters are nrs. 207, 235 and 268, in the text, reference is to the pages.

CEDRONI L., *Il concetto di democrazia nella seconda scolastica. La "Escuela Española"*, in *Studium*, n. 6, anno 91°, 1995.

CEREZO DE DIEGO P., *El pensamiento americano de un discipulo de Victoria: Alonso De Veracruz*, in *I diritti dell'uomo e la pace nel pensiero di Francisco de Victoria e Bartolomé de las Casas*, Studia Universitas S. Thomae in Urbe, Massimo, Milano, 1988.

CERRONI U., *Introduzione* a B. CONSTANT, *Principi di politica*, Editori Riuniti, Roma, 1970.

CHATEAUBRIAND F. R., *Mémoires d'Outre-Tombe*, vol. I, Paris, 1948.

CHEVALLIER J. J., *Les grandes oeuvres politiques. De Machiavel à nos jours*, Librairie Armand Colin, Paris, 1966.

CICERO M. T., *De Legibus*, in aedibus Livianis, Patavii, MCMLXVIII.

COLE G. D. H., *Socialist Thoyght: The Forerunners (1789-1850)*, vol. I, Macmillan & Co LDT, London, New York, 1953.

COLE G. D. H., *Socialist Thoyght: The Second International (1889-1914)*, Volume III, Part I, Macmillan & Co LDT, London, New York, 1956.

COLLETTI L., *Bernstein e il marxismo della Seconda Internazionale*, Introduzione a EDUARD BERNSTEIN, *Die Voraussetzungen des Sozialismus und die Aufgaben der Sozialdemokratie*, tr. it., Editori Laterza, Bari, 1967.

COMPAGNA L., *L'idea dei partiti. Da Hobbes a Burke*, Bibliopolis, Napoli, 1986.

COMPAGNA L., *Liberalismo ed aristocrazia*, in *Behemoth*, n°. 20, luglio-dicembre 1996.

COMPAGNA L., *Gli opposti sentieri del costituzionalismo*, Il Mulino, Bologna, 1998.

COMPOSTA D., *Il concetto di diritto nell'umanesimo giuridico di Francisco De Victoria O.P.*, in *I diritti dell'uomo e la pace nel pensiero di Francisco de Victoria e Bartolomé de las Casas*, Studia Universitas S. Thomae in Urbe, Massimo, Milano, 1988.

COMTE A., *Cours de philosophie positive*, 5e édition, 6 voll., Schleicher Frères éditeurs, Paris, 1907-1908.

CONSTANT B., *De la force du gouvernement actuel de la France et de la nécessité de s'y rallier (1796)*, *Des réactions politiques*, *Des effets de la terreur (1797)*, Champs - Flammarion, Paris, 1988.

CONSTANT B., *De la religion considérée dans sa source, ses formes et ses développements*, Bibliothèque romande, Lausanne, 1971.

CONSTANT B., *Principes de politique. Applicables à tous les gouvernements représentatifs et particulièrement à la*

Constitution actuelle de la France 1815, in *Écrits politiques*, Éditions Gallimard, Paris, 1997.

CONSTANT B., *De la liberté des anciens comparée à celle des modernes. Discours prononcé à l'Athénée royal de Paris en 1819*, in *Écrits politiques*, Éditions Gallimard, Paris, 1997.

CONTINISIO C., *Introduzione* a GIOVANNI BOTERO, *Della ragion di Stato*, Donzelli Editore, Roma, 1997.

COPPELLOTTI F., *E. Bloch: il terzo Evangelo ed il suo Regno*, introduzione a E. BLOCH, *Ateismo nel Cristianesimo*, Feltrinelli Editore, Milano, 1976.

CROCE B., *La filosofia di Giambattista Vico*, Editori Laterza, Roma-Bari, 1973.

CROCE B., *Storia del Regno di Napoli*, Editori Laterza, Bari, 1967.

CROCE B., *La scuola cattolico-liberale e la storia d'Italia e del mondo*, in *Storia della storio- grafia italiana nel secolo decimonono*, vol. I, Laterza, Bari, 1964.

CUSANO N., *La dotta ignoranza* e *Le congetture*, Rusconi Libri S. p. A., Milano, 1988.
The number in the quotations refers to the paragraphs.

CUSANO N., *La concordanza universale*, in *Opere religiose*, a cura di P. Gaia, UTET, Torino, 1971.

CUOCO V., *Saggio sulla rivoluzione napoletana del 1799*, Editori Laterza, Roma-Bari, 1980.

Cuoco V., *Frammenti di lettere dirette a Vincenzo Russo*, in appendice a Cuoco V., *Saggio sulla rivoluzione napoletana del 1799*, Editori Laterza, Roma-Bari, 1980.

D'Addio M., *Storia delle dottrine politiche*, vol. I, Ecig, Genova, 1992.

D'Addio M., *Storia delle dottrine politiche*, vol. II, Ecig, Genova, 1992.

D'Addio M., *Introduzione* a A. Rosmini-Serbati, *Filosofia della politica*, Marzorati Editore, Milano, 1972.

D'Addio M., *Rosmini e la Confederazione italiana*, in Aa. Vv., *Stato unitario e federalismo nel pensiero cattolico del Risorgimento*, Atti del XXVII Corso della "Cattedra Rosmini", 1993, a cura di G. Pellegrino, Sodalitas - Spes, Stresa - Milazzo, 1994.

D'Addio M. e Negri G., (a cura di) *Introduzione* a *Il Federalista*, il Mulino, Bologna, 1980.

Deguise P., *Postface* a Constant B., *De la religion considérée dans sa source, ses formes et ses développements*, Bibliothèque romande, Lausanne, 1971.

Del Noce A., *Giovanni Gentile. Per una interpretazione filosofica della storia contemporanea*, Il Mulino, Bologna, 1990.

De Luca S., *Il pensiero politico di Constant*, Editori Laterza, Roma-Bari, 1993.

Denis H., *Histoire de la pensée économique*, PUF, Paris, 2008.

DERRÉ J.-R., *L'ecumenismo mennaisiano*, in AA. VV., *I cattolici liberali nell'Ottocento*, S. E. I., Torino, 1976.

DE RUGGIERO G., *Storia del liberalismo europeo*, Feltrinelli Editore, Milano, 1971.

DE VICTORIA F., *Relectio de Indis*, C.S.I.C., Madrid, 1967.

DI DONATO F., *Un costituzionalismo di antico regime? Prospettive socio istituzionali di storia giuridica. Introduzione* a DENIS RICHET, *La france moderne: l'esprit des institutions*, Flammarion, Paris, 1973, tr. it., Editori Laterza, Bari-Roma, 1998.

DI VONA P., *Aspetti di Hobbes in Spinoza*, Loffredo, Napoli, 1990.

ELOURDUY E., *La soberania popular segun Francisco Suarez*, in FRANCISCO SUAREZ, *Principatus Politicus*, Introduccion y edicion critica bilingüe por E. Elourduy y L. Pereña, C.S.I.C., Madrid, 1965.

ERASMO D. DA R., *Μωρίας Ἐγκώμιον id est Stultitiae Laus*, ed. lat., a cura di O. Holtze, Lipsia, 1912.
The Roman numerals in the quotations refer to the chapters.

ERASMO D. DA R., *Institutio Principis Christiani*, in *Opera Omnia*, vol. V/1, A.S.D., Amsterdam, 1974.
The Roman numerals in the quotations refer to the chapters.

ERASMO D. DA R., *Aut regem aut fatuum nasci oportere*, in *Adagia, sei saggi politici in forma di proverbi*, Einaudi Editore, Torino, 1980.
The Latin text is from the Basileae ex Officina Froberiana edition, 1536. The numbers correspond to the numerical order in the Latin text.

Erasmo D. da R., *Dulce bellum inexpertis*, in *Adagia, sei saggi politici in forma di proverbi*, Einaudi Editore, Torino, 1980.
The Latin text is from the Basileae ex Officina Froberiana edition, 1536. The numbers correspond to the numerical order in the Latin text.

Euchner W., *La filosofia politica di Locke*, Laterza, Bari, 1975.

Fasnacht G. E., *Acton's Political Philosophy: an Analysis*, Hollis and Carter, London, 1952.

Fasnacht G. E., *Freedom and Socialism*, in *Lord Acton on Nationality and Socialism*, London, 1949.

The Federalist, A. Hamilton, J. Madison, J. Jay, with an *Introduction* by Garry Wills, Bantam Classic, New York, 2003.
The quotations refer to the number of artiche.

Ferguson A., *An Essay on the History of Civil Society*, London, 1767.

Ferrarotti F., *Introduzione* a Herbert Spencer, *Principi di sociologia*, vol. I, UTET, Torino, 1967.

Feuerbach L., *Das Wesen des Christentums*, in *Gesammelte Werke*, Band V, Akademie – Verlag – Berlin, 1973.

Fichte J. G., *Beitrag zur Berichtigung der Urtheile des Publikums über die französische Revolution*, in *Werke*, Band I/1, 1791-1794, F. Frommann Verlag, Stuttgart-Bad Cannstatt, 1964.

Fichte J. G., *Einige Vorlesungen über die Bestimmung des Gelehrten*, in *Werke*, Band I/3, 1794-1796, F. Frommann Verlag, Stuttgart-Bad Cannstatt, 1966.

Fichte J. G., *Der Geschlossene Handelsstaat*, in *Werke*, Band I/7, 1800-1801, F. Frommann Verlag, Stuttgart-Bad Cannstatt, 1988.

Filangeri G., *La scienza della legislazione*, in *Illuministi italiani. Riformatori napoletani*, vol. II - tomo II, Classici Ricciardi Mondadori, Milano-Napoli, 1997.

Firpo L., *Introduzione* a M. Lutero, *Scritti politici*, UTET, Torino, 1978.

Fubini Leuzzi M., *Introduzione* a C. Balbo, *Storia d'Italia e altri scritti editi e inediti*, UTET, Torino, 1984.

Furet F., *Penser la Révolution française*, Éditions Gallimard, Paris, 1978.

Gadille J. e Mayeur J. M., *Gli ambienti cattolici liberali in Francia: continuità e diversità di una tradizione*, in AA. Vv., *I cattolici liberali nell'Ottocento*, S. E. I., Torino, 1976.

Galanti G. M., *Considerazioni sulla nostra legislazione*, in *Illuministi italiani. Riformatori napoletani*, vol. II - tomo II, Classici Ricciardi Mondadori, Milano-Napoli, 1997.

Gasquet A. F., *Lord Acton and his Circle (Letters of Lord Acton)*, ed. by Abbot Gasquet, George Allen, Burns & Oates, London, 1906.

GATTI MARIANO e HILARY, *Introduzione* a J. MILTON, *Areopagitica*, Rusconi Libri s.r.l., Milano, 1998.

GAUCHET M., *La Révolution des droits de l'homme*, Bibliotèque des histoires, nrf, Éditions Gallimard, Paris, 1989.

GENOVESI A., *Discorso sopra il vero fine delle lettere e delle scienze*, in *Illuministi italiani. Riformatori napoletani*, vol. II - tomo I, Classici Ricciardi Mondadori, Milano-Napoli, 1997.

GENOVESI A., *Dall'Edizione della "Storia del commercio della Gran Bretagna scritta da John Cary"*, in *Illuministi italiani. Riformatori napoletani*, vol. II - tomo I, Classici Ricciardi Mondadori, Milano-Napoli, 1997.

GENOVESI A., *Delle lezioni di commercio o sia d'economia civile*, in *Illuministi italiani. Riformatori napoletani*, vol. II - tomo I, Classici Ricciardi Mondadori, Milano-Napoli, 1997.

GENOVESI A., *La logica per gli giovinetti*, in *Illuministi italiani. Riformatori napoletani*, vol. II - tomo I, Classici Ricciardi Mondadori, Milano-Napoli, 1997.

GENTILE G., *Storia della filosofia italiana*, a cura di E. Garin, vol. I, Sansoni Editore, Firenze, 1969.

GIACON C., *La seconda scolastica. I problemi giuridico-politici. Suarez, Bellarmino, Mariana*, Fratelli Bocca Editori, Milano, 1950.

GIERKE O. VON, *Johannes Althusius un die Entwicklung der naturrechlichen Staatstheorien*, Breslavia, 1880, trad. it., Giulio Einaudi Editore, Torino, 1974.

GILBERT F., *Machiavelli and Guicciardini. Politics and History in Sixteenth-Century Florence*, Princeton, New Jersey, Princeton University Press, 1965.

GIOBERTI V., *Del Rinnovamento civile de'Italia, Inediti*, a cura di L. Quattrocchi, volume 21 della Edizione nazionale delle opere edite e inedite di Vincenzo Gioberti, Edizione Abete, Roma, 1969.

GIOBERTI V., *Del Rinnovamento civile de'Italia*, vol. I, a cura di L. Quattrocchi, volume 22 della Edizione nazionale delle opere edite e inedite di Vincenzo Gioberti, Edizione Abete, Roma, 1969.

GIOBERTI V., *Del primato morale e civile degli italiani*, tomo I, Dalle stampe di Meline, Cans e Compagnia, Bruxelles, 1843.

GIOBERTI V., *Del primato morale e civile degli italiani*, tomo II, Dalle stampe di Meline, Cans e Compagnia, Bruxelles, 1843.

GIULIANI A., *Presentazione* a ALESSANDRO MANZONI, *La Rivoluzione Francese del 1789*, Edizioni Costa & Nolan, Genova, 1985.

GROTIUS H., *De iure belli ac pacis*, trad. fr., *Le droit de la guerre et de la paix*, Chez Pierre de Coup, Amsterdam, 1729.

GUICCIARDINI F., *Storie fiorentine*, in *Opere*, vol. I, a cura di E. Lugnani Scarano, UTET, Torino, 1983.

GUICCIARDINI F., *Discorso di Logrogno*, in *Opere*, vol. I, a cura di E. Lugnani Scarano, UTET, Torino, 1983.

GUICCIARDINI F., *Consolatoria*, in *Opere*, vol. I, a cura di E. Lugnani Scarano, UTET, Torino, 1983.

GUICCIARDINI F., *Considerazioni sui «Discorsi» del Machiavelli*, in *Opere*, vol. I, a cura di E. Lugnani Scarano, UTET, Torino, 1983.

GUICCIARDINI F., *Dialogo del reggimento di Firenze*, in *Opere*, vol. I, a cura di E. Lugnani Scarano, UTET, Torino, 1983.

GUICCIARDINI F., *Ricordi e altri scritti*, in *Opere*, vol. I, a cura di E. Lugnani Scarano, UTET, Torino, 1983.

GUICCIARDINI F., *Storia d'Italia (libri I-X)*, in *Opere*, vol. II, a cura di E. Lugnani Scarano, UTET, Torino, 1987.

GUICCIARDINI F., *Storia d'Italia (libri XI-XX)*, in *Opere*, vol. III, a cura di E. Lugnani Scarano, UTET, Torino, 1987.

GUIZOT F., *Histoire de la civilisation en Europe*, Didier et Cie, Libraires-Éd., Paris,

GUIZOT F., *Histoire de la civilisation en France*, tomi I, II e IV, Didier et Cie, Libraires-Éd., Paris,

GUIZOT F., *Histoire des origines du gouvernement représentatif en Europe*, vol. I, Paris, 1851.

HARRINGTON J., *The Political Writings of James Harrington*, edited by J. G. A. Pocock, Cambridge University Press, 1977.

HAYEK F. A. VON, *Law, Legislation and Liberty*, vol. I, *Rules and Order*, University of Chicago Press, Chicago, 1973.

HAYEK F. A. VON, *Law, Legislation and Liberty*, vol. II, *The Mirage of Social Justice*, University of Chicago Press, Chicago, 1976.

HEGEL G. W. F., *Briefe von und an Hegel*, Band I: 1785-1812, Felix Meiner Verlag, Hamburg, 1952.

HEGEL G. W. F., *Frühe Schriften, Werke*: 1, Suhrkamp Verlag, Frankfurt am Main, 1986.

HEGEL G. W. F., *Die Fhänomenologie des Geistes, Werke*: 3, Suhrkamp Verlag, Frankfurt am Main, 1986.

HEGEL G. W. F., *Enzyclopädie der philosophischen Wissenschaften im Grundisse, Werke*: 10/III, Suhrkamp Verlag, Frankfurt am Main, 1986.

HEGEL G. W. F., *Vorlesungen über die Philosophie der Religion, Werke*: 16, Suhrkamp Verlag, Frankfurt am Main, 1986.

HEGEL G. W. F., *Vorlesungen über die Geschichte der Philosophie, Werke*: 18/I, Suhrkamp Verlag, Frankfurt am Main, 1986.

HENKEL W., *Le missioni e la legislazione coloniale alla luce della prassi e della dottrina di Fray Bartolomé de Las Casas*, in *I diritti dell'uomo e la pace nel pensiero di Francisco de Victoria e Bartolomé de las Casas*, Studia Universitas S. Thomae in Urbe, Massimo, Milano, 1988.

HIMMELFARB G., *Introduction* a J. S. MILL, *On Liberty*, London, 1985.

HOBBES T., *Leviathan*, London, Penguin Books, 1980.

HOBBES T., *Elements of Law Natural and Politic*, Cambridge University Press, 1928.

HOBBES T., *Elementorum Philosophiae Sectio secunda De homine*, vol. II, *Opera latina*, Reprint of the edition 1839-45 in 1961.

HUME D., *Essays, moral, political and literary*, in *The Philosophical Works* of David Hume, vol. III, Edinburgh, London, 1826.

HUME D., *An Inquiry concerning the Human Understanding*, in *The Philosophical Works* of David Hume, vol. IV, Edinburgh, London, 1826.

JACOBI F. H., *Uber die Lehre des Spinoza in Briefen an den Herrn Moses Mendelssohn*, in *Werke*, Band 1/1, Meiner, Frommann-Holzboog, Hamburg-Stuttgart, 1998.

JACOBI F. H., *Von den göttlichen Dingen und ihrer Offenbarung*, in *Werke*, Band 3, Meiner, Frommann-Holzboog, Hamburg-Stuttgart, 2000.

JAMES É., *Histoire sommaire de la penséeéconomique*, Éditions Montchretien, Paris, 1959.
The quotations refer to the part, the chapter, and the paragraph.

JEMOLO A.C., *Introduzione* a CESARE BECCARIA, *Dei delitti e delle pene*, Rizzoli Editore, Milano, 1980.

JEMOLO A. C., *Il cattolicesimo liberale dal 1815 al 1848*, in *Rassegna storica toscana*, anno IV, III-IV, 1958, ora in

Scritti vari di storia religiosa e civile, scelti e ordinati da F. Margiotta Broglio, Milano, 1965.

KANT I., *Kritik der reinen Vernunft 1*, in *Werke*: Band III, Suhrkamp Verlag, Frankfurt am Main, 1968.

KANT I., *Die Methaphysik der Sitten*, in *Werke*: Band VIII, Suhrkamp Verlag, Frankfurt am Main, 1968.

KANT I., *Über ein vermeintes Recht, aus Menschenliebe zu lügen*, in *Werke*: Band VIII, Suhrkamp Verlag, Frankfurt am Main, 1968.

KANT I., *Kritik der Urteilskraft*, in *Werke*: Band X, Suhrkamp Verlag, Frankfurt am Main, 1968.

KANT I., *Zum ewigen Frieden. Ein philosophischer Entwurt*, in *Werke*: Band XI, Suhrkamp Verlag, Frankfurt am Main, 1968.

KANT I., *Idee zu einer allegemeinen Geschichte in weltbürgerlicher Absicht*, in *Werke*: Band XI, Suhrkamp Verlag, Frankfurt am Main, 1968.

KANT I., *Über den Gemeinspruch: Das mag in der Theorie richtig sein, taugt aber nicht für die Praxis*, in *Werke*: Band XI, Suhrkamp Verlag, Frankfurt am Main, 1968.

KANT I., *Der Streit der Fakultäten*, in *Werke*: Band XI, Suhrkamp Verlag, Frankfurt am Main, 1968.

KANT I., *Rezensionen zu J. H. Schulz: Versuch einer Anleitung zur Sittenlehre für alle Menschen*, in *Werke*: Band XII, Suhrkamp Verlag, Frankfurt am Main, 1968.

KOCHAN L., *Acton on History*, A. Deutsch, London, 1954.

LAMENNAIS F. R. DE, *Affari di Roma*, in *Scritti politici*, UTET, Torino, 1965.

LAS CASAS B. DE, *Brevísima relació de la destrucción de las Indias*, Cátedra, Madrid, 1982, trad. it., Arnoldo Mondadori Editore, Milano, 1987.

LAS CASAS B. DE, *De Regia Potestate*, C.S.I.C., Madrid, 1969.

LASKI H. J., *Political Thought in England, from Locke to Bentham*, Oxford University Press, 1950.

LESSING G. E., *Die Erziehung des Menschengeschlechts*, in *Gesammelte Werke*, vol. VIII, Berlin, 1957.

LOCKE J., *Two Treatises of Government*, in *The Works* of John Locke in Nine Volumes, vol. IV, Baldwin, Printer, London, 1824.
The quotations refer to the paragraph.

LOCKE J., *A Letter concerning Toleration, beimg a traslation of the Epistola de Tolerantia*, in *Four Letters concerning Toleration*, in *The Works* of John Locke in Nine Volumes, vol. V, Baldwin, Printer, London, 1824.

LOCKE J., *An Essay Concerning Toleration*, in H. R. Fox Bourne, *The Life of John Locke*, in 2 volumes, reprint of the Edition London, 1876, I, pp. 174-194, Scientia Verlag Aalen, 1969.

LONGANO F., *Dalla "Filosofia dell'uomo"*, in *Illuministi italiani. Riformatori napoletani*, vol. II - tomo I, Classici Ricciardi Mondadori, Milano-Napoli, 1997.

LÖWITH K., *Die Hegelsche Linke*, Friedrich Frommann Verlag, Stuttgart-Bad Cannstatt, 1962.

LÖWITH K., *Meaning in History. The theological Implications of the Philosophy of History*, The University of Chicago Press, Chicago, 1955.

LÖWITH K., *Von Hegel zu Nietzsche. Der revolutionäre Bruch im Denken des neunzehnten Jahrhunderts. Marx und Kierkegaard*, W. Kohlhammer Verlag, Stuttgart, 1950.

LUGNANI SCARANO E, *Introduzione* a FRANCESCO GUICCIARDINI, *Opere*, vol. I, UTET, Torino, 1983.

LUKÁCS G., *Der junge Hegel und die Probleme der kapitalistischen Gesellschaft*, in *Werke*, Band VIII, H. Luchterhand Verlag, Berlin, 1967.

LUPPI S., *Vis et Auctoritas: I paradossi del potere nella filosofia politica di Francisco De Victoria*, in *I diritti dell'uomo e la pace nel pensiero di Francisco de Victoria e Bartolomé de las Casas*, Studia Universitas S. Thomae in Urbe, Massimo, Milano, 1988.

LUTHER M., *Von der Freyheit eynisz Christen menschen, Martinus Luther, Vuittembergae, Anno Domini MDXX*, in *Doctor Martin Luthers Werke, Kritische Ausgabe*, VII, 1897.

LUTHER M., *Ermanunge zum fride auff die zwelff artickell der Bawrschafft ym Schwaben. Auch widder diereubischen und mördischen rotten der andern bawren*, in *Doctor Martin Luthers Werke, Kritische Ausgabe*, XVIII, 1908.

MACHIAVELLI N., *Parole da dirle sopra la provisione del danaio*, in *I primi scritti politici*, in *Opere*, vol. I, a cura di Corrado Vivanti, Einaudi-Gallimard, Torino, 1997.

MACHIAVELLI N., *Il Principe*, in *Opere*, vol. I, a cura di Corrado Vivanti, Einaudi-Gallimard, Torino, 1997.

MACHIAVELLI N., *Dell'arte della guerra*, in *Opere*, vol. I, a cura di Corrado Vivanti, Einaudi-Gallimard, Torino, 1997.

MACHIAVELLI N., *Lettere, legazioni e commissarie*, in *Opere*, vol. II, a cura di Corrado Vivanti, Einaudi-Gallimard, Torino, 1999.

MACHIAVELLI N., *Discorsi sopra la prima Deca di Tito Livio*, in *Opere*, vol. I, a cura di Corrado Vivanti, Einaudi-Gallimard, Torino, 1997.

MACPHERSON C. B., *Introduction*, to T. HOBBES, *Leviathan*, London, Penguin Books, 1980.

MAGRI T., *Introduzione* a *La favola delle api*, Editori Laterza, Roma-Bari, 1997.

MANDEVILLE B. (DE), *The Fable of the Bees, or, private Vices, publick Benefits* a work, Ed. by F. B. Kaye, Clarendon Press, Oxford, 1824, Liberty Fund, Inc., Indianapolis, 1992.

Manin B., *Montesquieu*, in F. Furet- M. Ozouf, cit., pp. 884-897.

Manzanedo M. F., *Florilegio de sentencias*, (ad usum privatum amicorum), Roma, 1998.

Manzoni A., *La Rivoluzione Francese del 1789*, Edizioni Costa & Nolan, Genova, 1985.

Manzoni A., *Osservazioni sulla morale cattolica*, Edizioni Paoline, Torino, 1986.

Marcucci S., *Introduzione* a J Bentham, *Un frammento sul governo*, Giuffrè Editore, Milano, 1990.

Marcuse H., *An Essay on Liberation*, Beacon Press, Boston, 1969.

Mariana J. de, *La Tiranía y los Derechos del Pueblo*, Secretaría de Educación Pública, Mexico, D. F., 1948.

Marx K., *Zur Kritik der Hegelschen Rechtsphilosophie*, in Marx K. & Engels F., in *Werke*, Band 1, Dietz Verlag, Berlin, 1972.

Marx K., *Zur Kritik der Hegelschen Rechtsphilosophie. Einleitung*, in Marx K. & Engels F., in *Werke*, Band 1, Dietz Verlag, Berlin, 1972.

Marx K., *Die deutsche Ideologie. Kritik der neuesten deutschen Philosophie*, in Marx K. & Engels F., in *Werke*, Band 3, Dietz Verlag, Berlin, 1969.

Marx K., *Thesen über Feuerbach*, in Marx K. & Engels F., in *Werke*, Band 3, Dietz Verlag, Berlin, 1969.

Marx K. & Engels F., *Manifest der kommunistischen Partei*, in Marx K. & Engels F., in *Werke*, Band 4, Dietz Verlag, Berlin, 1972.

Marx K., *Oekonomisch-philosophische Manuskripte*, in Marx K. & Engels F., in *Werke*, Schriften bis 1844, Dietz Verlag, Berlin, 1973.

Mathew D., *Acton. The Formative Years*, London, 1946.

Matteucci N., *Organizzazione del potere e libertà. Storia del costituzionalismo moderno*, UTET, Torino, 1988.

Matteucci N., *Introduzione* a Alexis de Tocqueville, *Scritti politici*, vol. I, UTET, Torino, 1969.

Matteucci N., *La Rivoluzione americana: una rivoluzione costituzionale*, Il Mulino, Bologna, 1987.

Mayeur J. M. e Gadille J., *Gli ambienti cattolici liberali in Francia: continuità e diversità di una tradizione*, in Aa. Vv., *I cattolici liberali nell'Ottocento*, S. E. I., Torino, 1976.

McIlwain C. H., *Constitutionalism: Ancient and Modern*, New York, Cornell University Press, 1947.

Meinecke F., *Die Entstehung des Historismus*, in *Werke*, Band III, R. Oldenbourg Verlag, München, 1965.

Merker N., *Introduzione* a J. G. Fichte, *La missione del dotto*, Edizioni Studio Tesi, Pordenone, 1991.

MERKER N., *Introduzione* a G. E. LESSING, *Religione, storia e società*, La libra, Messina, 1973.

MERKER N., *Alle origini dell'ideologia tedesca*, Editori Laterza, Bari, 1977.

MESNARD P., *L'essor de la philosophie politique au XVIe siècle*, J. Vrin, Paris, 1952, trad. it., *Il pensiero politico rinascimentale*, vol. II, Editori Laterza, Bari, 1964.

MESSINEO A., *La società delle genti nel pensiero del Suarez*, in *Civiltà Cattolica*, 1949, vol. IV, n. 2387.

MILTON J., *Areopagitica*, in *The Prose Works* of John Milton in two volumes, vol. I, Ed. by Refus Wilmot Griswold, J. W. Moore, No. 198 Chesnut Street, Philadelphia, 1847.

MINGUIJON S., *Balmes apologista*, in AA. VV., *Balmes filosofo, social, apologista y politico*, Madrid, 1945.

MIONI F., *Introduzione* a J. ADAMS, *Rivoluzioni e costituzioni*, A. Guida Editore, Napoli, 1997.

MIRRI E., *Introduzione* a *Religione popolare e Cristianesimo*, in G. W. F. HEGEL, *Scritti teologici giovanili*, Guida Editori, Napoli, 1972.

MONNEROT J., *Sociologie du communisme*, nfr, Gallimard, Paris, 1949.

MONTESQUIEU, *Dialogue de Sylla et d'Eucrate*, in *Oeuvres complètes* vol. I, Éd. Gallimard, Paris, 1990.

MONTESQUIEU, *Lettres persanes*, in *Oeuvres complètes*, vol. I, Éd. Gallimard, Paris, 1990.

MONTESQUIEU, *Discours sur Cicéron*, in *Oeuvres complètes*, vol. I, Éd. Gallimard, Paris, 1990.

MONTESQUIEU, *Considérations sur les causes de la grandeur des Romains et de leur décadence*, in *Oeuvres complètes*, vol. II, Éd. Gallimard, Paris, 1989.

MONTESQUIEU, *De l'Ésprit des Lois*, in *Oeuvres complètes*, vol. II, Éd. Gallimard, Paris, 1989.

MORUS T. (MORE T.), *Utopia. De optimo Reipublicae Statu*, The Latin Text and the English Translation, in *The Complete Works of St. Thomas More*, volume IV, Yale University Press, New Haven and London, 1965.

MULLER H. J., *The Use of the Past. Profiles of Former Societies*, New York, Oxford University Press, 1957.

NEGRI G., *Il federalismo nel Risorgimento da Gioberti a Montanelli*, in AA. VV., *Stato unitario e federalismo nel pensiero cattolico del Risorgimento*, Atti del XXVII Corso della "Cattedra Rosmini", 1993, a cura di G. Pellegrino, Sodalitas - Spes, Stresa - Milazzo, 1994.

NEGRI G., *Il sistema politico degli Stati Uniti d'America. Le istituzioni costituzionali*, Nistri-Lischi, Pisa, 1969.

NICOLAI P., *Dal deismo all'ateismo. Il processo al cristianesimo*, Millennium Romae, Roma, 1999.

NIVEAU M., *Histoire des faits économiques contemporains*, P. U. F., Paris, 1966.

OBERTI E., Introduzione a G. W. F. HEGEL, *Lezioni sulla filosofia della religione*, Zanichelli Editore, Bologna, 1973.

O'BRIEN C. C., *Introduction. The Manifesto of a Counter-Revolution*, in E. BURKE, *Reflections on the Revoluction in France*, Penguin Books Ltd, 1981.

OLIVETTI M. M., *Filosofia della religione come problema storico*, CEDAM, Padova, 1974.

OWEN R., *A new View of Society and other Writings*, J. M. Dent & Sons LDT, London, 1963.

PAINE T., *The Rights of Man, Part I (1791)*; *The Rights of Man, Part II (1792)*; in THOMAS PAINE; *Political Writings*, edited by B. Kuklick, Cambridge University Press, 1989.

PAGANO F. M., *Politicum universae romanorum nomothesiae examen*, in *Illuministi italiani. Riformatori napoletani*, vol. II - tomo II, Classici Ricciardi Mondadori, Milano-Napoli, 1997.

PAGANO F. M., *Progetto di costituzione della repubblica napolitana presentato al governo provvisorio dal comitato di legislazione*, in *Illuministi italiani. Riformatori napoletani*, vol. II - tomo II, Classici Ricciardi Mondadori, Milano-Napoli, 1997.

PAREYSON L., Introduzione a JOHN LOCKE, *Due trattati sul governo civile*, UTET, Torino, 1948.

Passerin D'Entrèves E., *Presentazione* a Aa. Vv., *I cattolici liberali nell'Ottocento*, S. E. I., Torino, 1976.

Passerin D'Entrèves E., *Le origini del cattolicesimo liberale in Italia*, in Aa. Vv., *I cattolici liberali nell'Ottocento*, S. E. I., Torino, 1976.

Pellicani, L., *Gramsci e la questione comunista*, Vallecchi Editore, Firenze, 1976.

Pellicani L., *Hobbes e la società borghese*, in *Modernizzazione e sviluppo*, anno 6, n. 1, 1996, pp. 3-8.

Pellicani L., (a cura di), *Dimensioni della Modernità*, Edizioni Seam, Roma, 1999.

Pellicani L., *Miseria del marxismo. Da Marx al Gulag*, Sugarco Edizioni, Milano, 1984.

Petruzzellis N., *Presentazione* a Erasmo Da Rotterdam, *Elogio della follia*, U. Mursia & C., Milano, 1970.

Pezzimenti R., *The Open Society and its Friends*, Gracewing, Leominster, 1997.

Pezzimenti R., *The Political Thought of Lord Acton. The English Catolics in the Nineteenth Century*, Gracewing, Leominster, 2001.

Pezzimenti R., *Organizzazione e struttura politca in Gramsci*, in *Orientamenti sociali*, anno 34, n°. 4, 1978.

Pico della Mirandola G., *De Hominis Dignitate*, S. Berlusconi Editore, Milano, 1995.

POSTIGLIOLA A., *Politica, storia e scienza della società in Montesquieu, Introduzione* a MONTESQUIEU, *Le leggi della politica*, Editori Riuniti, Roma, 1979.

POZZI R., *Introduzione* a F. GUIZOT, *Storia della civiltà in Francia*, UTET, Torino, 1974.

PROUDHON, P.-J., *Du principe féderatif*, Bonacci Editore, Roma, 1988.

PUFENDORF S. VON, *De iure naturae et gentium*, trad. fr., *Le droit de la nature et des gens ou sisteme general des principes les plus importants de la morale, de la jurisprudence, et de la politique*, Chez Pierre de Coup, Amsterdam, 1712.

QUADRI S., *Dottrine politiche nei teologi del '500*, Editrice Studium, Roma, 1962.

REVELLI M., *Introduzione* a *Putney. Alle radici della democrazia moderna. Il dibattito tra i protagonisti della rivoluzione inglese*, Baldini & Castoldi, Milano, 1997.

RIVA C., *Introduzione* a A. ROSMINI, *Saggio sul comunismo e sul socialismo*, a cura di C. Riva, Pescara, 1964.

ROSMINI-SERBATI A., *Saggio sul comunismo e sul socialismo*, a cura di C. Riva, Pescara, 1964.

ROSMINI-SERBATI A., *Delle cinque piaghe della Santa Chiesa. Trattato dedicato al Clero Cattolico (Con aggiunte e chiarificazioni inedite)*, a cura di Clemente Riva, Morcelliana, Brescia, 1971.

Rosmini-Serbati A., *Nuovo saggio sull'origine delle idee*, vol. II, edizione sesta, eseguita sulla quinta riveduta dall'Autore, Intra Tipografia di Paolo Bertolotti, 1876.

Rosmini-Serbati A., *Filosofia della politica*, Marzorati Editore, Milano, 1972.

Rossi P., *Prefazione* a K. Löwith, *Significato e fine della storia*, Edizioni di Comunità, Milano, 1979.

Rousseau J.-J., *Discours sur les Sciences et les Arts*, in Jean-Jacques Rousseau, *Du Contrat Social et autres oeuvres politiques*, Éditions Garnier Frères, Paris, 1975.

Rousseau J.-J., *Discours sur l'origine de l'inégalité parmi les hommes*, in Jean-Jacques Rousseau, *Du Contrat Social et autres oeuvres politiques*, Éditions Garnier Frères, Paris, 1975.

Rousseau J.-J., *Du Contrat Social ou Principes du droit politique*, in Jean-Jacques Rousseau, *Du Contrat Social et autres oeuvres politiques*, Éditions Garnier Frères, Paris, 1975.

Saint-Simon L. de, *Nouveau Christianisme. Dialogues entre un conservateur et un novateur. Premier dialogue*, Paris, Bossange père, 1825.

Sanguinetti F., *Introduzione* a Alessandro Manzoni, *La Rivoluzione Francese del 1789*, Edizioni Costa & Nolan, Genova, 1985.

Sarubbi A., *Manuale di storia delle dottrine politiche*, G. Giappichelli Editore, Torino, 1991.

SAVONAROLA G., *Prediche sopra Aggèo*, in vol. V, dell'*Edizione nazionale delle opere* di G. SAVONAROLA, a cura di L. Firpo, Angelo Belardetti Editore, Roma, 1965.

SAVONAROLA G., *Trattato circa il reggimento e governo della città di Firenze*, in vol. V, dell'*Edizione nazionale delle opere* di G. SAVONAROLA, a cura di L. Firpo, Angelo Belardetti Editore, Roma, 1965.

SCHIAVONE G., *La figura di James Harrington: scienza politica e utopia*, Saggio introduttivo a JAMES HARRINGTON, *La Repubblica di Oceana*, Franco Angeli Libri, Milano, 1989.

SCHUMPETER J. A., *History of Economic Analysis*, Oxford University Press, New York, 1954.
The quotations refer to the part, chapter and paragraph.

SCOPPOLA P., *Idea di partito politico*, in *Dizionario storico del movimento cattolico in Italia*, vol. I/1, *I fatti e le idee*, Casa Editrice Marietti, Torino, 1981.

SERONI A., *Introduzione* a TOMMASO CAMPANELLA, *La città del sole*, Feltrinelli Editore, 1979.

SIEYÈS E.-J., *Qu'est-ce que le tiers état?*, *Essai sur les privilèges*, au Siège de la Société, Paris, 1888.

SMITH A., *The Theory of Moral Sentiments*, New York, 1950.

SMITH A., *The Wealth of Nations*, Ed. by Robert Reich, The Modern Library, New York, 2000.

SOLARI G., *Introduzione* a IMMANUEL KANT, *Scritti politici e di filosofia della storia e del diritto*, UTET, Torino, 1971.

Soto D. de, *De justitia et iure*, vol. I, Inst. de Estud. Politicos, Madrid, 1967.

Spencer H., *The Principles of Sociology*, vol. I, Williams and Norgate, London, 1882.

Spencer H., *Political Institutions, Being Part IV of The Principles of Sociology*, Williams and Norgate, London, 1882.

Spencer H., *The Principles of Ethics*, vol. I, Williams and Norgate, London, 1892.

Spinoza B. de, *Ethica ordine geometrico demonstrata*, Quotquot reperta sunt recpgnoverunt J. Van Vloten et J. P. N. Land, editio tertia, tomus primus, Hagae comitum apud Martinum Nijhoff, MCMXIV.

Spinoza B. de, *Tractatus Theologico-Politicus*, Quotquot reperta sunt recpgnoverunt J. Van Vloten et J. P. N. Land, editio tertia, tomus secundus, Hagae comitum apud Martinum Nijhoff, MCMXIV.

Stuart Mill J., *Principles of Political Economy*, Edited with an Introduction by Jonathan Riley, Oxford University Press, Oxford-New York, 1994.

Stuart Mill J., *On Liberty*, in *On Liberty and Other Essays*, Edited with an Introduction by John Gray, Oxford University Press, Oxford-New York, 1991.

Stuart Mill J., *Utilitarianism*, in *On Liberty and Other Essays*, Edited with an Introduction by John Gray, Oxford University Press, Oxford-New York, 1991.

STUART MILL J., *Considerations on Representative Government*, in *On Liberty and Other Essays*, Edited with an Introduction by JOHN GRAY, Oxford University Press, Oxford-New York, 1991.

STUART MILL J., *The Subjection of Women*, in *On Liberty and Other Essays*, Edited with an Introduction by JOHN GRAY, Oxford University Press, Oxford-New York, 1991.

SUAREZ F., *Principatus Politicus*, Introduccion y edicion critica bilingüe por E. ELOURDUY Y L. PEREÑA, C.S.I.C., Madrid, 1965. Il testo contiene la terza parte della *Defensio fidei* che tratta del *Principatus politicus*.

SUAREZ F., *Tractatus de legibus ac Deo legislatore*, Lugduni, 1619.

TOCQUEVILLE A. DE, *La démocratie en Amérique I (1835), II (1840)*, in *Œuvres*, vol. II, Éditions Gallimard, Paris, 1992.

TOCQUEVILLE A. DE, *L'ancien régime et la Révolution*, Éditions Gallimard, Paris, 1996.

TOCQUEVILLE A. DE, *Discours prononcé à l'Assemblée constituante dans la discussion du projet de contitution (12 septembre 1848) sur la question du droit au travail*, in *Œuvres*, vol. I, Éditions Gallimard, Paris, 1991.

TOURN G., *Introduzione* a GIOVANNI CALVINO, *Istituzione della religione cristiana*, UTET, Torino, 1971.

TRANIELLO F., *Cattolicesimo liberale*, in *Enciclopedia Filosofica*, ristampa aggiornata della II[a] edizione interamente rielaborata, Lucarini, su licenza della Casa

Editrice "Le lettere", Firenze, 1982.

VASALE C., *Il significato del federalismo giobertiano nella storia d'Italia*, in AA. VV., *Stato unitario e federalismo nel pensiero cattolico del Risorgimento*, Atti del XXVII Corso della "Cattedra Rosmini", 1993, a cura di G. Pellegrino, Sodalitas - Spes, Stresa - Milazzo, 1994.

VENTURI F., *Introduzione* a *Illuministi italiani. Riformatori napoletani*, vol. II - tomo I, Classici Ricciardi Mondadori, Milano-Napoli, 1997.

VENTURI F., *Antonio Genovesi. Nota introduttiva*, in *Illuministi italiani. Riformatori napoletani*, vol. II - tomo I, Classici Ricciardi Mondadori, Milano-Napoli, 1997.

VENTURI F., *Francesco M. Pagano. Nota introduttiva*, in *Illuministi italiani. Riformatori napoletani*, vol. II - tomo II, Classici Ricciardi Mondadori, Milano-Napoli, 1997.

VERRI P., *Osservazioni sulla tortura*, Rizzoli Editore, Milano, 1988.

VICO G.B., *De antiquissima italorum sapientia ex linguae latinae originibus eruenda*, in *Opere filosofiche*, Sansoni, Firenze, 1971.

VICO G.B., *Principi di una scienza nuova d'intorno alla comune natura delle nazioni, in questa terza impressione dal medesimo autore in gran numero di luoghi corretta, schiarita, e notabilmente accresciuta (1744)*, in *Opere filosofiche*, Sansoni, Firenze, 1971.

Vico G.B., *Sinopsi del diritto universale*, in *Opere giuridiche*, Sansoni, Firenze, 1974.

Vico G.B., *De universi iuris uno principio et fine uno. Liber unus - De uno universi iuris principio et fine uno* e *Liber alter - De constantia iurisprudentis*, in *Opere giuridiche*, Sansoni, Firenze, 1974.

Villani P., *Introduzione* a Vincenzo Cuoco, *Saggio sulla rivoluzione napoletana del 1799*, Editori Laterza, Roma-Bari, 1980.

Weinstein D., *Machiavelli and Savonarola*, in *Studies on Machiavelli*, edited by Myron P. Gilmore, G. C. Sansoni Editore, Firenze, 1972.

Woodhouse A. S. P. (a cura di), *Putney Debates* in *Puritanism and Liberty: Being the Army Debates (1647-49) from the Clarke Manuscripts, with Spplementary Documents*, Dent, London, 1938.

Index of Names

ABBONDANTI W., 110, 139
ACTON J.E.E.D., LORD, 15, 87, 193, 308-309, 346-355, 368, 426
ACUTIS C., 65
ADAMS J., 17, 225-230, 241
AUGUSTINE OF IPPONA ST, 56, 76, 158,171, 323, 347, 442-443
ALATRI P., 349, 488-489
ALBERTONI E.A., 203
ALEMBERT J.B. LE ROND D', 488
ALTHUSIUS J. or ALTHUS, 79-85
ALTHUSSER L., 190
AMERIO F., 157
ANTISERI D., 20
ARISTOTLE, 18, 57, 65, 69, 98, 119, 227, 395, 448, 464, 518
ASHLEY COOPER A., LORD, 94

BACON F., 158, 448-450
BADALONI N., 162, 165
BAKUNIN M. A., 371
BALBO C., 329-331
BALMES J., 272, 293, 299-306
BARCLAY, 78
BARTOLO DA SASSOFERRATO, 23
BASTID P., 255

BAUER B., 419
BEAUMONT G. DE, 277
BECCARIA C., 206, 209-211, 511
BÉCHAUX A., 314
BEDESCHI G., 268
BELLARMINO R., 75-79
BENTHAM J., 87, 150-156, 334
BERLIN I., 13, 18-19, 195
BERNARD ST, 321
BERNARDINO OF SIENA, 50-53
BERNSTEIN E., 364, 374-377
BIEN D.D., 194
BISMARCK SCHÖNHAUSEN O. VON, 374
BOBBIO N., 392, 394-398, 401, 404-405
BODIN J., 72, 79, 82-83, 387-389
BOECLER G.E., 80
BOLINGBROKE H.S.J. DE, 110-113, 151
BONALD L. DE, 148, 268, 311-313
BONAPARTE, 253, 258
BONGHI R., 322
BOSSUET J. B., 381, 390-391
BOTERO G., 79
BOUDON R., 31, 34, 172
BOULAINVILLIERS H. DE, 251

BRANCA V., 441
BRUNI L., 23
BRUNO G., 481
BRYCE J., 13-14, 16
BUCCILLI N., 155
BUCHEZ P.J.B., 370
BURGIO A., 190
BURKE E., 87, 140-150, 215, 237-238, 301, 310
BURNS J.H., 151

CACCIARI M., 450-451
CAESAR C.J., 116
CALVIN J., 78, 384-386
CAMPANELLA T., 451-455
CANTONI R., 480-481
CANTÙ F., 65
CAPES J.M., 348
CAPOZZI E., 110-112
CAPPONI P., 39
CARENA C., 442
CARLETTI G., 206
CARPENTER W.S., 96
CARRANO A., 267
CASANOVAS I., 299
CASSIRER E., 114, 116, 195
CASTAÑO J.F., 61-62
CASTRO A. DE, 64-65
CASTRUCCIO CASTRACANI, 461-462
CATHERINE OF SIENA ST, 49-50, 321
CATHERINE II, 209
CATTANEO C., 329
CEDRONI L., 64, 72
CEREZO DE DIEGO P., 63
CERRONI U., 253, 261

CERVANTES M. DE, 59
CHATEAUBRIAND F.R., 306
CICERO M.T., 16-18, 54, 62-63, 68-69, 81, 90, 93, 95, 108, 116, 119, 122, 127, 146, 148, 155, 168, 175, 178-179, 185, 189, 192-193, 218, 224, 227-228, 304, 323, 335, 350, 503, 508, 510, 513-514
COCHIN A., 248
COKE E., 91
COLE G.D.H., 363-364, 366, 369-370, 372-373, 376
COLERIDGE S.T., 334
COLLETTI L., 376
COMMONS J. R., 392
COMPAGNA L., 111, 113, 120, 194, 236, 239, 250-251, 257-258
COMPOSTA D., 62
COMTE A., 268, 356, 366-367, 435-436
CONDILLAC É.B. DE, 243
CONDORCET M.J.A.N.C. DE, 244
CONDORCET S., 367
CONRING H., 80
CONSTANT B., 203, 258-266, 269, 277, 489, 500
CONTINISIO C., 79
COPPELLOTTI F., 425
CROCE B., 157-161, 163, 200, 206, 316-317
CROMWELL O., 393, 456
CUSANUS N., 47, 53-55
CUOCO V., 199, 211-221, 268
CYPRIAN ST, 54

D'ADDIO M., 24, 53-54, 60-61, 64, 90-91, 140, 144, 150-152, 160, 232, 235, 267, 276, 311-313, 322-326, 328, 351, 356, 367, 372-373, 387, 435, 437, 481-482, 484, 501, 516
DANTE A., 47, 240, 464
DARCY, 224
DEGUISE P., 261
DELFICO M., 206
DEL NOCE A., 319
DE LUCA S., 259-260, 264, 500
DENIS H., 139, 500
DERRÉ J.-R., 312
DE RUGGIERO G., 251, 307, 310
DESCARTES R., 119, 393-394
DE WITT BROTHERS, 479
DICKINSON, 230
DIDEROT D., 487
DI DONATO F., 500
DI VONA P., 484
DÖLLINGER J.I. VON, 348
DUBOS J.-B., 251, 273
DUPANLOUP F., 348

ELIZABETH I QUEEN, 448
ELOURDUY E., 68-69
ENDEN F. VAN DEM, 478
ENGELS F., 353, 374, 376, 423, 425, 431
ERASMUS D. OF ROTTERDAM, 55-59, 302, 441-443
EUCHNER W., 103
EUCRATES, 177
EUSEBIUS OF CAESAREA, 21

FASNACHT G., 347-348, 353-355
FERGUSON A., 109
FERRAROTTI F., 356, 361
FEUERBACH L., 420-421, 427, 432
FICHTE J.G., 219, 268, 515-520
FICINO M., 23, 55
FILANGERI G., 203-204, 206
FILMER R., 112
FIRPO L., 382-384
FOX BOURNE H.R., 103
FUBINI LEUZZI M., 330
FURET F., 245-249, 275, 289-290, 296-297

GADILLE J., 313-315
GAIUS, 172
GALANTI G.M., 205-206
GALIANI F., 203
GALILEO G., 75, 158, 393, 452
GASQUET A.F., 349
GATTI M., 92
GATTI H., 92
GAUCHET M., 250-251
GENOVESI A., 198-202
GENTILE G., 319
GHIRINGHELLI R., 110, 139
GIACON C., 79, 85
GIBBON E., 269
GIERKE O. VON, 80, 82-85
GILBERT F., 25
GIOBERTI V., 268, 317-320
GIOVANNI DEI MEDICI or LEO X, 56
GIRARDIN E. DE, 488
GIULIANI A., 316

GLADSTONE W., 309, 353
GOETHE W., 259
GOEZE J.M., 403
GOLDONI C., 469
GRAMSCI A., 216, 410, 435, 518
GRAVINA G., 213
GRIMALDI D., 202
GRIMALDI F., 202
GROTIUS H., 85-86, 160-163, 494
GUICCIARDINI F., 23-46, 137, 158, 463
GUICCIARDINI P., 23
GUIDI M., 155
GUIZOT F., 194, 245, 268-276, 302-304, 315, 334

HAMILTON A., 141, 231, 240-241, 350
HARRINGTON J., 89, 91, 455-456
HART H.L.A., 151
HAUBOLD DE MILTIZ E., 515
HAYEK F.A. VON, 107-108, 136, 172, 202
HEGEL G.W.F., 348, 353, 392, 401, 405- 419, 422-423, 427, 429-431, 434, 470, 475, 481, 484, 488, 501, 507, 513, 517
HENKEL W., 67
HENRY VIII, 443
HERDER J.G., 310,406
HERZEN, 371
HILFERDING R., 376
HIMMELFARB G., 354

HOBBES T., 16, 30, 91, 93, 95-96, 105-106, 112, 161, 231, 290, 391-401, 462, 475-476, 483, 504
HOFFMANN A.F., 403
HÖLDERLIN F., 407
HUBER U., 80
HUMBOLDT W. VON, 266-268
HUME D., 104, 110, 113-127, 150, 179, 201, 488

INTIERI B., 199
IRETON H., 89

JACOBI F.H., 115, 404-405, 409, 481
JAMES I STUART, 68, 448
JAMES É., 139
JAMES W., 21-22
JANNET C., 214
JAY J., 231-232
JEFFERSON T., 224, 226, 230-231, 240, 350
JEMOLO C.A., 209, 308
JEROME ST, 321, 442

KANT I., 21, 85, 267, 337, 410, 434, 501-515
KIERKEGAARD S., 405
KOCHAN L., 353

LA BOÉTIE E. DE, 46-47
LA FAYETTE J.P., 250
LALLY-TOLLENDAL A., 250
LAMENNAIS F.-R.DE, 312-313
LA REVELLIÈRE-LEPEAUX, 250
LAS CASAS B. DE, 65-67

Index of Names

LASKI H J., 149
LEIBNIZ G.W., 323
LENIN, VLADIMIR ILIČ ULIANOV, known as, 216, 245, 416, 421, 425, 428-429, 496
LEO X, 56
LEO XIII, 309
LEOPARDI G., 318
LESSING G.E., 403-405, 431
LILBURNE J., 89
LIVIUS T., 24, 461
LOCKE J., 46, 87, 89, 93-104, 123, 183, 350, 492, 504
LONGANO F., 202
LORENZO DE' MEDICI, 478
LOUIS XIV, 290, 366
LÖWITH K., 407, 409-410, 416-418, 420-422, 430
LUCANUS M.A. or LUCAIN, 109, 514
LUCIAN, 443
LUGARINI L., 414
LUGNANI SCARANO E., 25
LOUIS XIII, 452
LUKÁCS G., 417
LUPPI S., 62
LUTHER M., 56, 381-384, 443, 519
LYCURGUS, 449, 497

MABLY G.B. DE, 243-244, 500
MACHIAVELLI N., 16, 24, 27, 79, 105, 158, 161, 183, 197, 213, 215, 231, 322, 394, 399, 401, 456, 461-478, 504, 507
MACPHERSON C.B., 392
MADISON J., 231
MAGRI T., 107
MAISTRE J. DE, 148, 212, 268, 311-313, 331
MANDEVILLE B. DE, 104-110
MANIN B., 195
MANNHEIM K., 444
MANZANEDO M.F., 23
MANZONI A., 209, 314-318, 322
MARCUCCI S., 153-154
MARCUSE H., 430, 433-434
MARIANA J. DE, 73-75, 300
MARITAIN J., 461
MARK ST, 50
MARTIN V, 53
MARX K., 133, 136, 296, 353-354, 371, 374-375, 417, 421-425, 427-434, 441, 481, 484, 488-489, 493, 513
MATHEW D., 347, 352
MATTEUCCI N., 15, 90-91, 223-225, 231, 276-277
MAYEUR J.M., 313-315
MCILWAIN C.H., 18, 224, 237
MEINECKE F., 196
MENDELSSOHN M., 481
MERKER N., 403, 518-519
MESNARD P., 68, 75
MESSINEO A., 72
MICHELET J., 245, 334
MILTON J., 92-93
MINGUIJON S., 303
MIONI F., 17, 226-227, 229-230
MIRRI E., 410-411
MOLINA L. DE, 65

Monnerot J., 425, 434
Montesquieu Ch. L., 14, 16, 45, 47, 101, 146, 148-149, 157, 163, 176-195, 198, 201, 213-214, 227, 236, 269, 287, 319, 330, 412, 498, 502, 515
More T., 56, 59, 118, 442-447
Muller H.J., 361
Münzer T., 383

Navarro, M. de Azpilcueta, known as, 64-65
Necker J., 257
Negri G., 225, 231-232, 235, 320, 351
Newman J.H., 309, 348
Nicholas Lord, 448
Nicolai P., 115
Niveau M., 363

Oberti E., 411, 413
O'Brien C.C., 146, 150
Olivetti M.M., 406
Otis J., 230
Owen R., 298, 368-369, 447

Pagano F.M., 205
Paine T., 230, 237-240
Pallavicino Sforza P., 79
Palmieri G., 206
Paul III, 24, 66
Pareyson L., 98
Passerin D'Entrèves E., 310, 315
Paulet A., Lord, 448
Pecqueur C., 370

Pellicani L., 15, 22, 372, 392, 428
Pereña L., 68-69
Petrarch F., 55
Petruzzellis N., 56
Petty M., 89
Pezzimenti R., 19, 21, 216, 307, 309, 350
Pico della Mirandola G., 441
Pius ix, 318, 328
Plato, 57, 92, 118-119, 161-162, 212, 243, 386, 444-445, 447-448, 452-454, 456-457, 484, 494, 507, 511, 518-519
Plautus T.M., 54
Pocock J.G.A., 223
Polibius, 118
Pope, 111
Postel G., 47
Postigliola A., 184
Pozzi R., 268, 270
Proudhon P.-J., 364-365, 370-374
Pufendorf S. Von., 85-86, 160-161, 493
Pulteney W., 111
Putnam H., 13, 21-22

Quadri S., 64, 70-71, 76-77

Rabaut Saint-Etienne J.P., 250
Rainsborough J., 88
Rawley W., 449
Revelli M., 88-89
Richelieu A. J., 289, 452

RICHET D., 500
RIVA C., 327
ROGER-DUCOS, 253
ROSMINI-SERBATI A., 297, 307, 309, 318, 320-329
ROSSI P., 417
ROUSSEAU J.-J., 15, 120, 122-123, 145, 149, 195, 202-204, 243, 255, 258, 262, 299, 310, 373-374, 415, 420, 423, 487-500, 505-506, 515, 517

SAINT-SIMON L. DE, 365-368, 422
SALUTATI C., 23
SALVIATI M., 24
SANGUINETTI F., 316
SARUBBI A., 50
SAVIGNY F.K. VON, 271
SAVONAROLA G., 50-53, 441-442,
SCHELLING F.W.J., 407
SCHIAVONE G., 91, 456-457
SCHILLER F., 259
SCHLEGEL F., 259
SCHUMPETER J.A., 71, 110
SCOPPOLA P., 318, 329
SENECA L.A., 18, 83, 116
SERONI A., 451
SHAKESPEARE W., 59
SIEYÈS J.-E, 239, 250-258, 289
SIMPSON R., 348
SMITH A., 108, 121, 124, 127-139, 145, 156, 201, 412
SMITH T., 90-91
SOCRATES, 57
SOLARI G., 504-506

SOLON, 497
SOTO D. DE., 64-65
SPENCER H., 355-361
SPINOZA B. DE., 479-485, 513
STAËL G. MAD. DE, 259
STRAUSS D.F., 419, 424
STUART MILL J., 333-345
SUAREZ F., 65, 67-72
SWIFT J., 111
SYLLA C. F. or SCYLLA, 177-178, 182

TACITUS C., 79, 118, 126, 149, 158, 162-163, 228, 304
TELESIO B., 452
TERENCE P. A., 119
THIERRY A., 315
THOMAS OF A. ST, 56
TIBERIUS CAESAR, 79
TOCQUEVILLE A. DE, 14, 41, 45, 104, 142, 150, 194, 218, 233, 245-246, 276-298, 312, 328, 333-334, 340, 347, 350, 358
TOMMASEO N., 322
TOSTI L., 316
TOURN G., 384-385
TRANIELLO F., 310
THUCYDIDES, 393
TURGOT A.R.J., 228, 244

ULPIAN or ULPIANUS, 100, 168, 201, 512-513
URBAN VIII, 452

VASALE C., 320
VASQUEZ F., 63-64

Velasquez D., 65
Venturi F., 197-198, 205
Veracruz A. de, 63
Verri A., 208-209
Verri P., 206-209
Vico G.B., 14, 16, 18-19, 22, 73, 109, 112, 115, 146, 148, 157-177, 194-195, 198-199, 201, 205, 213, 215, 217-218, 220, 227, 269, 271, 310, 317, 322-323, 388
Vitoria F. de, 60-65
Villani P., 211-213
Voltaire, Arouet F., *known as*, 487

Walpole, 111
Warens Mad. de, 487
Washington G., 226, 231, 240
Weinstein D., 51
William of Orange, 95
Winstanley G., 89
Wiseman N. Card., 348